Rethinking
Democratic
Accountability

RETHINKING DEMOCRATIC ACCOUNTABILITY

ROBERT D. BEHN

BROOKINGS INSTITUTION PRESS
Washington, D.C.

ABOUT BROOKINGS
The Brookings Institution is a private nonprofit organization devoted to research, education, and publication on important issues of domestic and foreign policy. Its principal purpose is to bring knowledge to bear on current and emerging policy problems. The Institution maintains a position of neutrality on issues of public policy. Interpretations or conclusions in Brookings publications should be understood to be solely those of the authors.

Copyright © 2001
THE BROOKINGS INSTITUTION
1775 Massachusetts Avenue, N.W., Washington, D.C. 20036
www.brookings.edu

Library of Congress Cataloging-in-Publication data

Behn, Robert D.
Rethinking democratic accountability / Robert D. Behn.
    p.   cm.
Includes bibliographical references and index.
ISBN 0-8157-0862-9 (cloth)—ISBN 0-8157-0861-0 (pbk.)
    1. United States—Officials and employees—Discipline.   2. United
States—Officials and employees—Rating of.   3. Administrative
responsibility—United States.   4. Administrative agencies—United
States—Management.   I. Title.
    JK768.7 .B44 2001   00-011826
    352.3'5'0973—dc21   CIP

9 8 7 6 5 4 3 2 1

The paper used in this publication meets minimum requirements of the American National Standard for Information Sciences—Permanence of Paper for Printed Library Materials: ANSI Z39.48-1992.

Typeset in Minion

Composition by R. Lynn Rivenbark, Macon, Georgia

Printed by R. R. Donnelley and Sons
Harrisonburg, Virginia

Contents

To

Dick and Sadie Howe

*For an abundance of advice, and
one wonderful daughter*

Preface

It began innocently enough: a call from the American Society of Public Administration asking if I would deliver the first Donald C. Stone Lecture at ASPA's 1996 Annual Conference. "Sure," I responded. But then what? What could I possibly talk about? What might interest the public-administration community? I decided to focus on a philosophical debate within the profession—the fundamental conflict between the old "Champion" of traditional public administration and the "Challenger" of the new public management. Who, I asked, would prevail in the three rings in which these two traditions were competing: performance, managerial competence, and democratic accountability. And, thus, this project was born.

After all, preparing the lecture wasn't too complicated. So, why not write a conference paper—or two? The first was presented both at a meeting of the Association for Public Policy and Management and at a gathering of the International Public Management Network—and published in the *International Public Management Journal*. The second paper was delivered at a conference of the National Academy of Public Administration.

But once you have written a speech and a couple of conference papers, why not a book? So I sent a short manuscript to Brookings, which liked the concept but wanted a "real book." Now the project was getting more serious. And so was the work.

Fortunately, along the way, I've had assistance and advice from a variety of friends and colleagues. I benefited from the comments of those who sat through my presentations at the three conferences and at Duke University's Terry Sanford Institute of Public Policy. More specifically, I profited from the brilliant ideas, tangible assistance, caustic criticisms, and wacky theories of: Mark Abramson, William Ascher, Eugene Bardach, Richard Behn, Sandford Borins, Jonathan Breul, Anthony Brown, Justin Brown, Evan Charney, Helen Conrad, Phillip Cooper, Melvin Dubnick, Gerald Emison, Elizabeth Field, Carolyn Forno, Beverly Godwin, William Gormley, James Hamilton, Donna Harrison, Alexander Hawes, Alex Jones, Lawrence Jones, John Kamensky, Robert Korstad, Elizabeth Kujawinski, Helen Ladd, David Mathiasen, Frederick Mayer, Vicky Patton, James Pfiffner, Jolie Pillsbury, Alasdair Roberts, Steven Smith, Robert Stephens, Edith Stevens, Fred Thompson, Susan Tifft, Sara Watson, Edward Weber, Ellen Weiss, Michael Williamson, and Marc Zegans.

I also appreciate the help from all of the folks at Brookings Press: Becky Clark, Larry Converse, Nancy Davidson, Charles Dibble, Christopher Kelaher, Thomas Parsons, Janet Walker, and Susan Woollen.

To all of them, I am grateful. Sometimes I actually followed their advice. Sometimes I ignored it. (If I had followed all of their advice, I would have produced not a book but a twelve-volume set that could have been published only posthumously.) These folks are, of course, not accountable for any of the annoying errors or blatant inaccuracies that you may discover if you get past the first page. I am the accountability holdee—not them. (In the spirit of the accountability-holding business, however, I am open to any suggestions about how I might morph myself into the accountability holder. Accountability holdees are always on the lookout for someone onto whom they can deflect some blame. What are friends for?)

Finally, I can't let a book (or day) pass without saluting my favorite golfer, preferred traveling companion, diligent critic, and best friend. Judy: Thanks!

Robert D. Behn
Cambridge, Massachusetts

December 2000

Rethinking Democratic Accountability

1

What Do We Mean
by Accountability, Anyway?

What do we mean by "accountability"? What exactly do we mean when we say that we want "to hold people accountable"? We talk this way all the time. We are always talking about holding someone accountable. Yet, when we say it—"we are going to hold people accountable"—what do we really mean?

Accountability Holders and Accountability Holdees

Lots of people are in the accountability-holding business—either because their jobs give them this responsibility or because they have simply assumed it. Elected officials and candidates are always declaring that they will "hold people accountable." An agency's clients and other stakeholders repeatedly call for its managers to be "held accountable." The U.S. General Accounting Office prepares reports for Congress with titles such as *Federal Agencies Should Use Good Measures of Performance to Hold Managers Accountable.*[1] Scholars write books about *Holding Government Bureaucracies Accountable* and *Holding Schools Accountable.*[2] We have created government officials— auditors, inspectors general, independent counsels—whose sole task is holding other government officials accountable. Lawyers hold government officials accountable by suing them or by convincing juries to lock them up or at least give them a big fine.[3] And, of course, journalists believe it is their constitutional mission to hold everybody accountable.

During 1998, for example, questions about President Bill Clinton's campaign fundraising and personal behavior generated numerous calls to hold someone accountable. "Perjury," said U.S. Representative (and speaker designate) Bob Livingston when he announced his retirement from Congress, "is a crime for which the president may be held accountable, no matter the circumstances."[4] Former senator Bob Dole criticized Attorney General Janet Reno's failure to appoint an independent counsel to investigate the fundraising practices of the 1996 Clinton-Gore campaign committee and hoped that "someone in Congress will hold the attorney general accountable."[5] Allegations of Chinese espionage at U.S. nuclear laboratories caused Senate Majority Leader Trent Lott to remark that somebody "made some major mistakes, and somebody needs to be held accountable."[6]

Everyone wants people—other people—to be held accountable.[7] Mark Moore of Harvard University and Margaret Gates, a consultant to nonprofit agencies, write of "the public's demand for accountability," of "an unquenchable thirst for accountability that cuts across the political spectrum." Liberals and conservatives, they write, like accountability and want more of it. "Everyone agrees," they continue, "that the evils of corruption, arbitrariness, and inefficiency are inherent in government and that they can be exorcised through mechanisms of accountability."[8]

On the baseball diamond, the umpires hold the players accountable. But at the beginning of the 1999 season, the baseball players—calling for more accountability of the umpires—issued a ranking of the umpires in each league.[9] Peter Gammons, the ESPN baseball commentator, noted that "for a long time everyone in the [baseball] business has wanted umpires to be accountable the way the players and management people are accountable."[10] Predictably, the umpires were not pleased.

Our system of accountability has two types of people: Either you are an accountability *holder* or you are an accountability *holdee*. It's great to be an accountability *holder*. It's not so much fun to be an accountability *holdee*.[11]

Who can hold someone in government accountable? Anyone with a printing press, photocopy machine, microphone, law school diploma, video recorder, Internet access, or campaign filing fee. But what do these official and unofficial accountability holders really mean when they say, "We're going to hold people accountable"?

I'm not sure that I can offer a good definition.[12] And I'm not sure that any of these accountability *holders*—the politicians, the stakeholders, the auditors, the scholars, the lawyers, or the journalists—know exactly what it means to "hold someone accountable." The General Accounting Office observes, "Accountability is an important yet elusive concept whose meaning and characteristics differ depending upon the context."[13] That's not very helpful.

I suspect, however, that the people being held accountable know. These accountability *holdees* have a very clear picture of what being held accountable means to them—to them personally. They recognize that, if someone is holding them accountable, two things can happen: When they do something good, nothing happens. But when they screw up, all hell can break loose.[14] Those whom we want to hold accountable have a clear understanding of what accountability means: Accountability means punishment.[15]

This punishment can be a fine, a jail term, the loss of one's job—all of which are subject to the requirements of due process. But the punishment can also be the public humiliation of being grilled by a hostile legislator, of being sued by an aggressive lawyer, of being subpoenaed by an unctuous prosecutor, or of being defamed by an investigatory journalist—none of which requires much due process. When people screw up, there are a variety of ways to hold them accountable—to punish them.

The Ambiguous Abstraction of Accountability

Moreover, the definition of a "screwup" is constantly changing. Thus what someone can be held accountable for is also constantly changing. Legislatures and regulators can always change the formal laws and rules that establish accountability, although these legal standards of accountability are *relatively* easy to track. Further, lawyers can convince the courts to change how these laws and regulations are interpreted. And when these interpretations change, accountability holdees may find themselves held accountable for prior behavior under new standards.

The informal standards of accountability are, however, subject to political vagaries. Public officials may not realize that something is a "screwup" until someone holds them accountable for doing what many others have been doing for quite a while. Congratulations: You are the first person to be held accountable for doing something that, until today, lots of people did and the rest of us considered acceptable.

"Today's ethics police" not only exhibit "self-righteousness," writes Suzanne Garment of the American Enterprise Institute; they also "display impressive inventiveness in not simply catching criminals but trying to ensure that what is offensive or imprudent behavior today can be treated as scandalous or even criminal behavior tomorrow."[16] As a result, observe

Frank Anechiarico of Hamilton College and James Jacobs of New York University, "much conduct that was legal a generation ago is now corrupt." New York City's Department of Investigations is, they report, "even prosecuting misconduct that used to be considered suitable only for administrative disciplinary action like sick leave fraud and abuse."[17]

The traditional dictionary definitions of "accountable" are: "1. subject to giving an account: *answerable*"; and "2. capable of being accounted for: *explainable.*" And "accountability" is "the quality or state of being accountable, liable, or responsible."[18] In *The Dorsey Dictionary of American Government and Politics,* Jay Shafritz of the University of Pittsburgh defines accountability: "1. The extent to which one must answer to higher authority—legal or organizational—for one's actions in society at large or within one's particular organizational position. . . ." and "2. An obligation for keeping accurate records of property, documents, or funds."[19] In *The International Encyclopedia of Public Policy and Administration,* Barbara Romzek of the University of Kansas and Melvin Dubnick of Rutgers University define accountability as "a relationship in which an individual or agency is held to answer for performance that involves some delegation of authority to act."[20]

These formal definitions never mention punishment.[21] Instead, they emphasize the responsibility to answer, to explain, and to justify specific actions (or inactions), in part by keeping records of important activities.[22] Somehow the dictionaries have not caught up with the vernacular. When people seek to hold someone accountable, they are usually planning some kind of punishment.

What do we really mean by accountability? Romzek and Dubnick call accountability "a fundamental but underdeveloped concept in American public administration." William Gormley of Georgetown University says that "accountability has become a murky concept." Moore and Gates observe that "the terms of accountability are always changing." Kevin Kearns of the University of Pittsburgh calls "the notion of accountability the ultimate 'moving target.'" Moreover, he observes, "accountability has become a catch-all term referring to everything from cost control to professional ethics." This is because, Kearns continues, "while the standards of accountability often are formally codified in laws and regulations, they are also defined by implicit expectations of taxpayers, clients, donors, and other stakeholders."[23] Thus if expectations can change so can the standards to which individuals and organizations are held accountable. Little wonder that the late Frederick C. Mosher, long of the University of Virginia, called accountability "that will-o-the wisp."[24]

Being in the accountability-holding business can be fun. The accountability holders get to go around checking on other people—to see if the accountability holdees have done anything wrong. And to whom are these accountability holders accountable? They believe that they are accountable to no one. For example, the late Zechariah Chafee, long of Harvard Law School, once observed: "The sovereign press for the most part acknowledges accountability to no one except its owners and publishers."[25] One inspector general (IG) in the federal government told Paul Light of the Brookings Institution, "No one should evaluate an IG but God."[26] This position—of being accountable only to God—has a long, historical tradition: It is the perspective held by emperors, queens, and other divinely chosen potentates.[27]

The accountability holders themselves don't have to do anything particularly right. They just have to catch other people doing things that are wrong. The only way that these accountability holders can do something wrong is if they fail to discover or point out that someone else has done something wrong. They do have to be a little diligent. They do have to be a little dogged, a little inquisitive, a little skeptical, even a little cynical. But accountability holders don't really have to do anything right; they just have to catch other people doing something wrong.[28] Anyone with such a job description will never, on this planet, be unemployed. What a wonderful profession!

It does help to actually discover that someone did something wrong. In fact, it really helps to be the *first* person to discover that someone did something wrong. Coming in second does not count for much in the accountability business—though if you are a legislator, you can still be the first to hold the hearings.

If it turns out that the accountability holdee whom the accountability holders "caught" doing something wrong was not really doing anything that was actually wrong, well, the accountability holders were just doing their job: "Sorry. In government, you can't be too careful, you know. Our job is to hold people accountable." Raymond J. Donovan, secretary of labor under President Ronald Reagan, spent six years coping with congressional hearings, an independent counsel's reports, journalists' stories, and a district attorney's indictment. When it took a jury less than ten hours to acquit him, Donovan plaintively inquired: "Which office do I go to to get my reputation back?"[29]

What do we really mean by this ubiquitous admonition to "hold people accountable"? The phrase rolls off one individual's tongue and into another's ears without registering in either's mind. To "hold people accountable" has become a cliché and, like all clichés, is a substitute for thinking. Indeed, using the phrase suggests that no real thinking is going on. We hide our inability to create a clear understanding of accountability (both among citizens and within our own mind) behind a well-known phrase that is guaranteed to start a lot of heads nodding.

Certainly government does have some clear responsibilities, and we citizens expect that our government will fulfill them. We are concerned about the responsibilities, obligations, and duties of public agencies and public officials. We are concerned about how these agencies and officials carry out these responsibilities, obligations, and duties. We expect that these agencies and officials will preserve, earn, and build the public's trust while fulfilling the public interest.[30]

For the highest officials in American government, we impose accountability through an elaborate constitutional system of checks and balances—including periodic elections. But what about the public managers—both those who are politically appointed and those from the career civil service? What about middle managers and frontline workers? What are their responsibilities, obligations, and duties? How are they preserving, earning, and building the public's trust while fulfilling the public interest? What does it mean to hold these people accountable?

Sometimes we citizens know exactly what these responsibilities, obligations, and duties are. Sometimes we have defined them very precisely. But all too often we haven't—or at least we aren't all using the same definition. After all, there are a lot of different citizens who want to hold different public agencies and public officials accountable for lots of different things. "The accountability environment," explains Kevin Kearns, "is a constellation of forces—legal, political, sociocultural, and economic—that place pressure on organizations and the people who work in them to engage in certain activities and refrain from engaging in others."[31]

The accountability environment is certainly complex.[32] Yet, when we talk about holding people accountable, we usually mean accountability for one of three things: accountability for finances, accountability for fairness, or accountability for performance.[33]

Accountability for Finances

The words "accountability," "accountable," "account," and "accounting" all have the same root. They go back through Old English and Old French to

Latin—to *computāre*, which is also the root of the verb "to compute." (*Computāre* is the compound of *com*, which meant "together," plus *putāre*, which meant to "count, reckon, consider.")[34] So it is not surprising that the most obvious form of accountability focuses on financial accounting—on how the books are kept and how the money is spent.[35] Indeed, observe Eugene Bardach of the University of California at Berkeley and Cara Lesser of the Center for Studying Health System Change, "because financial controls are among the few tools of legislative control of administration, the desirable aim of protecting legislative power also has had the unintended consequence of making financial accountability a virtual synonym for the whole concept of accountability."[36]

Financial accountability is (relatively) straightforward. *The Dictionary of Accounting Terms* offers a simple, generic definition of accountability: "individual or departmental responsibility to perform a certain function. Accountability may be dictated or implied by law, regulation, or agreement."[37] Accounting provides the mechanism to account for the money: Where did it go? Was it spent on the people and things for which it was supposed to be spent? If yes, then everything is fine. If not, this can be very bad. Someone must be held accountable; that someone may have to go to jail. The question of financial accountability is whether the organization and its officials have been wise stewards of the resources with which they were entrusted.[38]

Accountability for finances has established the framework for other holding-people-accountable systems. First, decide what values we want individuals and organizations to uphold. Next, specify what it means to uphold these values by codifying them into very specific rules, procedures, and standards: Don't do this. Do do that. Then create numerous reporting mechanisms to demonstrate that these rules, procedures, and standards have been followed. Finally, give a separate organization the specific task of auditing these records to check whether the rules, procedures, and standards have been followed.[39] And, if these auditors discover any failures, lapses, or discrepancies, they identify the culprits so that we can hold them accountable—so that we can punish them.

What exactly do all of these rules, procedures, and standards accomplish? They specify our expectations for how public officials will handle our money. You can't have accountability without expectations. If you want to hold people accountable, you have to be able to specify what you expect them to do and not do. Because we have very detailed expectations for how our public officials will handle our finances, we need a lot of rules, procedures, and standards.

All of this sounds quite straightforward. The managers and employees of any public organization have been entrusted with something quite valuable: the taxpayers' money. They have the responsibility—the obligation—to use these funds wisely. They ought to be held accountable for doing so. When they don't, they ought to be punished.

Accountability for Fairness

We want to hold government organizations and their employees accountable for more than simply handling the finances properly. We also want to hold them accountable for a variety of other well-established norms of democratic government—specifically, for fairness. We want government to be fair to its employees and to its contractors. We want government to be fair to all of the clients of its various programs. We want government to be fair when it provides services to citizens, when it taxes citizens, when it accuses citizens of violating the law. We want government to be fair—exceptionally fair.[40]

To ensure that government and its officials pay careful attention to these ethical standards—to these democratic norms—we create rules to codify exactly what we mean, operationally, by fairness and equity. These rules create processes and procedures that, if followed, ensure that government has been equitable—that it has treated its citizens fairly. Indeed, the rules embody and define what we, as a society, mean by equity and fairness.

Thus the process of creating accountability for fairness has many similarities with the process of creating accountability for finances. First, decide what values we want government to uphold. Next, create rules, procedures, and standards to establish what the organization should and should not do.[41] Then, require the organization and its managers to keep a lot of records of what it did (and sometimes of what it did not do). Finally, audit these records to ensure that the organization and its managers did follow the rules, procedures, and standards. And, if we discover that they did not do so, we hold them accountable by punishing them.[42]

Again, to establish a basis for holding people accountable, we have to create expectations—very specific expectations. And, again, this is what the rules, procedures, and standards do. They codify our expectations for how public officials will treat citizens—what, exactly, we mean by being fair. Because we have very clear, very detailed expectations for how our public employees will deal with citizens, we need a lot of rules, procedures, and standards.

Again, all of this sounds quite straightforward.[43] The managers and employees of any public organization have been entrusted with something quite valuable—with ensuring our mutual commitment to fairness. Thus they have the responsibility to treat all citizens absolutely fairly. They ought to be held accountable for doing so. When they don't, they ought to be punished.

Accountability for the Use (or Abuse) of Power

Why do we worry about accountability in government? Because we fear that public officials—elected officials, appointed executives, or civil servants—will abuse their power. And many public officials do have a lot of power. They award contracts worth millions or billions of dollars to some but not to others. They decide to grant benefits to some and not others. They decide to prosecute some and not others. They decide to convict some and not others. They impose fines and disburse funds—to some but not to others. Public officials exercise a lot of discretion, and as Steven Kelman of Harvard University notes, we "fear granting discretion to public officials."[44]

Thus, as citizens, we seek to constrain the behavior of public officials, to limit their discretion, to prevent them from abusing their power. We have our elected representatives create rules and then attempt to hold people accountable for following these rules. "Politicians," write Guy Peters of the University of Pittsburgh and Donald Savoie of l'Université de Moncton, "can hold public servants accountable by imposing rules and regulations."[45] Paul Light observes that "the definition of accountability in government has remained relatively constant over the past fifty years: limit bureaucratic discretion through compliance with tightly drawn rules and regulations."[46]

What, however, are all of these rules and regulations designed to accomplish? Two things: the proper use of public funds and the fair treatment of citizens. Accountability for the use (or abuse) of power is nothing more than accountability for finances and fairness.

Accountability for Performance

Government is not only supposed to use money prudently and to treat everyone fairly; it is also supposed to accomplish public purposes. Accountability for finances and accountability for fairness reflect concerns for *how* government does what it does. But we also care *what* government does—what it actually accomplishes.[47] This requires a third kind of accountability—accountability for performance.[48]

We care about the *consequences* of government action. Are the policies, programs, and activities of government producing the results that they were designed to produce? How much did the elementary students learn?[49] How much cleaner is the river this year than it was ten years ago? How much healthier are the children this year than last? How much safer is it to walk the streets? The answers provide the basis for holding government accountable for performance.[50]

To hold a public agency accountable for performance, we have to establish expectations for the outcomes that the agency will achieve, the consequences that it will create, or the impact that it will have.[51] We cannot, however, do this with rules, procedures, and standards. To specify the level of performance we expect from a public agency, we need some kind of objective, goal, or target—a clear benchmark of performance. We need an explicit measure of how well the agency has done against the expectations we have set for it. For this purpose, rules, procedures, and operational standards are useless. Accountability for performance requires something qualitatively different.[52] To establish our expectations for what a public agency will accomplish—and thus to create a basis for holding it accountable for performance—we citizens need to specify the results that we want it to produce.

Accountability for performance means—or ought to mean—more than providing the appropriate and required services to the agency's direct "customers." Our expectations for the performance of public agencies cover more than keeping customers happy. Accountability for performance ought to mean achieving performance standards that are set at a higher level than a seller-buyer, provider-customer exchange. It ought to mean satisfying the performance expectations of the diversity of people in Kearns's accountability environment. Accountability for performance ought to cover the expectations of citizens; it ought to mean accountability to the entire citizenry.[53]

The Accountability Dilemma

Now the accountability-holding business hits a snag. Holding people accountable for performance while also holding them accountable for finances and fairness creates a dilemma. The accountability rules for finances and fairness can hinder performance. Indeed, the rules may actually thwart performance.[54] Paul A. Volcker, former chairman of the Federal

Reserve Board, and William F. Winter, former governor of Mississippi (and the chairmen, respectively, of the Volcker Commission and the Winter Commission[55]) think precisely that:

> Not even the most public-spirited government workers can succeed if they are hemmed in on all sides by rules, regulations, and procedures that make it virtually impossible to perform well. The most talented, dedicated, well-compensated, well-trained, and well-led civil servants cannot serve the public well if they are subject to perverse personnel practices that punish innovation, promote mediocrity, and proscribe flexibility. . . . [The] detailed regulation of public employees is not compatible with productivity, high morale, and innovation.[56]

This is *the accountability dilemma*—the trade-off between accountability for finances and fairness and accountability for performance.[57] The late Peter Self, long of the London School of Economics, concludes that "the tensions between the requirements of responsibility or 'accountability' and those of effective executive action can reasonably be described as *the* classic dilemma of public administration."[58]

Self is not alone in observing the conflict between accountability for finances and fairness with accountability for performance. Many others have commented on the accountability dilemma:[59]

— "Some politicians, anxious to appear morally pure, support dubious and cumbersome 'reforms,' regardless of the possible effect of those reforms on public administration," observe Frank Anechiarico and James Jacobs. In their book *The Pursuit of Absolute Integrity: How Corruption Control Makes Government Ineffective,* they write that "moral entrepreneurs are likely to be so consumed with stopping corruption" that they rarely even consider "the integrity/efficiency trade-off."[60]

— "Accountability is not commonly associated with invention or novelty or serendipity, but rather with carrying out assignments, which are more or less specifically defined, honestly, efficiently, effectively, and at minimal cost," writes Frederick Mosher; "there is a conflict between the value associated with accountability and the values of originality, experimentation, inventiveness, and risk-taking."[61]

— Elmer Staats, former comptroller general of the United States, notes that this trade-off also applies to the various "nongovernmental organizations" upon which government calls "to achieve policy and program objectives": "The ever-present issue is how government can hold these organizations accountable without loss of the essentials of independence, ingenuity, creativeness, and initiative that have historically been associated with independent groups."[62]

— "The potential tensions between traditional notions of public administration (doing things by the book) and new forms of public management (seeking results through innovation and risk management) are starting to emerge," reports the Public Management Service of the Organisation for Economic Co-operation and Development. "If there is too much control, nothing will get done; but if there is too little control the wrong things will get done."[63]

Observes Phillip Cooper of the University of Vermont, "some of the older tools of accountability are precisely the 'problems' targeted by the reformers."[64]

The Accountability Bias

For what should the accountability holders hold the accountability holdees accountable? For complying with the processes for finances and fairness? Or for producing results through performance? If you want to be in the accountability-holding business, it makes more sense to concentrate on process than on performance. This is because our accountability expectations for finances and fairness are much clearer than they are for performance. We have codified our expectations for finances and fairness into explicit rules. Often, however, we don't agree about the results we want a public agency to produce; thus we are unable to make our performance expectations as clear. In contrast, the accountability standards for money and equity are much more formal, much more specific, much more detailed, much more objective, much more established, and much more accepted.[65] Any umpire will generate more protests with a judgment call than with one for which the standards are clear and objective.

From his study of inspectors general, Light observed "an important lesson on accountability": The inspectors general "were safest when they stuck to the most traditional concept of compliance-based monitoring and the most vulnerable when they branched into bigger questions of performance or capacity building." Indeed, argues Light, "compliance monitoring can eclipse a broader vision of accountability."[66] Similarly, Moore and Gates observed that inspectors general employ "a definition of waste or abuse that depends on procedural rules," while establishing accountability for performance is inherently much more subjective. Thus, in seeking to determine "not simply how much the government spends but how much social value it creates through its expenditures," inspectors general must "leave some of their precious objectivity behind," and "along with their objectivity goes some of their power."[67]

Accountability holders have a better chance of catching an accountability holdee when they concentrate on finances and fairness. And given that accountability holders have so many potential targets, why worry about subjective ones? Why not concentrate on objective targets? In checking whether all of the accountability holdees have complied with all of the objective rules and regulations, accountability holders have more than enough work.

This creates *the accountability bias.* Accountability holders concentrate on finances and fairness. They give much less attention to performance. If you are in the accountability-holding business, you need to hold someone accountable for something. And, given the very specific rules about finances and fairness, it is much easier to hold someone accountable for violating these well-established, objective standards than to hold someone accountable for not achieving your personal, subjective hopes for performance.

What should be the performance standard? Who should set the performance standard? And even if we can create a widely accepted performance standard, why did the agency fail to meet it? Was it the fault of the agency's managers or frontline workers? Was it the fault of changing conditions, such as an economic recession? Or was it the fault of the legislature or the budget office that failed to provide adequate funding or flexibility? Little wonder that accountability holders tend to focus on finance and fairness. It is much easier to establish who should be accountable for a failure in finances and fairness than for a failure in performance.

Indeed, if you are an accountability holder, and if you want to hold a particular agency accountable for some failure in performance (that is, if you want to punish the agency or its leaders for failing to produce the quantity or quality of performance that you desire), you may find it much more efficient and much more effective to go looking for some failure in finances or fairness. You may need much less time to uncover and document some mistake in finances or fairness (even if the violation did not mean that any money was actually misused or any individual was actually harmed) than to do the same for performance. You may also find it much easier to convince others that this procedural error was an obvious and thus punishable failure (even if the failure was a minor one) than to convince them that the performance error was both obvious and punishable.

Indeed, reports Derek Bok of Harvard University, this is precisely how accountability holders behave: "Rather than looking for fraud and other forms of actual malfeasance, reporters and public investigators are checking on whether officials have filled out forms properly or observed the superficial rules of propriety. Genuine wrongdoers have been allowed to escape serious condemnation by confessing to the lesser offense of paying too little heed to appearances."[68] If you want to punish a public agency or a public official, don't go looking for failures to produce satisfactory performance. Search out failures to follow the rules for finances and fairness.

The Deterrent Effect

Holding people accountable is designed not solely to catch, reverse, and punish wrongdoing. It is also designed to *deter* wrongdoing. By holding a specific accountability holdee accountable for a specific case of wrongdoing, the accountability holder seeks to influence the behavior of all future public officials—to convince them to live up to our expectations for finances, fairness, and performance.

But what kind of incentives do our methods of holding people accountable really create? After all, these incentive-creating mechanisms ought to be evaluated not in terms of their intentions but in terms of their consequences. What kinds of behavior do these accountability mechanisms actually provoke?

First, aggressive holding-people-accountable strategies may convince many accountability holdees to focus on money and equity and to ignore results. With a little experience in government, most accountability holdees understand the accountability bias and learn how to respond creatively to its incentives.

Second, aggressive accountability strategies may encourage accountability holdees to be excessively cautious. Writes Mosher: "A person who is held strictly accountable and is punished for a poor idea or a failed experiment is not likely to have much incentive to create or broach new ideas or launch experiments in the future."[69] This is why Volcker and Winter suggest "trimming work and procurement regulations that discourage public servants from exercising initiative, assuming responsibility, and experimenting in the interests of better service delivery and greater cost-effectiveness."[70]

Indeed, accountability holdees may create their own, even more stringent rules. After all, who knows better than the people inside an organization how someone might violate the written or unwritten norms about the disbursement of funds or the treatment of people. Knowing about such additional opportunities for people to abuse power, they can easily take preemptive action to insure against potential scandals—or some uncomplimentary publicity.

For example, those responsible for government procurement must both be penurious when spending government funds and fair in awarding government contracts. These officials recognize that, if they purchase anything but the bottom-of-the-line model, they risk being "exposed" for wasting government money. And if they even appear to award a contract in a not perfectly fair manner, they may face both a direct legal protest and an indirect political challenge. This "risk of protest," observes Steven Kelman, "encourages [procurement] agencies to make the evaluation process [for government contracts] even more complex." Indeed, Kelman "was repeatedly surprised how many common procurement practices are not mandated by the procurement regulations, but come from a procurement culture that has developed in contracting offices."[71]

Third, aggressive holding-people-accountable strategies may damage government's operating capacity. Light suggests that the aggressive prosecution of those who violate the rules for finances or fairness may actually undermine government's ability to comply with these rules. "The deterrent effect of one successful prosecution," he writes, "may be as powerful as one hundred." But, "if those extra ninety-nine convictions come at the cost of basic program operating capacity" (for example, if they drive away talent or divert it from operating programs to policing the rules), they could create "more exposure to fraud and abuse," and be "detrimental to overall management improvement."[72]

Public officials who try to satisfy their own, personal standards for finances, fairness, and performance may nevertheless choose to avoid being held publicly accountable for performance. One governor told his department heads, "Never put a number and a date in the same sentence." The message was clear: If you don't promise to produce a certain result by a certain time, no one can hold you accountable for not doing so. Don't overpromise. Don't even promise. Don't establish any public expectations for performance. Don't give anyone the opportunity to hold you accountable for any kind of performance.[73]

What kinds of behavior do our accountability systems deter? Our traditional, American mechanisms of holding people accountable may deter malfeasance and misfeasance for finances and fairness. Nevertheless, they may also encourage nonfeasance for performance. Our traditional mechanisms of accountability for money and equity can easily deter public managers from producing accountability for results.

The Benefits and Burdens of Public Service

Public officials—regardless of whether they are elected or appointed—face greater ethical obligations than do similarly situated officials in the private sector. "To accept public office is to accept, along with greater benefits, greater burdens than those of ordinary life," writes Dennis Thompson of Harvard University. "Among the burdens to which [public] officials could be assumed to consent is the risk of punishment for actions that are in fact justified."[74] Wow! Public officials have consented to be punished for justified actions. I wonder what consent form they signed.

What is the ratio of Thompson's "greater benefits" to his "greater burdens"? Indeed, what are these greater benefits? How do they compare with the greater burden—the risk of being punished for, as Thompson clearly states, "actions that are in fact justified"? And how do people who might consider accepting public office think about these greater benefits and greater burdens?

In late 1988, president-elect George Bush found out. He discovered that "talented men and women" who were "perfectly honest" were nevertheless unwilling to go to work in his administration because of two fears: the "fear of the sheer complexity of federal ethics laws" and the "fear that a simple, honest mistake could lead to a public nightmare."[75] Bush was not the first president to face this problem. "It used to be," recalled Pendleton James, who served President Reagan as White House personnel director, "that if the president actually asked someone to come to Washington, the guy would agree. 'You don't say no to the president,' was the saying. Well, they sure say no to the president now. I've sat in the Oval Office and watched them do it."[76]

Nevertheless, Thompson argues that the threat of punishment creates some useful incentives: "Officials [in government] know in advance that they may lose their jobs because of events over which they could have had little or no influence, and they thus tacitly consent to the risk of this kind of political 'punishment.' Such risk, furthermore, may be a useful feature in the design of political institutions, encouraging officials to take every possible precaution to avoid mistakes."[77] Not only have public officials consented to being punished for justified actions, they have also consented to being fired for events over which they had no control.

Yet how "useful" is Thompson's little "feature"? Does it really encourage public officials to do everything possible to avoid mistakes? And at what cost? Shouldn't such an incentive-creating feature be evaluated not in terms of its intentions but in terms of its consequences—in terms of the behaviors that it actually provokes?

Certainly, Thompson's feature encourages public officials to avoid mistakes. But how many people are willing to "consent to the risk of this kind of political 'punishment'"? And, having experienced such punishment, how many people will continue to consent to the risk? Given Thompson's rules of public service, how many people will be attracted by its "greater benefits"? For high-performing public managers, these benefits are certainly not financial. Nor, in today's world, do such benefits come in public esteem. If we seek to improve the public service—if we hope to attract talented people to manage public agencies—we ought not to assume that the practice and theory of accountability as punishment creates only positive incentives. We ought to think carefully about the incentives—both positive and negative— created by our formal and informal systems of accountability. We ought to be careful not to threaten officials with punishment, either for actions that were justified or for events that they could not have influenced, lest we deter them from ever considering public service.

Exit—and Entrance

As Albert Hirschman of the Institute for Advanced Study reminds us in his classic book *Exit, Voice, and Loyalty,* when people are unhappy with an organization, they can respond politically with voice or economically with exit.[78] An individual voice is, obviously, less effective than a collective one; thus career civil servants have formed associations that can present their well-organized collective voice. For the individual, however, exit may be a much more effective strategy.[79] Why bother complaining—particularly when the political and institutional imperatives suggest that such complaints will be unheard: "Hey, don't whine. When you went to work for the government, you consented to be punished for justified actions and to be fired for things that you didn't control. So just shut up and do your job."

If public officials perceive that they may be punished for actions that were justified or for events that they could not have influenced, how will they respond? One obvious choice is exit. People with enough smarts or skills can simply exit public service for the private sector, leaving behind all of Thompson's "greater benefits." For example, the General Accounting Office found that an important reason why members of the federal government's senior executive service chose exit was their "frustration with criticism of federal workers by the press, politicians, and/or the public."[80] Why put up with constant hassle in your professional and private life when employment in the private sector has more extrinsic rewards and fewer accountability contradictions?

If people considering either elected or appointed public office think that they may be punished for actions that were justified or for events that they could not have influenced, how will they respond? One obvious choice is to avoid entrance. Such people can simply remain in the private sector, eschewing all of those "greater benefits" of public service. And those eschewing entrance are not just senior officials. In the wake of the espionage allegations at the Los Alamos National Laboratory, reports David Pines, co-director of its Institute for Complex Adaptive Matter, "Washington's reaction to the incident has created an atmosphere of suspicion" that, in combination with congressional efforts "to impose inefficient micromanagement strategies," has "threatened the essence of the lab." Among the damage, writes Pines, is "a 60 percent drop in the number of top researchers accepting postdoctoral fellowships."[81] Some simply decide that public service is not worth the effort.

In Britain, the heads of the executive (or Next Steps) agencies are hired competitively from the public and private sectors and given specific performance contracts. The heads of two of these executive agencies (the Social Security Child Support Agency and the Prison Service) were dismissed as the result of parliamentary criticisms that focused on issues other than whether they achieved their performance targets. When it came to recruiting replacements, reports Alasdair Roberts of Queen's University, the dismissals had a "chilling effect."[82] As James Q. Wilson of Pepperdine University puts it, "most people do not like working in an environment in which every action is second-guessed, every initiative viewed with suspicion, and every controversial decision denounced as malfeasance."[83]

Robert Samuelson, a columnist with *Newsweek,* explains "Why I Am Not a Manager." He lists a number of specific drawbacks: "resentment from below; pressure from above; loud criticisms of failure; silence of the successes." In addition, writes Samuelson, managers are "supposed to get results—to maximize profits, improve test scores or whatever. Everyone must 'perform' these days and be 'accountable' (which means being fired, demoted, or chewed out if the desired results aren't forthcoming)." Thus, although Samuelson has "a certain grudging respect for managers," it "baffles" him why anyone would want the job. After all, he observes, all managers must "serve twin masters"—the organization for whom they work and the individuals who work for them.[84] And, public managers have to be accountable to many more masters than just these two.

Moral Entrepreneurs and Infinite Jeopardy

It is, of course, impossible to document the extent to which aggressive accountability contributes to the exit of officials whose talents and energy we would like to keep in the public service. It is even more difficult to document the extent to which aggressive accountability contributes to decisions not to enter government by people whose talents and energy we would like to see in the public service. Still, Anechiarico and Jacobs clearly conclude that it does both. "Ethics legislation may do more than discourage qualified individuals from entering public service. In some circumstances it may force qualified individuals to resign." Indeed, they report that "passage of a New York State ethics law in May 1991 precipitated a rash of resignations among local officials all over the state."[85]

"The current atmosphere not only keeps some people from going into government but helps push government employees out the door," writes Suzanne Garment. Moreover, "the fear among civil servants over how ethics rules will be interpreted is not paranoia." Consequently, she emphasizes, "anxieties bred by scandal dominate our public choices and force even those federal policy makers who are honest to spend so much of their time, energy, and intellect trying not to look like crooks."[86] In fact, concludes Jonathan Rauch of *National Journal,* "no matter how hard even the most honest politician tries to obey the law, he can no longer go about his business without fear of one or more ruinous corruption investigations."[87]

Anechiarico and Jacobs are quite scornful of the "moral entrepreneurs" who are "committed to forms of disciplinary control that nurture and exacerbate bureaucratic pathologies and make fundamental public administration reform all but impossible." In "the pursuit of corruption-free government," they argue, these corruption hunters have created a "panoptic vision" of corruption control that "is not concerned with efficient governing, but with control alone" and that "treats public employees like probationers in the criminal justice system."[88]

Moreover, argues Anechiarico, the emphasis on corruption control suggests to citizens an image "of public professionals as self-serving functionaries." The result, he continues, is "a self-fulfilling prophecy, as fewer talented, creative young people are attracted to public service."[89]

How do the moral entrepreneurs and the ethics police conduct their business? Rauch lays out the process:

> Formal investigations can be triggered by ordinary political conduct, with no showing that a crime has been committed; once the investigation begins, it justifies its expansive scope on the grounds that, after all, some people are guilty; the investigation exacts from even the innocent a toll in money and time and anguish that is itself often hard to distinguish from a form of punishment; above all, a cascade of investigations-of-investigations creates a maze of infinite jeopardy. At no stage is there protection from bankruptcy or exhaustion, or shelter from the radiating circles of fear as the subpoenas pour forth.[90]

As if our need to create accountability for finances, fairness, and performance were not enough, we have recently added a fourth form of accountability—accountability for personal probity—that may further deter people from public service. Thomas Kean, the former governor of New Jersey, notes that although there have always been rumors about the affairs of individual public officials, and although "they were always in the supermarket tabloids," such affairs (real or alleged) never became serious, public issues. But, says Kean, "now, we have the type of atmosphere where Tom Brokaw, *The Washington Post, The New York Times,* and *The Boston Globe* feel they have to print them." Kean, now president of Drew University, worries that this latest form of accountability will deter people from public service. "I had a young honor student in my office," recalls Kean. "He is going to an Ivy League graduate school and he said to me, 'I always thought of myself as someone who had a future in government, and I don't think that is true anymore.'" This new form of personal accountability "is not helping," concludes Kean, who believes "the future of democracy depends on the people we get to serve it."[91]

People have choices. People make choices. Public officials make choices about the precautions they will take to avoid mistakes. And political institutions can encourage—through the prospects for punishment (or reward)—these officials to choose to reduce the chances of mistakes.

People have choices. People make choices. People make choices about where to work. They make choices about whether to remain in the public service or to exit it. They make choices about whether to enter it at all. And political institutions can encourage or discourage—again, through the prospects for punishment (or reward)—these people to choose to work in the public service.

If we could conscript our public servants, then we might want to design our political institutions to ensure that these officials take every possible precaution to avoid mistakes. But we cannot simply draft people to work for two years as political executives, or as public managers, or as frontline employees. We have to convince people that they want these jobs. If we design our political institutions solely to encourage public officials to take every possible precaution to avoid mistakes, we should not be surprised when they will do precisely that. Unfortunately, the best possible precaution for avoiding mistakes is simply to avoid taking a job in which you may be accused of making mistakes.

We American citizens have designed our political institutions—our formal systems and our informal practices—to ensure the ethical conduct of public officials and to establish their accountability. But these political institutions may have other, less beneficent consequences. If our institutions for creating accountability also encourage good officials to leave public service—and if they discourage good people from even considering public office—then such practices and systems deserve serious rethinking.

2

Performance and the New Public Management

For more than a century, American government has been shaped and constrained by the public administration paradigm.[1] Guy Peters calls it "the old-time religion" of "traditional public administration," which is based on "six old chestnuts" or "principles" that "have guided our thinking about the public service and its role in governance": (1) an apolitical civil service, (2) hierarchy and rules, (3) permanence and stability, (4) an institutionalized civil service, (5) internal regulation, and (6) equality.[2] But, like any paradigm that has been around for a while, it has developed weaknesses: inconsistencies, problems that it can't solve, and outright challenges. The latest such challenge, which has emerged in the last two decades, is called "the new public management." It emphasizes performance.

Traditional Public Administration and the Corruption Problem

In the late nineteenth century, the public administration paradigm evolved in response to the corruption that had invaded American government. In a famous 1887 essay titled "The Study of Administration," Woodrow Wilson observed that Americans had "just begun purifying a civil service which was rotten full fifty years ago." Moreover, he directly linked the elimination of corruption to the introduction of effective administration: "The poisonous atmosphere of city government, the crooked secrets of state administration, the confusion, sinecurism, and corruption ever again discovered in the bureaux at Washington forbid us to believe that any clear conceptions of what constitutes good administration are as yet very widely current in the United States." Thus Wilson urged a new approach to government administration: "This is why there should be a science of administration which shall seek to straighten the paths of government, to make its business less unbusinesslike, to strengthen and purify its organization, and to crown its dutifulness."[3]

In many ways, the public administration paradigm did solve the corruption problem. By separating the implementation of public policies from the political decisions that created those policies, just as Wilson recommended, the advocates of the (then new) public administration sought to prevent the politics of personal favoritism and gain from meddling in the administrative decisions about personnel, procurement, finance, and service delivery. As a result, American government in the twentieth century was indeed much less corrupt than it had been in the nineteenth. Of course, twentieth-century government was not completely free of corruption; but whenever public power was abused, the advocates of public administration could usually attribute it to some breakdown in one of their underlying principles—particularly to someone's failure to abide by the hierarchical rules.

The New Public Management and the Performance Problem

At the beginning of the twenty-first century, however, American government is plagued less by the problem of corruption than by the problem of performance.[4] American government may not be very crooked; but neither is it very effective. "If one thing has become clear about the federal government," concludes Derek Bok, "it is that Americans have little regard for its performance."[5]

Indeed, many citizens have decided that government's performance is not growing as fast as their taxes. When Larry Polivka and Jack Osterhold worked in the executive office of the governor of Florida, they concluded that "the current emphasis on educational testing is largely in response to the feeling among many policymakers that student achievement has not matched the major increases in educational expenditures over the last 15 years."[6] "More and more people are uncomfortable with the idea that spending equals results in education," observes Thomas Finneran, speaker of the Massachusetts House of Representatives.[7] In his 1996 state of the state address, Georgia's governor Zell Miller offered "three facts":

(1) Our citizens want better service from state government on the issues they care about.

(2) They are not willing to pay more to get those services, because . . .

(3) They are not convinced that they have been getting value for their tax dollars.[8]

Often, citizens conclude that government's bang-for-their-tax-buck performance is going down. Thus in 1999, when Anthony Williams was inaugurated as the mayor of Washington, D.C., he emphasized the need to improve the performance of the city's government: "We will need to develop clear performance measures for all who work in government, provide training for those who need it and hold our managers accountable for results."[9]

This challenge to the traditional public administration paradigm comes in a variety of guises, with a variety of complaints, a variety of remedies, and a variety of labels. Some have called for "deregulating government."[10] Others have advocated "reinventing government" and "entrepreneurial government."[11] Some have labeled this public sector "managerialism."[12] Still others have championed a "new public management."[13] Regardless of the label— regardless of the prescriptions—these various reforms have all emphasized better management that produces better results.

Moreover, this emphasis on better government performance is not restricted to the United States. In their best-selling book *Reinventing Government,* David Osborne and Ted Gaebler call it "a global revolution."[14] "A truly remarkable revolution has swept public management around the world," writes Donald Kettl of the University of Wisconsin. "From Korea to Brazil, from Portugal to Sweden, government sector reform has transformed public management."[15] In a review of the new public management, Frederick Thompson of Willamette University concluded that, worldwide, "the conduct of the public's business is undergoing a sea-change."[16]

What are the new chestnuts—the new principles—of the new public management? This isn't so obvious. Peters has defined four new "emerging models" of governance with which the English-speaking democracies have been experimenting. In describing characteristics of each new-governance model, Peters specifies features that are designed to enhance performance:

Model 1: "Market government" focuses on decentralization, pay for performance, and other private sector techniques.

Model 2: "Participative government" emphasizes flatter organizations, total quality management, and teams.

Model 3: "Flexible government" features virtual organizations and temporary personnel.

Model 4: "Deregulated government" stresses greater managerial freedom.[17]

Each model is derived from a different diagnosis of government's inadequacies,[18] and thus each offers different remedies. Yet, behind the management strategies of all of these models lies the desire to improve the performance of the public sector.[19]

Sandford Borins of the University of Toronto describes "the new public management" as "a normative reconceptualization of public administration consisting of several inter-related components."[20] "This new paradigm is not reducible to a few sentences, let alone a slogan," argues Borins. Nevertheless, he suggests, it contains five "key ideas":

— Government should provide high-quality services that citizens value.
— The autonomy of public managers, particularly from central agency controls, should be increased.
— Organizations and individuals should be evaluated and rewarded on the basis of how well they meet demanding performance targets.
— Managers must be assured that the human and technological resources they need to perform well will be available to them; and
— Public sector managers must appreciate the value of competition and maintain an open-minded attitude about which services belong to the private, rather than public, sector.[21]

Of Borins's five key ideas, the first offers a definition of improved performance—"high-quality services that citizens value"—while the other four suggest ways to achieve it.[22]

A New Public Management Paradigm?

Can such a diversity of tactics and strategies be called a new "public management paradigm"? Not if you define a *paradigm* as a single, micro-tactic, or even as a coherent collection of such tactics combined into a macrostrategy.[23] But you may reach an opposite conclusion if you are willing to define a *paradigm* in terms of a macro-aspiration.[24] Indeed, the Public Management Service of the Organisation for Economic Co-operation and Development concludes: "A new paradigm for public management has emerged, aimed at fostering a performance-oriented culture" that is "characterized by [among other things] a closer focus on results."[25] In this spirit, I am defining this "new public management paradigm" as the entire collection of tactics and strategies that seek to enhance the performance of the public sector—to improve the ability of government agencies *and* their nonprofit and for-profit collaborators to produce results.

Any effort to enhance the performance of government needs not a single tactic but an entire repertoire of strategies. After all, improving government performance is a complex undertaking. It means different things in different nations and different things in the same nation in different regions, or at different times, or for different policy problems. Every government may be looking to ratchet up performance another notch, but some may be several notches ahead of others. Different governments with different problems need different remedies. Different governments, having made different political decisions about what they will (and will not) do, and how they will do it, need different strategies. Whenever a government decides to do something specific, it needs a specific strategy that will maximize its performance in its specific (and unique) context. Who believes that a single, micro-tactic will work in every situation or for every need to improve performance?[26]

The new public management is a worldwide phenomenon but with different strategies employed in different governments in different situations. In the United States, it is epitomized by the reinventing government movement and Vice President Gore's National Performance Review. In Britain, it began with Prime Minister Margaret Thatcher's Financial Management Initiative and continued with what is called *Next Steps*. Other nations of the Westminster tradition, as well as those in Scandinavia, have adopted their own reforms.[27] But New Zealand has made the most drastic changes in its government structure and managerial philosophy.

During the late 1980s, New Zealand's Labour government enacted a number of managerial reforms, including a dramatic switch from traditional public sector bureaucracies to competition and contracting: The political minister organizes his or her ministry into distinct operating units, establishes specific performance targets to be achieved by these units, and then either enters directly into a performance contract with the head of that agency, or opens the assignment to competition among private and public entities. The head of each unit is given significant flexibility for achieving the annual performance targets and receives performance pay. The performance targets for which the agency head is responsible are outputs, with the minister responsible for the outcomes. Thus the New Zealand reforms employ the public administration concept of separating politics from administration: The minister has the political responsibility for overall policy, for achieving the long-range outcome objectives, and for establishing the annual output targets; the agency head has the administrative responsibility of producing these politically mandated outputs.[28]

Is this new public management paradigm, as Christopher Hood of the London School of Economics asks, "a public management for all seasons?"[29] Not if it is defined as a single diagnosis with a single solution. But if the challenge is to improve the performance of government,[30] then the entire repertoire of strategies designed to achieve this result in different situations can be wrapped together in a comprehensive catalogue that may prove quite valuable for many, if not all, seasons.[31]

Accountability for Performance or for Process

When Vincent G. Mannering took over as executive director of the Boston Water and Sewer Commission, he made changes. To improve efficiency, he organized the agency, reassigned managers, and cross-trained employees. And he filled some supervisory positions with outsiders, many of whom were his friends. In response, several employees filed formal discrimination complaints. "They don't like my team," responded Mannering to the criticisms. "I'm sorry—it's my team. I'm running the show and the numbers say I'm doing a good job."[32]

The "accountability dilemma" prompts the public manager's cry: "Don't hold us accountable for process. Just hold us accountable for performance." If only I didn't have to follow all of those damn, nit-picking regulations, goes this line of reasoning, my agency could really produce results.[33] "Governors can create a results-based government," reports the National Governors' Association, if (among other things) they "shift accountability from complying with rules and regulations to achieving results."[34] "If you want better management," argues David Osborne, "untie the managers' hands and let them manage. Hold them accountable for results—not for following silly rules."[35]

Ironically, accountability holdees are not the only ones complaining about the silly rules. When these regulations apply to accountability holders, they don't like them either. Paul Light reports that the federal government's inspectors general "wanted what every other federal manager wanted: freedom from the cumbersome rules and regulations governing the management of their units." When they tried to hire people, the inspectors general were confronted by "inflexible bureaucrats" who specialized in saying no.

Amazingly, these accountability holders never seemed to wonder why. Instead, reports Light, the inspectors general simply wanted out—"out of the cumbersome, rule-bound personnel system; out of the endless paperwork; out of the inflexible regulations and oversight; out of the clutches of the classification analysts in their departments." Like every other federal manager, Light continues, the inspectors general "wanted to be trusted to do the right thing." Still, several didn't trust their department's general counsel to provide independent legal advice; instead, they wanted their own.[36]

Inspectors general are not the only accountability holders who wish to avoid the rules that they rigorously impose on others. Legislators are notorious for exempting themselves from personnel, procurement, budgetary, and ethical statutes with which they require the executive branch to comply.[37] It is precisely for such accountability holders that someone designed the t-shirt declaring: "I know the rules (they just don't apply to me)."[38]

Thus from the call to improve government performance emerges the call to deregulate government:[39] If the public really wants government to produce better results, it should lessen the multiple regulations that frustrate any effort to improve performance. Paul Volcker and William Winter argue that "deregulating the public service while maintaining appropriate avenues of accountability is almost certain to improve the administration of the nation's federal, state, and local governments."[40]

American citizens, however, have not stopped worrying about corruption. They are not about to give up on their cherished beliefs that each public official should be accountable for the use of their tax dollars and for treating all citizens fairly. Their argument is quite simple:

> Sure improved performance is important. We certainly want improved performance. But we don't think that you public managers can only get that improved performance by getting rid of the rules that ensure financial probity and guarantee fairness. Okay, the rules make it a little harder. But they don't make it impossible. They just mean that you have to be a little smarter, a little more persistent. But, hey, that's why we taxpayers pay you those big bucks.

We want to have it not just both ways but all three ways. We want accountability for finances, and for fairness, and for performance.[41]

How can public managers ever hope to be successful? How can they ever pass the accountability test? After all, this accountability test is really two tests—one test for finances and fairness, another test for performance; one test for process, another for results. And these two tests often seem to be in direct conflict. Indeed, a public manager can easily respond: "I can choose to satisfy the accountability rules for finances and fairness. Or I can focus on performance. But I can't do both." It's like being expected to be the top athlete *and* the top scholar in school. Sure, a few people can do it. But most of us are mortal. We can do one. Or we can do the other. But we can't do both—and certainly not at the same time.[42]

So what do public managers do? How do they respond to the "accountability dilemma"?

First, I think, most choose to satisfy the tests of accountability for finances and fairness. Most public managers make sure that no one can hold them accountable (that is, punish them) for not handling the finances properly or for not sustaining the American virtues of fairness and equity (at least as codified in all of the regulations). Most public managers make damn sure that their organization is audit-proof—that anyone who audits anything will find not the slightest infraction of the rules. Then, if they still have any time, resources, organizational capacity, or flexibility left over, they will try to improve performance. Accountability holdees are well aware of the "accountability bias"—and respond to its implicit incentives. As one public manager told Frank Anechiarico, it is "better to look honest than to get anything done."[43]

A few, however, will be less than judicious about the rules for finances and fairness and will focus their time, energy, and resources on performance. They hope that the results they produce will protect them from any punishment for any of the rules that they may break along the way. Indeed, among both practitioners and academics, there is a certain respect for those public managers who figure out how to evade the various rules and regulations that inhibit performance and then deploy this flexibility to actually produce results, while escaping capture by the regulatory police. For example, Lisbeth Schoor, in her book *Within Our Reach,* writes: "What is perhaps most striking about programs that work for the children and families in the shadows is that all of them find ways to *adapt or circumvent traditional professional and bureaucratic limitations when necessary to meet the needs of those they serve.*"[44] Similarly, Martin Levin of Brandeis University and Bryna Sanger of New School University observe: "An increasingly common response to management's frustration with excessive oversight and regulatory requirements is for executives to seek innovative ways to circumvent the formal rules." Levin and Sanger analyzed a number of "successful executives" who, they found, had "a risk-taking emphasis on quick results," would "short-circuit organizational clearance points," "often operated outside the normal bureaucratic chain of command," and employed "creative subversion."[45]

Most public managers, however, accept that they are not superheroes. They conclude that they must choose. They decide that they cannot possibly satisfy all three forms of accountability—that they cannot comply with the accountability rules for money and equity and at the same time produce results. In the American system of accountability, observes Marc Zegans of Harvard University, "rule-obsessed organizations turn the timid into cowards and the bold into outlaws."[46]

Two Theories for Improving Performance

The new public management paradigm is a direct response to the inadequacies of traditional public administration—particularly to the inadequacies of public bureaucracies. Yet, as Kettl observes, the new public management comes in two distinct varieties, each based on a different theory about how best to improve performance and produce results. Moreover, in some ways these two theories are quite contradictory: Some nations, such as New Zealand and the United Kingdom, use contracts and incentives to "make the managers manage." Others, such as Australia and Sweden, empower their managers and "let the managers manage."[47]

Both the contracting and the empowerment varieties of the new public management attempt to give public managers the flexibility they need to improve performance.[48] Yet those who adopt the empowerment (let-the-managers-manage) approach are implicitly trusting them to exercise their judgment intelligently, to employ their flexibility with prudence, and to be motivated primarily by the intrinsic rewards of public service. By contrast, those who employ the contracting (make-the-managers-manage) strategy often do so with specific, tightly written performance contracts that leave little room for such trust and that motivate improvements with very extrinsic rewards.[49] The contracting approach correlates to Peters's Model 1 of "market government," while the empowerment strategy reflects the three key ideas—participation, flexibility, and deregulation—of his other three models.

Which theory has the United States adopted? Predictably, we have avoided ideological purity. In the United States reports Kettl, "reformers have sometimes eagerly looked to both sets of ideas as a shopping list from which they could cobble together their own reforms."[50] Jack Nagel of the University of Pennsylvania calls the American approach "cheerfully eclectic."[51] Nevertheless, Frank Thompson and Norma Riccucci of the State University of New York at Albany found four themes that are common to David Osborne's work, the Winter Commission, and the National Performance Review: (1) "internal deregulation of government agencies," (2) "the need to make the administrative agents of government more mission-driven or bottom line-oriented," (3) "decentralization and the empowerment of frontline workers," and (4) "competition and customer service."[52] Thompson and Riccucci's second theme emphasizes the need to improve performance, while the other three are mechanisms for achieving it; theme 4 is the contracting approach, while the first and third reflect the empowerment strategy.

To the advocates of letting the managers manage, civil servants are not automatons, merely implementing policies according to rules promulgated from above. Instead, behind this version of the new public management lies the assumption that civil servants are intelligent, that they understand the problems their agencies are charged with alleviating, that they have some useful ideas about how to fix these problems, and that they can, if given the freedom, quickly convert these ideas into effective action. Indeed, many advocates of the public management paradigm assume that, because frontline civil servants are close to the problems, they are in a very good position (perhaps the best position) to decide what approach to take in solving public problems.

Moreover, these advocates of empowerment make no attempt to pretend that administration can be disconnected from politics or policy. They accept that it is and seek to exploit this well-recognized, but carefully avoided, reality. Thus, under this version of the public management paradigm, civil servants are instructed to be responsive to individual citizens and encouraged to develop new, innovative approaches to solving public problems.

In contrast, those who advocate the make-the-managers-manage approach emphasize the superiority of markets to hierarchy (and of extrinsic to intrinsic rewards). Thus, instead of relying on front-line civil servants to make better decisions and on smaller, leaner, decentralized government agencies to improve performance, they adopt strategies that exploit the advantages possessed by private sector organizations. They seek to contract out more public services—employing, quite naturally, performance-based (rather than fee-for-service) contracts[53]—and to privatize more government functions.[54] Or they create "performance-based organizations"

(PBOs) that reward the chief executive financially if the organization achieves its performance targets.[55]

These contracts necessarily define performance by using output indicators. The desired social outcomes (to which the outputs are designed to contribute) may not be realized for years or even decades. Moreover, a contractor—be it a private firm, a nonprofit agency, or a governmental PBO—can actually produce its outputs, but it does not control the outcomes. Other institutions or forces can also affect these outcomes. Thus it would be unreasonable to make performance payments dependent upon outcomes that a contractor cannot control. The make-the-manager-manage strategy implicitly assumes that politics can, indeed, be separated from administration.

Still, the two strategies have some important commonalities. Under traditional public administration, notes Peters, "the principal managerial tasks were carried out by conforming to rules rather than by exercising discretion." In contrast, he writes, "the emerging models of governing tend to shift the thinking about management toward greater autonomy and discretion for lower-echelon officials."[56]

The advocates of a new public management paradigm are contemptuous of traditional public administration. They scorn the bureaucratic ideal that seeks to base the implementation of policy on impersonal rules. Some reject the idea that politics should be (let alone can be) separated from administration—that the mind of the civil servant should be disconnected from the solution to policy problems. Others reject the idea that public services are best delivered by public agencies.[57]

The advocates of the new public management are seeking to solve the problem of performance. For them, controlling corruption is much less of a challenge to today's government than producing results. Consequently, they are not overly concerned about discarding some of the public administration safeguards that deter corruption. More significantly, they have not worried about how their new performance paradigm can mesh with our traditional concepts of political accountability. Nor have they bothered to construct a new and corresponding paradigm of democratic accountability.

Empowerment, Contracting, Flexibility—and Accountability

Can we permit entrepreneurial, empowered, responsive civil servants and independent contractors to make decisions, to exercise discretion, and to be innovative and still maintain democratic accountability? Can we give public managers flexibility and still ensure accountability?[58] Can we encourage public managers to be entrepreneurial in producing results and still obtain the information necessary to establish accountability?[59] Can we delegate public functions to private sector organizations without losing the sense that public services are not merely individual transactions with individual customers but have a larger, public purpose?[60] Can we demand that public managers produce results without losing accountability for finances and fairness? These big questions haunt those who would advocate either form of the new public management.[61]

Indeed, these questions have been raised frequently:[62] Borins notes that Osborne and Gaebler, the original advocates of "reinventing government" have been criticized because (among other things) "the public sector entrepreneurship they advocate may conflict with traditional values, such as accountability to the electorate."[63] The late Frederick Mosher observed that "the growing reliance upon outsiders to carry out federal programs greatly complicates the problem of accountability for the expenditure of public money."[64] To Kenneth Ruscio of Washington and Lee University, "the inherent problem of democracy in the administrative state is reconciling the political imperative of accountability with the managerial imperatives of flexibility and responsiveness."[65] "Many administrative reformers," observes Laurence Lynn of the University of Chicago, "fail to notice that what they pejoratively deride as bureaucracy run amok is in fact the institutional manifestation of the continuous effort to create responsive, accountable government, to prevent abuse of discretion."[66]

The proponents of a new public management paradigm emphasize performance—the ability of their strategy to produce results. But they cannot ignore the troubling question of political accountability. They must develop a process, a mechanism, a system, a concept, a something that not only permits public agencies—and their collaborators in the for-profit and nonprofit sectors—to produce better results but also ensures accountability to citizens.

The champions of the new public management have challenged the public administration paradigm that has ruled our thinking for more than a century. Their argument is quite simple: The traditional method for organizing the executive branch of government is too cumbersome, too slow, too bureaucratic, too inefficient, too unresponsive, too unproductive. It does not give us the results we want from government. And today, citizens expect government to produce results. They are no longer tolerant of inefficiency or ineffectiveness. Thus, we need a new way of doing business, a new paradigm for the management of government.

Moreover, continue the advocates of the new public management, we will do a better job at performance—at producing the results and services that citizens value. We know this because we have created a new system of accountability to customers through surveys and user fees.

"But wait," respond the defenders of traditional public administration. "Your outmoded rules and cumbersome regulations are our accountability." As Herbert Kaufman, long of the Brookings Institution, noted: "One person's 'red tape' may be another's treasured procedural safeguard."[67] Our approach to doing the business of government, continue these public administration advocates, may have some deficiencies, but it does have one very big advantage: It is accountable to the citizens.

The defenders of the traditional public administration paradigm may be willing to accept that government could benefit, as the advocates of the new public management assert, by employing the management techniques of business. Nevertheless, these defenders insist that the nature of government, particularly the nature of accountability in government, is fundamentally different from the nature of accountability in business.

"Any role prescribed for public administrators must be compatible with democratic values," writes Larry Terry of Cleveland State University. Adapting the private sector concept of the entrepreneur to public administration, he argues, is both "misplaced" and "dangerous." Terry makes his position unambiguous: "we should abandon the misconceived quest to reconcile public entrepreneurship with democracy." Indeed, he emphasizes, "public entrepreneurs pose a serious threat to democracy because of the nagging accountability problem."[68]

Democratic accountability is not optional. It is an essential characteristic of any approach to structuring the executive branch of government. It does not make any difference how well your market forces, your flatter and more flexible organizations, and your managerial autonomy works for private sector organizations, assert the advocates of traditional public administration. Government is different. Government must be responsible not just to self-interested stakeholders—not just to fee-paying, survey-filling-out customers. Government must be accountable to the entire citizenry. If your system does not ensure accountability to citizens, then it is, by definition, unacceptable.[69]

And one important feature of this accountability is fairness. "The issue of equality," notes Peters, "raises important questions about accountability and the law."[70] How can public management be both flexible and fair? Isn't government supposed to treat all of its citizens equally? Isn't this why we have a government of laws (not of men, or women)? Can it be legal (or ethical) for people with the same characteristics and the same rights to be treated differently by government? Isn't the democratic value of fairness more important than the value of flexibility?[71]

Conversely, if we empower frontline employees, if we permit civil servants at all levels to exercise discretion, what happens to our traditional notion of democratic accountability? As Peters observes, "If civil servants and other appointed officials are indeed to become entrepreneurial then they must become less dominated by the dictates of these [political] masters. If this approach were practiced, it would alter fundamentally ideas of accountability."[72]

How should empowered and discretion-exercising civil servants (or independent contractors) be accountable to the citizenry?

Public Law and Hierarchical Accountability

Perhaps the most thorough critique of the new public management—or, at least, of its application to the government of the United States as exemplified by the National Performance Review—is offered by Ronald Moe of the Congressional Research Service and Robert Gilmour of the University of Connecticut. Moe and Gilmour perceive "a fundamental clash of cultures" between "the entrepreneurial management paradigm" and "the public law paradigm," which they advocate. Moreover, they are concerned that the "sheer audacity of the entrepreneurial management advocates" has "caught off guard" the defenders of traditional public administration.[73]

To promote "the effective and accountable management of government," Moe and Gilmour offer ten "principles of public administration." Four of these "axiomatic 'givens' in American public administration" are designed to ensure hierarchical accountability for the implementation of public law:

> The purpose of agency management is to implement the laws passed by Congress as elected representatives of the people. . . .
>
> Executive branch managers are held legally accountable by reviewing courts for maintaining procedural safeguards in dealing with both citizens and employees and for conforming to legislative deadlines and substantive standards. . . .
>
> Political accountability for the implementation of policy and law requires a clear line of authority from the president to the heads of the departments and agencies and from them to their subordinates. . . .

Public accountability requires that inherently governmental functions and tasks be performed by officers of the United States and their
government-employed subordinates.

To Moe and Gilmour, "political accountability necessarily assumes legally
based hierarchical reporting structures."[74]

Moe and Gilmour do not approve of the contracting variant of the new
public management, in part because "the private and government sectors
are based on fundamentally different streams of legal doctrine." Private law
is designed to structure the relations between private individuals; in contrast, public law is designed "to ensure continuance of a republican form of
government and to protect the rights and freedoms of citizens at the hands
of an all-powerful state." Moreover, they continue, "openness to congressional, judicial, and public scrutiny of department and agency decision-
making processes is a hallmark of the governmental sector operating under
public law; not so in the private sector." The federal government's "greater
dependence upon private contractors and consultants to perform basic
management functions," they argue, has increasingly "placed at risk" federal
agencies and programs.[75]

Nor do Moe and Gilmour like the empowerment version of the new
public management. They disapprove of efforts to adapt "the generic behavioral principles of management as taught in schools of business" to the task
of "administering government agencies." To Moe and Gilmour, the job of
the public manager is not to improve performance but to implement the
public law. "The actions of government officials must have their basis in
public law," they write. "The missions and priorities of agencies are determined by law, not by the president or by the department heads, either collectively or separately." Moe and Gilmour would not "trade away the con-
stitutionally protected, known means of ensuring accountability for yet to
be established measures of government performance." To them, "the value
of accountability to politically chosen leaders outranks the premium placed
on efficient, low-cost service."[76]

Yet, like the advocates of the new public management, Moe and Gilmour
conclude that "the federal government now faces a management crisis."
They simply "diagnose the causes of the crisis differently." The federal government's political leaders have ignored management, argue Moe and
Gilmour; the problem lies in "the long-term retreat of presidents from their
organizational management responsibilities and the downgrading of the
central management agencies," combined with the "vague or contradictory"

legislation enacted by Congress. Further, Moe and Gilmour believe that "the federal manager is overregulated and needs to be deregulated." Indeed, they argue that Congress and the president should undertake a "tough, systematic review" of the general management laws and their accompanying regulations. This task would be "inevitably time consuming, tedious, and difficult," they admit, but not impossible. "The real issue is how to make this legal system, with its hierarchies and rules, work to the advantage of the federal management, not the disadvantage. It is a legal problem calling for a legal answer." Still, they believe, such a legal answer can be found: "There are no legal or structural reasons preventing creative management from becoming a reality."[77]

Moe and Gilmour argue that "the hierarchical structure found in the executive branch is designed more to ensure accountability for managerial actions than to promote control over employees."[78] They are not interested in accountability to the various parties in a public agency's accountability environment. Instead, Moe and Gilmour want direct, sequential, hierarchical accountability to political executives, to the president, to the Congress, and thus to the citizenry.

Can We Have It All?

What do we mean by democratic accountability? Does this mean that public managers are solely accountable for implementing the law? Or do they have a larger and positive responsibility to improve the performance of public institutions and to produce the results that citizens desire? And if so, is it possible to create accountability for this kind of performance and still maintain accountability for finances and fairness?

This is an honorable debate that has been going on for decades.[79] But it is not some metaphysical schism over which of the three angels of accountability should get to dance on the head of some governmental pin (or whether all three can somehow agree to dance together at the same time). It is a practical concern that worries very practical people.

In an essay titled "The New Public Management and Its Critics," David Mathiasen, a former member of the senior executive service, notes that "traditionalists object that the indiscriminate application of TQM [total quality management] to public sector institutions violates the principles of law, equity, public interest, and due process on which public administration is based." Moreover, Mathiasen writes, "the new public management often carries an efficiency connotation that suggests cutting corners on citizen entitlements, or at the very least increasing flexibility on how they are administered." Yet it is not strictly the theologians of traditional public administration who object. At a ministerial symposium sponsored by the Organisation for Economic Co-operation and Development, reports Mathiasen, the ministers responsible for public management in their countries accepted the value of the new public management. Nevertheless, they were "unwilling to concede the more traditional responsibilities of the state, that is, as protector of the general interest, and keeper of law and order, as the champion of fairness and equity, and as the caretaker for disadvantaged or handicapped citizens."[80]

Has performance become so important that we have begun to ignore our concerns for finances and fairness? This worry is not new. The accountability dilemma has always been with us. More than a quarter century ago, Hugh Heclo of George Mason University wrote that with the end of the Nixon presidency "the imbalance between output concerns and process concerns is being rectified." He noted, however, that this was only "after some years during which concern for outputs had almost totally eclipsed concern over the standards governing the production of those outputs."[81]

The president of the United States has the constitutional obligation to "take care that the laws be faithfully executed."[82] Other elected executives (mayors, governors, county executives) have similar obligations. So too do their political appointees and their jurisdictions' civil servants. They are not entrepreneurs designing clever mechanisms for achieving their own wonderful objectives, argue the advocates of traditional public administration; they are obligated to implement the laws enacted by our duly elected legislators, and nothing less. But, continue the traditionalists, nothing more either. If, to do their jobs, to achieve their public purposes, public managers need new innovative mechanisms, or if they need to define new public purposes, they should tell the legislature. Let the elected officials worry about it. Meanwhile, public managers should concentrate on implementing the existing laws—on following the legally prescribed means for achieving the legally established purposes. As Woodrow Wilson himself asserted, "public administration is detailed and systematic execution of public law."[83]

What is the job of executive branch agencies, of the leaders and managers of these agencies, of their frontline workers, and of their collaborators outside government? To improve performance? Or to implement the public law? This fundamental question divides the advocates of the new public management from the defenders of traditional public administration. In a debate with Barry Bozeman of the Georgia Institute of Technology, Moe makes the challenge clear: The "objective standard I argue for is the 'law.' The objective standard Bozeman advocates is 'performance.'"[84]

This challenge cannot be dismissed.[85] For what are public manager's accountable: performance or the law? Or is it possible to have accountability for implementing the laws governing finances and fairness and still have accountability for performance too? As we focus on improving the performance of public agencies, can we continue to insist that these agencies handle our tax dollars with care and treat citizens equitably? Or must we accept that, as we attempt to improve government's accountability for performance, we must sacrifice some of our cherished accountability for finances and for fairness? Is it possible to have it all—accountability for finances, and for fairness, and for performance too?

Colin Diver of the University of Pennsylvania identifies "two contrasting perspectives" on public management: the "engineering" and the "entrepreneurial" models. Diver's "manager as engineer uses his specialized wizardry to effectuate the value choice of the people, as communicated through their elected representatives." In contrast, his entrepreneur "conjures up a kind of frontier image of the public manager alone in the political wilds, surrounded by concealed pitfalls and drawn by undiscovered wealth." There are other contrasts as well: "The engineering model is ethically preferable, but unrealistic," writes Diver, while the entrepreneurial view seems "the more faithful image of reality, yet is morally unacceptable." To resolve this dilemma, he observes, we can either "make the engineering model more realizable or rehabilitate the ethical status of entrepreneurship." Yet, to Diver, there is no choice: "We must make the unavoidable more acceptable."[86]

The advocates of any new approach to the management of the public enterprise must not only demonstrate that their strategy is more effective. They must also demonstrate how it is accountable to the citizenry. "The central challenge facing advocates of the performance paradigm," writes Alan Altshuler of Harvard University, "is to demonstrate its compatibility with the paradigm of accountability." This means, he continues, that "innovative thinking is needed about accountability no less than about programmatic efficiency."[87] Those who seek to create a new paradigm of public management have the burden of providing a correlative paradigm of democratic accountability.

3

The Traditional Public Administration Paradigm of Accountability

The intellectual heritage of the traditional public administration paradigm comes from the thinking and writing of Woodrow Wilson, Frederick Winslow Taylor, and Max Weber. These observers constructed the rationale for the current form of much of our government. Wilson argued that administration could be—and should be—separated from politics; after those responsible for politics made the policy decisions, the task of implementing their policies could be turned over to experts in the "science of administration."[1] This would be possible because, Taylor contended, "among the various methods and implements used in each element of each trade there is always one method and one implement which is quicker and better than any of the rest."[2] Finally, Weber asserted that bureaucracy was the most efficient organizational structure; thus a bureaucracy would be ideal for implementing Taylor's scientific principles.[3]

Efficiency, Hierarchy, and Accountability

Wilson, Taylor, and Weber all strove to improve efficiency. And, although efficiency is a value in itself, it has another advantage. This efficiency is impersonal. Thus it can only be fair. By separating administration from politics, by applying science to the design of its administrative processes, and by employing bureaucratic organizations to implement these processes, government would ensure not only that its policies were fair but also that their implementation was fair.[4] And, in America, the administration of government must be fair. "Public administration has a number of core values," write Guy Peters and Donald Savoie, and "one value high on many lists is fair treatment for all."[5]

This emphasis on efficiency has another advantage: It implies that the policy implementation can, indeed, be separated from policy decisions. If there exists a one best way (and thus a most efficient way) to carry out any policy decision, and if there exists an organizational apparatus for deploying all of these one best ways, government can, indeed, separate administration from policy.[6]

Furthermore, by separating administration from politics, we Americans can create an accountability process that is tidy, linear, and hierarchical: People elect their legislative representatives and chief executive; then these individuals (and their political assistants) undertake the political task of developing and deciding upon public policies; next the administrative apparatus of government implements each policy in the most efficient way; finally, in case anything goes amiss, the elected officials oversee the work of the administrators. John Uhr of the Australian National University summarizes the legislature's universal role in ensuring accountability:

> The central arena of accountability is the political assembly, which exists to provide the community with a *public* accounting of public officials. The political assembly is the filtering institution between community and government, and public accountability is at base a filtering exercise in which the assembly "audits" (literally, listens to) the accounts by responsible ministers and officials of the use of public offices and funds.[7]

It's basic, eighth-grade civics.

This concept of democratic accountability is clear, simple, and direct. Because government can separate administration from policy, and because the bureaucratic apparatus of government will find and adopt the most efficient way to implement any policy, the public need not worry about administration. Citizens need only to worry about the policy. And if they don't like their government's policies (or the way in which the legislature is overseeing the administration of these policies), citizens have a direct and effective means to correct the situation: They can vote their elected officials out of office. That is political accountability. That is direct accountability.

The public administration paradigm is internally consistent; the distinction between politics and administration permits the construction of a simple, appealing, hierarchical model of political accountability.[8] Thus, despite its flaws, the old paradigm has one, big advantage: political legitimacy. The accountability relationships are clear. The traditional public administration paradigm meshes well with our traditional paradigm of democratic accountability.

Madison's Separation of Powers

The American concern for democratic accountability began, of course, not during the Progressive era but at the founding of the Republic. James Madison framed the problem famously: "If men were angels, no government would be necessary."[9]

In *The Federalist Papers,* Madison and his colleagues, Alexander Hamilton and John Jay, advocated a constitution that would give the national government stronger powers than did the Articles of Confederation, which had been a reaction to the powers previously exercised over the colonies by the English government. The three sought to convince New York's voters that this new government needed to be and would be stronger—but not too much stronger.

Thus the new government would have three separate branches. Indeed, the "separate and distinct exercise of the different powers of government," Madison argued, is "essential to the preservation of liberty." Moreover, he wrote, the American federal system would provide for a further division of powers between the national government and the states.[10] Hamilton and Madison supported the Constitution's provision for both a House of Representatives and a Senate because it divided the legislative powers and thus permitted each house to check the other. Specifically, Madison cautioned in Federalist 49 that "the tendency of republican governments is to an aggrandizement of the legislative, at the expence of the other departments."[11]

Still, Madison worried. He worried that his theory of the separation of powers would not work in practice. In Federalist 48, he wrote, "a mere demarkation on parchment of the constitutional limits of the several departments, is not a sufficient guard against those encroachments which lead to a tyrannical concentration of all the powers of government in the same hands." To guard against such encroachments, Madison sought "to give each a constitutional controul over the others."[12]

Indeed, Madison followed his famous sentence about men, angels, and government with a more detailed analysis of the problem:

> If angels were to govern men, neither external nor internal controuls on government would be necessary. In framing a government which is to be administered by men over men, the great difficulty lies in this: You must first enable the government to controul the governed; and in the next place, oblige it to controul itself. A dependence on the people is no doubt the primary controul on the government; but experience has taught mankind the necessity of auxiliary precautions.

To design these "auxiliary precautions," Madison relied on a simple principle: "Ambition must be made to counteract ambition."[13]

To ensure that ambition would control abuses, Madison sought to construct a government in which the people who occupied a public office—be they in the legislative, executive, or judicial branch—would have a personal stake in the power and prerogatives of that office. Thus, to prevent "a gradual concentration" of power in one branch, Madison proposed "the subordinate distributions of power; where the constant aim is to divide and arrange the several offices in such a manner as that each may be a check on the other."[14]

Thus the United States Constitution provides for what we now call the system of "checks and balances," although Madison used this phrase in neither the Constitution nor *The Federalist*.[15] To Madison, it was not enough for the people to hold the government accountable through periodic elections.[16] Madison wanted to ensure that the three different branches and the two different levels of American government could also hold one another accountable.[17]

Wilson's Distinction between Politics and Administration

In "The Study of Administration," Woodrow Wilson laid out the "distinction" between politics and administration: "The field of administration is a field of business. It is removed from the hurry and strife of politics." Indeed, Wilson wrote of the "truth" that "administration lies outside the proper sphere of politics. Administrative questions are not political questions."[18]

Wilson described his distinction between politics and administration in several ways: "The distinction is between general plans and specific means."

"The broad plans of governmental action are not administrative; the detailed execution of such plans is administrative." Wilson did not try to define the distinction very precisely, because "this discrimination between administration and politics is now, happily, too obvious to need further discussion."[19]

In 1881 President James A. Garfield was assassinated by a disappointed office-seeker, and two years later Congress passed the Pendleton Act to reform the federal civil service. Thus, when Wilson was writing in 1887, civil service reform was very much on his mind. To Wilson, it "is a plain business necessity" that American government have "a body of thoroughly trained officials serving during good behavior." But what is *good behavior?* Wilson answered with his own definition of what is now called *neutral competence:* all civil servants should have a "steady, hearty allegiance to the policy of the government they serve." Moreover, such policy "will not be the creation of permanent officials, but of statesmen whose responsibility to public opinion will be direct and inevitable." Thus, concluded Wilson, civil service reform "is clearing the moral atmosphere of official life by establishing the sanctity of public office as a public trust, and by making the service unpartisan, it is opening the way for making it businesslike."[20]

Indeed, Wilson's "eminently practical science of administration" was designed to do more than provide guidance for structuring the civil service: "We are now rectifying methods of appointment; we must go on to adjust executive functions more fitly and to prescribe better methods of executive organization and action."[21]

Moreover, to Wilson, "the objective of administrative study is to rescue executive methods from the confusion and costliness of empirical experiment and set them upon foundations laid deep in stable principle." Thus, nearly a quarter of a century before the Interstate Commerce Commission held its 1910 hearings on railroad rates and made Frederick Taylor's ideas famous, Wilson advocated what Louis Brandeis labeled during those hearings "scientific management."[22] Wilson wrote of "a science of administration," and worried that "not much impartial scientific method is to be discerned in our [American] administrative practices."[23]

In search of such knowledge, Wilson hoped that Europe could provide models. For those who might "be frightened at the idea of looking into foreign systems of administration for instruction and suggestion," Wilson distinguished between uniquely American ends and helpful European means. To make this point, he offered a metaphor:

If I see a murderous fellow sharpening a knife cleverly, I can borrow his way of sharpening the knife without borrowing his probable intention to commit murder with it; and so, if I see a monarchist dyed in the wool managing a public bureau well, I can learn his business methods without changing one of my republican spots. He may serve his king; I will continue to serve the people; but I should like to serve my sovereign as well as he serves his.

Whatever administrative model was found in Europe, Wilson emphasized, "it must be adapted" to the U.S. form of federal government: "we must Americanize it."[24]

Taylor's Scientific Management

On Thursday, January 25, 1912, when Frederick Winslow Taylor was summoned to testify before the Special Committee of the House of Representatives to Investigate the Taylor and Other Systems of Shop Management, he advocated a variety of changes—a "complete mental revolution"; a "great mental revolution"[25]—in how the nation should organize its workplaces. Taylor was concerned about "the great loss which the whole country is suffering through inefficiency in almost all of our daily acts" and was convinced that "the remedy for this inefficiency lies in systematic management, rather than in searching for some unusual or extraordinary man."[26] Indeed, to illustrate scientific management, Taylor described for the committee both "the science of bricklaying" and "the science of shoveling." When shoveling coal or ore, reported Taylor, "there is one right way of forcing the shovel into materials of this sort, and many wrong ways."[27]

Taylor concluded that inefficiency was created by the "rule-of-thumb methods" and "traditional knowledge" that workers employed when they did their job. This, however, was not their fault. Instead, it resulted from "the old systems of management in common use" that gave each worker "the final responsibility for doing his job practically as he thinks best, with comparatively little help and advice from management." Taylor wanted management to undertake the task of designing the work. He wanted management to determine scientifically how each component of work could be carried out most efficiently, particularly by a "first-class" worker who was scientifically suited for the task.[28]

Under scientific management, wrote Taylor,

the managers assume new burdens, new duties, and responsibilities never dreamed of in the past. The managers assume, for instance, the burden of gathering together all of the traditional knowledge which in the past has been possessed by the workmen and then of classifying, tabulating, and reducing this knowledge to rules, laws, and formulæ which are immensely helpful to the workmen in doing their daily work.

In particular, Taylor thought that the managers of any enterprise had four "new duties":

> *First.* They develop a science for each element of a man's work, which replaces the old rule-of-thumb method.
>
> *Second.* They scientifically select and then train, teach, and develop the workman, whereas in the past he chose his own work and trained himself as best he could.
>
> *Third.* They heartily cooperate with the men so as to insure all of the work being done in accordance with the principles of the science which has been developed.
>
> *Fourth.* There is an almost equal division of work and the responsibility between the management and the workmen. The management take over [sic] all work for which they are better fitted than the workmen, while in the past almost all of the work and the greater part of the responsibility were thrown upon the men.

These are management's responsibilities, argued Taylor, because the workers do not have time or expertise to both figure out the best system and do their work.[29]

Taylor organized work around the concept of "the task"—which he called "perhaps the most prominent single element in modern scientific management." The task "specifies not only what is to be done but how it is to be done and the exact time allowed for doing it." Moreover, the job of defining each such task is the responsibility of management: "The work of every workman is fully planned out by the management at least one day in advance, and each man receives in most cases complete written instructions, describing in detail the task which he is to accomplish, as well as the means to be used in doing the work." To Taylor, "scientific management" was "task management."[30]

Moreover, management has the responsibility of matching people with the jobs for which they are best suited. This was the definition of a "first-class man"—someone who was scientifically suited for the job. And, although people would be second class at many jobs, everyone was first class at some job. "I have tried," Taylor told the House committee, "to make it clear that for each type of workman some job can be found at which he is 'first class,' with the exception of those men who were perfectly well able to do the job, but won't do it."[31]

Taylor's concept of "the task" lives on in the "job descriptions" of our civil service system. For in government, management (not the worker) has the responsibility of defining each task that each worker should perform. Management then lists these tasks on the job description and fills the job by scientifically selecting the individual whose qualifications best match these tasks. The worker's responsibility is to do these tasks—and only these tasks. Workers are not supposed to think about these tasks; that is strictly management's job. Civil service systems directly apply Taylor's concept of scientific management, which "involves the establishment of many rules, laws, and formulæ which replace the judgment of the individual workman."[32]

When management assumes its four managerial duties, Taylor wrote, "the results must of necessity be overwhelmingly greater than those which it is possible to attain under the management of initiative and incentive." Indeed, Taylor went even further: "The general adoption of scientific management would readily in the future double the productivity of the average man engaged in industrial work."[33]

Frederick Taylor not only invented scientific management. He should also receive credit, emphasizes Alasdair Roberts, for "another accomplishment: the creation of the role of the modern manager."[34] And, although he did all of his work in industrial settings, Taylor clearly believed that his "principles" applied to the management of churches, universities, and "government departments"—even to the management of baseball teams.[35]

Weber's Bureaucracy

As society became more complex, Max Weber argued, it needed more complex institutions. To Weber, this meant a shift from informal, personal organizations to bureaucracy. Weber's bureaucracy is a hierarchical organization staffed by experts with credentials who have regular, official duties that they carry out as trustees by impersonally applying rational rules over a specific jurisdiction.

"The principle of hierarchical office authority," wrote Weber, "is found in all bureaucratic structures: in state and ecclesiastical structures as well as in large [political] party organizations and private enterprise." Indeed, he asserted, "it does not matter for the character of bureaucracy whether its authority is called 'private' or 'public'"; hierarchy is still the structural principle. Specifically, "the principles of office hierarchy and of levels of graded authority mean a firmly ordered system of super- and subordination in which there is a supervision of the lower offices by the higher ones."[36]

The people who desire to work in Weber's hierarchy earn educational credentials, obtain an appointment, develop their expertise, and agree to carry out their duties in a loyal yet impersonal way. "Office management, at least all specialized office management," wrote Weber, "usually presupposes thorough and expert training." When accepting a position in a bureaucracy, he continued, an individual accepts "a specific obligation of faithful management in return for a secure existence." This individual is not loyal to his boss as a person but to the boss's position; that is, "modern loyalty is devoted to impersonal and functional purposes."[37]

Like Wilson, Weber advocates what Herbert Kaufman calls one of the "core values" of public administration: "neutral competence."[38] Specifically, Weber argues, "the honor of the civil servant is vested in his ability to execute conscientiously the order of the superior authorities, exactly as if the order agreed with his own conviction." Thus Weber also separates administration from politics; the "genuine official" in Weber's bureaucracy "will not engage in politics. Rather, this official should engage in impartial 'administration.'"[39]

To Weber, a bureaucracy behaves like a referee with a computer: "Bureaucracy is like a modern judge who is a vending machine into which the pleadings are inserted together with the fee and which then disgorges the judgment together with its reasons mechanically derived from the code."[40] Weber's bureaucracy—with its emphasis on the impersonal implementation of impersonal though rational rules—is both efficient and fair: "Experience tends universally to show that the purely bureaucratic type of administrative organization," writes Weber, "is, from a purely technical point of view, capable of attaining the highest degree of efficiency." Bureaucracy "is superior to any other form in precision, in stability, in the stringency of its discipline, and in its reliability."[41]

Nevertheless, politics can undermine both a bureaucracy's efficiency and its fairness. Indeed, Weber recognizes, political corruption can interfere with the work of experts impersonally following the rules. Although Weber believes that effective bureaucracies would be a benefit to politicians when they sought reelection, he suggests that this was not always the case:

The demand for a trained administration now exists in the United States, but in the large cities, where immigrant votes are "corralled," there is, of course, no educated public opinion. Therefore, popular elections of the administrative chief and also of his subordinate officials usually endanger the expert qualification of the official as well as the precise functioning of the bureaucratic mechanism.[42]

Little wonder that Weber sought to separate politics from administration.

Weber's bureaucracy is necessarily fair. It bases its decisions and discharges its business "according to calculable rules and 'without regard for persons'"— which it does by "eliminating from official business love, hatred, and all purely personal, irrational, and emotional elements which escape calculation."[43] Little wonder that our systems of bureaucratic accountability—particularly our systems for creating accountability for finances and fairness—are based on "calculable rules."[44]

The Fallacy of Efficient, Nonpolitical Administration

Unfortunately, traditional public administration has proven neither as efficient nor as nonpolitical as Wilson, Taylor, and Weber predicted. Often, it is both quite inefficient and quite political. For each of the intellectual founders of the public administration paradigm employed a logic that is plagued by a critical fallacy.

(1) *Weber's Fallacy: Bureaucracies are efficient.*

Is bureaucracy efficient? Today, we think not. Today, the word *bureaucracy* is synonymous with inefficiency. Among the technical advantages that Weber attributed to "the fully developed bureaucratic mechanism" was "speed";[45] yet, today, we think of bureaucratic processes as being interminably slow.

In Weber's bureaucracy, workers specialize, and the rationale for this specialization is its efficiency. Because different individuals specialize in different tasks, each individual need master only his or her narrow assignment. In a bureaucracy, workers need not know how to perform all of the tasks or understand how they mesh together. Instead, each can concentrate on doing one task very well.

Unfortunately, dividing the work of a bureaucracy into distinct, specialized tasks creates a new problem: coordination. If everyone performs all of the tasks, there is no coordination problem; each individual can coordinate these tasks in his or her own brain. But when the tasks are all divided up, coordination becomes difficult, and if the conduct of the different tasks is not coordinated, the organization can become very inefficient.[46]

Moreover, bureaucracy inhibits change. Indeed, bureaucracy is designed to inhibit change. Because no specialist understands the big picture, no specialist knows enough to contemplate major innovations in how the organization does its work (or in what work the organization should do). Moreover, because each specialist conducts work for several other specialists, change means changing not just the work of one specialist but the work of many. Thus even if someone could figure out how to improve the work of the bureaucracy, such changes would necessarily disrupt the routines of many specialists, all of whom have become quite comfortable with their personal routines.

(2) *Taylor's Fallacy: There is necessarily one, universal, best way.*

In an age when the answer to every scientific question has a single, universally correct answer (and a zillion wrong ones), we can easily believe that every management question should also have a single, universally correct answer. But management is less like science than like engineering. Moreover, the questions of engineering have many possible answers.[47] In some circumstances, some answers will be better than others. Yet, even for a single set of circumstances, there may be many, quite correct answers.

Thus the search for the one best way can undermine motivation. If there is one best way, and if it is management's job to figure it out, the workers have no responsibility other than to implement management's brilliant decisions. But if there exists more than one possible answer, and if many of these answers may be equally effective, how does an organization choose? Management might still make the choice and delegate implementation to the workers. But if there is more than one possible way, why not let the workers choose? Why not let the workers decide—thereby gaining the additional motivation that comes from their desire to prove themselves right.

It is a tribute to the simplicity and forcefulness of Taylor's ideas that we continue—implicitly, though rarely explicitly—searching for that elusive one best way.[48]

(3) *Wilson's Fallacy: Implementation is inherently not political.*

Finally, it is impossible to separate administration from politics and policy.[49] Administration is not just about efficiency; it inherently involves policy choices. Legislators and elected executives cannot—individually or collectively—think of all of the possible circumstances and special situations that may arise. No matter how hard the political leaders in the legislative and executive branches try, they cannot develop a set of policies and rules that is appropriate for every situation. Individual cases and specific circumstances may be covered by no policy at all—or by several, contradictory policies. Thus those charged with the mere efficient implementation of authorized policies must—by default—make policy decisions. As Paul Appleby, the late dean of the Maxwell School at Syracuse University, wrote a half century ago: "Arguments about the application of policy are essentially arguments about policy."[50]

Indeed, Wilson himself recognized that the division of responsibility between politics and administration is an inherently political question:

> The study of administration, philosophically viewed, is closely connected with the study of the proper distribution of constitutional authority. To be efficient it must discover the simplest arrangements by which responsibility can be unmistakably fixed upon officials; the best way of dividing authority without hampering it, and responsibility without obscuring it.

Nevertheless, Wilson hoped that "administrative study can discover the best principles upon which to base such a distribution" of power between political and administrative officials.[51]

But suppose such an administrative study did uncover some excellent (if not necessarily best) principles for dividing power between political and administrative officials. What would happen? Would these principles be quickly codified into law? We all doubt it. As Madison hoped, the distribution of constitutional authority—particularly between the legislative and executive branches—is a source of continual political competition. The conclusions of a study might influence a distribution of authority and power, but political negotiation and thus political power will be controlling. Indeed, one criticism of the National Performance Review—and other efforts by the advocates of the new public management to increase the discretion and flexibility allocated to executive branch officials—is that they encroach, however subtly, on the power of the legislature.[52]

The Evolution of Multiple Mechanisms of Accountability

Despite these three fallacies, we Americans anchor our implicit thinking (if not our explicit practice) about accountability on beliefs that have changed little in the last century.[53] From the ideas of Wilson, Taylor, and Weber—

plus the work of Frank Goodnow, Luther Gulick, and the Public Administration Institute[54]—we Americans have evolved the basic building blocks of our system of democratic accountability, keeping the old mechanisms of accountability while experimenting with new ones.[55] For example, in the Budget and Accounting Act of 1921, Congress created two new institutions of hierarchical accountability—the General Accounting Office and the Bureau of the Budget—both of which evolved, during the remainder of the twentieth century, new responsibilities and new mechanisms for holding agencies accountable for finances if not for fairness. Thus in the 1950s Herbert Kaufman could note that the "governmental structure" and other institutions of public administration have evolved through "a process of experimentation" that "goes on vigorously today."[56]

Indeed, we Americans have not been satisfied with our ability to exercise accountability through periodic elections. For example, at the beginning of the twentieth century the Progressives worried that direct, electoral accountability was not enough; so they added the extra accountability mechanisms of the recall and the initiative. With the recall, voters do not have to wait until the end of an elected official's term to hold him or her accountable. With the initiative, if legislators are not sufficiently accountable in the bills they have enacted, the citizens can engage in direct democracy: they draft a law, collect petition signatures, qualify for the ballot, and then convince voters to enact the law themselves.[57]

In response to the corruption of traditional politics, the Progressives also established independent agencies and government corporations. To temper the monopolistic tendencies of big business, they created independent regulatory commissions, such as the Interstate Commerce Commission (1887), the Federal Communications Commission (1927), and state public utility commissions. To insulate the administration of these regulatory bodies from political influence, the members of such a "commission" are appointed for fixed terms and cannot be removed (except for ethical violations). The legislature is accountable for establishing the proper regulatory policies; the commission is accountable for independently (and scientifically) implementing these policies.

In the same tradition of separating administration from policies, the Progressives created public authorities, such as the Port Authority of New York and New Jersey (1921), and the Tennessee Valley Authority (1933).[58] Again, political leaders would establish the purposes and policies of the independent authority; then a nonpolitical hierarchy of experts would scientifically administer the policies and thus achieve the purposes.[59]

To eliminate the political patronage and political favoritism that could undermine the technical effectiveness of the regulatory commissions and public authorities, we insulated them from politics. Just as independent civil servants would, in Wilson's words, help make government's "business less unbusinesslike,"[60] so would independent commissions and authorities. The Progressives placed these organizations and their responsibilities outside the formal lines of hierarchical accountability because they worried that otherwise their administrators would be *too* accountable—too responsive to the interests of their political superiors.[61] Instead, the Progressives sought to mitigate the problem of political accountability by placing their faith in the nonpatronage experts who would staff these independent agencies. These "scientists"—economists in the regulatory commissions, planners in the public authorities—would be professionals, hired not for their connections but for their credentials and expertise and for their commitment to professional standards. Such professional standards are, however, no more value-neutral than are political ones. [62]

Moreover, these professionals used their expertise to gain enormous power. "The absolute monarch is powerless opposite the superior knowledge of the bureaucratic expert," wrote Weber. "The 'political master' finds himself in the position of 'dilettante' who stands opposite the 'expert.'"[63] In addition, these professional experts carried out much of the work of these independent agencies in private. "Bureaucratic administration always tends to be an administration of 'secret sessions,'" observed Weber. "In so far as it can, it hides its knowledge and action from criticism."[64] And independent agencies have proven quite effective at hiding their actions—both through secret sessions and through professional expertise.

Thus, by creating these independent organizational arrangements (outside the normal lines of hierarchical accountability), we did not eliminate the politics; instead, we simply altered the arena in which the politics was played and the amount of influence that different interests could mobilize in the new arena. Indeed, because regulatory commissions are independent from direct political control by elected officials, the firms that they are assigned to regulate are able to "capture" them.[65] And independent public authorities are able to choose economic concerns over social ones—creating, for example, the frequent conflicts between port authorities and the citizens (often their neighbors) whose lives the authorities' work or plans have disrupted.[66] Regulatory commissions and public authorities are indeed accountable—accountable, however, to the constituencies they seek to cultivate, not to the citizenry.[67]

This, of course, is not a new problem. Nor is it limited to independent agencies. Even public agencies under the direct control of an elected executive can operate in secret or be captured by an organized and aggressive stakeholder. Thus we Americans have sought additional mechanisms to hold such public agencies accountable to a broader public and to a broader conception of the public interest. We enacted freedom-of-information laws and passed sunshine acts to prevent public officials from colluding in private with influential constituents. If we citizens—or our surrogates in the press—can always know what public officials are doing, we have a better chance of holding them accountable for their actions. Maybe we cannot punish them. Nevertheless, when we uncover a questionable decision or action, we can, at least, force them to provide an explanation.

Inspectors General and Special Prosecutors

Such accountability innovations failed, however, to check corruption. Thus we Americans created some new accountability holders: inspectors general and special prosecutors.

To establish accountability for finances—to cope with what Paul Light calls "the three horsemen" of the inspector-general concept: fraud, waste, and abuse—Congress established an office of inspector general (IG) in each federal department.[68] In their study of inspectors general, Mark Moore and Margaret Gates observe that Congress came to believe "that government programs were rotten with massive fraud, waste, and abuse and that neither the political executives nor the career civil servants who managed the programs could be relied on to root it out." Each inspector general has a staff, note Moore and Gates, that includes a mix of investigators, who seek "criminal prosecutions of individuals," and auditors, who seek "administrative sanctions against negligent managers or new procedures designed to prevent future problems."[69]

Although investigators and auditors both rely on after-the-fact monitoring,[70] they have distinctly different objectives, ethics, and operating styles. Light contrasts the "investigator mentality" with the "audit culture" and argues that such differences create a "rivalry"; within each IG office, the two professions are "pitted against each other" for resources. And from this struggle came what Light calls "a drift toward investigation." The investigators had "a much stronger external orientation" and a "penchant for visibility." Moreover, the investigators' record of "statistical accomplishment"—

measured in indictments and convictions—is easier to understand than the auditors' successes—measured in audits conducted, in "funds put to better use," and in "total investigative recoveries."[71]

In addition to selecting how to balance their staff, IGs have other strategic options. Moore and Gates argue that they "must decide if they are in business primarily to find previous errors, assign blame, and recapture lost resources, or whether it is more important for them to use information about past errors to design better policies and procedures for the future."[72] Light suggests that the inspectors general have a similar choice: They can choose not merely to perform fewer audits and more inspections, or vice versa; they can also choose to perform fewer audits *and* fewer inspections and, instead, focus more on evaluating performance.[73]

Implicitly, however, the inspectors general have adopted the traditional, public administration paradigm of accountability and focused on what Light calls "compliance monitoring." "The IGs have not done their job poorly," he writes, "but they may be doing the wrong job—putting too much emphasis on compliance and not enough on performance and capacity building."[74] Similarly, Moore and Gates suggest that the inspectors general should take a broader view of their responsibilities. Because of the IG's current approach, they write, "government may become 'accountable' in some narrow sense [for fraud, waste, and abuse], but actually lose 'accountability' in a broader sense which involves the quantity and quality of government programs."[75]

Why does compliance monitoring make sense? Because behind it lies the implicit assumption of scientific management: Once a task has been scientifically designed, we can establish accountability by determining whether those assigned this task have followed all of the scientific rules.

What happens, however, when a high-ranking political appointee fails to follow the scientifically created bureaucratic rules designed to separate administration from politics and, instead, engages in some form of fraud or abuse? Then, an inspector general might not have enough independence or clout; after all, the president can remove from office every inspector general in the federal government. For such cases, Congress created independent counsels, although so many of these individuals abused their office—to whom were they accountable?[76]—that when this legislation expired in 1999 Congress let it lapse. The fundamental dilemma was explained two millennia ago by Juvenal in the sixth of his Satires: "Sed quis custodiet ipsos custodes?" "But who is to keep watch over the watchers themselves?"[77]

Taking Accountability to the Courts

Our latest innovation in democratic accountability has been to sue the government. The Progressives created an abundance of regulatory agencies and empowered them to constrain citizens' freedom to use their private property. Before these agencies could act, however, Congress required them to follow formal procedures and, in 1946, after discovering that these agencies had created a complexity of different procedures, enacted the Administrative Procedure Act.[78]

The Administrative Procedure Act established formal rules that federal regulatory agencies had to follow before they could impose restrictions on the use of private property or the exercise of individual liberty. "The traditional conception of administrative law," writes Richard Stewart of New York University Law School, reflects "a common social value in legitimating, through controlling rules and procedures, the exercise of power over private interests by officials not otherwise formally accountable."[79] We Americans had already revolted against the efforts of the government of King George III to expropriate our property without our consent; we weren't about to let our own constitutional government do it.

Originally, the individuals with a right to challenge an administrative agency's decision—the individuals who had standing to appeal to the judiciary—were those whose property or liberty was threatened by regulatory action. But the New Deal expanded government's influence and thus the ways in which citizens were directly affected by government actions. The regulatory agencies created by the Progressives could affect an individual's or firm's economic interests by exercising their regulatory authority; the social welfare agencies created by the New Deal could affect an individual's or firm's economic interests by *not* exercising their benefit-granting authority. In the 1960s, legal theorist Charles Reich labeled such benefits "the new property" and argued that it deserved the same legal protections as did traditional property.[80]

Thus, three decades after the passage of the Administrative Procedure Act, the result, wrote Stewart, was "a fundamental transformation of the traditional model" of administrative law. "The Supreme Court has largely eliminated the doctrine of standing as a barrier to challenging agency action in court, and judges have accorded a wide variety of affected interests the right not only to participate in, but to force the initiation of, formal proceedings." Thus, concluded Stewart, administrative law became "a surrogate political process to ensure the fair representation of a wide range of affected interests."[81]

Now citizens—or, at least, their lawyers—could hold government officials accountable. Citizens no longer needed to rely upon traditional electoral and political processes. Now they had new methods of political accountability: the administrative processes created by the various administrative laws, as well as the mechanisms for the judicial review of administrative decisions. "Litigation," argues Joseph Sax of the University of California, "is in many circumstances the only tool for genuine citizen participation in the operative process of government."[82] The hell with elections! Just sue the government!

If there has been a fundamental change in the last fifty years in how we Americans hold government accountable for finances or fairness, it has been the growth in litigation.[83] Observing the United States at the beginning of the nineteenth century, Alexis de Tocqueville wrote: "Scarcely any political question arises in the United States which is not resolved, sooner or later, into a judicial question."[84] In response, Phillip Cooper was inspired to observe that, at the end of the twentieth century, every administrative question is resolved, sooner or later, into a judicial question.[85]

At any one time, the Texas Department of Mental Health and Mental Retardation is dealing with fifty to sixty lawsuits. Often these lawsuits are settled out of court, though such settlements do not really *settle* the issue. Instead, the judge often appoints a special master to hold the agency accountable for complying with a consent decree. The original lawsuit and the consent decree may have focused on only one aspect of the agency's operations, observe Gary Miller and Ira Iscoe, both of the University of Texas; yet the conduct of the special master can be quite "invasive." In the field of mental health, they argue, consent decrees have "allowed the litigation to grow to the point that it dominates all policy- and decision-making." "Lacking accountability to state government," continue Miller and Iscoe, special masters "are free to play the same political game as other government officials, but without the attendant risks that provide moderation and balance—namely the risk of not being reelected or reappointed to a position or being fired."[86] Like special prosecutors, special masters are accountability holders who are not themselves accountable.

By creating public programs using vague laws, legislators facilitate lawsuits. "The ambiguity and conflicts in the statutes," writes Mark Moore, "provide ample cause for interested parties to sue the government no matter what action an official takes." Thus "the management of the program ends up in court." The result, he continues, "is a very clumsy process that puts officials in a difficult and ultimately hopeless position: they can work very hard in setting up a process and making a choice, but they have little reason to believe that their decision will be accepted as legitimate, final, and binding."[87] Instead, the officials charged with implementing vague legislation have every reason to believe that their decisions will be challenged in court. Moreover, even if the legislation specifically permits the agency to exercise policy judgment, lawyers can still sue, claiming that the agency failed to faithfully follow every administrative procedure. If you don't like the policy, you can always sue over the process.

After the New York Senate confirmed Mary Jo Bane as commissioner of the state's Department of Social Services, I asked her when she would take office. "Next month," she replied, "but my name can already go on the lawsuits."

Bane has a sophisticated, if sardonic, view of litigation. To her, lawsuits are one more management challenge. Other public managers, however, take them personally. Some are simply terrified. Although "administrative agencies win the overwhelming number of judicial review challenges of their decisions," writes Cooper, these lawsuits have a significant impact on the morale and behavior of public managers:

> many managers feel frustrated, angry, and, to one degree or another, fearful about the threat of suit. Even if they win, they say, the amount of time and energy that is involved in avoiding litigation, preparing for it if it should occur, and responding to formal legal challenges even if the matter never gets to a courtroom, is enormous and unacceptable in a period of declining resources.[88]

How should a public manager allocate personal time and staff resources between covering the agency's rear against possible lawsuits and improving the agency's performance?

The Collapse of Hierarchical Accountability

Our American concept of democratic accountability evolved from Madison's separation of powers to Wilson's separation of administration from politics, with Taylor and Weber justifying that separation by describing how an independent administrative apparatus could be both efficient and accountable. As government engaged in more diverse and intrusive activities (which Madison, Wilson, Taylor, or Weber would never have contemplated), it also became more complicated. As a result, the chain of hierarchical accountability—from citizens to elected officials to appointed officials to government action—grew longer and stretched the public's confidence that it could ensure the accountability of those who made major policy decisions and took significant administrative actions.

In an analysis of accountability, Colin Campbell of Georgetown University identifies "two schools of thought." The "hierarchs" seek "to channel accountability so that it flows directly and exclusively up through superiors, then to ministers and, eventually, to legislators." The "pluralists" assert that "life is not that simple."[89] Guess what? The pluralists won.

Indeed, we Americans have created a complex collection of extrademocratic, nonhierarchical mechanisms of accountability. To classify them, Barbara Romzek and Melvin Dubnick define four kinds of accountability:

(1) *Bureaucratic accountability* is imposed formally through the hierarchy within organizations—particularly bureaucratic organizations.

(2) *Legal accountability* is imposed formally by laws or rules created by the legislature, the judiciary, or a regulatory agency such as a procurement office or civil service commission.

(3) *Political accountability* is imposed informally by various stakeholders in the accountability environment, working either directly or through elected officials.

(4) *Professional accountability* is imposed informally by the members of the organization itself, through their expertise and standards (which may be established by professional organizations or education and training).[90]

We Americans did not decide to create a systematic, four-part, pluralistic accountability system. Nor did we set out to tack on to the traditional public administration paradigm one new accountability mechanism after another. Instead, each evolved somewhat naturally from a perceived inadequacy, to a speculative idea, to some experiments, with the apparent successes being institutionalized (and the apparent failures being discarded). In the process, the public manager became less accountable to his or her nominal superior in the hierarchy, and more accountable to the various actors in what Kevin Kearns calls "a new accountability environment that is more dynamic and complex than at any time in history."[91]

"The modern public servant is faced with a barrage of demands for accountability," observes John Langford of the University of Victoria. "Public servants, like Christians in post-reformation Europe, are confronted by a bewildering variety of competing edicts, practices and pressures." The consequence, Langford continues, is "confusion about to whom public servants should be accountable." Today's public official must march to a "multitude of drummers."[92]

Our current system of democratic accountability is neither orderly, nor hierarchical, nor coherent. Instead, it consists of an overlapping set of independent and competing mechanisms—and a variety of independently operating accountability holders. Indeed, Light worries about our propensity for "adding more cross-checkers, auditors, investigators, and second-guessers" who collectively advance a "compliance-based approach" to accountability.[93] Currently, the de facto, if not de jure, doctrine of accountability relies more on an anarchy of aggressive attorneys than on democratic elections and a hierarchical chain of command.

Whatever happened to our concept of direct, electoral, and hierarchical accountability? Are we willing to delegate the accountability-holding responsibilities of our democracy to unaccountable lawyers whether officially appointed or self anointed? A headline in *Fortune* asked: "Who's running this country, anyway?" and responded: "We, the Lawyers."[94] Whatever happened to "We, the People"? Even without the problem of performance, Americans need to rethink what we mean by democratic accountability to the citizenry.

Madmen, Academic Scribblers, and Ideas

Despite the rise of the pluralists and the decline of the hierarchs, as we attempt at the beginning of the twenty-first century to develop new strategies for improving government's inadequate performance, the public administration paradigm remains extremely attractive. Why? Because it is blessed with a simple and compelling theory of political accountability, which the new public management has yet to match. We have evolved an accountability system obfuscated by complicated procedures, overlapping processes, contradictory standards, divergent demands, and competing accountability holders. Yet, when we talk about democratic accountability, we implicitly employ the mantras of traditional public administration: the separation of administration from politics, the scientific quest for efficiency, and the imperative of hierarchy.

On the concluding pages of his *General Theory of Employment, Interest, and Money,* John Maynard Keynes wrote:

The ideas of economists and political philosophers, both when they are right and when they are wrong, are more powerful than is commonly understood. Indeed the world is ruled by little else. Practical men, who believe themselves to be quite exempt from any intellectual influences, are usually the slaves of some defunct economist. Madmen in authority, who hear voices in the air, are distilling their frenzy from some academic scribbler of a few years back. . . . soon or late, it is ideas, not vested interests, which are dangerous for good or evil.[95]

Neither Wilson, Taylor, nor Weber was an economist, though all could be classified as "academic scribblers." All have been dead for more than three-quarters of a century. Yet people who know no more of the trio than that Wilson was president during World War I are, nevertheless, slaves to their ideas.

4

The Questions of Democratic Accountability

What do we mean by democratic accountability? What does it mean to say that, under the public administration paradigm, both politics and administration are accountable? Accountable for what? Accountable to whom? Accountable how? How, exactly, will government be held accountable? We employ the phrase "hold government accountable" as if its meaning were obvious. Yet before we can begin to hold anyone accountable for anything—particularly for performance—we need to answer a basic question of democratic accountability:

Q *How* will we hold *whom* accountable for *what?*

The advocates of the public management paradigm respond: Don't hold us accountable for process; hold us accountable for results. This, at least, appears to answer the "for *what?*" part of the question. In fact, however, it only raises another question: *Who* decides *what results* government should be accountable for producing? Who gets to set the expectations for performance? Thus the accountability question becomes, at least from the perspective of the new public management's emphasis on performance:

Q *How* will we hold *whom* accountable for producing *whose* results?

Finally, there is one additional issue involved in this accountability question: Who are "we"? Who, exactly, is going to do accountability holding? Will it be the citizens in general, either through the electoral process or in some other way? Will it be the citizens' elected representatives—specifically, their elected legislators—through the traditional process of oversight hearings? Will it be officially authorized watchdogs, such as auditors and inspectors general, or unofficial, self-authorized watchdogs, such as citizen groups and journalists? The advocates of the new public management paradigm need to answer the essential question of democratic accountability:

Q *How* will *who* hold *whom* accountable for producing *whose* results?

The question of democratic accountability for performance is really four distinct but interrelated questions:

Q1 *Who* will decide what results are to be produced?

Q2 *Who* is accountable for producing these results?

Q3 *Who* is responsible for implementing the accountability process?

Q4 *How* will that accountability process work?

The new public management paradigm needs a correlative accountability paradigm that addresses these four questions.[1]

Q1: Who *Will Decide What Results Are to Be Produced?*

Accountability requires expectations. Without specific expectations—be it for finances, or fairness, or performance—it is impossible to create accountability. Thus accountability for performance requires some explicit expectations about what results will be produced by when. "Without some standard of performance, it is difficult for constituents to hold elected officials or the bureaucracy accountable for their actions," emphasizes Glenn Cope of the University of Illinois. "This is one of the most difficult problems for democracy and bureaucracy—how to set policy achievement standards that are measurable in ways that citizens can understand and use to hold elected officials and appointed bureaucrats accountable."[2]

But *who* will set these performance standards? This may be the most troubling question raised by the new public management paradigm, for the advocates of the new public management assume that sometimes—perhaps often—civil servants will make these decisions. And yet, how do these unelected (and usually unremovable) government employees gain the authority to make such policy decisions? What authorizes government employees to set their own expectations for performance? Isn't this a policy decision? Don't elected officials (and their direct political appointees) have this responsibility? How can the advocates of the new public management discard so cavalierly what has been for more than a century a basic operating principle of American democracy?

The advocates of the new public management respond with an answer that is practical, not theoretical. They point out that, although civil servants are not supposed to make policy, they nevertheless do. This is the dirty little secret of public administration: Civil servants do make policy. Typically, they disclaim that they are doing any such thing. They insist that they are merely filling in the administrative details of overall policies established by their political superiors.[3] These little details, however, can determine what a policy really means—how it really works. Yet for over a hundred years, we have maintained the fiction that civil servants do not make policy.

It is a most convenient (though precarious) fiction. For once we confess to the unpleasant reality that, for civil servants to do their job, they *must* make policy decisions, we have to discard the public administration paradigm. Yet, by continuing to publicly profess both the principle and the practicality of the politics-administration dichotomy, the advocates of traditional public administration are able to offer an internally consistent (if disingenuous) theory.

The proponents of the new public management have, however, surrendered this advantage. They accept that civil servants do make policy decisions. Indeed, they advocate that civil servants should make policy decisions. And thus they have no escape. They need a new political theory that explains why and how this is (or can be) consistent with democratic accountability.

Indeed, the advocates of the new public management need a political theory that answers five, interrelated questions about how empowered, entrepreneurial, responsive civil servants can make innovative decisions in a decentralized yet democratic government:

— *The Question of Decentralized Decisionmaking:* What is the theory of democratic government that encourages decentralized decisionmaking while still maintaining accountability to the entire citizenry?[4]

— *The Question of Responsiveness:* What is the theory of democratic government that permits individual public employees to be responsive to the needs of individual citizens while still guaranteeing that government treats all citizens fairly?[5]

— *The Question of Empowerment:* What is the theory of democratic government that empowers civil servants to exercise discretion while still ensuring that we remain a government of laws?

— *The Question of Innovation:* What is the theory of democratic government that encourages frontline workers to be innovative in improving performance while still obligating them to achieve democratically authorized purposes?

— *The Question of Entrepreneurship:* What is the theory of democratic government that suggests public managers should be entrepreneurial (both in the public purposes they seek to achieve and in the means they deploy to achieve them) while still committing them to be accountable to the citizenry?[6]

The performance problem itself does not demand a new theory of democratic accountability; a focus on producing results does not require one. But giving civil servants the authority to make decisions about exactly *what results* to produce—and about exactly *how* to produce them—does obligate the advocates of the new public management to think seriously about the relationship between the effectiveness of their management strategy and the need for democratic accountability. "The problem," writes Guy Peters, "becomes how to structure government in ways that recognize the reality, and even the desirability, of the significant policy role for civil servants while simultaneously preserving the requirements of democratic accountability."[7]

Q2: Who *Is Accountable for Producing These Results?*

The answer to this second accountability question might appear obvious: the responsible agency. But the new public management is about more than empowered civil servants. Not only does the new public management reject the idea that civil servants are passive, scientific implementors of policy decisions; it also rejects the bureaucratic ideal of separate organizations responsible for implementing separate policies.

Behind the traditional concept of public administration, behind the traditional concept of organizational accountability is the implicit assumption that one organization is responsible for one policy—or that at least every policy is the responsibility of just one organization. It is another beauty of bureaucracy and hierarchical accountability. The law assigns the clear and full responsibility for implementing each policy (or each component of each policy) to one organization (or one component of one organization). And for each component of the organization, one individual is clearly in charge. Thus one individual is clearly accountable:

— The state superintendent is accountable for implementing education policy in the state.
— The district superintendent is accountable for implementing education policy in the school district.

— The school principal is accountable for implementing education policy in the school.

— The classroom teacher is accountable for implementing of education policy in the classroom.

Employing a hierarchical bureaucracy to implement a policy clarifies individual accountability.

This ideal arrangement is, of course, another fiction. For as the purposes we seek to achieve through government become more demanding and, thus, as the policies we establish become more complex, so do the organizational arrangements necessary to implement them. Again, however, the advocates of the public administration paradigm have it easy. They can continue to insist on using stovepipe policies. Perhaps we should label this another principle of public administration: not just the "separation of policies" but also the "separation of responsibility." Each piece of legislation creates one policy that is implemented by one organization that is managed by one individual. Call this "the one-bill, one-policy, one-organization, and one-accountability-holdee principle."[8]

Dennis Thompson argues that accountability mechanisms are most effective when they focus on the individual, not the organization. Emphasizing "personal responsibility" instead of collective responsibility, Thompson writes: "The pursuit of personal responsibility provides the best foundation for understanding the role that human agency plays in good and bad government, and the strongest basis for enhancing the accountability that democracy should demand of officials of government."[9] Moreover, as Onkar Dwivedi of the University of Guelph and Joseph Jabbra of Saint Mary's University in Nova Scotia observe, "there is some difficulty in attributing moral responsibility to an entity rather than an individual."[10] Accountability holders need an individual to be the accountability holdee.[11]

Individual or Collective Accountability?

Indeed, when we are concerned about the significant harm that government can do, we certainly want to focus on the individual or individuals who caused the harm. In his analysis of "moral responsibility" and "the problem of many hands," Thompson focuses on various wrongs that government can do— "harmful policies," "harmful consequences," "harmful decisions," "an admittedly wrong policy," or "a morally dubious course of action." What government officials are at fault for a government "failure"? How should we go about apportioning blame for a harmful outcome or just an objectionable outcome? Thompson recognizes that "because many different officials contribute in many ways to decisions and policies of government, it is difficult even in principle to identify who is morally responsible for political outcomes."[12]

Thompson, however, rejects collective responsibility. Instead, he argues that "responsibility for a policy depends in part on the contribution an individual actually made, or could have made, to the policy." Thompson is equally concerned with both an individual's action that contributed to a harmful policy and an individual's failure to take action that could have prevented (or mitigated) the harm. "Proponents of the collective model take that problem [of many hands] all too seriously," he writes. "When everyone in the collectivity or only the collectivity itself is responsible, citizens have no one to call to account." Thus, Thompson argues, "an approach that preserves a traditional notion of personal responsibility—with its advantages for democratic accountability—can accommodate many of the complexities of a political process in which many different officials contribute to policies and decisions."[13]

When we are worried about the abuse of power (for either finances or fairness), we do need individual accountability. After all, it is the individual person—the human agent—not the collective organization, that abuses power. It is the individual (or a conspiracy of individuals) who violates the public trust by deploying public funds corruptly or by treating people unjustly. And, if somehow the organization does this systematically, it is only because someone (or, at least, some group of someones) has created the systems and standard operating procedures (or culture and expectations) that induced or permitted the organization to collectively misuse funds or maltreat people. For finances and fairness, it is usually possible—and appropriate—to create, as Thompson suggests, individual, personal responsibility.[14]

Our desire to foster democratic accountability, however, goes beyond catching and punishing the perpetrators of petty corruption or harmful policies. We also want to create democratic accountability for government's performance. We are not just interested in identifying and assigning responsibility for all of the negative that government can do—for all of the harm that we want to prevent government from doing. We also want to create accountability for all of the positive that government can do—for all of the benefits we want government to provide.[15] And except for the most dedicated of anarchists, people want government to do some things and to do them well. Even the advocates of the most minimalist public sector still want government to defend the nation effectively and to ensure the integrity of private contracts. And when some private organization from which they really benefit gets in serious trouble, they inevitably want government to bail it out.

But who is accountable for performance? Can we identify which specific individual is responsible for a specific failure of performance? We can, of course, identify a frontline worker who failed to do his or her job: a teacher who failed to follow the curriculum, a forest ranger who failed to follow standard operating procedures, a soldier who failed to follow orders. But are government's performance failures primarily the consequence of the failure of individual civil servants to do their assigned tasks?

Again, some unpleasant realities intervene. It may be possible to determine what specific individual in what specific organization was responsible for what specific abuse of power—for what specific failure to uphold the accountability requirements for finances or fairness. It is, however, much more difficult to determine what specific individual was responsible for an organization's failure in performance. Because the economic, social, environmental, and security problems that we want contemporary government to solve—or at least to mitigate—are quite complex, we have chosen to attack these problems with institutional arrangements that are also quite complex. How, then, can any deficiency—or even failure—in performance be attributed solely to the deficiency (or failure) of any individual?

Paul Light argues that "the thickening of government"—by which he means the growth of both the number of layers in the hierarchy and the number of people in each layer—has an important "cost" in the form of a "diffusion of accountability." In fact, he believes that this thickening government "may mean that no one anywhere in government is accountable for what goes right or wrong." For example, Light observes that "the administrative inertia that comes with multiple internal checks and detours may mean that no one can be held responsible for a lack of action." The thickening of government, Light concludes, "denies presidents and Congress the opportunity to hold anyone accountable for what government does."[16]

Moreover, W. Edwards Deming, the guru of total quality management, argued that, in most organizations, most of the causes of inadequate performance—even inadequate performance by frontline workers—are the responsibility of top management. This is Deming's famous "85-15 Rule": Eighty-five percent of an organization's failures are caused by inadequacies in the system within which the frontline employees work. Only 15 percent of the failures are due to the inadequacies of the employees themselves.[17] Later in his life, Deming concluded that the percentage of problems caused by the system was closer to 94.[18] Massachusetts state senator Susan Tucker thinks Deming has this number about right. Commenting on the problems plaguing the state's Registry of Motor Vehicles, she observed: "Ninety-five percent of the problems the public sees are due to issues over which the front-line employees have no control." Yet, Tucker continued, "they always take the blame."[19]

David Osborne and Ted Gaebler, the authors of *Reinventing Government,* make a similar argument: "the people who work in government are not the problem; the systems in which they work are the problem."[20] If so, a failure of performance is usually an organizational not an individual failure. And, thus, to create accountability for performance, we need a theory of collective responsibility.

A failure to handle the public's finances properly or to treat citizens ethically is usually an individual failure. But a failure in performance—a failure to produce the results that citizens expected—is usually the collective failure of the entire organization. It is rarely the failure of a specific public employee or even a small group of employees. No individual can rectify the performance failures of an entire organization; so how can we hold an individual accountable for these failures?

Still, if the organization has failed, we want to point the finger of blame at someone: Something has gone wrong. Someone should be held accountable. Someone—damnit—should be punished.

Scapegoat Hunting

Thus Thompson's "pursuit of personal responsibility" risks becoming nothing more than the pursuit of a scapegoat. Indeed, the doctrine of personal responsibility provides the excuse to go scapegoat hunting. It encourages senior officials to emphasize their own diverse and demanding responsibilities, which prevent them from obtaining the necessary information or having enough time for anything more than a minor and distant involvement; instead they offer up a specific subordinate as the scapegoat who really knew what was going on and was really in charge.[21] Moreover, once the Biblical mandate has been fulfilled—once the scapegoat has been publicly identified, all of the sins of the mistake have been clearly placed on this individual, and he or she has been sent firmly packing into the wilderness—the holding-people-accountable duty has been discharged.[22]

If this failure was indeed the personal deviant act of a lone miscreant, then disposing of the scapegoat would prevent a repeat of the failure. If not, however, it would accomplish little more than to provide a forum for much self-righteous finger-pointing by a congregation of accountability holders, and to scare the hell out of other potential accountability holdees who can see themselves as potential scapegoats for a future governmental failure that has complex and multiple causes.

Moreover, the search for an individual scapegoat may well preclude any probe into the governmental systems, formal structures, programmatic ambiguities, policy contradictions, informal signals, and organizational cultures that created the circumstances that permitted, abetted, facilitated, stimulated, or actually caused the failure. Such an accountability investigation—such a search for collective accountability—is much more difficult and will result in a more sophisticated explanation with a more complicated solution. Such an accountability investigation will not produce the drama of heroes and villains, with neat headlines, and ten-second sound bites. Such an accountability investigation will—almost by definition—be boring.

Yet, if the fault, as Deming, Tucker, Osborne and Gaebler, and others argue, is the system, the fault lies with those who created the system. But who did that? Was it the leadership team of the agency, who failed to create the organizational culture and programmatic structure that would produce the desired performance? Or was it the legislators, elected chief executive, political appointees, and overhead-agency officials who created all of the formal institutions and particular policies within which the agency's leaders were forced to work? Was it the organization's stakeholders who demanded more miracles than any public agency could reasonably be expected to deliver? Was it all of these accountability holders who created the accountability systems and accountability culture within which the agency's leaders were constrained to manage? Or was it the citizens themselves who demanded a government that works better but doesn't cost anything?

Any major failure in organizational performance has multiple causes. And many different people connected with the organization—from top leadership and legislative overseers, to frontline workers and stakeholders, to auditors and journalists, to citizens—understand some (if not all) of these causes. They ought to have a positive obligation to identify and help fix them.

This is particularly true under the new public management. For example, if career managers and frontline workers are to have the discretion—indeed, the responsibility—to identify and fix specific problems that cause distress to individual citizens, they should also have the responsibility to identify and fix systemic problems that cause distress to entire groups of citizens.

The maintenance building at North Carolina's Dorothea Dix Hospital was built in 1921. Over the years, water severely damaged the roof, yet the building received no major renovations. In 1991 hospital officials requested funds to repair the roof so it would not collapse. In 1999 the funds were approved. A week later the sagging roof collapsed (fortunately, no one was injured).[23] Who should have been held accountable? The officials who managed the Dix campus? The budget bureau? The state legislature? Or citizens?

Robert Citron was the entrepreneurial treasurer of Orange County, California, whose aggressive investment strategies made millions for his county and for other municipal governments that joined his investment pool. Assuming that interest rates would fall, he began speculating in derivatives and reverse repurchase agreements; when, in 1994, interest rates rose, the county was forced into bankruptcy. Who should have been held accountable? Citron, the elected official, who was not (apparently) a financial expert? The county board of supervisors to whom Citron explained his investment strategy in his annual financial statements? The county's staff auditor, who posed no questions? Peat Marwick, which also reviewed the county's books and which also posed no questions? Investment firms, such as Merrill Lynch and CS First Boston, both of which made millions of dollars underwriting county bonds without raising questions? Or, do the citizens of the county share some of the accountability? Observe Steven Cohen and William Eimicke of Columbia University:

> the entire Orange County community seems to have been infected with a get-something-for-nothing, get-rich-quick fever during the entire period of investment boom and bust. The governments and the people who elected them wanted high-quality public services, but they did not want to pay the taxes that produce such services. Perhaps the ethical climate of the entire community, not just the actions of one public servant, was a major contributor to the crisis.[24]

If the citizenry creates expectations for government's performance while also imposing constraints that prevent honorable public officials from achieving the expected levels of performance in an honorable manner, they will get one of three possible results: (1) these officials will fail to achieve the performance expectations; (2) these officials will experiment with less-than-honorable means of achieving the expectations; or (3) these honorable officials will simply exit, to be replaced, perhaps, by some less honorable ones. In any of these cases, the citizenry will seek to call its public officials to account—in the first case, for failing to produce the desired performance; in the other two cases, for behaving dishonorably. Yet does not the citizenry have some responsibility? If so, how will a county's or a country's citizens call themselves to account?

When a U.S. Air Force F-15 crashed in Germany on May 30, 1995, killing the pilot, an investigation revealed that two mechanics had installed flight control rods incorrectly and that this mistake had caused the fatal crash. But the error was not only quite easy to make, it was common, having been made many times in the previous decade. Moreover, senior officers knew about the problem, yet they failed to correct it. Indeed, Air Force safety officers had recommended specific solutions, but higher officials had ignored them. Who should have been held accountable? Predictably, the Air Force accused the two mechanics of negligent homicide. On the day that the court martial was to begin, one of the mechanics killed himself.[25]

In some cultures, the traditional concept of accountability has required the senior responsible official to commit hara-kiri—or at least to resign. In contemporary America, our concept of accountability can drive the lowest-level official to suicide.

Collaborative Accountability

For two reasons, the one-bill, one-policy, one-organization, one-accountability-holdee principle doesn't work for performance. First, it doesn't work because even within a specific organization there is not just one individual who is responsible for performance. It also doesn't work because most public policies are not implemented by just one organization. To realize the ambitious public purposes that Americans seek to achieve today, we no longer enact one bill that creates one policy that is assigned to one organization with one accountability holdee. Instead, we enact multiple bills that establish multiple policies that are assigned to multiple organizations.[26] How can we ever hope to establish "personal responsibility"?[27]

In fact, most failures in performance are failures of collaboratives.[28] In the United States, most public policies are no longer implemented by a single public agency with a single manager, but by a collaborative of public, nonprofit, and for-profit organizations.[29] Indeed, the advocates of the U.S. version of the new public management believe that producing results requires collaboration.[30] It may require the collaboration of agencies from different levels of government—for example, from federal, state, and municipal environmental agencies.[31] It may require collaboration of several

agencies at the same level—for example, from state agencies of environmental protection, agriculture, water resources, and commerce. It may also
require the collaboration of private and nonprofit organizations.

Moreover, argues Sandford Borins (one of the advocates of the new public management), "In areas where coordination is needed, it is becoming
increasingly evident that informal coordination and partnerships are a better alternative than central coordination."[32] Yet, concludes Eugene Bardach,
"substantial public value is being lost to insufficient collaboration in the
public sector."[33]

How is a collaborative accountable for producing what results?[34] How
can the concept of accountability be applied to a collaborative?[35] How is a
collaborative defined? Who is part of the collaborative? Who is not? *Who* in
the collaborative is accountable? *Who* gets to hold the collaborative
accountable?[36] Gerald Caiden of the University of Southern California
argues that two of the "intractable problems of ensuring public accountability" are "collaborative government" and "contracted government." In such
"multi-layered governmental systems," he writes, "no one body can be sin-
gled out as being in charge of the whole, for nobody is."[37] As long as we
Americans maintain our federal system, which diffuses responsibilities
among the national and state governments (and local governments too),[38]
as long as we insist on contracting out responsibility for a variety of public
services, and as long as we believe that some public purposes are best
achieved through the collaboratives of public, private, and nonprofit organizations, we will have a very difficult time assigning individual accountability for performance.

In an analysis of collaboratives, Bardach comments on this problem:
"Although traditional [accountability] methods do provide symbolic reas-
surance, it is not clear that they are very functional as genuine tools of
accountability." Collaboratives can provide "novel opportunities to add new
methods of accountability to the existing portfolio," suggests Bardach,
"especially if we think of *accountability* as a complement to the effort to
improve quality and not merely as [a] substitute for it or as a necessary drag
on it." Indeed, Bardach suggests three ways to foster "accountability as a
form of organizational learning: peer accountability, a clearer focus on
results, and the greater involvement of consumers or clients or customers."[39]

In a traditional, hierarchical bureaucracy, there is little formal ambiguity
about who is in charge. The manager at each level is the accountable *individual.* But in a collaborative of individuals—or in a collaborative of organizations (that may themselves be bureaucracies or collaboratives)—identifying

an accountable individual or even accountable individuals is not easy. And *for what* should such individuals be accountable? Are they responsible collectively for producing the overall result? Or is each component of the collaborative responsible only for producing its own, specific component of that overall result. In a post-bureaucratic world (even if that world consists of collaboratives of bureaucracies) identifying who is accountable for what results is not easy. In this post-bureaucratic world, the question of accountability for performance becomes even more complicated:

> Q *How* will *who* hold *whom* in what collaborative accountable for producing *whose* results?[40]

The new paradigm of public management requires not just a new theory of democratic accountability; it requires a new theory of *collaborative* accountability.

Q3: Who *Is Responsible for Implementing the Accountability Process?*

Under the traditional public administration paradigm, the answer to the third accountability question is straightforward. Both elected officials and the electorate have a responsibility. Elected officials oversee the implementation of policy by public agencies, and the electorate oversees the elected officials. In such a linear, hierarchical system, the chain of accountability goes straight up from civil servants to political appointees to elected officials to the electorate.

Again, reality is slightly different. Almost any public policy is complicated; thus both the implementation of that policy and the oversight of that implementation are also complicated. Individual citizens cannot devote much time to systematic, comprehensive oversight. And the legislative branch does not do much more. Indeed, the critique of congressional oversight as a mechanism for establishing accountability is long, distinguished, and not very encouraging. For example, in his classic study of legislative oversight, Morris Ogul of the University of Pittsburgh reports: "Most members [of Congress] assigned a relatively low priority to oversight and hence spent little time on it."[41] This is another reason why civil servants end up making policy decisions: Legislatures supplement their vague and contradictory policy guidance with random (and often contradictory) oversight.

In a Brookings publication, *Improving the Accountability and Performance of Government,* several commentators examined the relationship between congressional oversight and accountability. For example, Harvey

Mansfield Sr., long of Columbia University, concludes: "The incentives for a member of Congress to continue to expend attention, time, and energy on oversight duties are weak, unless he happens upon a case that draws wide public attention." Regarding the behavior of members of Congress, Bruce Smith, long of the Brookings Institution, writes:

> The attention span of most of them is such as to discourage the systematic assessment of agency performance against defined standards. Congressional oversight, whatever its flaws, can be immensely useful and certainly play some part in fostering accountability. But it tends to be sporadic, capricious, and at times meddlesome. Members of Congress generally do not have the time to make a major effort to review agency performance systematically.[42]

In 1999 *National Journal* reported on the "increasingly poor congressional oversight over federal programs." In particular, it concluded that Congress is failing at one of its most basic oversight responsibilities: reauthorizing federal programs. Congress permits the legislation authorizing both major and minor programs to lapse but waives its own budget rules to permit such programs to continue through the appropriations process. Indeed, in early 1999 *National Journal* counted 115 programs that continued even though Congress had not reauthorized them.[43]

Still, not everyone agrees that Congress (or other legislative bodies) fail to provide adequate oversight. For example, Joel Aberbach of the University of California concludes that over the last several decades "the incentives to undertake oversight increased," and, as a result, "the quantity of oversight has increased sharply since the 1960s." Still Aberbach concedes the "somewhat chaotic nature of congressional oversight of policy and administration."[44]

Mathew McCubbins and Thomas Schwartz of the University of California offer a different defense of congressional oversight. The critics, argue McCubbins and Schwartz, use the wrong model of oversight. These critics believe that Congress should be out on the streets like a "police patrol" looking for errors in executive-branch implementation. Congress, however, employs an entirely different "fire-alarm" strategy. It "places fire alarm boxes on street corners, builds neighborhood fire houses, and sometimes dispatches its own hook-and-ladder in response to an alarm." McCubbins and Schwartz explain how Congress implements "fire-alarm oversight":

instead of examining a sample of administrative decisions, looking for violations of legislative goals, Congress establishes a system of rules, procedures, and informal practices that enable individual citizens and organized interest groups to examine administrative decisions (sometimes in prospect), to charge executive agencies with violating congressional goals, and to seek remedies from agencies, courts, and Congress itself. . . . Congress's role consists in creating and perfecting this decentralized system and, occasionally, intervening in response to complaints.

Moreover, McCubbins and Schwartz continue, both for Congress collectively and for its individual members, this decentralized strategy is a perfectly logical: Other people do most of the work; other people incur most of the costs; other people absorb most of the blame. And, when there is credit to be claimed, Congress can claim it. To a member of Congress, write McCubbins and Schwartz, "time spent putting out visible fires gains one more credit than the same time spent sniffing for smoke."[45]

But what are the costs of fire-alarm oversight? As any fire chief knows, putting out fires is obviously costly, though presumably the costs are less than the savings. An undetected fire is also costly, and thus an effective alarm system can save a lot. And, McCubbins and Schwartz imply, the congressional system of "fire-alarm oversight" catches most fires.

But what about fire prevention? Shouldn't Congress invest a little of its own time and resources creating systems that actually prevent fires from ever starting? (The advocates of the new public management would argue that any municipal fire chief has a fiduciary responsibility to the public and, thus, ought to be entrepreneurial in finding innovative ways not only to put out fires but also to prevent them.)

Moreover, as any fire chief knows, responding to false alarms can also be very costly. People can get hurt, and equipment can get damaged. Moreover, there is the opportunity cost; people and equipment sent chasing false alarms are not available to fight real fires. This, apparently, does not bother McCubbins and Schwartz. Yet by giving every interest group their own personal fire-alarm box, and by encouraging them to pull the lever anytime they think they see some smoke—or (like a group of churlish teenagers) need a little attention or excitement—Congress encourages executive branch agencies to invest scarce resources in fire-fighting personnel and equipment—resources that might could be redirected to actually improving performance.

The Insufficiency of Stakeholder Accountability

Of course, some citizens do care deeply about specific policies and their implementation. But these stakeholders, who form what Hugh Heclo of George Mason University calls "issue networks,"[46] do not seek to exercise influence strictly by voting. Instead, they create their own accountability process independent of the constitutional one. They seek to influence directly the implementation choices made by political appointees and civil servants by offering information and advice. And they seek to influence the policy decisions of elected officials by offering information and advice—and by providing organizational and financial support during elections. Because these stakeholders have a deep, personal interest; because electoral account-ability, though formally direct, dilutes any individual's influence; because elected officials are not inherently interested or actively engaged in regular oversight; because civil servants must make policy decisions (often with lit-tle official guidance); and because these decisions are susceptible to influ-ence, such organized stakeholders are usually the most actively involved in creating accountability—although their means are completely estranged from the accountability mechanisms conceived by the founders of the pub-lic administration paradigm. In most situations, observes John W. Gardner, the former secretary of Health, Education, and Welfare, "the executive agency is only nominally accountable to Congress; in reality both are accountable to the third player at the poker table—the special interest. Needless to say, it's usually not a poker game to which the public has been invited."[47]

The National Credit Union Administration (NCUA) is very responsive to its customers; it is very accountable to its stakeholders. The NCUA regulates and insures the nation's 7,200 credit unions, which are essentially banks for people with a common employer or association. In late 1996 a federal appeals court ruled that the NCUA's fourteen-year-old policy of permitting company credit unions to sign up people employed elsewhere was illegal. Yet within a month, the NCUA, after meeting privately with two credit union trade groups, promulgated an interim rule permitting credit unions to enroll people from a common trade, industry, or profession. In nullifying this interim ruling, U.S. District Court Judge Thomas Penfield Jackson labeled the NCUA a "rogue federal agency," denounced its attempt to "cir-cumvent" his earlier decision, described its meeting with stakeholders as "surreptitious, underhanded and collusive"[48] and said that the agency "has functioned as a trade association for the industry."[49] Perhaps direct stake-holder accountability does have a few defects.[50]

In addition to attempting to hold an agency accountable directly by (for example) participating in its traditional administrative rulemaking,[51] or indirectly by (for example) making its views and concerns very clear to key legislators and committee chairs, stakeholders have another direct accountability channel: Sue the agency. Individual citizens, organized interests, and entrepreneurial lawyers can all seek to hold a public agency accountable by asking the courts to nullify some action because the agency failed to follow the requirements of the Administrative Procedure Act or some other process designed to ensure fairness. "Democracies around the world," writes Robert Reich of Brandeis University, "have systems of judicial review to guard the rights of minorities against the majority. Public servants— elected, appointed, and career—are accountable to judges."[52] (Of course, these stakeholders, like other accountability holders, may be using the rules for fairness to attack a policy that they oppose.)

The advocates of any new public management paradigm could simply embrace this reality. They could reject as utopian the traditional concept of elected officials and citizens being responsible for implementing democratic accountability and accept that any policy's stakeholders are the only people with sufficient interest to worry about accountability for performance.[53] But the result looks slightly sleazy. "Interest groups and accountability," argues Michael Baer of Northeastern University, are "an incompatible pair."[54] After all, why should the best organized—even if they have the biggest direct stake in a policy—be delegated (even unofficial) responsibility for implementing accountability?[55] Whatever happened to accountability to the entire citizenry?[56]

Q4: How *Will That Accountability Process Work?*

Under the traditional, public administration paradigm, the answer to the fourth accountability question is again straightforward. The accountability process works (or is supposed to work) in a direct and explicit way. Elected officials are responsible for overseeing the implementation of each policy that they established. Then, if the citizens are unhappy with the policy, with the implementation of that policy, or with the oversight of that implementation, they vote these officials out of office. The accountability process functions both through elected officials and through the electorate.

Again, this does not quite work as well in practice as in theory. After all, elected officials establish many policies. Sometimes these policies are conflicting or contradictory. Sometimes an agency is given responsibility for implementing a policy without being given adequate resources. This complicates the accountability process. It complicates the part of the process for which elected officials are responsible. It also complicates the citizenry's role.

If elected officials support a particular policy—and if they have provided adequate resources for implementation—their oversight of that policy could be relatively straightforward. The elected officials need to check whether the responsible agency is using its resources wisely, whether it is implementing the policy intelligently, and whether the policy is producing the desired effects. If not, the elected officials need to change the agency's top officials, the mix of resources, or the policy itself.

But how do elected officials oversee policies with which they disagree? Should they strictly oversee the implementation of the policy, checking to see whether the policy is achieving the purposes that its creators designed it to achieve? Or should they also reexamine those original purposes? And if their oversight produces a critique, are they critiquing those implementing the policy or the policy itself? Any answer is confusing, since it is difficult (if not impossible) to separate out such motives.[57]

And for what should elected officials be accountable to citizens? For each individual policy? Or for the overall collection of policies that they have supported? For the totality of policies established by government? Or for the single policy about which each citizen cares the most?[58] Once a large collection of diverse policies is implemented, what role do citizens have in the accountability for these policies?

In a parliamentary democracy, the line of accountability is much clearer. The government—the party with the parliamentary majority and, thus, in charge of the executive branch—is responsible for all of the policies. Citizens may like some of these policies but not others; still, they know who is responsible. And the loyal opposition constantly seeks to make its differences with these policies explicit. If the opposition fails to make its key disagreements clear, it will be unable to convince the electorate to replace the party in power.[59] In a parliamentary democracy, citizens must still choose between bundles of policies, and few citizens will be completely satisfied with every policy in that bundle or with the implementation of every one of these policies. Nevertheless, the citizens' role in achieving accountability through periodic elections is more straightforward.[60]

The United States does not have a parliamentary democracy. Thus American citizens cannot easily make the accountability process work electorally. When they vote, they cannot easily send effective signals about the policies (or the implementation) with which they disagree.

Thus in the United States, the accountability process works primarily outside of the constitutional framework. And there exist few checks or balances within these extra-constitutional accountability mechanisms. In some circumstances, different stakeholders may check or balance one another. But if several stakeholders can collude, if they can negotiate an agreement that reflects each stakeholder's major interests, they can create an accountability process that is not checked or balanced by other forces and that fails to incorporate the broad interests of all of the citizens.

Again, the advocates of the new public management paradigm could simply accept and sanctify this reality. But doing so would not make this process of accountability any more democratic.

Accountability for Performance

How will accountability for performance work? The answer is not obvious. We cannot simply adopt—or even adapt—the mechanisms of accountability for finances and fairness to performance. As Phillip Cooper writes, "accountability may look very different in a system that attacks rules, flattens hierarchies, and empowers officials at lower levels of ministries and departments."[61]

5

Discretion and Trust

U nlike Frederick Taylor and Max Weber,[1] Woodrow Wilson believed in administrative discretion. His "science of administration" was not the mindless following of minute rules; instead, his "eminently practical science of administration" would "discover, first, what government can properly and successfully do, and, second, how it can do these proper things with the utmost possible efficiency and at the least possible costs either of money or of energy."[2]

Woodrow Wilson and the Necessity of Discretion

Wilson specifically advocated the delegation to the administrative apparatus of government the discretion necessary to employ, develop, and adapt the most effective and efficient means of implementing policies. He argued that "the administrator should have and does have a will of his own in the choice of means for accomplishing his work. He is not and ought not to be a mere passive instrument."[3] Moreover, Wilson continued, without such a delegation of discretion, it is impossible to establish accountability: "large powers and unhampered discretion seem to me the indispensable conditions of responsibility." Thus, "to be efficient," Wilson's study of administration had to "discover the simplest arrangement by which responsibility can be unmistakably fixed upon officials; the best way of dividing authority without hampering it, and responsibility without obscuring it."[4]

Wilson wanted to separate administration from politics and politics from administration. His administration would only execute politically enacted laws. And his politicians would not meddle in that execution: "Although politics sets the tasks for administration," wrote Wilson, "it should not be suffered to manipulate its offices."[5] Like reformers throughout our nation's history, Wilson wanted to make government more businesslike—to take the politics out of administration.

Wilson also cautioned against "the error of trying to do too much by the vote." To explain his reasoning, he offered a metaphor: "Self-government does not consist in having a hand in everything, any more than housekeeping consists necessarily in cooking dinner with one's own hands. The cook must be trusted with a large discretion as to the management of the fires and the ovens."[6] Indeed, if you do not trust the cook with discretion, if you tell the cook precisely how to manage the fires and the ovens, then the cook is no longer responsible for the dinner. You are.[7]

Discretion and the Accountability Catch

Harvey Mansfield Sr. also notes the importance of discretion: "How can an officer or agency be accountable unless he, she, or it has some independence, some freedom of judgment or choice?" Otherwise, for any error, there exists "a variety of third-party scapegoats"; the officer or agency simply blames those who issued the orders or meddled subtly. Indeed, for the public manager with no discretion, the list of available excuses is endless. Such a manager, concludes Mansfield, is "not responsible; let higher authority, or someone else, answer."[8]

This is the "accountability catch": *Without discretion there can be no accountability.* If political superiors refuse to delegate to public managers the discretion to manage their organizations and to implement their programs—either by imposing rules on them that cover every circumstance, or by requiring that they seek specific approval for all decisions and actions—they cannot hold these managers accountable.

Yet delegating discretion requires trust. To delegate discretion to the cook, the housekeeper must trust the cook; similarly, to delegate discretion to a public agency, citizens must trust the agency. And, clearly, housekeepers trust their cooks more than citizens trust their public agencies. As Wilson observed, "All sovereigns are suspicious of their servants, and the sovereign people is no exception to the rule."[9]

To Wilson, this suspicion was not necessarily evil: "If that suspicion could be clarified into wise vigilance, it would be altogether salutary; if that vigilance could be aided by the unmistakable placing of responsibility, it would be altogether beneficent." But by itself, Wilson continued, suspicion "is never healthful either in the private or in the public mind." Suspicion has to be combined with trust: "*Trust is strength* in all relations of life." Thus, both in framing constitutions and in creating administrative systems, Wilson argued, it is necessary to design them to foster trust: "as it is the office of the constitutional reformer to create conditions of trustfulness, so it is the office of the administrative organizer to fit administration with conditions of clear-cut responsibility which shall insure trustworthiness."[10]

Accountability requires both discretion and trust.

James Madison and the Culture of Mistrust

Unlike Woodrow Wilson, James Madison did not believe in trust.[11] To Madison, the problem was power, for "the accumulation of all powers" he wrote in Federalist 47, is "the very definition of tyranny."[12] Thus Madison did not even attempt to create Wilson's "conditions of trustfulness." Instead, he designed a constitution that reinforces suspicion. Madison created multiple institutions with specific responsibility for balancing and checking one another. He designed these institutions not to cooperate but to compete— to be suspicious, not trustful. That competition, Madison believed, would prevent the tyranny of accumulated power, create accountability, and compensate for our lack of trust.[13]

How can Americans trust a government that is specifically designed to incessantly expose itself as untrustworthy?

After all, institutionalized suspicion undermines trust. Kenneth Ruscio writes: "In the chain of relationships linking lawmakers, administrative officials, and citizens, how can there be trust when the design of political institutions depends so heavily on an expectation that power will be misused?"[14] Indeed, any institution charged with being suspicious will, unless it is completely incompetent, uncover suspicious behavior. "Distrust, like lawyers, breeds more of the same," writes David Dery of Hebrew University of Jerusalem.[15] As Suzanne Garment notes, "tightened rules and beefed-up corps of investigators guarantee that we will hear a steady stream of ethics charges." Indeed, she continues, we have developed "the habit of making large scandals out of what were once thought of as garden-variety misdeeds."[16]

How can Americans trust a government that is specifically designed to incessantly expose itself as untrustworthy?

Moreover, we continually create new government institutions with the sole, specific job of distrusting other government institutions. These institutions gratify our distrust of government—and reinforce it. For example, the office of the independent counsel was designed, observes Garment, "to cater specifically to modern mistrust"—indeed, "to perpetuate and broaden the mistrust on which it was built." And "all good reporters," she explains, "should mistrust official explanations." As a result, continues Garment, the institutions of mistrust—"a more aggressive press, tougher ethics laws, increasingly powerful congressional investigating committees, and a proliferation of prosecutors and other government sleuths"—have become "a self-reinforcing scandal machine."[17]

Like all organizations, government is constantly making all kinds of mistakes. Yet government's small procedural errors may have more impact than major policy failures. Everyone understands the cost of a minor case of fraud, waste, or abuse; reasonable people, however, can easily differ over the consequences of a major policy failure. Senator William Proxmire made headlines every month when he gave his Golden Fleece award to some federal agency for wasting the public's money. Yet he got the most press—the most public attention—not for the million-dollar mistakes, but for the small ones that everyone could understand. One of Proxmire's most widely remembered Golden Fleece awards went to the National Endowment for the Humanities for a $25,000 grant to study why tennis players lie, cheat, and act rudely.[18] Indeed, the repeated, daily discovery of small errors in following the details of established, bureaucratic rules (or common sense) may do more to undermine trust in government than ongoing policy debates over large, substantive issues.

Moreover, once someone exposes a failure in bureaucratic discretion, it is widely disseminated and widely accepted. Everyone understands that a 3¢ screw ought not to cost the Pentagon $91 (as the Grace Commission claimed it did) or that the Navy ought not to pay $436 for a $7 hammer (as Peter Grace said it did). Such horror stories of egregious waste make eye-catching headlines and easy fodder for Jay Leno and David Letterman. And when the simple story of the $91 screw or $436 hammer turns out to be distorted or just plain wrong, as Steven Kelman discovered,[19] who offers, sees, or recalls the correction? Everyone, however, remembers the original "mistake." Indeed, journalists later rounded up the $436 hammer to the $600 hammer.[20]

In his critique of the new public management, Donald Savoie has commented on the problem of errors:[21]

> Public administration operates in a political environment that is always on the lookout for "errors" and that exhibits an extremely low tolerance for mistakes. . . . [I]n business it does not much matter if you get it wrong ten percent of the time as long as you turn a profit at the end of the year. In government, it does not much matter if you get it right 90 percent of the time because the focus will be on the 10 percent of the time you get it wrong.[21]

Indeed, in government, it doesn't much matter if you get it right 99 percent of the time because the focus will be on the 1 percent of the time you get it wrong. This is why the Ten Commandments of Government are: "Thou shalt not make a mistake. Thou shalt not make a mistake . . . Thou shalt not make a mistake."[22]

Still, mistakes happen. Mistakes will be discovered. Mistakes will be reported. Mistakes will be punished. The institutions we have created to uncover such errors will track down enough of them to make government look uniquely error-prone. In 1984, for example, the Grace Commission made 2,478 recommendations that it concluded would save the federal government $424 billion.[23] Impressive! And very memorable. Observes Paul Light: "those who want headlines in the war on fraud, waste, and abuse will find plenty in the narrow stories of graft and corruption that often flow from compliance monitoring. The media appears always willing to report another story on the subject."[24] Indeed, notes Suzanne Garment, "when there is a scandal on the scene, it drives out the human appetite for more mundane sorts of political news."[25]

The result is a "culture of mistrust" that, Garment argues, "has made the always difficult job of governing measurably harder." Public officials are constantly looking over their shoulder, wary about committing their recommendations or even thoughts to paper; competent officials leave the government, and talented recruits are deterred from entering. "The fear among civil servants over how ethics rules will be interpreted is not paranoia," concludes Garment. "The great American scandal machine," as she calls it, has "done little to improve the performance of our government"; indeed, it "has almost certainly made our government worse instead of better."[26]

How can Americans trust a government that is specifically designed to incessantly expose itself as untrustworthy?

They don't[27]—as poll after poll reveals. In the spring of 1999, for example, Peter Hart and Robert Teeter conducted a national survey and reported "low levels of public trust and confidence in government." Hart and Teeter asked 1,214 adults: "How much of the time do you think you can trust the government in Washington to do what is right—just about always, most of the time, or only some of the time?" Less than a third answered either "just about always" or "most of the time."[28]

Trust is a delicate commodity—easily destroyed, yet hard to regenerate. "Trust is fragile," writes Paul Slovic of Decision Research. "It is typically created rather slowly, but it can be destroyed in an instant—by a single mishap or mistake. Thus, once trust is lost, it may take a long time to rebuild it to its former state." Slovic calls this the "asymmetry principle": "When it comes to winning trust, the playing field is not level. It is tilted toward distrust."[29] We Americans, however, believe that this natural asymmetry is not enough. We have designed our institutions to tilt the playing field even more toward distrust.

Nevertheless, all governments require trust. Woodrow Wilson understood this. Moreover, the increased discretion of the new public management requires some major increases in the citizenry's trust. Unfortunately, we have few public institutions devoted to the task of building trust. To change our thinking about how we should conduct the business of government—to replace the traditional public administration paradigm with the new one of public management—we need to invent mechanisms and institutions to enhance the public's trust.

The National Performance Review (NPR) was designed, in part, to enhance trust. In its original report, *From Red Tape to Results: Creating a Government That Works Better & Costs Less,* Vice President Gore stated that the NPR was not only about reducing the budget deficit "but also about reducing the trust deficit."[30] Alasdair Roberts worries, however, that the new public management "reforms will simultaneously improve the quality of public services and reduce the costs of services, *and* reduce public trust in government." How can this be? Because, Roberts writes, the "new methods of service delivery often abandon institutional arrangements that are widely thought to be essential for preventing abuse of power." Consequently, "in their attempt to make government 'work better and cost less,'" he continues, "governments made structural changes that have rekindled long-standing concerns about the potential for abuse of public and private power."[31]

The Fear of Discretion

Why does government have so many rules—so many regulations? They result, reports Steven Kelman, from our "fear of discretion"—our "fear of allowing public officials to use good sense and good judgment." Kelman examined the procurement systems of government and found a lack of discretion that "undermines the government's ability to get the most for its money and reduces the quality of government performance." Our fear of discretion is behind more than the excess of procurement regulation; our collective fear of discretion is the underlying cause of the volumes of rules and regulations that govern the behavior of all government officials.[32] As Kelman writes, "we fear discretion because we do not trust officials to live up to high standards of probity unless we keep a close eye on them."[33]

Thus, continues Kelman, we have created "a system of public management based on rules."[34] If we trusted our government more, observed Herbert Kaufman, "we would not feel impelled to limit discretion by means of lengthy, minutely detailed directives and prescription"—government's infamous red tape.[35] Exhibit A is the Administrative Procedure Act of 1946, which permits the judiciary to "hold unlawful and set aside" decisions by federal agencies that reflect "an abuse of discretion."[36]

This is also why we have created a system of accountability based on rules.[37] Paul Light calls this the "control definition" of accountability: "accountability is seen as the product of limits on bureaucratic discretion—limits that flow from clear rules (commands), and the formal procedures, monitoring, and enforcement that make them stick (controls)."[38]

And the creation of rules to limit discretion and establish accountability begins with legislation. Ronald Oakerson of Houghton College argues that "the purpose of legislation is to craft a specific governance structure around basic units of accountability," and that this governance structure has three features: "legal mandates" specifying things that administrators and agencies *must* do; "legal proscriptions" specifying things that they *must not* do, and "permissive authority" permitting *discretion* within defined boundaries.[39]

Most (but certainly not all) of the mandates and proscriptions concern finances and equity. Do spend money on this; don't spend money on that. Do treat people this way; don't treat people that way. Sometimes, however, such mandates and proscriptions do concern performance.[40] For example, the 1958 Delaney Amendment to the Food, Drug and Cosmetic Act of 1938 forbade the Food and Drug Administration (FDA) from approving any food additive that "is found to induce cancer when ingested by man or animal."

Thus, when tests in Canada demonstrated that saccharin caused cancer in rats, the FDA had no discretion; it had to ban saccharin—and to create a large, public controversy, which impelled Congress to repeatedly enact legislation to delay the ban.[41]

Between the boundaries imposed by mandates and proscriptions, public agencies exercise their discretion. Here they use Oakerson's "permissive authority"—presumably in ways designed to achieve their public mission. To ensure accountability, Oakerson continues, requires "policing the boundaries of discretion" (to ensure that the agency does not violate these boundaries) as well as creating "accountability for how discretion is exercised" within these boundaries.[42]

And how do we ensure that the discretion is exercised only within the accepted boundaries and is exercised responsibly there? Bureaucracy—with its hierarchy and rules—is the traditional answer. Each level in the hierarchy constrains and oversees the discretion exercised by lower levels. From their training and expertise, from their bureaucracy's detailed rules and regulations, and from their knowledge of how previous exercises of discretion have been accepted or annulled, everyone in the hierarchy learns how much discretion he or she has. And they all learn that if they exercise too much discretion they will be held accountable—that is, punished.

Distrust lives. Distrust thrives.

Legislators and Their Fear of Discretion

In testimony prepared for Congress concerning the need to "improve performance and accountability across the federal government," David Walker, comptroller general of the United States, reported that the General Accounting Office had found "serious challenges that must be confronted to achieve more efficient, effective, and economical federal operations and to build greater public respect for, and confidence in, their government." In particular, Walker outlined four "major challenges" to improving government's "performance and strengthening accountability":

— Adopting an effective results orientation.
— Improving the use of information technology to achieve results.
— Strengthening financial management for decision-making and accountability.
— Building, maintaining, and marshaling the human capital needed to achieve results.[43]

But what, exactly, created these performance challenges? Describing the need for a more "effective results orientation," Walker explained the source of the problem:

> Ineffective and outmoded organizational and program structures frequently have undermined agencies' effectiveness. Challenges agencies confront range from the need for clearer lines of accountability to streamlining organizations in response to changing circumstances. All federal agencies share the ongoing need that their organizational structures and program approaches efficiently support the accomplishment of mission-related goals.

For the human capital challenge, Walker advocated "creating a performance-oriented culture":

> Moving successfully to a more performance-based approach requires that organizations better align their human capital policies and practices with their missions and goals. New ways of thinking must be adopted about the goals to be achieved; the organizational arrangements, program strategies, and partnerships needed to achieve those goals; and how progress will be measured. Likewise employee incentive and accountability mechanisms need to be aligned with the goals of the organization. The failure to constructively involve staff in an organization's efforts to become more performance-based means running the risk that the changes will be more difficult and protracted than necessary.[44]

What a wonderful mix of generalities and the passive voice!

Who created the "ineffective and outmoded organizational and program structures" that are undermining agency effectiveness? Walker doesn't say. But his language permits the members of Congress to infer that the fault is in the agencies—not in themselves. Who should create the clearer lines of accountability and streamline the agencies? Again, Walker's words are ambiguous. Nevertheless, they suggest—or permit a member of Congress to infer—that federal managers ought to be doing this. Why are federal agencies not doing a better job of aligning their human capital practices with their missions? Walker doesn't say. But someone could easily read between the lines and conclude that maybe, just maybe, it is because the government's managers are incompetent. And who should adopt the "new ways of

thinking"? Walker's mastery of the passive voice permits multiple interpretations. Yet I suspect that few members of Congress thought: "Wait a
minute! He means *me*."[45]

Why are public managers not changing employee incentives to reinforce
agency missions? Why are they not overhauling their organizational and
program structures? Is it because they are incompetent or stupid? Or is it
because every time they try to improve their agency's effectiveness by modifying some basic feature of their human capital practices, or their organizational structures, or their program approaches, they get slapped down—
by either a congressional committee or by an overhead agency enforcing
some regulation mandated by Congress.

Elmer Staats, one of Walker's predecessors as comptroller general, re-
marked on the problem. "Granted that oversight and accountability are
essential, the remaining question is how Congress can be persuaded to focus
on program formulation and results and avoid the temptation to 'micromanage' the executive branch," wrote Staats after he left GAO. "Too frequently it gets bogged down in details of administration, missing the forest
for examining the trees."[46]

In principle, the members of Congress are all in favor of Walker's ideas
for implementing "performance-based management" and adopting a
"results orientation." Just ask any one of them:

— Do you think that federal agencies should streamline their organizations in response to changing circumstances to ensure that their organizational structures and program approaches efficiently support
mission-related goals?

— Do you think federal agencies should adopt a performance-based
approach and align their human capital policies with their missions
and goals?

They will, of course, answer yes.

When, however, any specific agency starts to streamline its organizational
structure or to adopt performance-based personnel practices, some stakeholders will inevitably scream. In response, some member of Congress will
intervene to prevent this unauthorized exercise of discretion.

Public Managers and Their Fear of Discretion

Citizens and journalists fear government discretion. Legislators fear executive-branch discretion. Overhead regulators fear line-agency discretion.
Moreover, political executives fear the discretion exercised by career man-

agers and frontline workers. Even elected chief executives fear the discretion of the political executives whom they personally appoint.

Every newly elected chief executive and his or her team of cabinet secretaries worry that the previous administration has brainwashed the permanent, career officials, who will now resist or sabotage their initiatives. Even when politically appointed managers accept that their career subordinates are quite willing to follow their leadership and implement their new policies, they may still worry that these subordinates lack the subtle capacity to do so with discretion. Political superiors will always worry that their technically omniscient subordinates will not possess the political sophistication to exercise discretion with the proper prudence. And elected chief executives and their personal staff will always worry that their own political appointees to managerial jobs will, in the famous words of John Ehrlichman, President Nixon's policy director, "go off and marry the natives."[47]

In an analysis of "the tensions between discretion and accountability" in human services agencies, Olivia Golden, now with the Administration on Children, Youth and Families of the U.S. Department of Health and Human Services, sought to understand how public managers can obtain the flexibility that they need to experiment with new service-delivery strategies and that their caseworkers need especially when working with hard-to-serve groups. She concluded that elected officials resisted allocating significant managerial discretion for a variety of reasons, including their ability to "see the potential risk of a bad outcome more vividly than the potential benefit of a good one" and their recognition that "the present way of doing business is the result of a complicated truce among different political groups and [that] any innovation would represent a movement away from the truce and would make some group angry." Similarly, she found that elected officials resisted delegating discretion to frontline workers for other reasons, including a "distinct concern . . . for equity and consistency of decisions across geographical areas and across workers," a concern "whether decisions made individually by workers will respond to the goals and priorities held by elected officials," and a concern "for program quality," which may, "paradoxically, lead to bureaucratization."[48]

Even career public managers fear the discretion of their career subordinates. It matters not whether the discretion is dishonest, improper, stupid, unthinking, or merely undiscerning. All can create havoc, not only for the subordinate who exercised the discretion imperfectly but also for the career superior who failed to properly supervise that discretion.

All public managers—both political appointees and career civil servants—face what David Mathiasen calls "the political risks inherent in flexibility."

Subordinates may not abuse their discretion in an illegal or immoral manner. Rather, they may simply exercise it in what seems to them (and would seem to you if you knew about it) a perfectly reasonable way—only to cause the agency to be harassed by angry stakeholders, impugned by the press, summoned to a legislative oversight hearing, or hit by an expensive lawsuit. And the accumulative impact of a series of such lawsuits, argues Mathiasen, can further limit discretion: "As the number of disputes that are settled in the courts increases, and the pressure to codify government policies in ever greater detail increases, the degree of administrative discretion decreases, and new public management becomes more difficult to carry out."[49]

Lawsuits impose financial costs on an agency. They also impose political costs on its top executives. Agency heads don't like having their organization sued; it doesn't look good, and often the plaintiffs get the more favorable journalistic coverage. Even if the government wins in court, it may still lose in the court of public opinion. "Acme Corp. Sues Government Agency" makes a great headline; the same cannot be said for "Court Finds No Basis for Acme Corp. Suit against Government."

Public managers at all levels may not actively *distrust* their subordinates (though some clearly do), but they certainly *mistrust* them.[50] They worry that all of the rules and regulations imposed on their organization may not be enough to prevent some embarrassing exercise of discretion. Consequently, they add their own rules—just to make doubly sure that their subordinates don't get them or their organization into any trouble. From his study of procurement, Kelman concludes that "few program and technical people have any idea that many of the [procurement] injunctions they are receiving do not have the force of law or regulatory requirement."[51]

One of the core principles of total quality management (which is a component of some variations of the new public management) is the creation of mutually supportive relationships with suppliers.[52] Yet, observes Mathiasen, traditional accountability mechanisms—or, at least, the ways in which such accountability mechanisms are frequently deployed—directly undermine such partnerships: "The emphasis on procurement tendering procedures, and the frequent existence of administrative law procedures to contest bid awards substantially restricts the ability of public managers to exercise the discretion necessary to build TQM-like relationships with suppliers."[53]

In 1996, prompted by Britain's Next Steps program, Vice President Gore's National Performance Review proposed creating federal performance-based organizations (PBOs) to give specific agencies more discretion to achieve their goals.[54] One of the early candidates to become such a PBO was the Saint

Lawrence Seaway Development Corporation (SLSDC), an agency within the U.S. Department of Transportation (DOT). SLSDC wanted to escape from some of the administrative burdens and reporting requirements imposed by DOT. Yet SLSDC did not have to become a PBO to obtain this flexibility; DOT had the authority to grant it. Why had it not done so? Because, the General Accounting Office reported after talking with DOT officials, "the department does not want to set the precedent of relieving any of its administrations from crosscutting departmental requirements."[55] If public managers give additional discretion to one unit, other units will request it too. So, to avoid creating a precedent, and the nasty arguments that will follow, managers simply deny such flexibility to all of their subordinates.

This fear of discretion is a global phenomenon. One analysis of the Next Steps program in Britain found that the departments were reluctant to delegate discretion to their executive agencies because of a "lack of trust that agencies will make good and responsible use of freedoms."[56] At a ministerial symposium sponsored by the Organisation for Economic Co-operation and Development, reports Mathiasen, the top political executives responsible for public management in the world's developed nations worried about "the tension between decentralizing and delegating service delivery (with its greater acceptance of risk-taking) and pressures for accountability to the taxpayer." They also worried about "a similar tension between the desirability for flexibility and experimentation on the one hand and the problems of avoiding politically embarrassing mistakes."[57]

The Inevitability of Discretion

As James Madison's progeny, we Americans distrust our government and seek to keep it from exercising discretion. But we cannot prevent it from doing so. Public officials—from elected officials, to political appointees, to career managers, to frontline workers—exercise discretion.[58] To do their jobs, they have to. They have no choice. Legislatures cannot enact laws with enough details and bureaucratic superiors cannot promulgate enough regulations to cover all of the circumstances with which public officials must deal every day.[59]

In reality, the legislative branch often fails to provide the executive with anything close to definitive policy guidance.[60] In the Multiple-Use Sustained-Yield Act of 1960, Congress decided that the national forests "should be administered for outdoor recreation, range, timber, watershed and wildlife and fish purposes."[61] How's that for legislative direction? This policy guidance is simultaneously both vague and contradictory.[62] To implement the act—to encourage multiple uses while ensuring sustained yields—the National Forest Service must make policy.[63]

Similarly, the elected officials in the executive branch often fail to provide their key appointees with definitive policy guidance. In 1979 Mayor Edward Koch of New York appointed Ellen Schall to be commissioner of the Department of Juvenile Justice (the agency responsible for pretrial detention of juvenile offenders). At Schall's swearing-in ceremony, the mayor gave her only two sentences of policy guidance that were simultaneously vague and contradictory: "Don't let them out. Do as much for them as you can."[64]

More than two decades ago, Michael Lipsky, now of the Ford Foundation, pointed out that "street-level bureaucrats"—police officers, teachers, and social workers—"have wide discretion over the dispensation of benefits or the allocation of public sanctions." Indeed, he argues, "street-level bureaucrats make policy." They exercise this discretion, Lipsky writes, "because the nature of service provision calls for human judgment that cannot be programmed and for which machines cannot substitute."[65] So much for Max Weber's vending-machine bureaucracy making its mechanically derived judgments.

Moreover, observes Lipsky, in our effort to control the behavior of street-level bureaucrats, we have created rules that are "so voluminous and contradictory that they can only be enforced or invoked selectively." This also requires the exercise of discretion. Thus, concludes Lipsky, "to the extent that tasks remain complex and human intervention is considered necessary for effective service, discretion will remain characteristic of many public service jobs."[66]

Sometimes we citizens give street-level bureaucrats discretion because we can't make up our mind. How, for example, do we want the police to behave? "The community claims to want disciplined police officers impartial in their enforcement of the laws and skilled in the restrained use of force," notes Mark Moore, "but it also wants protection from criminals." To resolve this contradiction, the community implicitly colludes with the police to produce what Moore calls the "dirty deal" of policing: "So long as the police are willing to put their lives on the line to protect the good citizens from the bad, the good citizens will not ask too many questions about how they do it."[67] Of course, whenever some egregious police misconduct comes to our attention, we immediately call foul—"That's not what we meant"—and hold accountable the officers who engaged in the misconduct by punishing them.

If a policy controversy exists and we can't resolve it ourselves, our elected officials are unlikely to resolve it either. So we all leave it to the bureaucrats. Or to the courts. Supreme Court Justice Harry Blackmun recalled a member of Congress telling him that incoherent legislation is not always unintentional. Instead, Blackmun was told, legislators will purposely employ "unintelligible language" and then turn it over to the court to "tell us what we mean."[68]

Discretion is inherent in all of government, not just to government that embraces the new public management. Whenever we create a government, writes Gerald Caiden, "some selected people have to be empowered and entrusted to act on behalf of the collectivity." These public officials, continues Caiden, "must be given the discretion to judge what seems best for the community."[69]

For example, prosecutors possess some of the broadest and most consequential discretion. "Every day," observes Garment, "government prosecutors have to decide whether individuals should be indicted." These decisions depend upon a multitude of factors: "the matter's importance to some government policy," "the credibility of witnesses," and "the overall likelihood of conviction." Some of these factors "are cynical or shockingly Machiavellian," while others are "extraneous to the issue of how bad the crime was." Moreover, continues Garment, "sometimes these questions cannot be answered with any certitude, and prosecutors have to make their decisions according to unspoken judgments, hunches, and predispositions."[70] Even accountability holders have to exercise discretion.

Americans may accept intellectually that public officials have to exercise discretion. Behaviorally, however, we continue to reject this reality. We ask our top public officials to limit the discretion of bureaucrats, and they oblige (or at least try to). To limit the discretion of judges, they enact mandatory sentencing laws;[71] to limit the discretion of social workers, they create detailed rules and procedures to ensure that only the right people get exactly the right amount of assistance for only the right amount of time; to limit the discretion of teachers, they establish very specific curricular requirements about what concepts in what subjects should be taught during what months.

Americans need to accept the inevitability of governmental discretion. It is impossible to create a government—particularly the American, federal government with its wide array of social aspirations and institutional arrangements—and still prevent the public officials who manage these arrangements from exercising discretion. Public officials exercise discretion. Public officials have to exercise discretion.

Americans: Get over it!

Only when we do—only when we accept the reality that all public officials must exercise discretion—will we be able to discard our futile attempts to eliminate such discretion and take on the more intellectually demanding and politically treacherous task of creating some accountability mechanisms that may help to ensure that this discretion is exercised in an intelligent, sophisticated manner that does, indeed, achieve our public purposes.

The Necessity of Trust

To function, business requires trust.[72] Any business firm needs to create trust internally.[73] And it needs to develop trust with the other firms with which it must deal.[74] We tend to think that business conducts its business on purely economic terms with formal legal contracts (providing severe penalties for any breach), arm's-length, impersonal relationships, and tough bargaining that rewards only cunning and power. Yet many in business rely on trust rather than contracts. In an often-quoted article titled "Non-Contractual Relations in Business," Stewart Macaulay of the University of Wisconsin asks why detailed contracts and legal sanctions are used so rarely in business and concludes that "in many situations," they are "not needed." Indeed, to many in business, reports Macaulay, a carefully planned contract "indicates a lack of trust and blunts the demands of friendship, turning a cooperative venture into an antagonistic horse trade."[75] Trust, writes Carolyn Shaw Bell of Wellesley College, "is the rarely identified foundation of a market economy."[76] From a study of "lean production" of automobiles in Japan, James Womack and his MIT colleagues found that Japanese firms created a system for dealing with their suppliers that "replaces a vicious circle of mistrust with a virtuous circle of cooperation."[77] And in an analysis of the effectiveness of teams in business, Jon Katzenbach and Douglas Smith of McKinsey & Company note "the trust upon which any team must be built."[78]

To function, any organization—private, public, or nonprofit—requires trust. "Trust holds organizations together," writes David Carnevale of the University of Oklahoma.[79] "Trust is the catalyst in organizational performance," observe Dennis Daley and Michael Vasu of North Carolina State University; "trust establishes an organizational climate that encourages cooperation and allows employees to devote their undivided attention to the task at hand."[80] Francis Fukuyama of George Mason University writes that "the most effective organizations are based on communities of shared ethical values." Moreover, he continues, "these communities do not require extensive contract and legal regulation of their relations because prior moral consensus gives members of the group a basis for mutual trust."[81]

To function, collaboratives require trust.[82] Eugene Bardach argues that trust and trustworthiness are essential for creating an interagency collaborative. "Trust is confidence that the trustworthiness of another party is adequate to justify remaining in a condition of vulnerability," writes Bardach. Thus, to create a functioning collaborative, he concludes, the collaborators must engage in four activities: "(1) assessing the trustworthiness of [other] individuals and the institutions they represent, (2) persuading others of one's own trustworthiness, (3) learning how to trust, and (4) taking collective measures to develop trust."[83]

To function, a society requires trust.[84] "Society," says Carolyn Shaw Bell, "runs on trust."[85] This is the basic thesis of Fukuyama's book *Trust:* "One of the most important lessons we can learn from an examination of economic life is that a nation's well-being, as well as its ability to compete, is conditioned by a single, pervasive cultural characteristic: the level of trust inherent in the society." Indeed, Fukayama writes, "all successful economic societies" consist of economic communities that "are united by trust," that are "formed not on the basis of explicit rules and regulations but out of a set of ethical habits and reciprocal moral obligations internalized by each of the community's members." And to the extent that a society must rely on rules and regulations, he argues, it pays a price. "Widespread distrust in a society," argues Fukuyama, "imposes a kind of tax on all forms of economic activity, a tax that high-trust societies do not have to pay."[86] Trust, writes Sissela Bok of Harvard University, "is a social good to be protected just as much as the air we breathe or the water we drink. When it is damaged, the community as a whole suffers; and when it is destroyed, societies falter and collapse."[87]

To function, government also requires trust.[88] Obviously, it needs to create trust internally, so that its components can function. And it needs to create trust externally, for many government activities require significant cooperation of its citizens. "Trust is central to legitimate democratic government, to the formation of public policy, and to its implementation," writes Kenneth Ruscio. "A high level of trust does not eliminate mechanisms for accountability, but it can make them less intrusive, providing discretion for managers and a greater willingness to delegate."[89] To function, government requires trust between the executive and the legislative branches, between elected and appointed officials, between political and career managers, between managers and frontline workers, between the federal and state governments, and between state and local governments.

With organizations, this trust must go both ways. Superiors must trust their subordinates to exercise their discretion intelligently and judiciously. Similarly, subordinates must trust their superiors to exercise their discretion intelligently and judiciously. "Trust is a reciprocal attitude," emphasizes David Carnevale. "People comprehend and reflect the trust aimed at them," and thus "employees reciprocate the kind of trust directed toward them."[90]

Why do so many American labor unions insist that management follow so many narrow rules when dealing with their members? Because the workers don't trust management. Because they want to limit management's discretion. Traditionally, American labor unions have "strongly preferred promotion based on seniority rather than skill," writes Fukuyama. "To promote workers on the basis of ability requires trusting management to make difficult judgment calls about individual abilities, which they were not willing to concede." And "the unions' insistence on detailed work rules and job classifications," he continues, has "hampered the introduction of teams and flexible production."[91]

The modern workplace—with employee empowerment, total quality management, and lean production—requires labor-management teams to which both parties bring their knowledge and expertise. Yet federal labor laws, specifically the National Labor Relations Act of 1935, inhibit the use of such teams. Why? Those laws are relics of the labor-management struggles of the 1920s and 1930s; labor assumed that management could not be trusted and thus lobbied for legislation that constrained management's discretion. Today these laws limit experimentation with organizational arrangements that could help both build trust and improve performance.

One of the core principles of the new public management is that public officials *should* exercise discretion. Tight, hierarchical supervision is out. The intelligent exercise of discretion is in. Oakerson observes: "The strengthening of hierarchical management, once understood as an absolute good, is regarded today with greater skepticism in view of its high costs, primarily in the form of elaborate clearances and the proliferation of administrative rules that tighten and restrict the boundaries of discretion on the part of those who act."[92] Yet, throughout American government, the administrative rules that tighten and restrict discretion continue to exist—indeed, to proliferate.

To improve performance, the new public management requires trust. Yet if citizens lack this trust, they will not appreciate the calls for flexibility, deregulation, and empowerment.

Trust and the Moore Paradox

In fact, the new public managers employ a style that may further undermine public trust. To improve performance, public managers need not only flexibility, deregulation, and empowerment. To produce results in today's complex policy environment, public managers need particularly high levels of dedication, energy, even audacity. The prototype of the new public manager is not merely entrepreneurial. He or she is often brash and aggressive—taking conspicuous chances, publicly accepting responsibility for both successes and failures, and thumbing a nose at detractors or those who warn of the necessity of caution.

"Public *management* is different from public *administration*," emphasizes Donald Savoie, one of the critics of the new public management. Savoie contrasts the operating styles of public *managers* and public *administrators:* "Unlike the traditional public administration language that conjures up images of rules, regulations and lethargic decision-making processes, the very word 'management' implies a decisiveness, a dynamic mindset and a bias for action."[93] Yet we citizens are not sure that we trust such governmental entrepreneurs.

All this creates what Mark Moore describes as an "interesting paradox": "On one hand, because personal leadership and responsibility seem to be key to successful innovations, they should be valued. On the other hand, the arrogance and flashy style that often accompany personal leadership often attracts hostility and suspicion in the public sector." To be a successful innovator in both business and government, observes Moore, an executive needs a "willingness to take the initiative and accept responsibility while remaining modest about his or her contributions and generous in crediting others." Yet, he continues, "executives in the public sector must err even more on the side of modesty" lest they "trigger close press scrutiny and antipathy." This creates the Moore Paradox: "the public expects a style of management in the public sector that would be ineffective if managers actually engaged in it."[94]

Public managers who exercise little initiative produce few results and thus undermine the public's confidence in government. Public managers who are leaders may produce results but through their style still undermine the public's trust. "The entrepreneurial model," writes James Stever of the University of Cincinnati, "can never legitimate public sector administration in the eye of a skeptical public. The public may envy, even admire the entrepreneur, but the actions of the entrepreneur are illegitimate in that the entrepreneur cannot be expected to function as guardian of the broader public interest."[95]

The three entrepreneurs whom Eugene Lewis of the University of South Florida features in his discussion of *Public Entrepreneurship*—Hyman Rickover, J. Edgar Hoover, and Robert Moses—illustrate the Moore Paradox. All three created major public agencies and achieved significant results—results of which others could not even dream. To do so, reports Lewis, all three achieved "degrees of autonomy and flexibility which are popularly believed to be impossible in government bureaucracies." They employed "buffering and autonomy-seeking strategies," observes Lewis, and managed to make such "behavior appear reasonable, sensible and even occasionally patriotic." Indeed, Lewis concludes that two steps in becoming a public entrepreneur are "the creation of an apolitical shield" and a continuing "struggle for autonomy."[96] Yet Rickover, Hoover, and Moses did all of this in a way that we now think of as decidedly undemocratic.

How do we Americans want to resolve the Moore Paradox? Do we want public managers to be entrepreneurs who actively exercise and protect their discretion and in the process create high-performance organizations that produce results? Or do we want public managers to assiduously obey all of the rules and regulations even if this ensures that they accomplish little?

Perhaps there is some happy (if narrow and vaguely defined) medium: leadership that produces some results but is not too aggressive. But with all of the other considerations and interests that modern public managers must balance, should we also assign them the additional burden of getting this one precisely right?

Deconstructing the Discretion-Accountability Trade-off

Is there a trade-off between discretion and accountability?[97] Ruscio writes of "the paradox created by reformers who want to simultaneously give public managers greater flexibility and make them more accountable."[98] If we give our public officials too much discretion, goes this logic, we will lack sufficient standards with which to establish accountability. But again, as Woodrow Wilson observed, if we give our public officials no discretion then they have no accountability.[99]

Maybe, however, this isn't a zero-sum game. Maybe every additional increment of discretion does not automatically reduce how much accountability we get. Maybe we ought to think about how we could authorize discretion to *enhance* accountability. Maybe we ought to rethink the relationship between discretion and accountability.

Some general principles might help guide such a rethinking. For example, agencies and collaboratives that have proven more competent in producing the results for which they were created, while also adhering to our norms for finances and fairness, could be allocated more discretion. Organizations with inadequate track records (for either finances, or fairness, or performance) deserve less. Demonstrated competence warrants more trust.

When delegating discretion, we need not rely strictly on an agency's history of matching our expectations for finances, fairness, and performance. We might want to offer more discretion to agencies pursuing purposes that are relatively noncontroversial and for which measures of performance are clearer and more widely accepted. And we might delegate less discretion to agencies that possess greater opportunities for corruption—either because they possess significant coercive powers over citizens, or because they can more easily hide their abuse of discretion.

Such theoretical principles will, however, be very general. What works best will vary among policy areas and among agencies. We will need to experiment. Only through a variety of efforts to enhance accountability by authorizing discretion will we learn what kind of discretion to authorize under what circumstances.

But will the results of any such experiments prove politically (as well as analytically) convincing? How much discretion will the legislature or the citizenry consider delegating to executive branch agencies? How will they think about the possibility of enhancing accountability by allocating discretion? Will they think of this as an opportunity or a threat?

Trust, but Verify

The traditional strategy for holding public officials accountable is to constrain their actions so narrowly that they cannot possibly violate our trust. James Q. Wilson explains how this micromanagement approach works: Government agencies hire professionals for their "esoteric knowledge"—because "they know how to do things that must be done." At the same time, he continues, "democratic government requires bureaucratic accountability"—meaning that "no one wholly can be trusted to make important choices free of legal and administrative constraints." But aren't these in conflict? Yes. And we usually resolve "this anomaly," Wilson concludes, "by hiring professionals for their expert knowledge but denying them the right to use that knowledge as they see fit."[100]

This micromanagement approach to accountability is plagued by an obvious flaw that is both conceptual and operational. Yet we continue to rely upon it. Indeed, it creates one of the "big questions" of public management: "How can public managers break the micromanagement cycle—an excess of procedural rules, which prevents public agencies from producing results, which leads to more procedural rules, which leads to . . . ?"[101]

Micromanagement is not, however, the only way to achieve accountability. There exists an alternative strategy. To determine whether public officials have both lived up to our expectations for finances and fairness and still managed to improve performance, we could allocate to them the discretion they need to do their jobs and then check whether they have employed that discretion properly. Given the obvious failure of the micromanagement strategy, perhaps we ought to give the second strategy a serious try. This is the approach advocated by Oakerson: "Democratic administration depends first upon giving discretion to implementing agencies and then holding them accountable for the exercise of that discretion."[102]

President Ronald Reagan considered the Soviet Union to be "the evil empire." Yet he negotiated a treaty with Mikhail Gorbachev to eliminate intermediate-range nuclear missiles. To explain the treaty, Reagan employed "the wisdom in an old Russian maxim": "Trust, but verify." If the United States were prepared to adopt this approach to holding the public officials of a nuclear superpower accountable over such a life-and-death issue, perhaps we might consider adopting a similar trust-but-verify strategy to holding our own public officials accountable for finances, fairness, and performance.

6

Retrospective Accountability for Performance

Public administrators are responsible for process. The conventional method of creating accountability for process is relatively straightforward: The legislature establishes general guidelines for various processes to be followed for finances and equity, regulatory units in the executive branch codify them with more detailed regulations, and the agency itself establishes more processes and additional regulations for all of these processes. Then an agency keeps records to demonstrate that it has followed these processes faithfully and consistently and occasionally issues a report summarizing these records.

Meanwhile auditors examine these records to see whether all of the processes were followed (and to detect any dishonest behavior). Others—journalists, watchdog organizations, and stakeholders—scrutinize the agency, identifying instances when the agency failed to implement its own processes. When a pattern of errors emerges, or a particularly egregious case is identified, or a small but juicy mistake is uncovered, legislative committees hold hearings and take corrective action. Sometimes people who failed to follow the prescribed processes are fired or disciplined. Moreover, because all of this is well known, agencies are motivated to comply with the established processes.

Traditionally, we use a retrospective mechanism to ensure democratic accountability for the use of discretion. After the manager or frontline

employee exercises discretion, elected officials (and their appointees) determine if it has been used badly. For process—that is, for finances and fairness—we resolve the discretion-accountability trade-off by establishing specific expectations, permitting public administrators to exercise discretion in
meeting these expectations; then, after the fact, we check whether they have
done so—whether they have indeed, met our expectations. Trust, but verify.

Adapting the Existing Mechanism of Retrospective Accountability

Public managers are responsible for results. So why can't the conventional
method of retrospective accountability be also applied to results? Why
can't we just adapt the traditional mechanisms of democratic accountability to our new focus on performance? The legislature would establish
general guidelines for the results to be achieved during the next fiscal year,
some executive-branch organization would codify them with more
detailed performance goals, and the agency itself could establish additional goals and more details for all of these goals. Then an agency would
keep records to demonstrate that it is making progress toward achieving
these performance goals and would occasionally issue a report summarizing its accomplishments.[1]

Meanwhile, auditors would examine these records to see whether the
goals were indeed achieved (and to detect any dishonest behavior).
Others—journalists, watchdog organizations, and stakeholders—would
scrutinize the agency, identifying instances when the agency failed to
achieve its own goals. When a pattern of failure emerges, or a particularly
egregious failure is identified, or a small but juicy failure is uncovered, legislative committees would hold hearings and take corrective action. Sometimes people who failed to achieve their goals would be fired or disciplined.
Moreover, because all of this would be well known, agencies would be motivated to achieve their performance goals.

Thus, legislatures (and executive-branch superiors and overhead agencies) would employ the traditional, retrospective mechanism of democratic
accountability to make certain that executive agencies follow all of the
processes designed to ensure the proper use of all finances and to ensure
fairness to all employees and citizens. It is generic. Now, however, this
process has been adapted to create retrospective accountability to make certain that executive agencies achieve specific performance goals.

This accountability process requires the legislature to establish at least
general purposes; but legislatures already do that. It also requires executive-

branch superiors to establish some goals; but some already do that.[2] And it requires executive agencies to establish specific goals that can indicate progress towards realizing these general purposes; but some agencies already do that. Then, once an agency has chosen its goals for the fiscal year, the accountability process for performance can follow the accountability process that has already been perfected for finances and equity.

To make retrospective accountability work for performance, the legislature ought to do two additional things. During the fiscal year, the legislature ought to review the agency's choice of goals. And, after the fiscal year, it ought to evaluate the agency's achievement of these goals:

— *Reviewing the choice of goals:* After the agency has chosen its performance goals, the legislature ought to determine whether these goals make sense. It can assign staff to analyze the goals, consider alternatives, and assess the process the agency employed to pick the goals. It can hold hearings to learn whether the stakeholders and the general public are satisfied with the goals. Then, if the legislature is unsatisfied with the agency's choice, it can ask the agency to rethink its goals and report back. If it is extremely unhappy with the agency's goals, it can pressure the agency to change them, sanction the agency, attempt to convince the elected chief executive to change the agency's managers, or enact legislation changing the goals for the current fiscal year.

— *Evaluating the achievement of the goals:* After the fiscal year is over, the legislature needs to determine whether the agency has achieved its goals. It can ask the agency for a report, request an audit of that report, and assign some staff to provide an independent evaluation of how well the agency did. It can hold hearings to determine whether the stakeholders and the general public are satisfied with the agency's performance. Then, if the legislature is unsatisfied, it can determine the causes and ask the agency to develop a plan to improve performance in the next fiscal year. If it is extremely unhappy with the agency's performance, it can pressure the agency to make specific management changes, sanction the agency, attempt to convince the elected chief executive to change the agency's managers, or enact legislation creating new and different goals for the next fiscal year.

It seems straightforward to adapt the existing, retrospective mechanisms for establishing democratic accountability for finances and equity to the new needs of creating a retrospective mechanism for establishing democratic accountability for performance. Trust, but verify.

Retrospective Accountability in Business

Moreover, this generic accountability mechanism is similar to the way a business firm creates accountability for performance. The managers of various divisions and other units reach an agreement with their superiors about their goals for the year.[3] Then, once the fiscal year has begun, upper management monitors each division's performance. And, at the end of the year, it conducts an audit, determines which divisions have met their goals and which have not, takes corrective action when necessary, and negotiates new goals for the next year. If a division achieves its goals (and does not do anything illegal) it has been a success—it has been accountable for its stewardship of the owners' resources and for its broader obligations to society. Trust, but verify.

John W. Gardner, the former secretary of Health, Education, and Welfare, suggests that the accountability mechanism employed in business could work in government:

> I have served on a number of corporate boards, and I am struck by the fact that such boards—made up of people quite as busy as members of Congress—require management to serve up to them a considerable variety of indexes of performance that can be appraised at a glance. The necessity to provide such indexes is a lively stimulus to accountability. And in the business world it is not just the board of directors that expects such data. A vast network of individual investors, pension fund managers, security analysts, and the like assume that they will have available on a regular basis certain indexes of performance. No chief executive officer doubts that the requirement for providing such indexes makes it more likely that he will behave accountably in certain directions. If Congress required that agencies work up and publish comparable indexes of performance, then all groups engaged in the tasks of oversight would be acting on more adequate data.[4]

Trust, but verify.

The Politics of Process and the Politics of Performance

Why can't accountability for performance work like accountability for process? Why can't accountability for performance in government work similarly to accountability for performance in business? Why can't we trust and then verify?

Because process is different from performance. And because business is different from government. More relevant, the politics of process are different from the politics of performance.[5] The initial step of establishing specific goals makes this obvious. For there is always the annoying question: *Whose* goals? *Who* will decide what results are to be produced? As the National Governors' Association notes, "Implementing results-based accountability systems requires agreement among key stakeholders on what results are valued, how performance on state government functions and activities will be measured, and what performance levels are expected."[6]

The legislature could, of course, do this. After all, the legislature does establish processes. Sometimes it creates very detailed processes. Sometimes it formulates only general processes and lets the executive branch add more specifics—all of the time reserving the right to oversee, modify, or cancel these specifics. Can't the legislature do for performance what it does for process? Sometimes it could create very detailed goals. Sometimes it could formulate only general goals and let the executive branch add more specifics—all of the time reserving the right to oversee, modify, or cancel these specifics. Why doesn't the legislature do this?

Because the legislature does not want to. The legislature as a collective body (and each individual legislator as well) does not want to establish specific goals. As Donald Savoie emphasizes, government's "objectives are unclear because politicians prefer it that way."[7] Clarifying objectives is managerially sound but politically irrational. For in clarifying objectives, the politicians must choose from among competing constituencies and conflicting values. From experience, elected officials have learned that they can win more praise, support, and votes by being fuzzy about what results government will produce than they can by being specific.

Any discussion about a specific target for a specific year for a specific program or a specific agency reintroduces political disagreements that have been carefully minimized by incorporating the vague (rather than precise) purposes into the authorizing legislation. A legislative preamble that outlines general, multiple, and perhaps even contradictory purposes can make a lot of people happy. The purposes set forth in legislation are not multiple and general because no legislator had a clear idea of what goal he or she wanted to achieve; instead, the preamble contains multiple, general purposes because, although many legislators could identify one or several specific goals to be achieved, they could not all agree on a few common ones.

Moreover, legislative leaders use multiple and vague purposes to build the majority coalition necessary to enact or modify a program. Because the preamble to a bill lists multiple purposes, each member of the coalition can claim (completely sincerely) that he or she has been able to ensure that the legislation will achieve an important purpose that has been expressly advocated by a major constituency or generally endorsed by the electorate. And because all of these multiple purposes are expressed in vague language, each member of the coalition can claim (again, completely sincerely) that any purpose that an important constituency or the electorate finds objectionable will not be pursued seriously by the implementing agency. Vague purposes grease the legislature's wheels.

Further, vague purposes permit individual legislators to squeak loudly when the implementing agency chooses to focus on the "wrong" purposes. When some constituent complains, explains Morris Fiorina of Stanford University, "the congressman lends a sympathetic ear, piously denounces the evils of bureaucracy, intervenes in the latter's decisions, and rides a grateful electorate to ever more impressive electoral showings." Thus "congressmen appropriate all the public credit generated," writes Fiorina, "while the bureaucracy absorbs all the costs."[8]

In *Power without Responsibility: How Congress Abuses the People through Delegation,* David Schoenbrod of the New York Law School argues that by enacting vague legislation that delegates policymaking responsibility to executive agencies, members of Congress make generous promises but shift to the executive branch any blame for failing to produce results. "Delegation enhances legislator's opportunities to support the benefits of an action and oppose its costs, which is political heaven," observes Schoenbrod.[9] For example, "Congress can proclaim to be in favor of clean air, but against the costs of achieving it," he writes. "Congress can be in favor of removing asbestos from public schools, but not appropriate the funds to achieve that goal." Consequently, he continues, "government ends up making promises it cannot afford to keep, and voters lose the ability to discipline legislators for imposing costs." Legislators, Schoenbrod contends, "use every opportunity to take credit and shift blame."[10]

Accountability holders love to close the barn door after the horse has escaped. The legislature creates many horses (or, at least, a helluva lot of little ponies), stables them in a large number of barns, and mandates that each barn have a large number of doors. As a result, even if only a small percentage of these doors are left open for only a small percentage of the time, there still exist multiple opportunities for horses to escape. And when they do—when an accountability holdee leaves the wrong door open at the wrong time—a legislator or some other accountability holder can come in, denounce the accountability holdees for their stupidity in leaving the door open, and nail it shut. These accountability holders are never responsible for creating any specific door or even for any door's design; these details have been delegated to the agency. So obviously the accountability holders cannot possibly be responsible for any particular door being left open. But they can earn a lot of political or professional credit for nailing a lot of them shut.

Performance Goals and Bureaucratic Hoop Jumping

As the chairman of the Committee on Governmental Affairs, Senator William Roth of Delaware was the main force behind the 1993 Government Performance and Results Act (GPRA), which requires federal agencies to specify the results they will produce. Roth wanted Congress to establish specific goals for specific agencies. "Under the [proposed and subsequently enacted] legislation," wrote Roth in an addendum to his committee's report,

> Federal agencies would be required to develop measurable goals for their programs. I believe we should go one step further, and also require that Congress itself play a direct role in the establishing of at least some of those goals. Congress creates and funds the programs, so it ought to give some indication as to what it expects them to accomplish. . . . Congress has an obligation to tell the American taxpayers what results we intend for the money we spend, and this requirement should be included in the legislation.[11]

Sounds reasonable enough. But senators and representatives (including those on Roth's own committee) hastened to decline Roth's invitation. Their debates over vague purposes are contentious enough; they hardly wanted to create even more fractious debates over specific goals.

Still, as GPRA suggests, a legislature can create accountability for results without first specifying the results to be achieved; instead, it can have the agencies specify them. This shifts the ticklish burden of choosing between competing purposes and values from the legislative branch to the executive. But at least one legislative body—the United States Congress—has demonstrated its willingness to do precisely this. Maybe other legislatures, under pressure to produce results but unwilling to specify particular ones, will take this approach. The legislature surrenders some influence and control; but it avoids some nasty disagreements.

Will all of this create accountability? Will creating performance goals ensure accountability for results? After all, the executive agencies may be just as reluctant as the legislature to create nasty disagreements and the inevitable attacks that come from choosing goals. They, too, may equivocate. The legislature can create a process, a form, and a deadline requiring each agency to specify one or several goals. But the legislature cannot force the agencies to take the requirement seriously or to tackle the task intelligently. Agencies can choose uncontroversial and inconsequential goals. They can choose easily attainable goals.

In 1973 the U.S. Office of Management and Budget created a government-wide program of management by objectives. In the second year of this program, President Gerald Ford approved 172 "presidential objectives" for twenty federal agencies. The Department of Housing and Urban Development, for example, had several ambitious if ambiguous objectives, including improving the competitiveness of the maritime industry and promoting business ownership by minorities. In contrast, the Department of Justice had some very specific if narrow objectives, including building more prisons and increasing from sixteen to more than twenty-five the number of states with federal-state law enforcement committees.[12] Indeed, most of the 172 objectives were either very specific, short-term work measures or very general, global aspirations.

Congress can enact GPRA, but it can't force federal agencies to think more seriously about their goals. It can only force them to follow some procedures such as to develop a performance plan. Like all federal agencies, the Commodity Futures Trading Commission (CFTC) has such a plan. Its first goal is to "protect the economic functions of the commodity futures and option markets."[13] And how will it know if it has done this? For fiscal 1999, CFTC reported on a number of "performance indicators" for different activities that contributed to this goal. These activities included the "number of compliance and warning letters sent on reporting requirements," which totaled 2,705 for the year (compared with CFTC's target of 2,950) and the "number of documents obtained through subpoena or inspection," which totaled 27,455 (compared with the commission's target of 90,000).[14] Such a unique combination of global aspirations and mundane work-measures does little to produce real results or establish accountability for performance.[15]

When charged with creating performance goals, public managers can easily avoid the intent of their superiors. Given all the hoops that legislatures and overhead agencies have forced line-managers to jump through over the years, these managers have developed a lot of expertise in hoop-jumping. They can easily figure out how to jump through (or around) this one.[16]

The Politics of Rules and the Politics of Results

Does the executive branch similarly avoid legislative intent when it promulgates the rules and regulations that create the framework for process accountability? Not really. Every regulation has a historical rationale; every regulation is designed to prevent a recurrence of a previous error—some failure to handle money properly or to be fair to an employee or citizen. There is no limit to the number of regulations that either the legislature or the executive can create. That's why government has thousands—no: zillions—of regulations.

Managerially, more regulations are a pain. They consume valuable time and resources. And more regulations provide more chances for people within an agency to make a small but politically consequential mistake— one that captures the attention of an accountability holder and thus consumes valuable time and resources of the accountability holdee.

Politically, however, more regulations are always better. More regulations mean more accountability for finances and fairness. The legislature does not resist more regulation; indeed, it *seeks* more: It creates more on its own, and it presses the executive branch to create more too. It does so, however, not in response to pressure for more regulation in general; instead the pressure is for a large number of small, discrete regulations, all of which just happen to add up to more—a lot more.

Similarly, more regulators are always better—politically, that is. Managerially, more regulators are a pain. Still, more regulators mean that government is being more careful about accountability for finances and fairness. Authorizing another auditor or creating another inspector general is easy to justify: "We have to ensure that this outrage will never happen again." "We have to prevent any more lapses in accountability."

Can the same thing happen with goals? Perhaps. An executive agency that is charged with creating goals and that doesn't want to offend any stakeholders or neglect any values can simply follow the legislature's example: It too can create multiple and vague goals. But if an organization has a hundred goals, it really has none. When this happens, the legislature must either come up with its own specific goals or accept the executive's multiple vague ones. Or, if the legislature demands that the agency pick one and only one goal, the agency can do exactly as requested: choose only one goal, and create precisely the kind of fight the legislature has been trying to avoid.

Rules and results have quite different political attributes. The controversies surrounding rules are different from the controversies surrounding results. And thus the politics of rules are different from the politics of results. Consequently, it may not be easy to make a few small modifications in the existing accountability mechanisms used for process and have them work smoothly for performance. "Although congressional oversight is not as faint and fragile as it is sometimes said to be," concludes John Gardner, "it almost never provides a systematic assessment of agency performance against defined standards, and it is unlikely that this will change."[17]

Verifying Expectations

To create accountability with a trust-but-verify strategy, we need to establish the expectations. Only then can we later verify that people or agencies have complied with them.

We expect that public administrators will be responsible for processes. So we explicitly institute rules to codify our expectations about how they will implement the processes for which they will be accountable. Then, retrospectively, we verify that they have done so.

We expect that public managers will be responsible for performance. Unfortunately, we cannot codify our expectations about performance by creating rules similar to those we employ to codify our expectations for public administrators. For public managers, we have different expectations—expectations about results. To establish these expectations, we need to create goals.

These goals, however, do not directly constrain the public managers' discretion, at least not in the same way that rules do.[18] Certainly we want public managers to direct their efforts toward these goals. But in pursuing such goals, they have some discretion—a lot of discretion.

Thus we worry. Trusting the public managers to achieve their goals and then verifying that they did isn't enough. We care *how* they do this. And this gets back to finances and fairness. This gets back to constraints. If we are going to trust public managers, we will have to trust them to both achieve their performance targets and to do so while allocating their finances appropriately and while treating people fairly. When we trust public managers, we are trusting them with a lot more than we trust public administrators. And, therefore, we will have to verify a lot more. We will have to verify not just performance but also finances and fairness. To employ the trust-but-verify strategy to hold public managers accountable for performance, we will have to verify a lot more.

Compliance Accountability and Micromanagement

Accountability for finances and fairness is about the use and treatment of government's inputs. Accountability for performance is about the production of government's outputs and outcomes.[19] Inputs are different from outputs and outcomes.[20] Consequently, accountability for inputs is different from accountability for outputs and outcomes.

Accountability for finances and fairness concerns how government uses and treats its inputs: Does government deploy its monetary inputs honestly? Does it obtain its human (and material) inputs fairly? Does it deal equitably with the various human resources who are its clients: students; the disabled; the criminally accused; and driver's-license, passport, and building-permit applicants? We have some clear expectations about how government ought to handle these monetary and human inputs, which we can codify in very specific rules. Then, we can determine whether public officials have lived up to these expectations by checking whether they have complied with these rules. Accountability for finances and fairness is compliance accountability.

Accountability for performance, however, concerns what outputs and outcomes government has produced with its inputs. It is about whether government has achieved our desired results. We may have some clear expectations about what results government ought to produce, some of which we may be able to specify in very clear performance targets. Then, we can determine whether public officials have lived up to these expectations by checking whether they have achieved these targets. To create accountability for performance, we must specify our expectations in terms of results—not in terms of rules, or regulations, or processes. Accountability for performance is not compliance accountability.

We could attempt to convert accountability for results into accountability for rules. We could define accountability for performance as accountability for creating outputs and outcomes in the most economical, or most efficient, or most effective manner—for following the rules about how to produce the results. Then it would be compliance accountability. We could create expectations for how economical a public agency was (the money it spent to produce specified results), or for how efficient it was (the results produced per dollar), or for how effective it was (whether it followed established best practices in producing the results). But such accountability would not really be about performance. It would not be about the results produced. It would be about *how* the results were produced. Compliance accountability for performance is just micromanagement.

Finances and fairness are different from performance. Thus accountability for finances and fairness is different from accountability for performance. Compliance accountability can indeed create incentives that encourage public officials to abide by our expectations for finances and fairness. But compliance accountability for results will not create incentives that encourage public officials to improve performance. If we don't trust public managers to pursue improved performance in a diligent and intelligent manner, we may be tempted to create some rules for them to follow and to charge some accountability holder with checking to see whether the managers have complied with these rules. But, we ought not to confuse such micromanagement with accountability for performance.

Neutral Competence and Bureaucratic Anonymity

Gerald Caiden considers anonymity to be a shortcoming of our current system of public accountability: "The depersonalized nature of public administration shields officials from the consequences of their actions and prevents members of the public [from] identifying which officials are specifically responsible for particular operations."[21]

Woodrow Wilson well understood the need to eliminate bureaucratic anonymity:

> Public attention must be easily directed, in each case of good or bad administration, to just the man deserving of praise or blame. There is no danger in power, if only it be not irresponsible. If it be divided, dealt out in shares to many, it is obscured; and if it be obscured, it is made irresponsible. But if it be centered in heads of the service and in heads of branches of the service, it is easily watched and brought to book.[22]

Yet despite Wilson's influence, he did not convince people to create a system of government agencies that highlights responsibility in the heads of each agency. Why? Why doesn't American government highlight accountability for performance?

Because, expressly separating politics from administration inherently (if not consciously) obscures accountability. Under the politics-administration dichotomy, politicians are accountable for policy and for everything that flows from policy. The civil servants just carry out that policy scientifically. How can public administrators be accountable? How can they be accountable for the performance of a program or policy that they did not design?

Bureaucracies are, almost by definition, anonymous. Neutral competence[23]—the ultimate civil-service value—is almost the same as bureaucratic anonymity. When we visit a government bureaucracy and get angry with a government bureaucrat for applying (neutrally, if mindlessly) some obscure rule to us, we know (analytically, if not emotionally) that we really cannot blame the bureaucrat. Our treatment—no matter how absurd—is a consequence not of the bureaucrat's bureaucratic DNA. The system of rules (and of punishments for violating these rules) has motivated the bureaucrat to behave bureaucratically. Why should the bureaucrat accept accountability for the system of rules that someone else higher up in the hierarchy devised without ever asking frontline workers for their suggestions? At the same time, how can the person at the head of any agency really be accountable for the behavior of the individuals with civil-service protection who work several layers down in the agency's hierarchy[24]—particularly when these civil servants follow rules imposed by the legislature or some outside regulatory unit?

Finally, how can an individual legislator really be accountable for the vague mandates established by the legislature, let alone for the rules created by executive branch overhead agencies? Guy Peters of the University of Pittsburgh and John Pierre of the University of Strathclyde ask this question: "If elected political leaders have such limited control over the public administration, is it reasonable to hold them accountable for the decisions and actions of the public service, and if elected officials should not be held accountable, who then is accountable?"[25]

Who is accountable anyway?

Eliminating Anonymity; Highlighting Accountability

"The two enemies of accountability are unclear objectives and anonymity," writes Sandford Borins. And, he argues, "by promoting specificity of goals and by reducing anonymity, the new public management is strengthening accountability."[26] Creating specific goals for specific organizational units establishes accountability and reduces anonymity.

Specific performance goals are definitely a managerial plus. With specific goals, an agency's managers can motivate people and mobilize resources. With specific goals, an agency's managers can evaluate progress, learn what works and what doesn't, and improve performance. With specific goals, an agency's managers can document progress. With specific goals, an agency's managers can demonstrate that they are making good use of the public's money. Indeed, with specific goals, an agency's managers can explain what they could accomplish with more flexibility and resources.[27]

Although different advocates of a new public management paradigm may have different paradigms in mind, they all share a common focus on performance, on results, and, thus, on goals: The job of public managers is to improve organizational performance, to produce results, to achieve specific goals. But exactly how will the new public management help to reduce anonymity?

A system of specific performance goals to be achieved during the current fiscal year can highlight the agency director's accountability. Whether this goal is established by the legislature or the agency itself, the head of the agency is accountable for achieving it. The rest of the organization, however, is still off the hook. For what are those at lower levels in the hierarchy accountable? Are they simply accountable for implementing the director's plan for achieving the goal? If so, their life has hardly changed. They remain anonymous and still are not accountable.[28]

Yet if specific goals can help to eliminate the problem of anonymity at the top levels of an agency, why can't they do the same at all levels in the hierarchy? After all, everyone is a middle manager. Every manager of every unit has superiors and subordinates. So why not create specific goals for every level of the organization? Such subordinate goals would be tied directly to the organization's overall performance target.[29] Indeed, if these subordinate goals were intelligently selected, the organization would—simply by achieving all of these subordinate goals—automatically achieve its overall goal as well.

These lower-level goals need not be reported to the legislature. (They could be, but the legislature would never be able to examine more than a few in depth.) But establishing these subordinate goals—and, perhaps, by posting everywhere each unit's progress towards achieving its goals[30]—an organization would create accountability at lower levels and thus eliminate anonymity (at least within the organization). Moreover, if something went wrong, if the agency failed to achieve its goal for the fiscal year, the hierarchy of goals would permit the agency (or the legislature) to identify the cause of the failure. If some subunits failed to achieve their individual goals, then they and their superiors would be accountable. If all subunits achieved their goals, then the agency's director would be accountable for failing to create a system of subordinate goals whose achievement would produce the agency's overall goal.

Creating specific performance goals helps to eliminate anonymity. Requiring a public agency to have a specific goal to accomplish by the end of the fiscal year can highlight its accountability. Similarly, requiring lower levels in the agency's hierarchy to also have specific goals that they will accomplish by the end of the fiscal year can highlight their accountability. At all levels of government, specific performance goals help to reduce anonymity.[31]

Earning the Public's Trust

"Administration in the United States must be at all points sensitive to public opinion," argued Wilson.[32] Obviously the legislature is sensitive to public opinion. So is the judiciary; as one of Wilson's contemporaries, Finley Peter Dunne's Mr. Dooley observed: "th' supreme coort follows th' iliction returns."[33] Ought not the civil service also be sensitive to public opinion?

But how sensitive to public opinion ought administration to be? Wilson calls this "the fundamental problem" of public administration: "What part shall public opinion take in the conduct of administration?" Wilson's answer was that the public should be engaged, but not too engaged:

> The problem is to make public opinion efficient without suffering it to be meddlesome. Directly exercised, in the oversight of daily details and in the choice of daily means of government, public criticism is of course a clumsy nuisance, a rustic handling of delicate machinery. But as superintending the greater forces of formative policy alike in politics and administration, public criticism is altogether safe and beneficent, altogether indispensable. Let administrative study find the best means for giving public criticism this control and for shutting it out from all other interference. . . .
>
> The ideal for us is a civil service cultured and self-sufficient enough to act with sense and vigor, and yet so intimately connected with the popular thought, by means of elections and constant public counsel, as to find arbitrariness or class spirit quite out of the question. . . .
>
> . . . comparative studies of the ways and means of government should enable us to offer suggestions which will practically combine

openness and vigor in the administration of such governments with ready docility to all serious, well-sustained public criticism.[34]

As Wilson's words illustrate, striking the right balance between vigor and docility is difficult. When is government being open? When is public criticism serious? When is it well sustained? When is the civil service being arbitrary? What, indeed, is the best means for giving public criticism appropriate control while shutting it out from inappropriate interference? It is difficult to create accountability mechanisms that strike the right balance.

Still, we have tried. We have created formal processes and detailed rules to ensure both vigor and docility. We require public agencies to hold hearings, issue draft policies, and provide the public with formal opportunities to comment—all to ensure the appropriate docility to public criticism. (Then, once the agency has followed these procedures, it has the obligation to exercise its discretion with competence—to behave with adequate vigor.) Public officials do learn to follow meticulously the rules and processes for public involvement, but this hardly ensures meaningful participation. The formal systems for public involvement fail to truly connect government agencies to public opinion and popular thought (assuming that the public has a specific, well-thought-out opinion).

The new public management's emphasis on achieving specific goals may, however, have an important effect on the public's attitudes toward government. For much of the public's discontent with its government can be traced to its belief (whether justified or not) that it does not get much from its government, that it does not get its money's worth from its government, that its government cannot produce results. One poll reported that the American public believes that of every dollar the government spends, it wastes 48¢.[35] Canadians have a higher opinion of their government's efficiency; they believe that of each dollar Ottawa spends, it wastes only 47¢.[36]

"Americans give the government dismal performance ratings," reports the Pew Research Center for the People and the Press. From a poll that it took in 1997, the Pew Research Center found that "an overwhelming majority of the public says that government does a fair or poor job managing its programs and providing services (74%). Almost as many agree that when a program is run by government it is usually inefficient and wasteful (64%)." Moreover, Pew found that "most people say it is performance that determines their opinions" about government; this led Pew to "underscore the importance of government performance to improved public attitudes about government."[37]

In the 1980s, when the Massachusetts Department of Welfare was measuring and reporting the performance of its ET (Employment and Training) program, its public reputation improved significantly. The agency's leadership established annual and monthly goals for placing welfare recipients in jobs—goals for both the department as a whole and for its fifty local offices. It reported its results annually—and very publicly. "The polls say that 85 percent of the people are in favor of our ET program," reported the governor's chief of staff: "Can you name another state where 85 percent of the people are in favor of welfare?"[38]

Any public agency that demonstrates its ability to achieve specific results may improve the public's attitude toward its own organization and toward government in general. "Public trust in government is dependent upon information," argues the National Academy of Public Administration. Thus it urges public agencies "to measure and publicize progress toward program goals"—to create "performance indicators" that will help "citizens to determine whether government is worthy of their trust." The Academy seeks "empirical evidence—not merely anecdote or personal experience"—that citizens can use "to inform their impressions and assessments of government."[39]

Indeed, one of the basic reasons that any organization measures its own performance is to promote its reputation for competence.[40] A focus on performance—combined with monitoring systems that dramatize the results that different public agencies achieve—may influence the public's thinking. "Faith in public institutions will be restored when they perform better," argues David Carnevale. "Confidence in government will improve when it is able to get the credit it deserves for producing quality work."[41] By producing results—by achieving specific, pre-established performance goals—public agencies may begin slowly to convince the citizens that government performance is not an oxymoron.

7

A New Compact of Mutual, Collective Responsibility

What *might* accountability mean? What might it mean to hold someone accountable? What might it mean to be accountable? Who should be accountable? And for what? How might accountability for performance work not only in theory but also in practice?

To whom must public managers be accountable? The answer is "everyone."[1] Even citizens who do not have any children in the local school system have a stake in the finances of that school system, in the schools' equitable treatment of its students, and in the performance of these schools. Indeed, because the schools are charged with teaching not only mathematics and composition but also citizenship, even citizens who live in a different part of the nation have a stake in the school system's fairness and performance (if not in its finances). Even citizens who do not live near Yosemite National Park, even citizens who have never visited Yosemite, even citizens who know they will never visit Yosemite have a stake (if only a small stake) in it (if only so their grandchildren might enjoy it or because they believe in the park's intrinsic value). Public managers are, inherently, accountable to a diversity of stakeholders. Indeed, this is one of the biggest distinctions between public and private management.[2]

For what must public managers be accountable? Although the answer may not be everything, it certainly is a lot of things. Public managers will always be accountable for finances, fairness, and performance.

For what attributes of finances, fairness, and performance will public managers be accountable? This question is being continually debated, and the answers continually revised. Moreover public managers *can*—and *should*—influence the answer. Indeed, they should exercise leadership to help rethink the answer.[3]

Influencing Our Thinking about Accountability

Public managers *can* influence the things for which they are accountable and the ways in which they are accountable for these things. How should they be accountable for their finances? What is the theoretical purpose and practical definition of the various types of fairness for which public managers will be accountable? For what specific levels of performance should they be accountable? Public managers can influence the operational answers to these questions. They cannot eliminate any of the three forms of accountability. But they can shape both the *what?* and the *how?* of their accountability.

Public managers *can* influence what financial accountability means. They will never be able to eliminate financial accountability. They will always be required to provide an accounting for what they did with the public's funds. Still, they can influence the specifics of that accountability process—everything from how often the reports must be filed to what these reports must contain. They will not be able to reduce the frequency of financial reporting to once every five years. They will not be able to reduce the number of numbers they must report to just one: total dollars spent. But if they can make an intelligent argument for a system of financial accountability that is both less bothersome and more effective at identifying the most frequent and most egregious errors,[4] and if they can make that argument through the right channels and in the right forums, they can have an influence.

Similarly, public managers *can* influence the operational practicalities of ensuring equity and fairness (and perhaps even the democratic definition of these principles).[5] The nature of accountability for fairness is no more God-given than the definition of financial or performance accountability. The debate about the meaning of equity can take on theological overtones. Indeed, those engaged in the debate will, quite naturally, recruit to the fray theologians who share their creed.[6] But except for those definitions of equity that can be derived directly from the Ten Commandments, none are carved in stone. Most are open to debate. Thus most are open to influence.

Because public managers understand the operational implications of various standards and procedures, they could—and should—exercise some influence.

Clearly, however, public managers can have the most influence over the nature of accountability for performance. After all, an agency's managers understand (or should understand) their organization's capabilities. They know what the agency can and cannot do—what results it can and cannot produce. Thus they could explain to the various stakeholders what expectations for performance would be reasonable (or unreasonable), and what flexibility and resources would be needed to achieve higher—but still reasonable—levels of performance. Thinking strategically, the leaders of a public agency might seek to negotiate the terms under which they and their organization are accountable for performance.

Mark Moore argues that public managers should "embrace rather than shun accountability" for achieving specific objectives. Why? Because establishing a willingness to be accountable for achieving particular objectives helps public managers acquire the political support necessary to accomplish these objectives. Because embracing accountability helps them acquire more resources and more discretion in the use of existing resources. Because it increases their ability to challenge their own agencies to improve performance. For public managers who "seek strategic changes in organizations," writes Moore, "embracing accountability seems to be an important tool."[7]

Indeed, public managers ought to be accountable for suggesting very specific ways to create accountability. We citizens should expect them to suggest how their accountability for finances might be improved, how their accountability for equity might be improved, and how their accountability for performance might also be improved. Public managers clearly have some important insights about how these accountability processes could be improved.[8] Why should this knowledge be ignored? Why should it be wasted?[9]

Today accountability means forms, rules, and punishment. Public managers have to fill out the right accounting forms to prove that they have followed all of the rules about finances, fairness, and (maybe) performance. And, whenever they make a mistake—whenever they don't fill out the right forms or fail to follow all the rules—they are punished.

Accountability could, however, be something other than forms, rules, and punishment. It could be an agreement between the leadership team of a public agency and its direct political overseers. It could be an agreement between a public agency and its accountability environment. It could be an agreement in which *both* the managers and the overseers—indeed, *all* those in the accountability environment—have obligations. It could be an agreement in which no one is categorized as an accountability punisher or an accountability punishee. It could be an agreement that focuses less on forms, rules, and punishment and more on mutual obligations. It could be an agreement concerning not just finances and fairness, but finances, fairness, and performance.

A Performance Contract

Such an agreement could be a *performance contract.* Indeed, with the new public management, governments in Britain, New Zealand, Canada, and the United States have created such performance contracts. Usually, these agreements are strictly between a political superior and a managerial subordinate—between an elected chief executive and a cabinet secretary, or, in the Commonwealth nations, between a cabinet minister and an agency head. Often, the objective is to create a "performance-based organization," or PBO.[10]

Such a PBO is a formal, legal contract; the PBO's executive agrees to abide by certain (but fewer) rules and to achieve specific performance goals.[11] And if the PBO executive abides by the rules and achieves the performance goals, he or she earns a performance bonus. The PBO concept is based on the theory that giving the organization's top executive a personal, financial incentive to improve performance will indeed result in improved performance.[12] Although PBOs are one of the core components of the new public management, and although Vice President Gore's National Performance Review proposed creating several, by the beginning of 2000 the United States government had created only two: the Office of Student Financial Assistance in the Department of Education, and the Patent and Trademark Office in the Department of Commerce.

Nevertheless, during the 1980s, even before the publication of *Reinventing Government*[13] or the coining of the phrase "new public management," governors were creating performance contracts with their states' cabinet secretaries. Such a performance "contract" was not a legal document. It was simply an informal "agreement" between the governor and a department head outlining what specific results the department would produce during the coming fiscal year. Yet even such informal performance agreements involved the trade-off between accountability and flexibility.

"How much discretion should be given to agency directors"? ask Larry Polivka and Jack Osterhold. When they worked in the executive office of the governor of Florida, Polivka and Osterhold worried about how "to create an effective balance between agency discretion and gubernatorial leadership"— a "balance between autonomy and accountability in the executive branch." And one way to do this was with "a set of performance agreements" between the governor and the head of each agency, which, they argued, had become "an indispensible management tool for the governor." These performance agreements were built around a limited number of performance measures designed for "actually making quantitative, 'bottom-line' assessments of the impact of resource utilization." For example, the head of the agency responsible for environmental regulation, in seeking "to improve the quality and quantity of Florida's drinking water supply," had two fiscal-year targets: "(1) To reduce the number of maximum containment level violations by 30 percent; (2) To develop maximum containment levels for six additional organic contaminants."[14]

By 1985, concluded Polivka and Osterhold, these performance agreements had, in Florida, "become the executive branch's most rigorous and useful method of ensuring program accountability." State agencies "must be allowed substantial autonomy," they argued; at the same time, agencies "must be limited by accountability mechanisms" including "clearly articulated [gubernatorial] policies and program impact measures" that "the governor would review with the agency directors in his quarterly policy meetings." This way, Polivka and Osterhold concluded, it is possible to obtain "program impact accountability without destroying agency autonomy."[15]

Because such performance agreements are informal, the two parties— the elected chief executive and the politically appointed department head— have the flexibility to adjust its terms as circumstances change. If the legislature fails to appropriate all of the funds requested in the governor's budget, the performance targets can be lowered. If another agency makes an error in finances or fairness that generates public attention, some of the agency's flexibility may have to be temporarily retracted. Because these performance agreements are informal, and because they are negotiated between just two individuals and in private, they can be based on trust.

When, however, a performance agreement is a real, legal contract, the nature of the relationship changes significantly.[16] Craig Thomas of the University of Massachusetts argues that "extensively detailed contracts imply a lack of trust." Otherwise, why would the contract have to be so detailed? Why would the contract have to be so extensive? To illustrate "the spiral of distrust" that captured the American automobile industry in the 1970s, Francis Fukuyama of George Mason University cites the 1982 labor contract between the Ford Motor Company and the United Auto Workers, which "consisted of four volumes, each two hundred pages in length supplemented at the plant level by another thick collective bargaining agreement specifying work rules, terms and conditions of employment and the like." Fukuyama notes that legal institutions, including contracts, serve "as a substitute for trust," although "rules and contract have not done away with the need for trust in the modern workplace."[17]

An informal performance agreement between a political executive and an agency manager can help significantly to improve performance. It can focus the attention of the agency, its managers, and its frontline employees on specific performance goals. It can focus the attention of the political executive and various support agencies on the flexibility needed to achieve these goals. It can create mutual, interpersonal accountability between supervisor and subordinate. But neither an informal performance agreement nor a formal, two-party performance contract will really do much to enhance *democratic* accountability—to create more accountability to the citizenry.

A Compact of Mutual, Collective Responsibility

To create accountability to citizens, we need a new concept of democratic accountability: *a compact of mutual, collective responsibility.* I have chosen each of these four words carefully:
   — A "compact" is not a legal document but an ethical commitment.
   — "Responsibility" involves obligations willingly accepted, not punishment imposed.[18]
   — A "mutual" commitment entails a personal sense of duty to others, not a detached debt to some abstract rule.
   — A "collective" duty dramatizes that the members of the compact are accepting responsibility as a team and abandoning the search for individual scapegoats.
Accountability is imposed on you unilaterally. Responsibility is assumed by you voluntarily.

A compact of mutual, collective responsibility is not an explicit performance contract. It is not a formal legal document that delineates the constraints for finances and fairness to which the public manager must adhere, along with the performance objectives that he or she must achieve (combined, perhaps, with some monetary reward for achieving these performance objectives). It is not a collection of rules that regulates the behavior of its signatories. It is not a linear, hierarchical, uni-directional concept with a superior accountability holder and a subordinate accountability holdee.

Instead, this "responsibility compact" is an understanding in which every member makes a mutually supportive commitment to every other member and to their common purpose. It is a compact under which every member personally assumes some specific obligations to the group as a whole and to each of the other individuals in the compact.[19]

A compact of mutual, collective responsibility does not create adversarial accountability. It is a supportive institution that individuals join voluntarily. It is not a vehicle that competitors can use to impose accountability on each other. Instead, it is a collaborative in which people recognize their own personal responsibilities. It is a compact in which people seek to identify their common interests and foster cooperation so that they can deal better with their conflicts.[20]

A responsibility compact is not a performance contract but a more sophisticated and subtle agreement—one with both explicit and implicit clauses—that concerns not only finances, fairness, and performance but also the public trust, public interest, and democratic duties. It is more than a piece of paper signed by the leaders of a public agency and their political superiors in the executive branch, or by an agency's manager and its authorizing committee in the legislature. It imposes obligations not only on the agency, its managers, and its employees. It also imposes obligations on all of the other individuals and organizations in the accountability environment—upon legislators, stakeholders, journalists, and citizens. It is a compact of *mutual* responsibility.[21]

A compact of mutual, collective responsibility lays out the overall mission of the agency and specific performance targets for the next year.[22] It not only holds the public manager accountable for getting things done but also provides the public manager with the authority, resources, and organizational capacity necessary to do so.[23] It both proscribes and prescribes: It not only limits the public manager's authority but also enhances it. It specifies not only the forms the agency is expected to fill out but also the nature of the behavior in which all of the agency's personnel are expected to engage.[24]

A responsibility compact is more than an oath of office. It is a compact that every public manager accepts when taking the job. It is a compact not only with the leadership of the agency but also with the frontline personnel.

It is a compact that holds public officials, public managers, and public employees quite responsible and, if necessary, accountable—yes, even punishable—for failure to satisfy the demands of finances, fairness, and performance while giving these same individuals and groups an important and essential role in shaping the overall nature and specific standards of these demands.[25]

A compact of mutual, collective responsibility holds *everyone* in the accountability environment accountable—even punishable—for failure to contribute to satisfying the demands of finances, fairness, and performance. It is a web of mutual responsibility—a web in which each member of the accountability environment is accountable to every other member.[26]

A responsibility compact holds an agency's political superiors in the executive branch responsible and, if necessary, accountable when they change the rules. It holds political superiors responsible and, if necessary, accountable when they impose additional performance requirements. It holds executive branch superiors responsible and, if necessary, accountable when they cut budgets or job positions or otherwise alter the resources upon which the agency was relying to achieve its performance targets.[27] It holds overhead agencies responsible and, if necessary, accountable not simply for regulating the line agencies but also for helping them produce results that citizens value.[28]

A compact of mutual, collective responsibility holds legislators responsible and, if necessary, accountable if they impose unreasonable missions or goals on public agencies. It holds legislators accountable if they fail to provide executive agencies with the resources they need to achieve their goals. It holds legislators responsible and, if necessary, accountable if they set unreasonable deadlines for achieving these goals. It holds legislators accountable if they attempt to micromanage an agency. It holds legislators responsible and, if necessary, accountable if they set an executive branch agency up to fail.[29] It is a compact in which the legislative and executive branches are partners in improving performance instead of adversaries in allocating blame.

A responsibility compact holds journalists responsible and, if necessary, accountable not only for exposing dramatic failures of government agencies and egregious abuses of individual employees but also for highlighting important accomplishments and for educating citizens about who, specifically, will need to do what if government is to improve performance. It holds stakeholders responsible and, if necessary, accountable for making unreasonable demands. It holds stakeholders responsible and, if necessary, accountable (and perhaps even punishable) for filing lawsuits every time an agency makes a decision that is not one-hundred percent to their liking.

A compact of mutual, collective responsibility holds citizens responsible and, if necessary, accountable for paying attention not only to agency performance that affects them directly but also to government performance as a whole. It is a compact under which citizens not only have their constitutional right to complain about the poor performance of public agencies but also a democratic obligation to ensure that public agencies have the resources necessary to produce results.[30]

A compact of mutual, collective responsibility is not sealed in a single, dramatic signing but one that is constantly being earned, continually being examined, and frequently being revised.

Creating Charter Agencies

Kevin Kearns, James Q. Wilson, and Mark Moore all advocate some kind of new accountability arrangement, some kind of new compact that is negotiated between the managers of a public agency and key overseers in the accountability environment. Each advocates something similar to a "responsibility compact."

Kevin Kearns wants public managers to take both "tactical and strategic approaches to accountability challenges." Accountability, he tells public managers, "can and should be managed strategically, with a view toward prospective analysis of external opportunities and challenges as well as internal strengths and limitations." Kearns wants public managers "to reconceptualize accountability as not only a legal and moral imperative but also as a strategic organizational resource to be protected, nourished and enhanced."[31]

When the standards of accountability are explicit, Kearns wants public managers to think strategically and negotiate the specifics of these standards. When the standards are implicit, Kearns notes, managers "have the freedom to design and implement their own accountability systems, but they would be wise and prudent to prepare themselves to defend—that is, account for—these systems according to some set of criteria." This "calls for prudent action that can simplistically be described as doing the right thing even when the right thing is technically unenforceable."[32]

For what are the accountability standards most explicit? For finances and fairness. For what are these standards most implicit? For performance. Kearns's logic implies that public managers ought to attempt to influence the specifics of the accountability standards for finances and fairness while attempting to create new systems to provide accountability for performance.

James Wilson also argues that public managers should negotiate the terms of their agencies' accountability. Drawing upon the concept of the charter school, which negotiates a new set of accountability arrangements (as well as freedom from many regulations) with the state's educational overseers, Wilson advocates what I would call a "charter agency." Like a charter school, such a charter agency would negotiate a new accountability arrangement—a new charter. In return for a willingness to be accountable for higher standards of performance, the charter agency would not be required to jump through as many of the accountability hoops for finances and fairness. Wilson wants to put "agency executives in a situation in which the rewards for attaining goals are increased and the penalties for ignoring constraints are reduced."[33]

Moore has a similar idea. He, too, wants public managers to take the initiative to negotiate a new accountability arrangement. He wants them to suggest what their organization might do, what results it might produce, what improved performance might mean. He believes that "ideas about what would be worth doing could be initiated by managers."[34] Moore suggests that the manager of a public agency might note that the organization had a distinct capability that could be deployed in a new way to achieve a new public purpose.[35] (The leaders of many organizations do not, however, think this creatively. The U.S. military has the capacity to move much tonnage—of people, equipment, and supplies—around the globe very quickly; still, the leaders of the U.S. military resist adapting this outstanding organizational capability to the task of humanitarian relief.)[36]

In their efforts to rethink accountability, Kearns, Wilson, and Moore would give public managers a role in defining the results for which they will be accountable. All three propose that public managers take the initiative in suggesting the results their agencies will produce. They also imply that these managers should clarify what they will be unable to accomplish as well as what resources they will need to achieve the goals to which they are committing their organizations.

Trading Performance for Flexibility

Charter schools are the classic example of trading performance for flexibility. In return for improving performance, the managers of a charter school are given increased flexibility. After all, everyone "knows" that one of the primary reasons that public schools perform so poorly is because they have so many bureaucratic rules.

In *Politics, Markets, and America's Schools,* an influential book advocating school autonomy, John Chubb and Terry Moe conclude the public schools are plagued by "a bureaucracy problem." This problem "is not that the system is bureaucratic at all, but that it is too heavily bureaucratic—too hierarchical, too rule-bound, too formalistic—to allow for the kind of autonomy and professionalism schools need if they are to perform well." Indeed, "the more autonomous" schools are, Chubb and Moe argue, "the more likely they are to have effective organizations." Thus, "to liberate the schools," they propose "a new system of public education, one that is built on school autonomy and parent-student choice rather than direct democratic control and bureaucracy."[37]

This charter-school logic applies across government: The people who manage public agencies may not need more resources as much as they need more autonomy to use their existing resources more effectively.[38] This is the logic of the "charter agency": Public managers should be given significant freedom from many rules and, in return, should be accountable for performance. Public managers should be given the flexibility to structure their organizations, to motivate their people, and thus to produce results.[39]

Indeed, the call to trade performance for flexibility is not limited to education. Various scholars and managers have suggested the creation of such a charter agency—one that promises improved performance in return for increased flexibility.[40] This is a key theme of John DiIulio's *Deregulating the Public Service,* David Osborne and Ted Gaebler's *Reinventing Government,* and Osborne and Peter Plastrik's *Banishing Bureaucracy,*[41] as well as other publications.[42] It is a key theme of the National Commission on the Public Service (the "Volcker Commission"), the National Commission on the State and Local Public Service (the "Winter Commission"),[43] and Vice President Gore's National Partnership for Reinventing Government.

Sometimes, we do make this flexibility-for-performance trade—but only for the top performers. In South Carolina, the top 25 percent of the schools not only receive cash awards but also need not petition the state whenever they desire an exemption from a regulation.[44] Similarly, Mississippi exempts high-performing school districts from many state regulations.[45]

If, however, all of the rules and regulations are getting in the way of government performance, why not just get rid of them for everyone? Why do only some schools, only some school districts, only some public agencies get the flexibility? Why not simply eliminate the rules—not all of them, perhaps, but the vast majority of them?[46]

Because each rule is designed to ensure accountability for a specific aspect of finances or fairness. The advocates of trading performance for flexibility assume (if only implicitly) that the vast majority of the rules have little legitimacy. Yet every single rule was created to prevent the repetition of a very specific lapse in accountability for finances or fairness. None was enacted to hinder the performance of a public agency. Each new rule was created to accomplish a very noble purpose. Why should some public managers be relieved of the responsibility for handling money properly or for treating employees and citizens equitably? What's more important: probity in administering finances and impartiality in dealing with citizens, or results?

The Charter Agency Dilemma

Britain has been one of the leaders in experimenting with the new public management. Indeed, the executive agencies that it created under its Next Steps program were designed, in part, to trade flexibility for performance. Yet, reports Alasdair Roberts, "the British experience suggests that substantial deregulation is difficult to achieve."[47]

The early experience in the United States with the Government Performance and Results Act of 1993 (GPRA) suggests similar difficulties. In an analysis of "the managerial accountability and flexibility pilot" of GPRA, which would have essentially created a few charter agencies, the General Accounting Office (GAO) notes that Congress designed the legislation "to fundamentally shift the focus of federal management accountability from a preoccupation with rigid adherence to prescribed processes to a focus on achieving desired outcomes and results." Moreover, continued GAO, "in crafting GPRA, Congress recognized that if federal managers were to be held accountable for achieving results, they would need the authority and flexibility to achieve those results." Yet, concluded GAO, this "pilot did not work as intended." Indeed, the Office of Management and Budget (OMB) approved not a single pilot.[48] Why? GAO listed several reasons.

First, some federal agencies figured out that it "was much easier" to get the same flexibility by becoming a "reinvention lab" under the administration's National Performance Review. Second, many agencies that proposed a pilot failed to recognize that the rules from which they were seeking relief "often were imposed by the agency itself." Third, concluded GAO, OMB "did not actively work with agencies" to ensure that their proposals fit within the guidelines for this pilot—in part, because "OMB believed" that these proposals "were generally limited to seeking waivers from minor annoyances rather than significant barriers to improved performance."[49]

Furthermore, reported GAO, "for about three-quarters of the waiver proposals, OMB or other central management agencies decided that the waivers were not allowable for statutory or other reasons." In creating the flexibility for these GPRA pilots, Congress explicitly did not permit OMB to waive any statutory regulations. Indeed, before waiving any rule, OMB was required to seek a determination from the regulatory agency. For example, when the Federal Aviation Administration requested a wavier of the "requirements that preclude establishing a new performance appraisal system," the Office of Personnel Management denied it "under Chapter 47, Title 5, U.S.C." When the Internal Revenue Service requested a waiver from requirements "impeding IRS and state tax agencies from being housed in the same building," the General Services Administration (GSA) denied it because it "is mandated by law to provide space and related services to federal activities." When the Bureau of Engraving and Printing asked for a waiver from the "requirements impeding the ability to purchase insurance against negative fluctuations in exchange rates when contracting with foreign vendors," the Department of the Treasury denied it because "its policy does not allow granting waivers that would create the appearance of currency speculation." And, when the Patent and Trademark Office asked for a waiver from GSA "schedules for purchase of items," GSA denied it because these "schedules are contractual requirements that would be breached if [the] waiver request were granted."[50]

Several federal agencies—the U.S. Mint, the Bureau of Engraving and Printing, and the U.S. Customs Service—asked for a waiver from their personnel ceiling.[51] Surely such a waiver makes perfect sense. The agency already has a ceiling on the funds it can spend on personnel. Why not simply let it use these funds in the way that it thinks best? Why impose on an agency a system of double budgeting? Why constrain it with both a dollar budget and a personnel budget? Why not give the agency the flexibility to use its personnel dollars in a way that will best improve performance? Would not such a waiver be completely compatible with the concept of trading flexibility for performance? OMB answered no.

Why? Because in the Federal Workforce Restructuring Act of 1994, Congress imposed a reduction in total federal personnel of 272,900 full-time equivalent (FTE) employees. And, "OMB concluded," reported GAO, "that it could not manage the governmentwide FTE reduction requirements if one or more agencies were given the authority to exceed their FTE limits."[52]

Trading flexibility for performance isn't as easy as it sounds. The damn details—if only the statutory limitations—keep getting in the way. Sometimes these details are rules that embody an overhead agency's basic raison d'être. Sometimes these details are an overhead agency's concern for government-wide consistency: "If we give your agency this flexibility, we'll have to give it to every agency." Sometimes these details are codified into law. Sometimes these details are some overhead agency's interpretation of some law. We love our accountability rules for finance and fairness too much to surrender even a fragment—even if it might enhance accountability for performance. After all, if we can't rely on objective rules, how will we be able to hold managers, employees, and agencies accountable for finances and fairness? The objective rules are what make accountability impartial; they make accountability something more than the exercise of raw political power.[53]

How much accountability for finance and fairness *must we* give up to get more accountability for performance? How much accountability for finance and fairness *are we willing* to give up to get more accountability for performance? What specific aspects of accountability for finance and fairness *must we* be willing to give up? What specific aspects of accountability for finance and fairness *are we willing* to give up? This is the *charter agency dilemma.*

Drafting the Initial Responsibility Compact

A compact of mutual, collective responsibility sounds very nice. But such a compact is not created by specific words nor even through the negotiations over these words. Instead, a responsibility compact emerges from a sincere effort by those in the accountability environment to work together to do what is necessary to produce the results that they collectively desire. It is an agreement to improve, an agreement to experiment with ways to improve.[54] It has to be based not on formal legalisms but on trust.

Lawyers can't write the responsibility compact. They may think that writing contracts is their unique talent, moral obligation, official duty, and legal right. The accountability compact, however, is not a legal document but a web of mutual obligations. If you want to create a real compact of mutual responsibility, you first have to get the lawyers out of the room.[55]

Lawyers, observes political columnist David Broder, "use language differently from other people." For most people, Broder writes, language is a tool with which we "convey our thoughts and sentiments as clearly as possible." Lawyers, in contrast, "use language to stay out of trouble—to pin down the other party in a transaction and to avoid being pinned down themselves."[56] Yet the objective in creating a compact of mutual, collective responsibility is not to pin down the accountability of others while avoiding being pinned down yourself; instead, the objective is for everyone to agree on what they will accomplish together. This is not something that lawyers are trained to think about.

Legislators do not have the exclusive prerogative to write this compact. A responsibility compact is not a set of burdens that the legislative branch imposes on executive branch agencies. Neither is it the result of an unbalanced negotiation between legislative overseers and agency minions. It is a compact of *mutual* responsibility, of *collective* responsibility. Both the legislature and the executive have obligations. Each is responsible to the other.

The responsibility compact involves all those in the accountability environment. Stakeholders do not have the right to write the accountability compact—or even to dictate their own special clauses. Neither do elected executives, journalists, citizens, or public managers. All, however, should be engaged in the discussion, contribute to the compact's provisions, and be bound (not legally but morally) to its fulfillment.

The initial draft of the compact will be pasted together by some subgroup from the agency's accountability environment. To produce a useful agreement, however, the discussion needs to be very frank, very explicit. For in creating this draft, the participants need to clarify their mutual assumptions, expectations, and contributions. They need to eliminate ambiguity, to expose and work out their differences, to build rapport and trust. Still, even though this will be very hard work, they will produce only a draft and seal it with little more than a handshake. Moreover, those who do shake hands will need to give this deal a chance.

To create the necessary rapport and trust, to work out their differences, to make the necessary compromises, this subgroup may have to work initially in secret. After all, as James Madison observed about the work of the Constitutional Convention: "no Constitution would ever have been adopted by the Convention if the debates had been public."[57] But once this subgroup has agreed to the various components of the responsibility compact, they will have to make these provisions known to everyone in the accountability environment.

Relying on a small subgroup to draft the initial compact has other advantages. By working in a small group, the initial members will create personal relationships and learn to trust each other.[58] Moreover, with a very specific task—to draft the responsibility compact—the group has the opportunity to evolve into a real team. "When people do real work together toward a common objective," write Jon Katzenbach and Douglas Smith, "trust and commitment follow."[59]

Then the group needs to convert that trust and commitment into collective accountability. "No group," write Katzenbach and Smith, "ever becomes a team until it can hold itself accountable." Katzenbach and Smith carefully distinguish between individual accountability and mutual accountability, emphasizing the "crucial difference between 'the boss holds me accountable,' and 'we hold ourselves accountable.'" Team accountability, they argue, comes from the "sincere promises that we make to ourselves and others, promises that underpin two critical aspects of teams: commitment and trust." This, however, requires us to overcome our human propensity for individualism that, they argue, "discourages us from putting our fates in the hands of others." And, they note, "mutual promises and accountability cannot be coerced any more than people can be made to trust one another."[60]

People cannot be conscripted to join the group that drafts the initial compact. They can only be invited.

In deciding to prepare an initial compact of mutual, collective responsibility, the group accepts a specific assignment and gains a considerable benefit. "Specific performance goals," write Katzenbach and Smith, "provide clear yardsticks for accountability." This is why "teams enjoying a strong common purpose and approach inevitably hold themselves, both as individuals and as a team, responsible for the team's performance." In working to achieve a general purpose and a specific goal, the members of the team develop trust and commitment. As the members invest time, resources, and energy in their common task, they build commitment; as they work through problems, they develop trust. From the process, each member earns the right to not only express his or her views but also to make claims on the team's common efforts and important decisions.[61]

From the process, the members of the initial group draft an explicit Compact of Mutual, Collective Responsibility. Simultaneously, they also evolve their own, personal, implicit compact of mutual and collective responsibility.[62]

Negotiation, Experimentation, and Renegotiation

The initial Compact of Mutual, Collective Responsibility is just a draft. It is not a fixed, solemn document, signed in an impressive ceremony then sealed away in some safe deposit box to be retrieved only when it needs to be presented in court because one party is suing another for breaching it. Instead, any compact of mutual, collective responsibility is an explicit but revisable understanding. The compact is explicit because all of the parties have signed on as partners (though not on some lawyer's dotted line). The compact is an understanding of what the parties are, collectively, attempting to accomplish. The compact is an understanding of what the parties are, individually, committed to doing and contributing.

The responsibility compact is an understanding that, for example, if one party is unable to fulfill its obligations, the obligations for other parties depending upon these contributions are also modified. The compact is an understanding that, if some parts of the compact prove unrealizable, the parties will renegotiate something that is.[63] The compact is an understanding about what results are to be pursued under what constraints and with what resources. The compact is an understanding about not only the responsibilities of the public agency and the public manager (about what results they need to produce under what constraints); it is also an understanding about the responsibilities of political officials, legislators, stakeholders, citizens, and maybe even journalists (about what results they need to produce and under what constraints). It is an understanding that the entire process is a search for improved performance. The responsibility compact is an understanding for nothing more permanent than continuous experimentation.

Moreover, participation in the responsibility compact will no longer be limited to the initial team. For as the aspirations of the group grow, so must its membership. Indeed, if the compact is really to become a substitute for traditional hierarchical accountability, it needs to solicit participation from all of those in the accountability environment. It needs to expose its proposals for specific performance targets and its needs for specific resources to the scrutiny of those who have an interest in the targets or the resources. This can, of course, create problems. The initial group was small; it could evolve into a mutually supportive team based on commitment and trust.[64] Now it has to grow. It has to invite in people who will not understand the team's mores, habits, and jokes—and who certainly will not possess the initial team's commitment.

Most significantly, the personal trust among the members of the initial group will not be shared by the newcomers. The newcomers will not trust the "secret cabal" that created the draft compact. The original members will resent the newcomers (if only subconsciously) for their failure to contribute time and energy to the draft. And, of course, the various newcomers will not trust each other. Maintaining the group's cohesiveness will require continual experimentation and negotiation.

Further, anyone has the right to reopen negotiations. And they can reopen negotiations boldly and publicly—with a press release or a hearing—when they feel that the spirit of the compact is being violated. Or they can reopen these negotiations subtly and quietly when they discover that the compact is proving inadequate, either because it is not preventing the kind of behavior that it was designed to proscribe or because it is not achieving the kind of performance that it was designed to encourage. The compact is less a final document than an ongoing experiment.

Indeed, to work out such an accountability compact, to continually review and revise such a compact, requires much experimentation. And, for such experimentation to prove successful—for it to actually contribute to improved performance—the various parties in the accountability compact will have to cooperate at least as much as they compete.[65]

Special Education in Madison, Wisconsin

In the world of special education, accountability relationships are frequently adversarial. This is particularly true since 1975 when Congress passed the Education for All Handicapped Children Act.[66] In enacting this legislation, Congress assumed that the relationship between a school system and its special-education stakeholders was inherently adversarial. Thus, to provide a framework for this conflict, Congress created a highly legalistic system of detailed rights, procedural safeguards, and formal due process. As a result— surprise!—the accountability relations in special education have become quite legalistic and adversarial. The school system is the accountability holdee. The parents of special-education students, the special-education advocacy organizations, and their accumulation of attorneys are the accountability holders. And these accountability holders know how to use the multitude of due process provisions to hold the accountability holdees accountable for following every one of the detailed and complex special-education regulations.

But not in Madison, Wisconsin. Here, reports Joel Handler of the University of California, special education is cooperative not adversarial, informal not legalistic, discretionary not rule-bound, experimental not doctrinaire. Moreover, he argues, this is the way it should be; special-education "decisions should be discretionary." This is because, writes Handler, "for a great many of these children (for example, the mildly retarded), we really do not know why they are not performing well in school or what to do about it." Thus "the evaluation and education programs for the child should be judgmental, professional, flexible, experimental." In Madison, he reports, they are.[67]

How does this work? First, explains Handler, the Madison school system recognizes that it is engaged in a continuous, fifteen-year association with its special-education students and thus with their parents. Consequently, it actively seeks to create a cooperative relationship; after all, if the school is to be successful with the special-ed student, it needs not merely the acquiescence but the active participation of the parents. Madison has designed a variety of mechanisms to negotiate with the parents an agreement to an assessment of the student's condition and to an appropriate educational strategy. Indeed, because any discussion between parents and the school's multidisciplinary team of experts is necessarily an emotional one, and because the experts are, well, the experts, the conversation is unlikely to be one among equals. Thus such discussions include a "parent advocate," who helps the parent both emotionally and technically.[68]

For every student, writes Handler, Madison takes an "individualized, flexible, experimental approach." Consequently, the educational services provided to each student are continuously open to review. Parents always have the opportunity to question—indeed, to challenge—the mix of services offered their children. In fact, the school system encourages such a "continuous, bargaining relationship," because it wants to constantly engage parents in their children's development. In Madison, "a commitment to listen to each other," reports Handler, has helped transform the relationships "from winners and losers to partners." Yet the school district does not try to suppress conflict. Instead, in Madison, "conflict is used to help communication," as are the parent advocates. After all, school officials recognize "the problems of maintaining active parental participation, which they view as a continuing struggle." But such parental collaboration is not designed to ensure *procedural* accountability; instead, when the school district "developed its ideal of parental participation, it was thinking of the *substance* of special education, what was required to educate children with handicapping conditions."[69]

For special education, the Madison school system has sought to create a compact of mutual, collective responsibility. People in Madison don't call it this, of course. They don't even think that they are doing any such thing; they are simply responding to the realities of special education: To make special education work, the schools need cooperative, not adversarial, relationships. To make special education work, the schools need to be responsible and responsive to their primary stakeholders, the parents.[70] To make special education work, the schools need parents to accept responsibility too. To make special education work, the schools and the parents need to accept their mutual and collective responsibility. The result looks like a responsibility compact.

Madison, Wisconsin is, of course, a special case—just as is New Zealand, or Sunnyvale or Visalia, California, or any of the other jurisdictions to which the advocates of the new public management point with enthusiasm. But Madison isn't *that* special. The DNA of the teachers, administrators, and parents of Madison is not significantly different from yours or mine. They didn't just stumble into some cooperative, public-management Eden. To the extent that Madison is Eden—and it is clearly much closer to being Everytown, U.S.A.—it was created, not discovered. Moreover, to the extent that Madison's parents, teachers, and administrators did manage to evolve something that looks like a responsibility compact, they did it in a political context that *assumes* adversarial accountability. They did it in a policy environment for which all of the formal rules and informal expectations *promote* adversarial accountability.

Thus, special education in Madison offers an existence theorem: It is *possible* for a compact of mutual, collective responsibility to exist. It is *possible* to create one.[71] If some people—any people—can evolve a set of informal relationships that fosters a mutual and collective sense of responsibility that works in special education, shouldn't other people be able to so in a less presumptively adversarial environment?

Who Will Be Responsible?

In his discussion of "bureaucratic responsibility," John Burke of the University of Vermont argues that "individual responsibility, properly defined, offers a fruitful strategy for reconciling bureaucracy and democracy"—for reconciling managerial discretion with democratic government. To Burke, public managers need "a democratically grounded conception of responsibility";

they need to take political authority seriously and to accept obligations beyond the formal rules. "By appealing to a democratically inspired sense of responsibility," Burke "emphasizes accommodation rather than antagonism, [and] seeks consensus rather than conflict."[72]

But why are Burke's bureaucrats the only ones required to accept such personal responsibility? Can we really expect accommodation and consensus if some seize political advantage through antagonism and conflict? If we wish to encourage public managers to accept responsibility for adhering to both the rules and the principles of democracy, we need to ensure that they will not be disadvantaged or punished for their cooperation. We need to ensure that others—legislators, journalists, private attorneys, elected executives and their political appointees, individual stakeholders and stakeholder organizations—accept the same responsibility.[73]

We need to ensure that citizens, too, accept responsibility. But will they?

8

The Cooperation Challenge

Mutual accountability requires cooperation. A compact of mutual, collective responsibility is designed to foster that cooperation among the web of people and organizations in the accountability environment. The parties to such a compact would seek to establish the terms under which they—and, they hope, others in the accountability environment—would cooperate to enhance government performance, subject to some agreed-upon constraints to ensure the proper use of finances and the equitable treatment of people. Indeed, without such a responsibility compact for performance, those seeking to improve performance may be unable to move beyond an obsession with the rules for finances and fairness.

Who, however, will agree to cooperate? Who will sign on to a "compact" that guarantees nothing more than experimentation? Who will trade individual accountability for mutual accountability? Who (besides a public manager) will trade his or her well-understood (and relatively limited) individual accountability (often defined by professional peers) for some vague sense of mutual, collective responsibility that will be devised, refined, and revised sometime in the future by people with unknown or even incompatible values? Who has an incentive to cooperate?

And even if people do sign on to such a responsibility compact, will they remain bound by this informal (and not very enforceable) agreement? Who has an incentive to continue to cooperate?[1]

Cooperation and Self-Restraint

Many of the potential parties to a responsibility compact have an incentive to participate in the negotiations that will create it. They want to ensure that their interests are not trampled and that their results are included in the definition of *performance*. Yet how many of the potential parties will enter into the negotiations with any objective other than protecting their own prerogatives? Alasdair Roberts has described the "negotiations" over the creation of federal performance-based organizations and Britain's Next Steps agencies—a much less complex and threatening arrangement than a full compact of mutual and collective responsibility. His chronicle suggests that legislators, overhead regulators, and executive branch superiors are unwilling to forfeit their future ability to exercise control.[2]

A responsibility compact is more than a commitment to experimentation; it is also a commitment to self-restraint. Such a compact attempts to impose obligations and constraints on all of the organizations and individuals in the accountability environment. It attempts to enjoin the parties from instantly and publicly questioning the competence, intelligence, or integrity of others engaged in the experiment. By creating a web of mutual obligations, those who design the compact attempt to restrain not only themselves but others from being too quick to respond to any slight or failure by publicly assigning blame. Who will agree to such self-restraint?

Suppose, however, that a compact of mutual, collective responsibility is, somehow, negotiated. Suppose that all those in a public agency's accountability environment agree to hold themselves collectively accountable for achieving a specific performance target. What happens when something goes slightly sour? When something goes wrong (or appears that it might be about to go wrong), who will abide by this noble declaration of self-restraint?

— What journalist will delay publishing a story about a screwup, accepting instead that this is an experiment and that experiments inevitably produce mistakes—knowing that a competing journalist is about to break this juicy story?

— What stakeholder organization will eschew a press conference to denounce a public agency for some failure to achieve a result or fulfill an obligation—knowing that the publicity from such holding-people-accountable press conferences is what mobilizes the essential resources of money and people?

— What manager of an overhead agency will refrain from enforcing some minor regulatory requirement for finances or fairness, even if no funds were stolen or no individual was subjected to any discrimination—knowing that a journalist, legislator, candidate, or superior might discover not only the original infraction but also this regulatory beneficence?

— What legislator will decide not to conduct some holding-people-accountable hearings about an obvious mistake, choosing instead to ask for a private meeting with the agency's leadership to figure out how to fix the problem—knowing that some other legislator is also planning to hold hearings?

— What officer of a union of public-service employees will forgo a job action over job reassignments made possible by improvements in performance—knowing that several Young Turks are planning to run for union office next year?

— What auditor will decide not to issue a complete report detailing several agency decisions to contract with firms that were not the lowest bidder and instead to work with the agency's procurement staff to develop some specific procedures for establishing the legitimacy of such decisions—knowing that an inspector general is also investigating the same agency's procurement choices?

— What candidate for the legislature will put off denouncing the incumbent who, instead of holding an agency publicly accountable, sat down for a "secret," closed-door meeting with the agency's managers—knowing that only through such dramatic revelations is an election-day upset possible?

Who will exercise such self-restraint?

These questions pose the *cooperation challenge.*[3]

Blame, Trust, and Vulnerability

A compact of mutual, collective accountability is explicitly designed to encourage cooperation. It is designed to encourage cooperation in improving performance, in dealing with problems. Whenever something goes wrong, all those involved in this web of mutual responsibility—managers, frontline workers, elected and appointed executives, legislators, and stakeholders; even journalists, auditors, inspectors general, and citizens—share responsibility for the failure. (In reality, all of those in the accountability environment—regardless of whether they have joined the responsibility compact; regardless of whether they admit it—do have some responsibility for any failure.) By sharing this responsibility privately, they can build mutual trust and learn to solve problems collectively. By sharing this responsibility publicly, they ensure that none of the individual parties bears too much of the blame.

Nevertheless, any party to the compact can reduce the amount of blame assigned to it by being the first to blame the others. When something actually does go wrong—as it inevitably will[4]—everyone in the accountability environment has a clear incentive to blame someone else. Everyone has an incentive to blame the agency—and to blame the agency first. In today's accountability-holding business, the rewards go to those who speak with supreme confidence, to those who blame others, to those who point the finger of blame first. The rewards do not go to those who confess to uncertainty; they do not go to those who offer subtle analyses about the need to experiment with potential strategies for creating promising but unproven improvements; and these rewards certainly do not go to those who attempt to explain that mistakes are the inevitable price of progress. Yet if we continue to employ what John Mayne of the office of the auditor general of Canada calls "a 'blame apportionment' approach to accountability,"[5] we will never be able to conduct the experiments necessary to create a more productive form of mutual accountability.

In *Improving Government Performance,* John DiIulio, Gerald Garvey, and Donald Kettl offer a specific recommendation concerning this blame-apportionment approach to accountability: "Elected officials, notably the president and members of Congress, must lead the campaign for improved government performance by resisting the temptation to pick on isolated horror stories for immediate gain at the expense of discouraging managers from solving problems and taking risks."[6] But will these elected officials really resist this temptation? Will elected officials resist the temptation to pick on isolated horror stories when they know that doing so will yield immediate gain? Will these elected officials trust that other accountability holders will also resist this temptation? Indeed, will others in the accountability environment—crusading journalists, aspiring candidates, entrepreneurial lawyers, beleaguered union officers, or aggressive stakeholders—resist the temptation to pick on isolated horror stories for immediate gain?

Trust creates vulnerability. To join a responsibility compact, a public agency's accountability holders have to trust the others in the accountability environment. Furthermore, this trust makes them vulnerable. For not only is the agency exposing itself to public blame for some mistake that it has made; each accountability holder is also exposing itself to public blame for not exposing the agency's original mistake.[7]

To join a responsibility compact, a traditional accountability holdee has to trust its accountability holders. For the responsibility compact to function effectively, the agency's leadership will need to explain to the other members what problems the agency (and thus the compact)—needs to solve. To get the desired assistance from the traditional accountability holders who have joined the compact, the accountability holdee will need to describe these problems explicitly, honestly, and completely. This requires trust, and such trust makes the agency vulnerable.

— Why should the head of a public agency voluntarily cooperate with a powerful legislator by explaining that the agency's personnel division just can't produce?

— Why should a public manager cooperate with a prominent journalist by revealing that a new computer system is eighteen months behind schedule?

— Why should an agency's leadership cooperate with the president of a stakeholder organization by describing how the field staff is becoming less productive?

Why should public managers trust their agencies' accountability holders?

Trust creates vulnerability. And public managers are vulnerable enough already. Why should public managers want to be even any more vulnerable? Why should public managers cooperate with accountability holders in a way that can easily expose them to more public blame? As the obvious accountability holdees, an agency's managers have to do more than exercise self-restraint. To make the responsibility compact function effectively—to have it help solve the problems that impede the agency's ability to improve performance—these managers have to be forthcoming in identifying the agency's performance problems. Why should they increase their vulnerability by explaining their problems to precisely the people who can ensure that they receive an even bigger apportionment of public blame?

The cooperation challenge—created by the well-established accountability-holding technique of assigning blame—can inhibit the experimentation that a responsibility compact is designed to encourage. Moreover, just one defection from the compact's commitment to mutual, collective responsibility may cause it to unravel.[8] Indeed, the obvious incentive to be the first to defect by assigning blame to others may prevent the compact from ever coming into existence.

Professional Norms and Public Expectations

Why might accountability holders fail to sign on to a responsibility compact? Carefully calculated self-interest is not the only explanation.

Professional norms is another. And most accountability-holding professions have powerful norms.

Journalists, for example, love to think of themselves as the public's watchdogs. Any journalist who joined a responsibility compact would be ostracized by colleagues—maybe even fired. Cooperating with government may produce a few short-term gains, but it has significant long-term costs in journalistic integrity. What self-respecting journalist would even think about participating in an agreement for mutual or collective responsibility with a public agency?

Journalists do, of course, cooperate with government officials. They do it all the time. That is how they get good stories. A journalist will give a public official favorable coverage in return for some exclusive stories. Similarly, public officials cooperate with journalists. An official will give a journalist some exclusive stories in return for some favorable coverage. If the coverage isn't favorable enough, the official will give these exclusives to other journalists. Conversely, if the stories aren't exclusive enough, the journalists will give their favorable coverage to other officials.

Such cooperative arrangements are only implicit; they aren't even discussed. They just happen. Moreover, to be useful, they don't have to last long. One exclusive story traded for one instance of favorable coverage benefits both parties. An unplanned, irregular series of brief, one-night stands can be a quite profitable way for a journalist and a public official to cooperate.

Similarly, legislators cooperate with public officials. So do the leaders of stakeholder organizations. So even do auditors, inspectors general, special prosecutors, and occasionally even candidates.[9] And although some of these cooperative relationships may be ongoing, they are only implicit. And, if at any time, it makes sense for either party to stop cooperating, it does: No hard feelings; it's just business. And the cooperation will resume when it is again in both parties' interest.

Professional norms prevent such cooperation from becoming too cozy, too explicit. Key stakeholders and the staff members of the relevant legislative committees might attempt to establish very close, long-term relationships with an agency. But auditors, inspectors general, and special prosecutors have to maintain an appropriate professional distance.

Bruce Smith points out how this need to maintain professional distance affects the work of the General Accounting Office (GAO). By the early 1980s, reports Smith, GAO had "become more forward looking and less exclusively preoccupied with finding fault for past mistakes." But to the extent that such a forward-looking focus involves a concern with policy development and implementation, he continues, GAO "requires close and mutually respectful relations with executive departments." Specifically, says Smith, "cooperation between the GAO, the OMB, and the OPM would be particularly useful in matters of personnel policy, budget reform, financial management, contracting and procurement policy, and accounting standards." Such cooperation, however, "is not easily compatible with the role of staff arm for the Congress and watchdog for executive abuses." Thus, "in most of these areas there is inadequate cooperation."[10]

Auditors audit their accountability holdees, they don't cooperate with them. They aren't supposed to cooperate. Citizens don't expect them to cooperate. Their professional norms deter them from cooperating. How can GAO both audit the executive branch and cooperate with it? We citizens clearly expect auditors to audit, not cooperate. We expect that all of our accountability holders will not get too cozy with their accountability holdees.

Still, accountability holders could resist the temptation to pick on every isolated horror story. Do we really want every accountability holder to immediately jump on every small or potential mistake? Yet some of those in the accountability environment—particularly legislators, candidates, and journalists—do not believe in self-restraint, at least not in self-restraint on *their own* behavior. Even if a legislator, candidate, journalist, auditor, or prosecutor has signed on to the compact in principle, whenever the experiment produces its first error, personal incentives and professional norms may quickly take over.

Legislators, candidates, journalists, auditors, and prosecutors make their living by assigning blame.[11] Some may be able to resist the temptation to point the finger of blame at another party to the responsibility compact (particularly when there exist other failures that are not subject to the compact's constraints and that can easily be exposed). Others, however, will simply follow their profession's standard operating procedures and seek to be the first to earn credit for exposing failure. As Bruce Smith observes, "Congress is by nature a body composed of numerous individuals with an incentive for uncovering mischief within the administrative agencies."[12]

The Prisoner's Dilemma

The challenge of creating and holding together a responsibility compact has a number of similarities to a well-known puzzle from game theory. Merrill Flood and Melvin Drescher of the RAND Corporation devised this problem, and Arthur W. Tucker of Princeton University named it "the prisoner's dilemma":[13]

You and a friend rob a bank, speed off in a car, bury the loot, and make a solemn compact that, if captured, neither will turn state's evidence. A few days later, you are both captured and placed in separate cells so that you cannot talk with each other. The authorities, however, have very little evidence. Indeed, unless one of you confesses, you will both serve only two years in prison for stealing the getaway car. So, the district attorney offers each one of you a deal: If you turn state's evidence and finger your partner as the ringleader, you will go free (on unsupervised probation), while your partner will spend five years in jail for bank robbery. Of course, both of you realize that if you both confess, you will both serve four years in jail. What should you do?

The answer is complicated because this is not a game of pure competition. It is not a zero-sum game, in which whatever you win your partner must lose (and vice versa). It is a non-zero-sum game: a relationship involving both competition and cooperation. The two of you need to figure out whether some kind of cooperative strategy will be best for both of you. Indeed, that is why you made your original we-will-not-squeal agreement. Unfortunately, now that you have both been arrested and have learned the specifics of your situation, you can no longer talk and work out the best cooperative strategy. You have made a mutual pact; but you each have a clear incentive to defect.

Suppose you know that your partner has turned state's evidence and *will* finger you as the ringleader: What should you do? Should you keep your commitment to not turn state's evidence, or should you defect and squeal on your partner? If you *do not* turn state's evidence, you will go to jail for five years (while your partner will go free). But if you *do* finger him, you will go to jail for only four (and so will he). Thus, if you know that your partner will turn state's evidence, you will obviously be better off—spend one year less in jail—if you *do* so too.

Now suppose that you know that your partner *will not* finger you: What should you do then? Should you keep your commitment, or should you defect? In this situation, if you *do not* finger your partner, you will now go to jail for two years (and so will he). But if you *do* turn state's evidence, you will go free (and he will spend five years in jail). So, again, you will clearly be better off—spend no time in jail rather than two years—if you *do* finger him as the ringleader.

Regardless of what your partner does, regardless of whether he keeps his commitment or defects, you will be better off if you defect.

Your partner, however, has the same deal and is smart enough to work through the same logic. So he too realizes that, regardless of what you do, he will be better off—he will spend less time in jail—if he defects and fingers you. Of course, you both realize that the other is making this calculation and, as a result, that you will both defect. Unfortunately, you have no way to hold each other to your original commitment to never defect.

As a result, both of you will spend four years in jail. If you both kept your original commitment not to finger each other, you would each spend just two years in jail. Yet neither of you can be sure that the other will not defect. Moreover, neither of you has a mechanism for enforcing your original commitment. Consequently, both of you have a clear incentive to defect. This is why this problem is called the prisoner's *dilemma* (and why the mafia always makes good on its commitment that, if you ever finger one of them, they will break your mother's kneecaps).

The same prisoner's-dilemma logic could apply to a compact of mutual, collective responsibility. Most of the members (though not necessarily the journalists, candidates, auditors, or prosecutors) will be better off if they all maintain their commitments. If all of the parties keep their agreement, the performance of the agency will (presumably) improve, and all of them will be better off. After all, they all value the additional results that the improved agency will produce; that's why they joined the compact. Yet each also has a personal incentive to defect, for any single defector can gain some additional political advantage—provided that another member doesn't defect first. Of course, every member of the compact understands this logic; so each is carefully watching the others to see who might defect. Moreover, any member who concludes that another is about to defect has a big incentive to defect immediately.

Thus the logic that threatens to tear apart the compact made by the two prisoners is very similar to the logic that threatens to tear apart any responsibility compact formed among those in a public agency's accountability environment. The big difference is that the responsibility compact has more than two partners. Thomas Schelling of the University of Maryland has labeled this kind of problem the "multi-person prisoner's dilemma."[14]

The Tragedy of the Commons

The challenge of holding a responsibility compact together is also similar to "the tragedy of the commons." Biologist Garrett Hardin of the University of

California coined this phrase to describe the class of problems created when too many people take advantage of a free resource.[15]

In colonial New England, the town "commons" was owned in common. Because every citizen of the town "owned" an equal share of the commons, each citizen had an equal right to use the commons. Each citizen had the right to graze a cow on the commons. Indeed, each citizen had the right to graze many cows on the commons, and many citizens would. Thus the commons would became over-grazed and be of little use for grazing. The tragedy of the commons is a non-zero-sum game; it is not a game of pure competition but one of both competition and cooperation.

All of the citizens of the town would be better off if they could simply agree to cooperate and only graze one cow each on the commons. It is difficult, however, to get every citizen to commit to such a "compact of the commons." After all, the details of the compact matter. Who gets allocated one cow's worth of grazing rights? Each citizen? Each landowner? Each family? Each adult? And are these grazing rights transferable? Can a cobbler sell his grazing rights to a farmer? The objective is to create a fair agreement. But what is fair?

Then comes the challenge of enforcing the compact. After all, everyone has an obvious incentive to defect—to try to sneak an extra cow onto the commons. Everyone has an obvious incentive to become a "free rider"—to exploit the commons by putting in only a fair share (through fair taxes) while taking out more than a fair share (through excessive or unfair grazing).

In a small New England town, with a small commons, with a small number of families who know each other, and with only a few cows, enforcement might not be a big problem. But if the size of the commons grows, or if the number of families and cows grows, the town will need some means of identifying the owner of each cow. And it will need someone to monitor the grazing. This agreement is not automatically self-enforcing.[16]

Everyone has an obvious incentive to identify any defector. Yet anyone who publicly identifies a defector pays a cost, and that personal cost may be greater than any personal gain. First, any self-appointed enforcer has to devote time and resources to making an accurate identification of someone's extra cow. And any self-appointed enforcer who publicly labels another citizen as a cheater may be accused of being a squealer (with bad motives). And what does this squealer really gain? His or her cow will just have a few more blades of grass to eat. Is that worth it?

Enforcing a "compact of the commons" is difficult. Every member of the compact has an obvious incentive to defect. Every member of the compact knows that every other member has an obvious incentive to defect. Thus every member of the compact has an incentive to defect before the others do. And few have an incentive to devote resources to enforcing the compact.

All this is true for a compact of mutual, collective responsibility. Suppose a town creates a responsibility compact to help its "commons agency" improve the performance of the town commons and thus to increase the milk production of the town's farmers. Members of the town council have an incentive to defect, to blame the manager of the commons agency for incompetence for planting the wrong grass (while also enacting special legislation to permit the town's largest employer to graze five cows). The town's Independent Cow Grazers Association has an incentive to accuse the city council of being beholden to special interests (while ignoring its own members' special moonlight grazing). The town's inspector general has incentive to become a precisian when auditing the commons agency's records of who grazed their cows when, as well as to issue scathing reports accusing the agency's manager of not buying grass seed from the lowest bidder. And, although the editor of the town paper may be willing to take on all comers, he or she might worry that the town's biggest employer will pull its full-page milk ads. "The tragedy of the commons" is essentially "the tragedy of the responsibility compact."

The Problem of Collective Action

In the prisoner's dilemma, two individuals often fail to cooperate because each partner's calculation of individual, immediate self-interest reveals that he or she will benefit not from cooperating but from defecting. In the tragedy of the commons (or the multi-person prisoner's dilemma), many individuals often fail to cooperate because, again, each partner's calculation of individual, immediate self-interest reveals that he or she will benefit not from cooperating but from defecting. Yet, if somehow they could all commit to cooperate—if they could somehow ensure that every partner kept his or her commitment—every individual would be better off.

Mancur Olson of the University of Maryland calls this the problem of "collective action." How can you get self-interested people to act collectively for their common welfare, when (1) the benefits from any individual's action are spread among the others in the group, and (2) each individual's benefit from his or her cooperation is less than the cost of that cooperation? For example, how can you get the citizens of the New England town to cooperate when the total benefits of any individual's restraint in using or policing the commons, though larger than the costs to that individual, are spread among all of the citizens of the town? Olson's short answer is: You can't. "Unless the number of individuals in a group is quite small, or unless there is coercion or some other special device to make individuals act in their common interest, *rational self-interested individuals will not act to achieve their common or group interests.*"[17] You can get collective cooperation, says Olson, but only under three different and very particular circumstances.

First, a small group might voluntarily cooperate in their common interest. If the town is small enough, the cost to the group of grazing one additional cow will be significant; the gain, however, will also be significant, though it will go strictly to the owner of the additional cow. So every citizen benefits from grazing an additional cow. In a small town, however, the cost of policing the arrangement may be very low. Indeed, every citizen of the town might be able to identify every cow and its owner. Thus for any citizen the cost of policing the arrangement could be quite low—even less than the benefit that he or she would personally gain from preventing over-grazing. In this case, the one-citizen, one-cow policy would be almost self-policing and thus almost self-coordinating. (The two robbers in the prisoner's dilemma fail to cooperate not because the group is not small enough and not because the net benefit to each is not large enough, but because they have no mechanism for coordinating and policing their behavior.) If the town is small enough, once the agreement is created, each individual farmer might not have to do very much to ensure that others will cooperate.[18]

Second, a large group will cooperate if they are subjected to some form of coercion. If the town council deputizes a sheriff to tag each citizen's cows, to police the commons, and to drive out any citizen's second cow (and first cow too), the cow owners in the town will cooperate.[19] A citizen who sees an extra cow on the commons need only make an anonymous call to the sheriff (or to the private firm to which the town council has awarded the contract to police the commons).[20]

Third, a large group will cooperate if "some other special device" makes them do so. But what kind of device? And what makes it so special? Olson's special device is an individual benefit that each person gets as a condition for cooperating. In the case of the village commons, this would require a slight change in the rules: Any citizen who grazed only one cow on the commons would be eligible for special assistance from the town's agriculture specialist, could use the town's high-tech cow-milking machine (for all of the citizen's cows), and could market all of his or her milk through the town co-op. If these individual benefits to an owner of three cows exceed the cost of finding other pastures for two of them, the owner will gladly cooperate.

Usually, however, none of these three conditions apply. In such circumstances, people who, as Olson describes them, "rationally seek to maximize their personal welfare" will not cooperate.[21]

Self-Interest and Competition

When we try to understand or predict political behavior, we naturally think about rational people who are trying to maximize their personal welfare. Much of our thinking about political behavior derives from the assumption that people act primarily in their self-interest—not on some conception of the public interest. People make rational choices. People make self-interested choices. And, unless people are part of a small group, or unless they are coerced, or unless they have some extra, special, motivating inducement, these rational, self-interested, welfare-maximizing people will not cooperate.[22]

Instead, they will compete. This seems quite reasonable—quite legitimate. People are naturally competitive. They have to be. Their self-interest drives them to be.

Moreover, this competition creates some obvious benefits. Economic competition constantly motivates us to increase efficiency in the production of goods and services. Competition among the species, and within each specie, encourages adaptation and natural selection. So does the competition among journalists for the best scoops and most prestigious assignments. So does the competition among politicians. So does the competition among public agencies to demonstrate that they have the competence to warrant more resources and flexibility. We believe in the invisible hand not only in economics but also in genetics, journalism, and politics.

Competition is as natural as keeping score. We always keep score. Indeed, we invent all sorts of ways to keep score. When students get back a test, what do they ask each other? When you go to a baseball game, at what do you constantly glance? Do you know anyone who goes to a bowling alley, bowls a game, and doesn't keep score? Do you know anyone who follows political campaigns and doesn't read the polls? Do you know anyone who manages a business and doesn't keep track of the firm's key financial indicators? Whether in games and sports or in politics and business, we are all competitive. We all keep score.

Why might a member of a responsibility compact defect? Because they are in competition with each other—or with others who have not signed on to the compact. Journalists are in competition with other journalists. Candidates are in competition with other candidates. Legislators are in competition with other legislators—not directly for reelection but for the attention that brings status, recognition, and thus reelection. So are other accountability holders such as auditors, inspectors general, and prosecutors. Both electoral politics and policy politics are competitive.

But neither societies nor political institutions are built only on competition. Both also depend upon cooperation. Indeed, cooperation, too, has benefits. And both competition and cooperation have costs. The challenge for any society is to balance the competition and the cooperation—to balance the benefits and costs of competition with the benefits and costs of cooperation. The same applies to the design of political institutions: All competition, and we shoot each other; all cooperation, and each person sits around politely deferring to everyone else.

Competition, however, is usually easier to organize than cooperation. Indeed, competition may require no organization at all. Competition evolves from the interaction of rational, self-interested, welfare-maximizing people. Competition happens. Competition just happens. Can cooperation just happen?

Competition or Cooperation

Given the challenge of organizing any kind of collective action, who would even think about attempting to create a compact of mutual, collective responsibility? Given their self-interested motivation, who would join such a compact? Given the well-known collective action problems of the prisoner's dilemma and the tragedy of the commons, who would even think that such a compact could ever foster true cooperation? Given all of the professional norms and public expectations, who will voluntarily surrender their privilege of holding others accountable and replace it with an arrangement in which they would also have responsibilities—and thus would also be accountable? Given the bias toward competition, who will cooperate?[23]

As history has shown, the accountability holders of old—the emperors and queens—never surrendered their privilege without a fight. What chance do we have of convincing today's accountability holders of doing so?

Isn't the whole idea of a responsibility compact splendidly naive?

9

Fostering Cooperation with Conventions and Norms

Cooperation does happen. Friends cooperate. Professional colleagues cooperate. Enemies cooperate. Even strangers cooperate. Cooperation doesn't always happen. Competition also happens. Nevertheless, cooperation happens too.

People with different interests cooperate. Organizations with different interests cooperate. Legislators with different interests cooperate. Nations with different interests cooperate.[1] Somehow, they manage to break the conventional chains of the cooperation challenge. Even strangers can manage to avoid being captured by the prisoner's dilemma.

But when? How? Does cooperation just happen? Or must Jupiter align with Mars? Under what circumstances does cooperation happen?[2] How does cooperation happen? Can the individuals and organizations in a public agency's accountability environment cooperate? If so, how might we foster cooperation that would enhance accountability for performance?

Markets, Government, and Cooperation

David Brown of New School University summarizes the conventional wisdom about cooperation: "The assumption persists that voluntary cooperation among strangers is very unlikely without the profit incentive of private markets, in which self-interest is served, or the coercion of government, with which self-interest is subdued."[3] Again, self-interest is central to this assumption about cooperation. Cooperation happens, says the conventional wisdom—but only because either the market provides a mechanism to encourage self-interested people to cooperate or because the government provides a mechanism to discourage self-interested people from competing.

People cooperate in their economic lives. Adam Smith's invisible hand of the market encourages the cooperation of economically competitive units. By making an intelligent trade, two individuals (or two firms) can both enhance their economic position. Individuals and institutions, which are competing for resources, can compete more effectively by seeking out others with whom they can cooperate. By employing some special device, like pay, a firm can convince self-interested, welfare-maximizing individuals to cooperate. Market competition can foster economic cooperation.

What, however, did people do before governments and markets? Are these the only two arrangements that foster cooperation? Don't friends just cooperate?

Another common view is that cooperation can just happen in small groups of people who have learned to trust each other. And it does. Yet even cooperation among neighbors doesn't just happen. "In practice, small scale societies do not exemplify the idealized vision of community," writes Mary Douglas, the British social anthropologist. "Some do, some do not foster trust." For those who think otherwise, Douglas offers a riposte: "Has no one writing on this subject ever lived in a village?"[4] Has no one writing on this subject ever been a member of a neighborhood association, a church congregation, or a university faculty?

Evolving Cooperation

"Cooperation does occur," writes Robert Axelrod of the University of Michigan in his classic book, *The Evolution of Cooperation.* It is possible to create cooperation or, at least, to evolve cooperation. Axelrod's "cooperation theory" offers a strategy that encourages cooperation between two individuals with different interests engaged in a series of interactions with the characteristics of the prisoner's dilemma. In this "iterative prisoner's dilemma," the two players do not encounter each other just once. They will interact multiple times—and they know it. Thus each has an opportunity to learn what strategies produce selfishly beneficial outcomes. Indeed, each player has an opportunity to teach the other what strategies will produce mutually beneficial outcomes.[5]

To encourage cooperation by the other player, Axelrod reports, a player can employ a strategy with four components:

(1) Be "Nice": From the beginning, trust the other player and cooperate as long as he or she cooperates.

(2) Be "Retaliatory": But, if the other player defects, immediately punish him or her by defecting yourself at the next opportunity.

(3) Be "Forgiving": Then, immediately return to your trusting, cooperative self.

(4) Be "Clear": Moreover, make this strategy (of cooperation combined with immediate punishment for any defection) very clear to the other player.

Axelrod calls this strategy *tit for tat*: a player "cooperates on the first move and then does whatever the other player did on the previous move." A tit-for-tat player incurs some personal costs when punishing the other for a defection but does so to create what Axelrod calls "cooperation based on reciprocity."[6]

If two individuals play this game multiple times, they each have an opportunity to learn the other's strategy. If they know that they will play the game multiple times, they each have an incentive to figure out the other's strategy so as to take it into account in future encounters. If they know that they will play the game multiple times, and if one player can devise a mutually beneficial strategy, he or she has an incentive to make it known to the other player. And if that strategy is tit for tat , they each have an incentive to follow it religiously so as to convince the other to trust them to continue to employ it. Out of such multiple interactions, these competitors can develop a "norm of reciprocity."[7] Thus cooperation evolves. Competitors evolve into partners.

But can these results—derived from a tournament of game theorists playing the iterated prisoner's dilemma and some theoretical calculations—help real people evolve real cooperation with other real people in their personal and professional lives? Axlerod offers four "simple suggestions" for such individuals: "do not be envious of the other player's success; do not be the first to defect; reciprocate both cooperation and defection; and do not be too clever."[8]

Moreover, he writes, "if the facts of Cooperation Theory are known by participants with foresight, the evolution of cooperation can be speeded up." In particular, he offers several suggestions "to promote cooperation by transforming the strategic setting itself." His most important recommendation is to ensure that people will interact again and soon: "The evolution of cooperation requires that individuals have a sufficiently large chance to meet again so that they have a stake in their future interaction." When involved in a prisoner's dilemma, people are more likely to cooperate if they know that they will interact with the other individual again.[9]

Further, Axelrod suggests that, to encourage more cooperation, society should "teach people to care about each other." It should "teach reciprocity." If people cared more about each other, if they understood the importance of reciprocal (rather than competitive) relationships, they would be more apt to recognize and understand that their own wins do not depend upon forcing others to lose. Indeed, reports Axelrod, "in a non-zero-sum world, you do not have to do better than the other player to do well for yourself." Tit for tat works "by eliciting cooperation from the other player."[10]

Cooperation with Friends and Strangers

We compete with both strangers and friends. And although the official rules of the game are the same, when competing with friends we abide by an additional set of informal norms.

With strangers, we comply with the formal rules of the competition (though we may be quite willing to violate them if we think we can get away with it). Even modern warfare has rules (although if we are losing we may perceive little reason to abide by them). We never expect to see this stranger again, so there is little reason to do the hard work necessary to establish a basis for cooperation. Thus the competition becomes zero sum.

Our interactions with our friends are not, however, zero sum. If they were, these people would not be our friends. When competing with friends, we abide by the formal rules of the contest and by the informal norms that we have evolved for ourselves. We want to be friends for a long time and, thus, want to promote reciprocity. Indeed, when interacting with a friend, we may each (without even consulting the other) decide to abide by our own personal sense of what is proper; we do so to dramatize the kind of reciprocity that we believe is appropriate, valuable, and fair.[11]

When, however, our friend defects from either the formal rules or our informal norms, we are particularly offended. (And, suggests Axelrod, we ought to signal our unhappiness by reciprocating with some kind of proportional punishment.) To be friends, we have to agree to a common set of rules under which we both compete and cooperate. If we cannot agree on these rules, then we effectively end our friendship.

If at the end of the competition, we will completely sever our relationship—if we know we will never deal with the other party again—we can be completely brutal. If it will help us win the competition, if no one else with whom we must deal in the future is watching,[12] and if the rules have no moral force, we can ignore any rule. Winning is the only thing. But if we have to deal with the other party again, the definition of winning changes.

Indeed, sometimes it is impossible to terminate a relationship. Even if we will never be personal friends, we may be forced to be professional colleagues. We have no choice. We will meet again and again. And we don't want to let our desire to win a minor competition ruin this necessary (and necessarily long-term) relationship. And, again, we want to establish that the relationship is based on reciprocity. When we emerge from the competition, we want our friends to think of us as intelligent, vigorous, and fair competitors. Why might losing nations abide by the international rules of warfare? Because, after the war is over, the losing nation has to deal with the winner.[13]

Thus people behave differently when they play the iterated prisoner's dilemma than when they play it only once. If you play only once and defect on your partner, he or she has no way to retaliate—at least not until the jail term is over. But in the iterated prisoner's dilemma you know that you must deal with your partner in the future—in many futures. This converts your opponent into a partner. This is why you want to convert your partner into your friend. You cooperate because it is in *your* best interest. Moreover, you go out of your way to convince your partner that you are the cooperative type—that you will cooperate in the future. This is also in *your* best interest. This is why you signal your strategy. You want all of the people with whom you work to know that as long as they cooperate, you will too.

At the same time, you want to be sure that these people also know that you are committed to punishing any defection. "When a man's partner is killed he's supposed to do something about it," Sam Spade explains to Brigid O'Shaughnessy in Dashiell Hammett's *The Maltese Falcon*. "When one of your organization gets killed it's bad business to let the killer get away with it. It's bad all around—bad for that one organization, bad for every detective everywhere."[14]

Why do new-car salesmen have a better reputation than used-car salesmen? Both sell cars. Is the difference in reputation derived from the difference in the quality of cars? No. It comes from the difference in the nature of their relationships with their customers—specifically from the difference in the endurance of those relationships.

The used-car salesman has no reason to play fair. The used-car salesman will never deal with you again. He doesn't expect repeat business. He doesn't care about repeat business. Thus he has no reason to practice reciprocity. The used-car salesman simply wants to get as much money as possible—now. As Axelrod writes, "if the other player is not likely to be seen again, defecting right away is better than being nice."[15]

Why don't new-car salesmen get the same bad rap? Because the people in the new-car showroom want your repeat business. Even if the sales personnel on the floor don't expect to be there when you trade in this car for your next one, the owner and manager of the franchise do. They want you to come back. They want to establish an enduring relationship—to convince you that with this dealer you have a relationship based on reciprocity. Any individual working the sales floor has, of course, an incentive to get as much money from you as possible. The same is true for the manager and owner. This is a game of both competition and cooperation.

The new-car dealer knows that you can play tit for tat. You can easily reciprocate the dealer's cooperation, both by returning to buy your next car from this cooperating dealer and by telling your friends about this dealer's cooperative behavior. At the same time, you can easily reciprocate the dealer's defection by defecting too. Unless the dealer establishes a reputation for being fair,[16] you won't come back (and your friends will never come the first time).

Thus the dealer will insist that all sales personnel treat you fairly (or, at least, much more fairly than the used-car folks). The dealer does want you to come back.[17] The dealer is in the business for the long run.[18] As David Brown notes, "being known as a cooperator, rather than a defector, is to our advantage over the long run."[19]

Creating Professional Friendships

To foster cooperation with the people with whom you must work, you need to create professional friendships—ongoing relationships based on reciprocity. And to establish such professional friendships—to create relationships based on professional reciprocity—you need to play tit for tat.

Professional friendships need not preclude a willingness to discipline defectors. Tit for tat applies to both cooperation and defection.[20] Any punishment should, however, be limited and proportional to the offense. Maybe it cannot be precisely a *tat* for a *tat*. But the *tit* of retaliation ought to be proportional to the *tat* of defection. A professional punishment should signal what behavior is unacceptable and clarify how such (unacceptable) behavior will be dealt with in the future. Tit-for-tat punishment is not designed to create personal friendships; indeed, it might undermine them. But it can evolve professional friendships—professional, working relationships.

Creating friendships—even professional friendships—takes time. Indeed, professional friendships may take longer. Personal friendships may involve little more than singing in the choir once a week or bowling with a group once a month. The reciprocity required of such friendships is relatively modest: a little punctuality, a little skill, a little conviviality. Some integrity might be helpful, but the weekly bowling game requires only a minimum of integrity. Moreover, it is relatively easy to dump the cheater from the bowling group or the delinquent from the choir.

In contrast, professional friendships may be intricate and complex. They may require more trust—trust about the reciprocal nature of the relationship over many aspects of behavior. Thus creating professional friendships takes time; you need multiple and varied interactions to build up the trust in mutual reciprocity necessary to work together cooperatively on complicated projects. You can play bridge with someone you met this evening. If you go rock climbing, if you need someone to belay you up a sheer and unknown cliff, you need someone whom you have learned to really trust.[21]

Professional relationships are more like those among rock climbers than among a singing or bowling group. After all, the reciprocal agreements under which professional relationships function are based on some form of trust—not necessarily trust on every level, but certainly a trust that your partnership will continue to function within some widely understood professional norms of reciprocity.

"Friendship is not necessary for cooperation to evolve," writes Axelrod. Instead, "the evolution of cooperation requires that individuals have a sufficiently large chance to meet again, so that they have a stake in their future interaction." Nor does Axelrod put much faith in trust: "The foundation of cooperation is not really trust, but the durability of the relationship."[22] Yet the durability of the relationship fosters trust—trust in a commitment to reciprocate in the future that is derived from a history of interactions.[23] Perhaps this is the best way to think about professional friendships. Two individuals have a professional friendship if: (1) in the past, they have interacted sufficiently (played enough rounds of tit for tat) to have demonstrated their mutual commitment to reciprocity; and (2) they know that their relationship will continue well into the future.[24]

Creating Reciprocity within a Responsibility Compact

Is it possible to evolve cooperation among the partners in a multi-player prisoner's dilemma? Is it possible to use a tit-for-tat strategy to encourage cooperation among the many potential members of a compact of mutual, collective responsibility? Is it possible to use such a strategy to foster a responsibility compact? Is it possible to adapt tit for tat to create a web of mutually reciprocal relationships among those who have formally committed themselves to such a compact? (If so, can the compact's members employ such a strategy in dealing with others who may even disdain the compact?)

To foster cooperation, the potential members of a responsibility compact might employ a tit-for-tat strategy similar to that used effectively in the two-person prisoner's dilemma. To start, be nice: Trust the other parties, assume that everyone else will cooperate and, thus, cooperate with them. Second, be retaliatory: If any other party defects, retaliate immediately against this uncooperative individual. Then be forgiving: Immediately return to trusting this defector. Finally, be clear: Explain to everyone the principle underlying tit for tat.

A web of mutual and collective responsibility might evolve from a network of professionals working toward common purposes in a way that created and reinforced norms of reciprocity. From multiple opportunities to play tit for tat, these individuals might become professional friends. From these frequent interactions, they might learn to trust each other—to trust that the others would, indeed, reciprocate each *tat* with an appropriate *tit*. Indeed, the members of the compact might actively foster such trust if, whenever playing tit for tat, they would explicitly explain their principle of reciprocity, thus signaling their commitment to behave similarly in the future. Indeed, these professional friendships would depend on the recognition that the members would continue to work with each other well into the future.

The compact would need to make sure that any punishment on a defecting member was administered professionally. Such punishment should be only for noncooperative behavior that is a manifest violation of the compact's clear (if evolving) norms. Accountability requires clear expectations; if the members of a responsibility compact are going to hold each other mutually accountable for abiding by their common norms, they need to specify these norms. Administering a *tit* as a punishment for a *tat*, when that *tat* was never defined as a violation of the compact's norms, does not reinforce reciprocity; it only creates confusion. Moreover, when punishing a defector, the compact needs to explain explicitly to the offending individual (and all the other members) what makes such "uncooperative" behavior unacceptable. The compact needs to make clear to the defector the damage that he or she has done; it needs to explain the connection between the original defection (and its damage) and the retaliatory punishment to all of the members of the compact.

The Challenge of Enforcing Reciprocity

What might such "punishment" look like? Suppose one member of a responsibility compact decides to expose some small error in finances or fairness, or to publish a nit-picking evaluation of the agency's failure to improve performance, or to personally attack another member. Who should do what?

The nature of the punishment would depend upon the nature of the defector as well as the nature of the defection. In theory, the defector's *tat* should bring swift retaliation in the form of an identical *tit*. In reality, the members of the compact are unlikely to possess a *tit* that precisely matches the defector's *tat*. Thus they will search for an available *tit* that imposes on this particular defector a cost that is roughly equivalent to the cost produced by the original *tat*.

To what kind of retaliation are various members of the compact vulnerable? Usually, the agency and its leadership will be vulnerable to multiple forms of retaliation; this is why they are unlikely to defect. Legislators might also be vulnerable; their legislative colleagues can publicly upbraid these violators and deny them common legislative courtesies (such as committee assignments or funds for district projects). Other defectors, however, might not be very vulnerable to any *tit* that the other members of the compact could impose. What punishment could the members of a responsibility compact impose on a defecting journalist, candidate, auditor, or special prosecutor?[25]

To create reciprocal relationships both parties must be able to retaliate. You cannot employ a tit-for-tat strategy, if you cannot retaliate—if you possess no punishing *tit*s with which to respond to a defecting *tat*. And some of the core members of any responsibility compact—those who are the most interested in improving the agency's performance—may simply lack any *tit*s with which to respond to the *tat*s inflicted by some in the accountability environment. How could the agency's managers, or the leaders of a key stakeholder organization, or even an influential legislator possibly retaliate against a defection by an aggressive auditor, an investigative journalist, or a special prosecutor?

You don't need a compact to create mutually reciprocal relationships. It doesn't matter whether the auditor or the journalist or the prosecutor joins the compact or not. What matters is whether some member has a *mutual* relationship with each of them so that he or she can reward cooperation and punish defection. To overcome the challenge of creating cooperation, you need the ability to play tit for tat. If no one who seeks to create a responsibility compact can punish some important defectors, the tit-for-tat strategy collapses. And so does any obligation to the norm of reciprocity.

Further, for reciprocity and cooperation to evolve, each member of the accountability environment would have to recognize that he or she will be unable to avoid dealing with other members in the future. For institutional members, this will necessarily be true. Whether the compact continues or dissolves, the agency and the institutions in its accountability environment will continue to interact. The same, however, need not be true for individuals within these institutions. They can easily exit. Suppose the director of a stakeholder organization is about to resign to take a position requiring no future contact with anyone currently active in this accountability environment; such an individual might defect on some critical interaction knowing that the future *tit* with which the responsibility compact would respond to his defecting *tat*, will impose costs only on his former organization but not on himself.

Thus the tit-for-tat strategy of the two-player prisoner's dilemma may not work for the multi-player version created when those in a public agency's accountability environment attempt to form a compact of mutual, collective responsibility. Membership in the compact may be too fluid; too many individuals will spend too short a time in the compact to learn and internalize its norm of reciprocity, let alone feel constrained by some potential future *tat*s.

The challenge of creating cooperation is the challenge of enforcing reciprocity.

Cooperation in Large Groups

Cooperation may not always evolve in small groups; still, it is easier to foster cooperation in small groups than in large ones.[26] As Axelrod writes, "It is easier to maintain the norms of reciprocity in a stable small town or ethnic neighborhood."[27] Indeed, he goes further, arguing that what works in small groups won't work in large ones: "The policy advice based on reciprocity that works so well in the two-person Prisoner's Dilemma simply does not work for the *n*-person version of the game when there is more than a handful of people involved."[28]

Why? Why won't the approach that works between individuals to produce personal friends, to produce professional friends, to produce norms of reciprocity also work in large groups to produce networks of personal friends, to produce webs of professional friendships, to produce informal compacts of mutual, collective, and cooperative friendships that have internalized the norm of reciprocity?

As usual, the answer depends upon the circumstances. But for large groups, the circumstances are not favorable. The group does not have to be too large before no one person knows everyone else. Size makes communication difficult. Size inhibits conspicuous reciprocity (and thus the interpersonal trust that future acts will be reciprocated). Size makes it difficult to organize an agreement about the norms of cooperation. Moreover, if the benefits of cooperative behavior accrue equally to those who cooperate and those who don't, if the cooperators cannot prevent the defectors from getting such a benefit, each individual has the incentive to become a free rider. Size makes it difficult for the cooperators to identify the defectors, let alone to impose simple sanctions (such as calling them nasty names). Finally, even the most altruistic individuals, even those who are personally invested in the task of making the cooperative process work, can be easily discouraged by the lack of progress—by the lack of *visible* progress.[29]

In small groups, it is easier to employ reciprocity to promote cooperation: I won't graze my second cow on the commons as long as you don't. And if we live in a two-person town, we can easily play tit for tat. If I graze a second cow on the commons today, you can retaliate, graze a second one tomorrow, but then forgive me and return to grazing only one cow. Moreover, you can explain to me—simply and clearly—exactly what you are doing and why. "The effectiveness of strategies of reciprocity," writes Kenneth Oye of MIT, depends upon "the ability of actors to distinguish reliably between cooperation and defection by others and to respond in kind."[30] In our two-person town, each of us can easily determine if the other is cooperating or defecting; and each of us can easily reciprocate.

If, however, we live in a larger town—with just a dozen people—can you reliably determine whether I am defecting today? If there are thirteen cows grazing on the common, you can easily determine that someone has defected. But who? And what if eleven cows are grazing? Does that mean that one of us has simply decided not to graze a cow today? Maybe two of us chose not to graze a cow, and another, after counting cows, sneaked in an extra.

Moreover, if you do determine reliably that I am grazing an extra cow, how do you reciprocate? How do you retaliate? Can you punish me by grazing a second cow tomorrow? Will I think of this as punishment? Will I "learn" from this experience? Even if you explain it, will I get it? And will everybody else get the signal? Or will they just conclude that you are defecting too? Indeed, even if all eleven of you agree to retaliate, what do you do? Do you all graze a second cow tomorrow? If so, the cost of the punishment imposed on me, is eleven times greater than the cost that my original defection imposed on each of you (as is the cost to each of you of punishing me). You need to invent a form of retaliation that punishes me more than it punishes all of you.[31] This requires the eleven of you to agree upon a specific form of punishment, and that may not be easy.

Clearly, the group does not have to become very large before creating and imposing retaliatory punishments becomes difficult. The multi-player prisoner's dilemma "cannot be resolved with simple reciprocity," concludes Axelrod, because there exists "no way for the cooperating players to focus punishment on a defecting player."[32]

Creating Group Identity

One common strategy for encouraging cooperation is first to create some kind of group identity—a feeling of camaraderie. Such a group identity could be based on a common mission, a common ethical standing, a common adversary, or simply a sense of belonging.[33]

Within a group with a clear, common identity, the cooperation depends neither on its small size nor on coercion—two of the three circumstances that Mancur Olson argues can get "rational self-interested individuals" to cooperate "to achieve their common or group interests." Instead, the cooperation derives from Olson's third condition: "some other special device" that gives the group's members individual benefits.[34] These individual benefits need not, however, be extrinsic. They can be purely intrinsic, psychological benefits—for example, the emotional lift from being accepted or recognized as a member of a group with a certain, unique cachet.[35] "Public-spirited collective action," notes Dennis Chong of Northwestern University, "offers little in the way of direct tangible selective incentives." Instead, he continues in his study *Collective Action and the Civil Rights Movement,* "the most prominent benefits are usually social and psychological." But, Chong also notes, some individuals do face some costs if they choose not to join and cooperate; for people who see themselves—and want to be seen by others—as leaders, failure to participate in the collective enterprise can result "in damage to one's reputation, ostracism, or repudiation from the community."[36]

Thus those seeking to organize a responsibility compact could create a sense of common identity among those who are committed to improving the performance of a specific public agency and thus also create a norm of cooperation that will facilitate the desired improvement in performance. Moreover, in an effort to recruit additional members, they could seek to establish that this was a public-spirited undertaking to which all of the distinguished leaders in the agency's accountability environment had committed their efforts and reputations.

Again, however, some people—journalists, overhead regulators, candidates, legislators, and prosecutors—may feel no kinship with others in the accountability environment. Journalists may feel much more loyalty to their own profession—and to their professional norms, which preclude participation in any such cabal. The regulators in overhead agencies are committed to their organizations' values of government-wide consistency in the application of their rules for finances and fairness, and fear that any endorsement of flexibility might establish a precedent for others.[37] Certainly a candidate attempting to defeat a member of the compact will have no allegiance to its norms of cooperation. And although some legislators (the "insiders") closely identify with their legislative body and its norms of cooperation, other legislators (the "outsiders") have established a reputation—to say nothing of a self-image—as a challenger of the inside strategy of the legislative leadership.[38] Finally, many prosecutors and inspectors general possess their own self-identity; indeed, they "constitute a self-conscious interest group," write Frank Anechiarico and James Jacobs, that "advocates comprehensive surveillance, investigation, and 'target-hardening' strategies."[39]

Many in a public agency's accountability environment are members of groups with stronger self-identities than a potential responsibility compact. Many are members of other groups with strong norms that conflict directly with the compact's norms of cooperation. Others belong to groups with a more established reputation for sanctioning defection.[40] Thus most journalists, regulators, political candidates, legislative outsiders, inspectors general, and prosecutors are unlikely to be persuaded to identify themselves with others in an agency's accountability environment or to join their compact of cooperative reciprocity.[41]

The Challenge of Creating Group Norms

Despite all of the analysis and arguments suggesting that competition is more natural than cooperation, cooperation does happen—even in large groups. Indeed, as David Brown emphasizes, we even cooperate with strangers.[42] And we do this even when it may not be in our immediate interest. Moreover, despite Axelrod's pessimism about the applicability of the tit-for-tat strategy to a multi-person prisoner's dilemma, he still observes that "social norms do emerge and are often quite powerful means of sustaining cooperation"—and not just in small groups.[43]

How do such norms emerge?[44] How do they get established?[45] How are they sustained?[46] Why couldn't a norm of cooperative reciprocity emerge among the individuals and institutions within a public agency's accountability environment? Norms can facilitate cooperation on an international scale, affecting the behavior of nations and international institutions.[47] Why couldn't norms facilitate cooperation among the potential members of an accountability compact?

After all, abiding by norms can be quite inconvenient. Millions of us recycle our milk bottles and beer cans. We do so not because our back-of-the-envelope benefit-cost analysis reveals that we personally obtain a net benefit by recycling,[48] and not because we are required to do so by law,[49] but simply because we have accepted the norms of the environmental movement.[50] Recycling is a multi-person prisoner's dilemma: Collectively, we will all be better off if everyone recycles; individually, however, each one of us will be even better off (if only slightly) if we defect from the recycling norm (but let everyone else do it). After all, recycling is a pain: green glass here; aluminum there. And some of us do defect. Many of us, however, while recognizing that the personal costs we incur by recycling exceed our personal benefits, still carefully abide by the recycling norm.

The classic social norm is the line. When we Americans get to the movie theater or the supermarket checkout, we automatically form a line. We don't cut in. We are strangers, yet we cooperate. Even big guys, people who could easily impose their will on the shorties in the line, don't cut in. We all simply take our place at the end of the line. Why? Because forming an organized line was the first thing we learned in kindergarten? Or because, as Brown suggests, the "convention" of a line offers a simple solution to a collective action problem?[51]

Like most useful conventions, the line benefits everyone. "Our social conventions promote regularities of conduct that are consistent with self-interest while at the same time producing, for the most part, desirable outcomes," observes Brown. Conventions can replace unpredictable behavior with predictable behavior, which, he notes, "is in everyone's favor." Indeed, he continues, "conventions organize and simplify many instances of potential confusion or chaos."[52]

David Lewis of Princeton University thinks of conventions as "regularities of behavior, sustained by an interest in coordination and an expectation that others will do their part."[53] The line fits perfectly. It certainly is a regularity. It reflects our individual and collective interest in coordination. It is based on the expectation that others will do their part.

Still, why should self-interested, welfare-maximizing individuals abide by the convention of the line? Because it does have an overarching purpose: The line eliminates the fighting that will inevitably occur if we do not queue up in an orderly manner. But we also honor the convention of the line because it is based on a norm that is widely accepted as fair: first come, first served.[54] Cutting in line isn't fair; everyone understands this.[55] Even before you got to kindergarten, you learned the convention of the line by watching your parents (though the kindergarten teacher may have been the one to explain the norm behind the convention that you observed your parents follow).

The line itself is a powerful norm. Even when the stakes are high, we may all voluntarily cooperate. A friend of mine got up early to get in line for tickets to a Jimmy Buffett concert. Indeed, she was first in line. But the ticket distributor had developed a distaste for early lines; thus, to discourage them, it created a rule: The first thirty people would not get tickets on a first-come, first-served basis. Instead, these thirty people would go into a lottery, so that each of these people had the same, one-thirtieth chance of getting the best tickets. Thus, getting up early to be the first in line would be no better than getting up later and being number 30. Nevertheless, when the ticket office opened and the sales clerk began to explain the lottery, the people in line revolted. No, they said, we like our place in line. We want to get our tickets in this order. It's only *fair*. Obviously, the people in places 16 through 30 could, with the lottery, increase their chances of getting better tickets; yet they, too, supported the line. Even the thirtieth person in the line didn't complain, even though the lottery could only give this individual better seats. My friend ended up with seats in the middle of the front row.[56]

Norms are powerful. The line is a widely accepted convention because it is supported by a powerful norm. Norms can even cause people to forget their welfare-maximizing self-interest.

Rules and Enforcement

The line is an effective convention because it is relatively easy to police. Indeed, it is often self-policing. Every member of the line will quickly observe any individual who attempts to cut in. Any individual who is contemplating such behavior recognizes that many people will observe the violation and that if just one person speaks up, all the others will join in.

Indeed, if a convention solves a relatively unimportant problem (such as the order in which people buy their movie tickets and thus choose their theater seats), it may require little policing. For most lines, the advantage to be gained by cutting in isn't worth the public (and self-) reprobation. Moreover, as long as the violations of the convention are rare and relatively unimportant, the convention may function quite well without any policing. For most lines, people can simply ignore the infrequent, individual violators (and simply write off their antisocial behavior to poor toilet training) without destroying the overall effectiveness of the convention.[57]

In other circumstances, however, a simple convention may not be adequate. If the thing to be obtained at the end of the line is very valuable, several individuals—perhaps some very big individuals—may decide to breach the convention. In response, others may be willing to physically and aggressively enforce the first-come, first-served principle, and the decorum of the line may quickly disintegrate into chaos. If the line determines who gets Red Sox World Series tickets—not who gets which seats, but who gets any seats at all—we may need to convert the informal convention into a formal rule and develop formal mechanisms for policing compliance.[58]

Who, however, will do this policing? This is a standard "make-or-buy decision." The people who signed on to the convention and created the rule could "buy" policing by hiring some cops. Real police—complete with all of the symbols of authority, from uniforms to weapons—will deter most people from violating the rule of the line and will quickly punish any who do.

Alternatively, those who support the convention and rule could "make" the policing by doing it themselves. Indeed, they may be the best people to do so. Real police are simply mercenaries. The people in the line have a real, personal stake in ensuring that everyone abides by the first-come, first-served principle. "When you yield to a convention," writes Brown, "you invest in its being a success."[59]

At Duke University, undergraduate students line up to get into Cameron Indoor Stadium for basketball games. And for the really important games—against, for example, that hated pale-blue team from the University of North Carolina at Chapel Hill—they line up not just days but weeks in advance. And, to be able to spend days or weeks in line, they pitch tents. This "line," however, creates two questions. How do the students know who is in front or behind whom in this line—which hardly looks like a line, and more like an upper-class Hooverville? (It is actually called Krzyzewskiville or K-ville, for the Duke basketball coach, Mike Krzyzewski, a.k.a. "Coach K.") And what do students have to do to maintain their place in the line? There are no police. Instead, the students themselves have evolved a complex system of rules that resolves these two questions (which apply to any line). They have a formal process for getting in line (and thus for determining each person's order in the line) and a formal series of tent checks to ensure that you (or at least someone representing your tent) has maintained your place in line.[60]

Whether we make or buy the policing, however, we have to ensure that it is fair. Thus we also need a set of rules that establish what kinds of behavior are unacceptable and thus punishable. "What representative government often seeks to do by enacting laws," writes Brown, "is to reassure the majority of us that no one will take advantage of our voluntary cooperation."[61]

Those who have signed on to the convention of mutual, collective responsibility will be invested in its success. Having established the norm of reciprocity, they will have the incentive to police the behavior of the compact's members. They won't, however, be able to hire any police. They will have to do the work themselves.

Unfortunately, those who once agreed to a responsibility compact need not continue to do so. The compact is not like a line for World Series tickets. It does not provide unique access to an extrinsic benefit. Thus only those directly interested in the collective benefit of improved agency performance—or who get intrinsic benefits from contributing to this cause—will accept its norm of reciprocity. Only those seeking to improve performance will help enforce the compact's norm of reciprocity. Even journalists or auditors who thought that improving agency performance was a worthy purpose would not reject their own professional norms in favor of the compact's internal norm of reciprocity. And the members of the compact have few sanctions with which to police the behavior of nonmembers.

Norms and Conventions in Politics

Cooperation happens. It happens in the United States House of Representatives, where for anything to happen at least 218 self-interested, welfare-maximizing, big-ego individuals have to cooperate. Moreover, they have to cooperate with at least 51 other self-interested, welfare-maximizing, even-bigger-ego individuals from the Senate. How does this happen? The norm of reciprocity helps explain how the competitors manage to cooperate.

In politics, reciprocity is a powerful norm: "To get along, go along." Indeed, politics *is* reciprocity. Edmund Burke, the British statesman, may have thought that an elected representative owed "his judgment" to his constituents. But that was over two centuries ago. Today, most elected officials believe that they owe their supporters reciprocity.[62]

Indeed, reciprocity is the glue that holds together a legislature of competitors. It goes by a couple of names: logrolling, back-scratching. In the U.S. Senate, "reciprocity is a way of life," writes Donald Matthews, long of the University of North Carolina. "Much advice giving and advice taking is reciprocal: Senator 'A' advises Senator 'B' on labor bills while 'B' advises 'A' on agricultural matters. Thus are many of the senators bound together in an endless web of interdependence." This "spirit of reciprocity" combines with other "unwritten rules of behavior," Matthews concludes, to create "the folkways of the Senate," which "soften the inevitable personal conflict of a legislative body so that adversaries and competitors can meet (at the very least) in an atmosphere of antagonistic cooperation or (at best) in an atmosphere of friendship and mutual respect." But a senator who breaks a part of this "implicit bargain," Matthews continues, "can expect, not cooperation from his colleagues, but only retaliation in kind."[63]

How do legislatures control the tendency of some members to carry their take-no-prisoners campaign strategy into their first (or tenth) legislative session? To encourage cooperation and discourage excessive competition, legislatures establish very specific conventions of conduct. No senator is permitted to call another member "the honorable jerk from West Dakota" (at least not on the floor).[64] If the leaders of a legislative body fail to enforce their rules of legislative civility, they can lose all control, and the session will deteriorate into anarchy. "Courtesy, far from being a meaningless custom as some senators seem to think it is, permits competitors to cooperate," explains Matthews. "The chaos which ensues when this folkway is ignored testifies to its vital function."[65]

In the three decades since Matthews reported on the folkways of the Senate, political life in America has become less civil. And so has political life in the Senate.[66] Moreover, other changes in American politics have weakened reciprocity within legislatures. Term limits, for example, may inhibit the ability of legislatures to maintain conventions and norms.

"There is great pressure for conformity in the Senate," one influential senator told Matthews. "It's just like living in a small town."[67] Legislatures today, however, are becoming less like small towns and more like tourist groups. Everyone has been thrown together in close quarters for a short period of time. If they fight constantly, life will be miserable; so they reciprocate in the protocol of daily life. But they all know that the tour will be over soon—that they may never see each other again. So they have little incentive to develop professional working relationships—to undertake the task of employing short-run reciprocity to evolve long-term cooperation.

As a result, term limits may impede the evolution of compacts of mutual and collective responsibility. The new guys won't get it. They just won a major competition and, in the process, learned some "lessons." Often, one such "lesson" is to attack *first*. Don't wait until your opponent goes negative. This is one of the "rules" of modern political campaigning: "Go negative early, often, and right through election day, if necessary."[68] Whether this maxim actually works is irrelevant. If most winning candidates learn this "lesson," it will become self-fulfilling.[69]

Moreover, new legislators may carry this lesson over from their campaign strategy into their legislating strategy. Indeed, they may go looking for opportunities to go negative. Thus, while the members of the responsibility compact are working collectively to solve a problem, a new legislator (as soon as he or she discovers some accountability error) may go negative. The new legislator can not only expose the problem but also denounce all of those working "behind closed doors" to fix it.

Aside from the "lessons" from negative campaigning, term limits themselves may inhibit cooperation. A new legislator is dealing with a term-limited leadership that won't be around to play tit for tat much longer. Why should a new legislator bother to cooperate today with people who won't have much opportunity to reciprocate tomorrow? Lame ducks lose their bargaining power because everyone knows that they will soon lose their ability to reward cooperators and retaliate against defectors.

A Responsibility Compact as a Convention or Norm

Conventions backed by principled norms are powerful devices for fostering cooperation. Conventions can get complete strangers to cooperate. Conventions can get egotistic legislators to cooperate. Could a convention also encourage those in a public agency's accountability environment to cooperate?

Could a compact of mutual, collective responsibility evolve into a convention? Could it become accepted as a standard mechanism for handling a collective action problem and eliminating the uncertainty over how to behave? Could it become accepted as an effective strategy for coping with a multi-person prisoner's dilemma?

Could a responsibility compact foster any norms? Could it nourish the evolution of a norm of reciprocity to promote our common interest in improving the performance of public agencies?

The line solves a common coordination problem. Everyone shares this problem, and the convention of a line provides a simple solution, which most people accept. Could a responsibility compact similarly solve our common problem of creating accountability for performance?

Unfortunately, a responsibility compact does not solve a problem that everyone shares. Many of these individuals may not think a problem exists. Others may think that accountability for performance is a minor problem compared with accountability for finances and fairness. Still others who accept the need to create accountability for performance may think it is best obtained with more rules and oversight, more surveillance and punishment. Even those who understand the challenge of creating an accountability mechanism that actually improves performance may not think it is a problem for which a responsibility compact would be a useful solution. Indeed, some people may think that such a compact would *create* an accountability problem.

A compact of mutual, collective responsibility will never become a convention unless it is generally perceived as collectively advantageous to society—unless it is widely accepted as a solution to our important and universal problem of improving accountability for performance. Unfortunately, the concept of a responsibility compact has a variety of natural opponents. Moreover, the members of such a compact will be unable to retaliate against those in the accountability environment who defect from the compact's norm of reciprocity. Consequently, we may never have an opportunity to experiment sufficiently with the idea to actually learn whether it could become a convention—to learn whether establishing some norms of reciprocity within a public agency's accountability environment could help to improve performance.

10

Evolving a Charter Agency

Creating a compact of mutual, collective responsibility is a complex task—maybe an impossible one. So perhaps we should undertake something less daunting. Perhaps we should attempt to create something less complicated. Something that suggests how a responsibility compact might work. Something that achieves similar but modest objectives. Something that helps us learn whether we could ever hope to create a responsibility compact. Something that teaches us how we might, someday, create a compact of mutual, collective responsibility. Something that is something like a mini responsibility compact.

Something like a charter agency.

The Charter Agency

A charter agency would be similar to a charter school. In return for promising to produce particular results, the agency would gain some flexibility from traditional regulations. A charter agency would accept some additional accountability for performance; in trade, it would be required to comply with fewer of the accountability constraints for finances and fairness.

A charter agency, however, would not be created as charter schools have been. And though a charter agency might appear to be similar to a performance-based organization (PBO), it would not be created as PBOs have been. Indeed, a charter agency would not be *created*; instead, it would *evolve*.

The process for creating charter schools is quite formal. The legislature decides to improve the state's elementary and secondary education and enacts legislation. Such legislation establishes a formal process for creating charter schools. It establishes how many such schools can be created and where. It establishes the rules with which these charter schools must comply; it establishes which rules they can waive (and under what circumstances). It establishes how these schools will be funded. And the legislation establishes expectations for performance.[1] The entire formal process is written into law.

The same is true for PBOs. Everything about their operation—from rules that are waived to specific performance targets—is spelled out in detail before a PBO receives its charter.

I am not, however, proposing to *create* charter agencies. I am proposing to *evolve* them. I am seeking to evolve mini responsibility compacts that will evolve into charter agencies. I am seeking to evolve a few mini responsibility compacts that might help us learn how to evolve more of them—and thus to evolve more charter agencies. I am seeking to evolve mini responsibility compacts that might help us learn how to evolve full-fledged compacts of mutual, collective responsibility.

Maybe we cannot create a compact of mutual, collective responsibility composed of everyone within a public agency's accountability environment. But maybe we can evolve a mini responsibility compact among those most interested in improving the agency's performance.[2] If so, maybe such a mini compact can evolve into a charter agency. If so, maybe a few of them would evolve into compacts of mutual, collective responsibility. Then again, maybe none ever will. Maybe, however, we can evolve the concept of a charter agency into a something that is as widely accepted as a convention.

Success, however, will take time. If charter agencies are to evolve into a convention that we Americans accept as a way to improve accountability for performance while maintaining accountability for finances and fairness, it will take time. "Most social practices," writes David Brown, "require some period of time in order to become established as conventions."[3]

Evolving a Convention

How does a convention get established? Brown suggests three ways: "unplanned coordination: coordination by agreement; and coordination by central authority."[4] Would any of these help to convert a charter agency into a convention?

Would some kind of unplanned, spontaneous coordination work? "Most conventions depend on tacit agreements among strangers that are rarely discussed and debated," writes Brown, "and that is why they remain so invisible to us in everyday life."[5] A charter agency, however, would be more than one of Brown's invisible, purely implicit conventions. A charter agency requires more than "tacit agreements among strangers." A charter agency compact will not really emerge spontaneously.[6]

Delegating the coordination necessary to create a charter agency convention to some central authority would certainly produce an agreement that is more explicit—indeed, too explicit. A centrally authorized charter agency would lack the flexibility to experiment with different ways of creating accountability for finances, fairness, and performance. Moreover, the exercise of some central authority would not foster a mutually supportive mini compact of personal, mutual, and collective responsibility.[7]

Thus, I think, any effort to evolve charter agencies (that, later, might collectively evolve into a convention for improving accountability for performance) will have to emerge from "coordination by agreement"—from a series of informal agreements. Further, each such agreement can only evolve through much discussion and debate. The people who create any kind of mini responsibility compact will have to get to know each other. They will need many long conversations—including, perhaps, some acrimonious debate—to craft their initial agreement. They will have to evolve some mutual expectations for behavior. As Brown argues, "each person's contribution needs to be specified so that each person can reasonably expect others to do their part."[8]

Those who are attempting to evolve a charter agency will experiment. Individuals will do things, and the collective will decide which actions are beneficial cooperations and which are harmful defections. And the group will experiment with reciprocity—attempting to see if can reward a cooperating *tat* with a cooperative *tit*, and punish a defecting *tat* with a defecting *tit*. This is how, as any agreement evolves, the members of the mini responsibility compact will establish individual responsibilities and experiment with, create, clarify, and enforce their mutual expectations for cooperative behavior.

Only after society has evolved a variety of charter agencies will we be able to consider whether their successes and their similarities warrant our converting these experiments into a concept worthy of being a convention. If the advantages of charter agencies become obvious, they could evolve into a convention—a model that various agency heads and legislators can employ to improve performance.[9]

The Initial Charter Team

Who from an agency's accountability environment would be part of its mini responsibility compact—its charter team? There are several logical candidates: the director of the agency; some of the legislators who chair the agency's key oversight or appropriations committees; the heads of some influential stakeholder groups; the leaders of important collaborating organizations in the private and nonprofit sectors. None of these people is essential. The initial group need not include all of the important legislators, though it would be useful to include some. The initial group need not include representatives from all of the key stakeholder organizations, though it would be useful to include some. It need not include representatives from all of the agency's collaborating organizations, though (particularly if they are helpful for improving performance) it would be useful to include some. It need not even include the agency's director, though eventually it will have to (either because the existing director begins to understand or because the agency gets a new one).

The initial members of the charter team will be individuals who believe that the agency needs to improve performance. They might also agree that improved performance depends upon changing the agency's accountability arrangement. They might even agree that to improve performance, the agency needs to trade increased accountability for performance for some flexibility in accountability for finances and fairness. But the only real requirement for membership is an agreement that if the agency is to improve its performance, someone has to do *something*.[10]

Each potential member of the charter team will be willing to cooperate if the others do. Conversely none will cooperate if the others won't. It is a multiperson prisoner's dilemma.[11] Each potential member's cooperation is conditional upon the cooperation of the other members. But how will they all arrange to cooperate? Does this require leadership? Or is mere talk adequate?

"Cooperation is more conditional when developing new conventions," argues Brown. Nevertheless, he continues, "a conditional framework for voluntary cooperation among strangers can arise if there is adequate feedback."[12] If several potential members of the compact talk enough among themselves, they may be able to convince each other that everyone is genuinely, if conditionally, committed. Such discussions could provide the feedback necessary to convince each individual that everyone else will do his or her fair share. And thus, in some formal ceremony or, more likely, over a long dinner, each individual could sign up to do *something*.

This *something* may be quite undefined. Indeed, perhaps, the only thing that those at the dinner really have in common is a sense that *something* has to be done to improve performance.

Those who have signed up to do something will form the leadership core of the charter team—of some kind of fledgling, ill-defined, mini responsibility compact. Many will know each other. Many will have already worked together. Some will have learned to respect the professional talents of some others. And if they can figure out what *something* do to first, they may be able to evolve a charter agency.

"Problem solving in public life is more social than cognitive," argues Brown. To craft a solution, we must "learn that cooperation is necessary to produce a satisfactory outcome—not optimal from the perspective of narrow self-interest, but satisfactory in that a problem can't otherwise be solved."[13] To foster such social problem-solving, the first step is not to commission a task force of public policy wonks or to appoint an advisory committee of stakeholders but to assemble a salon of professional friends. If the members of this charter team can get together not in a conference room but for some informal dinners, they may have a chance to evolve the social relationships that encourage cooperation.

The Oregon Option is a responsibility compact between the federal government and the state of Oregon—or, as the National Academy of Public Administration calls it, "an experiment in results-driven governance." In a memorandum of understanding (that is explicitly "not a legally binding or enforceable agreement"), the two partners set out "to redesign and test an outcomes oriented approach to intergovernmental service delivery." In return for flexibility in how it uses federal funds, Oregon agreed to improve performance (with the same level of funding). It is a basic accountability trade-off: flexibility in rules and administrative procedures for improvements in performance. The objective was to experiment with replacing procedural accountability with performance accountability.[14]

When the people from the state and federal governments launched this program, they made an effort to create friendships—professional friendships and even personal friendships. "We began with a conscious effort to get to know people," reported Connie Revell, then the executive director of the Oregon Option. Most relationships in government, she observed, are based on the assumption "that other people are going to cheat you." So Revell, her colleagues from Oregon, and the federal managers from the National Partnership for Reinventing Government set out to build friendships. When Revell visited Washington, for example, she would stay at the home of her federal partners; and when the feds went to Oregon, they would stay with Revell. "I read bedtime stories to their kids," noted Revell. "I even went to one of their weddings."[15]

The initial members of this kind of charter team need not, however, be close personal friends. They do, however, need to establish professional friendships. Each initial member of the compact needs to have (or build) a professional relationship with every other member—to work enough with each of these individuals to be able to predict from their past, and consistent, behavior that each will be a cooperative colleague in the future. And each will have to accept that they will all have to continue working together in the future. Then each will be able to combine his or her knowledge of the other's past behavior with the assurance of the need to continue to work together to confidently predict that they will all be cooperators, not defectors.

The Need for Leadership

Still, who will organize the dinners? Perhaps the discussions will simply evolve. Perhaps people will just start talking. As various members of a public agency's accountability environment meet, converse, argue, and gossip, each might recognize the need to change significantly the accountability mechanisms that hinder performance. Independently but simultaneously, each might recognize that they could, if they acted collectively and cooperatively, effect such a change. And thus they might evolve themselves into a mini compact of mutual, collective responsibility that then evolves the agency from a traditional, fully regulated public agency into a charter agency. But if this were true—if mini responsibility compacts could just emerge—wouldn't a few have emerged already?

So how might this evolutionary process begin? Who would do what? Who talks with each potential member over lunch? Who gets everyone together for dinner? Who exercises the initial leadership? Evolving the mini responsibility compact that then evolves into a charter agency will require some leadership—even if it doesn't look like what we think of as traditional (heroic) leadership.[16]

Even if each potential member of a charter team recognizes that the collective benefits of attempting to create something like, perhaps, a charter agency clearly outweigh the collective costs, each may also calculate that the short-term personal costs of attempting to do so easily exceed the short-term benefits. Why would anyone go first? Everyone might be quite willing to join if everyone else has already joined (or, at least, is committed to joining). But who would unilaterally commit to get the process going? Who will go first?

A charter agency might just evolve. But it is more likely to evolve if someone takes the initiative to help this along. And the logical person to exercise such leadership is the head of the agency. Others might also have an incentive to go first; dissatisfied stakeholders, disgruntled middle-managers, disaffected frontline supervisors, disillusioned legislators, or disenchanted citizens could decide that the opportunity to make some small but significant improvements in performance was worth at least some initial effort. Still, the agency's head—or better, the agency's leadership team—has the most obvious incentive.

Demonstrating Competence

The usual first step for doing anything new in government (or in business) is to create an ad hoc team, an interagency committee, or a stakeholder task force that will develop The Plan. You can't do anything without The Plan. You can't do anything without first getting everyone to agree to The Plan. And that, of course, means that you have to make sure that all of the key decisionmakers—everyone who has to agree to The Plan—are represented on the planning team.

As a consequence, this team becomes a committee, which becomes a task force, which becomes too big—too unwieldy. The meetings last forever. Everyone has a veto. The Plan has to satisfy everyone. As a result, The Plan satisfies no one. The Plan accomplishes nothing.

The Constitution of the United States does not require you to start with The Plan. Honest! You could look it up. You don't need a huge task force. You don't need to consult everyone. You can just start.

In particular, the agency's leadership could start by improving performance. They could start by identifying a few small but significant barriers to performance. They could start by identifying a few barriers that have been erected internally. And then they could eliminate some of these barriers. Without any additional resources, without any additional flexibility, the leaders of the agency could visibly demonstrate that they are competent—

indeed, that their agency is competent. They could do this by making some noticeable improvements in performance—and by doing so without first obtaining or demanding any additional resources or flexibility.

But how? How can they ratchet up performance without more resources or more flexibility? Robert Schaffer, the author of *Breakthrough Strategy,* argues that every organization has a "hidden reserve of unused or misused capacity." How does he know that this underutilized capacity exists? Because, he explains, it "is 'miraculously' revealed in crises." Unfortunately, Schaffer continues, most organizations don't know how to tap this hidden reserve. Yet, he believes, it is relatively easy: The organization's leadership needs to identify an "urgent and compelling goal," break this down into a "short-term, first-step subgoal" that can be achieved quickly; make that goal measurable, and take advantage of "what people are *ready, willing, and able* to do." The result, he observes, is that people throughout the organization produce a specific result that they thought was unachievable, earn a sense of accomplishment, and learn how to improve performance.[17]

If the agency's previous managers have devoted their time to policy—if they have concentrated on creating interagency committees and organizing stakeholder task forces; if they have created multiple variants of The Plan— they will have ignored the simple tasks of management. If so, the new leadership team will be lucky. They can pick some particular areas for improvement, establish some baseline measures of performance, knock over some of the biggest or weakest barriers, measure their new performance, and then dramatize their new level of performance to anyone who will listen.

It might, just might, make them look competent.[18]

The first step is *not* to get a charter agency bill through the legislature. Indeed, the first step is *not* to even talk about becoming a charter agency—*not* to even talk about asking for some additional flexibility. Instead, the first step is simply to demonstrate that the agency can accomplish something significant— to demonstrate that the agency and its leadership are clearly competent. And to do this, the agency's leadership needs to ratchet up performance.[19]

Does this initiative have to come from the agency's leadership? No, it could come from stakeholders, middle managers, legislators, union officials, frontline supervisors—from anyone who can get some people to cooperate in a small but significant effort to ratchet up performance (and thus demonstrate competence). But the agency's leadership has an obvious incentive to take this initiative and is (or ought to be) able to actually accomplish something.

Looking for a Few Good Allies

With this modest improvement in performance, the agency's leadership has created some specific evidence that it is worthy of support. Thus these leaders can go looking for partners—for charter members for their charter team.

First, however, they need to decide what they want: What additional flexibility does the agency need to improve performance further? Does it want freedom from the personnel ceiling? If so, who is the most likely ally? Who is most likely to understand and act on the argument: "Here's how much we have improved performance so far. Now, without any additional money, but merely the flexibility to allocate our people in innovative ways, we can improve it further to here." The leadership could take this logic to the president of the agency's union and the chair of the house appropriations committee. These two individuals might be convinced—particularly if each was convinced that the other was convinced—to permit a little experimentation, provided it did improve performance and did not abuse any of the union's members. In the process, the union president and the appropriations chair would become charter members of the charter team.

The agency's leaders would not, of course, talk about creating a charter agency. They would simply talk about improved performance. They would not ask the appropriations chair for some new kind of formal status. Instead, they would simply ask for some help to ratchet up performance another notch—for some minor flexibility on personnel ceilings that could be added as boilerplate to the agency's next appropriations bill. That's all. Nothing big. Nothing fancy. Nothing to alarm anyone. Nothing that might appear precedent-setting. Just some help in improving performance.

Then the leadership team has to make good on its part of this accountability bargain. The agency must continue to treat all of its employees fairly. And it has to produce the promised improvements in performance.

If the agency does so—if it reciprocates the flexibility granted it by the union and appropriations committee—it will have created the core of its performance team, its accountability team, its charter team. The agency has found some people who have been willing to commit to the collective task of improving the agency's performance. They may not think of themselves as members of a compact. They certainly don't have a formal "charter." But each of these two key members of the agency's accountability environment has recognized the benefits to be gained by their mutual cooperation and has been willing to commit some of his or her limited authority to make an essential trade-off—less rule-constrained accountability for fairness in return for more results-driven accountability for performance. Each will have decided to "sign up."

Recruiting People to "Sign Up"

In *The Soul of a New Machine,* the Pulitzer Prize–winning study of the creation of a new minicomputer at Data General, Tracy Kidder described this concept of "signing up" and how it worked. Signing up was a commitment, he explained: "By signing up for the project you agreed to do whatever was necessary for success." For example, Kidder reports that one engineer, Chuck Holland, had helped another, Carl Alsing, choose the Microteam, organize and carefully review its work, and mediate important battles. But why? "Nobody had ordered him to do all this," reports Kidder. "Alsing had made the opportunity available, and Holland had signed up." Organizations are held together, writes Kidder, by "webs of voluntary mutual responsibility, the product of many signings-up."[20] In real organizations, each individual has a responsibility to everyone else—not just to superiors but also to subordinates and peers. Thus the job of the leader is less to give orders than to convince people to sign up.

No one can order anyone else to join an agency's charter team. People have to volunteer. People have to sign up. But even within hierarchical organizations, volunteering works better than an order. Thus, even in business, people are rarely ordered to do things.[21] Instead, they "sign up" to do them. Moreover, this signing-up is much more powerful than an order; in signing up to do something, the individual makes a personal commitment to produce the result.

Thus, in creating a charter team, the challenge is to get people to sign up—to convince them to voluntarily accept a responsibility to every other member of the team. Yet this may not be quite as difficult as it sounds. The leaders of the effort can exploit what Brown calls "unexamined optimism that draws others into an organized effort."[22] Indeed, before approaching anyone about joining the charter team, the leadership of the agency should noticeably improve performance, thereby creating such "unexamined optimism."

Moreover, people who already want to improve the agency's performance may well recognize both the necessity of some kind of charter team and the difficulty in patching together the initial core members. And, as Brown suggests, this may be an advantage: "Paradoxically, the conditional nature of cooperation is a strength, not a weakness, when enlisting others' cooperation. After all, if everyone else is going to do something why do they need me? But if my cooperation is important for enlisting or maintaining others' cooperation, then I become important, not just marginal."[23] Each potential member of the charter team may well recognize that his or her contribution is essential. Each may recognize that if he or she doesn't do something, performance will not improve. They may not be willing to do more than their "fair share." But they may also accept that, as charter members of the charter team, their "fair" burden will be greater than that borne by later joiners.

Still, the nascent leaders of the effort and the core of the charter team will bear the greatest burden of all. They must be "unconditional cooperators"— people, explains Dennis Chong, "whose actions are not contingent upon the actions of others." In his effort to discover "whether rational people will participate in public-spirited collective action," Chong found that these unconditional cooperators "are usually needed to initiate collective action. Such individuals step into the breach and pay the heavy start-up costs, while everyone else waits for more favorable circumstances before contributing."[24] A charter agency will never be evolved by conditional cooperators who are unwilling to do any more than the minimum fair share.

Thinking about the challenge of getting an abstract collection of individuals to join together in an abstract compact of mutual and collective accountability is very difficult. How do you start? With whom do you start? Such questions cannot be answered in the abstract. They can only be answered in a specific context: a specific performance challenge with a concrete history, particular problems and special opportunities; specific people, with specific interests, objectives, idiosyncrasies, and patterns of behavior associated with specific institutions with their own interests, idiosyncrasies, histories, and patterns of behavior. For the abstract problem, there is no obvious place to start; indeed, there is no way to start. For each specific problem, however, the specifics suggest possibilities: People to talk with first. The issues to raise first (and the ones to avoid). The self-interests, altruistic objectives, or personal resentments to appeal to first. The obvious issue, prominent personality, visible organization or other conspicuous feature to focus on first.[25] These will be only guesses; but from knowledge of the specifics, they can be intelligent guesses.

People who do sign up for a charter team are not, however, likely to defect. They became charter members of the charter team because they cared about improving the agency's performance. Thus, explains Albert Hirschman in his classic book *Exit, Voice, and Loyalty*, each will continue "to care about the activity and 'output' of the organization *even after he has left it."* Any member is free to defect from the charter team, but he or she is not free from caring about the team's success in improving performance. This means, Hirschman argues, that *"full exit is impossible."* Moreover, such members, *"especially the more influential ones,"* will recognize that *"the organization to which they belong would go from bad to worse if they left."* They realize that their defection would actually contribute to the "deterioration in the quality of the organization's output."[26]

Consequently, to the extent that the few core members who have signed up for the charter team care deeply about improving the performance of "their" agency, the compact may be less fragile than it initially appears. Each member of the charter team may recognize that many of those in the agency's accountability environment (journalists and auditors, for example) will never join them in a full-fledged compact of mutual, collective responsibility. At the same time, each of them will also recognize that the team's collective ability to evolve a charter agency, to gain some flexibility, and to improve performance depends purely on the team's effort, which, in turn, depends significantly on his or her own personal effort. To the few members of the charter team, to those who are dedicated to improving the agency's performance, defection may simply not be an option.

The Search for Small Wins

What next? The agency's leadership, the union leadership, and the chair of the House Appropriations Committee have formed the core of the charter team. What is the next logical incremental step in improving agency performance: What should be the next performance target? What additional flexibility or resource does the agency need to achieve these additional results?

The charter team needs what Karl Weick, long of Cornell University, calls "a strategy of small wins." Weick suggests that "social problems seldom get solved, because people define these problems in ways that overwhelm their ability to do anything about them," which creates feelings of "frustration" and "helplessness." In contrast, he argues, "the prospect of a small win has an immediacy, tangibility, and controllability." Consequently, Weick recommends that we break our big problems down into "a series of controllable opportunities of modest size that produce visible results." When one small win has been achieved, he suggests, "forces are set in motion that favor another small win."[27] Indeed, these forces create advantages both internally and externally.

Within an agency, the series of small wins builds competence and confidence. People are no longer intimidated by their ambitious mission, which
appears to exceed their meager capabilities. Small, specific, achievable targets, Weick argues, give people "an opportunity for visible success from
which they draw confidence." Indeed, he continues, "small wins are stable
building blocks"; they "preserve gains." Further, "small wins are like minia-
ture experiments"; the "feedback is immediate and can be used to revise
theories." And a history of small wins provides people with "assurance of
success" in the future.[28]

A series of small wins also helps an agency to establish, among those in its
accountability environment, a reputation for competence. Each win, Weick
confesses, "may seem unimportant." Nevertheless, he declares, "small wins
have power." In a city like Washington, occupied with "people with short
time perspectives," Weick argues, small wins have an advantage because they
are "compact, tangible, upbeat, noncontroversial, and relatively rare." And a
series of visible successes, he continues "reveals a pattern that may attract
allies, deter opponents, and lower resistance to subsequent proposals."[29] A
series of small wins can convince key people to join the charter team.

This small-wins approach, reports the National Academy of Public Administration, was adopted by the creators of the Oregon Option. For example, the group that was focusing on child health "developed a timetable for
achieving measurable progress. They wanted to show tangible results
quickly in order to build confidence in the process and gain support for the
longer-term challenges." Thus they identified three performance targets that
they could achieve in two years.[30]

As a charter team grows, it may experience some difficulty attracting
new members. Initially, its small core will be able to exploit its sense of
group identity and common purpose. But each new set of members may be
less committed. Every member of the charter team will have multiple and
conflicting affiliations and norms. Each new member, however, will realize
that his or her individual contribution is not as essential to the survival of
the charter team. Thus, as the charter team grows, its core members will
need to employ additional membership appeals. They may not be able to
provide many extrinsic advantages, but they can offer the intrinsic benefit
of being associated with a high-performing team that (at least within the
agency's accountability environment) has developed some social or professional status.

Weick's "logic of small wins" is similar to Schaffer's emphasis on "a series
of breakthrough projects" focused on "short-term performance improve-

ments" that "establish a pattern of success and a sense of momentum."[31] The organization never overpromises.[32] It simply undertakes yet another project designed to improve performance in a small but obvious way, building both internal capacity and external respect, and creating the opportunity to do it all over again.[33]

The Curse of Becoming an Official Charter Agency

At no time, however, should the agency's leadership or the charter team seek to be designated an *official* Charter Agency. They don't need this. They already have what they want. They have managed to slowly trade their increased accountability for performance for some flexibility in their regulations for finances and fairness. They have been careful to keep accurate books and avoid contracts that would cause obvious embarrassment, while managing to win some freedom in how they deployed their financial resources. They have been careful to treat citizens and employees fairly, while managing to win some freedom from the complicated regulations that limit their ability to get the most productivity from their employees and collaborators.

So why would they want the legislature to give them some new, distinctive status as a Charter Agency? In fact, they don't want this. Such a formal designation would only draw attention to all of the flexibility they have already earned. If they still need some additional flexibility, they need to evolve further the membership of their charter team. They need to determine what kind of additional freedom they really need, discover who in their accountability environment needs to approve it (both officially and informally, administratively and politically), and then figure out how to recruit these individuals to their mini, but growing, responsibility compact.

A state government (or a municipal government or a federal department) could have a number of charter agencies, and yet no one in the state capitol would be using the term. That's because each such responsibility compact would have evolved in its own way: Each would have made some initial improvements in performance, created its own charter team, gained some flexibility, improved performance some more, expanded its membership, gained some additional flexibility, improved performance again, and continued winning flexibility that it converted into improved performance. Each would have evolved its own distinct strategy of small wins. Each would look quite different. Each would be using its own unique language. These charter agencies would not exist because the state legislature enacted the

"Charter Agency Act." These mini responsibility compacts would not have been formally sanctioned by the Governor's Commission on Performance Accountability. They would have just evolved.[34]

An abstract discussion about trading enhanced results-driven accountability for less rule-obsessed accountability for finances and fairness will go nowhere: Why can't you have all three? Why can't you follow the rules for finances and fairness *and* also improve performance? This kind of theoretical debate accomplishes little.

A charter agency will only gain flexibility in the rules governing its accountability for finances and fairness by accepting more accountability for performance. Only by first demonstrating more accountability for performance—by achieving new levels of performance—would a potential charter agency manage to win some specific but narrow flexibility in the rules for finances or fairness. This flexibility comes not from an abstract debate. It evolves from a series of small but specific *quid pro quo*s. Every time the charter team gains some additional flexibility, it does so by committing itself to a new level of performance. And the members of the charter team are able to make this bargain—to convince the people charged with ensuring accountability for finances and fairness—because they have already demonstrated their ability to make good on their part of the bargain. To evolve a charter agency, the charter team has to practice tit-for-tat reciprocity.

Democracy and the Choice of Performance Targets

Who decides what results are to be produced? Or as Alasdair Roberts asks in an analysis of performance-based organizations, "Who sets performance targets?"[35] These will be determined through negotiation. But who gets to sit at the bargaining table?

For a charter agency, it is the members of the charter team—or, eventually, the members of the (bigger but still mini) compact of mutual, collective responsibility—who choose the next performance targets. The people who will authorize the additional resources and increased flexibility needed to achieve the next performance target will also select it. After all, the three items—resources, flexibility, and performance target—have to make a coherent whole. It makes little sense to assign a particular goal to an organization without creating the capacity to achieve this goal. Thus, whenever the charter team considers taking on a slightly more ambitious goal—one for which the current members of the team are unable to provide the essential resources—it needs to seek new members. Thus the members whom it recruits next will be the ones to set the new target; for they will be the ones who will provide the necessities for achieving it.

Still, each new increase in performance is a small one. Thus any increase in resources or flexibility is similarly incremental. As a result, only a few people may care about this small supplement. Who will hold hearings to expose as a budget-breaker an extra one-percent funding increase for an agency with a reputation for competence? Who will call a press conference to denounce as evil some small flexibility that has been granted to an agency with a track record of success? Yes: Even a one-percent increase in spending will be contested at every step in the budget process. And those guardians of the overhead regulations will oppose any deviation from strict obedience. Still, in a world of constant battles over resources and flexibility, who will decide to devote their limited resources fighting a coalition of forces that promises to use small increments in flexibility and resources to produce yet another increment in performance?

But wait: Isn't this undemocratic? Shouldn't the elected officials set the performance targets? Who do the self-appointed members of the charter team think they are? Who selected them to establish the agency's mission and goals? Aren't we talking about *democratic* accountability? When does the *democracy* come in? When does the citizenry get its say?

The answer, of course, lies in our American structure of democracy.[36] The charter team necessarily consists of many of the key actors in the agency's accountability environment. Some will be legislators. Certainly *they* are legitimate; they were elected by citizens. Some may be executive-branch officials appointed by the elected chief executive. They, too, possess democratic legitimacy—at least if they carry out the direct orders or pursue the general wishes of their elected boss. Some may be civil servants, chosen for their expertise and their willingness to follow the guidance of elected officials. Given their insulation from electoral decisions, however, their democratic accountability is suspect. Some will be key stakeholders. They, however, do not represent the citizens; instead, they represent very particular organizations with narrow and personal interests. We call these *special* interests. What role do they have in *democratic* accountability?

As the charter team becomes more successful and evolves into a mini responsibility compact, it will naturally meet with more challenges. As the charter agency continues to ratchet up its performance, as its accomplishments and performance targets become more significant, it will become more visible. And because many of the traditional accountability holders—journalists, auditors, inspectors general, and prosecutors—will never join a responsibility compact, the charter agency will face more examinations of its operations.

The charter agency's strategy of small wins cannot last forever. If the charter team is effective, its wins will accumulate. And so will its flexibility. Eventually, people will take notice. And, if the charter agency has accumulated significant relief from a number of financial and fairness regulations, people will begin to ask questions: Is this ambitious agency really accountable for its handling of the public's money? Is this agency really accountable for treating citizens fairly? Has it abused its discretion? Does it really need all of this flexibility?

A strategy of small wins is an effective way to improve performance. A strategy of small wins is an effective way to earn flexibility. But a strategy of small wins will not protect a public agency from scrutiny. Indeed, a successful strategy of small wins will eventually increase a public agency's visibility and thus expose it to more scrutiny—and that scrutiny will focus not only on its flexibility from the rules but also on its choice of performance targets.[37]

The democratic accountability for the selection of performance targets will come not through prior approval but through after-the-fact scrutiny.

The Demand for Consistency

Bureaucracies love consistency. If you can't have consistency, how can you have bureaucracy? Bureaucracies have rules, lots of rules, rules designed to ensure consistency—to ensure that in similar situations all parts of the bureaucracy behave consistently. How can a large department with lots of agencies have some charter agencies with one set of rules and some ordinary agencies with a different set of rules? Wouldn't that be inconsistent?

Yes. That is why the overhead units in any large governmental organization won't like the charter-agency concept. "If we grant some extra discretion to one agency," goes their argument, "we'll have to grant it to everyone."

Moreover, the overhead units will fight very hard for their consistency. They have to. Their raison d'être is the regulation of the line agencies. Their job is to ensure that the line agencies all behave consistently. If a few of these line agencies become charter agencies, each with a different set of rules, what purpose will the overhead units serve? Why even bother to have overhead units?

Thus, even once a charter agency is established, the overhead units will still fight its discretion. They will go looking for abuses of discretion—or even for minor inconsistencies that make the department look bad. Meanwhile, they will be continually bombarded by requests from the remaining ordinary, non-charter agencies for an exemption from this rule or that: "If that agency doesn't have to abide by this rule, why do we have to?" To resolve such inconsistencies, the overhead units will attempt to pull some discretion back from the charters.

Then the fight may escalate to the department head. At this level, a charter agency will need political protection. Unless the agency has a political godfather, its only political protection will come from its performance. To maintain its flexibility, a charter agency will need to demonstrate improved performance—consistently and repeatedly improved performance.

Bureaucratic consistency is a powerful norm. It resonates with everyone. It resonates with legislators, citizens, stakeholders, journalists, and auditors. It resonates with almost everyone in a public agency's accountability environment. Even those who seek improved performance—even those who recognize that bureaucratic, lowest-common-denominator rules hamper performance—will still appreciate the norm of consistency.

A charter agency will never defeat the demand for consistency. For a charter agency, it will be a war without end—a war that it can never win. The overhead units may win a decisive battle (by reorganizing the charter agency out of existence), but the charter agency can never experience the same kind of conclusive victory. Sometimes a charter agency will be attacked by some sneaky guerrillas who create a new set of rules that just happen to undermine much of the charter agency's well-won flexibility. Sometimes a charter agency will face a full-scale artillery bombardment at a legislative hearing. Regardless, a charter agency—and its exemption from some rules—will be constantly under attack. The charter agency can win battles, but it can never win the war.

To cope with these unremitting attacks, a charter agency will have to launch repeated counteroffensives. It will need to constantly remind everyone in its accountability environment of its performance—of its continually improving performance. It will have to issue periodic reports.[38] It will have to constantly hold special events to dramatize its success. It can never let up. In the never-ending war with the champions of consistency, a charter agency will need to constantly remind everyone that a key to its performance is its freedom from oppressive rules.[39]

The Inevitability of Mistakes

Everyone makes mistakes. Every organization makes mistakes. Doctors and hospitals make mistakes. Only a small percentage of their diagnostic and treatment decisions are mistakes. Yet, in a report titled *To Err Is Human*, the Institute of Medicine concluded that, every year, such mistakes kill between 44,000 and 98,000 hospitalized Americans.[40]

With the charter agency's increased flexibility—with political executives, career managers, frontline workers, middle managers, and collaborators empowered to exercise initiative—a few people will make mistakes. Even if the percentage of these entrepreneurs who make mistakes is very small, the number of such errors can still be quite significant. What happens then? "Initiative and empowerment will entail mistakes," write Guy Peters and Donald Savoie, "and many of them will be highly visible in the media."[41]

When this happens, how will the charter team respond? How will the advocates of the new public management respond? "Unless the civil service sees that the political leadership is willing to spend political capital to make the reforms work," argue Peters and Savoie, these initiatives "will peter out."[42]

Do the political leaders visibly support the civil servant who employed the approved flexibility? Do they rally round the agency manager who exercised the authorized discretion? Do they publicly defend the official who made an honest (if, in hindsight, obvious) mistake? Or do they set these few, vulnerable individuals up to take the fall? Everyone will be watching. When an aggressive chair of a legislative committee holds a hearing, will the political sponsors of the charter agency attend the hearing, sit next to the victims, and forcefully defend their efforts to improve performance? This is the test.

Existing Charter Agencies

The American federal system has evolved numerous charter agencies— agencies that used their improved performance to gain some measure of flexibility, which they plowed back into even better performance, which earned them still more flexibility. No one calls them charter agencies. They are just public organizations that are managed more effectively and led more creatively.[43]

Many suburban school systems are charter agencies. They aren't charter schools. But each has entered into an informal, implicit compact of mutual and collective responsibility with its town's citizens. The school system implicitly promises performance: We will prepare your children to get into college and perform well when they get there. The school system might even promise: We will prepare your children to get into an elite college and to perform well when they get there. In return, the town promises additional financing and flexibility.

The school system is still accountable for finances and fairness. The town can't eliminate any of the rules imposed by the legislature or the state department of education. The school system has to abide by all of the state's accounting rules, and it has to use the funds it receives from the state for their designated purposes. It has to abide by the personnel rules the state establishes for its school districts. But by providing extra tax revenues, the citizens provide their school system with some freedom from the more onerous constraints imposed by the accountability rules for finances and fairness.

A middle-class community that wants better-than-average results from its schools can clearly trade some flexibility for some additional accountability for performance. By raising their taxes and putting them into the schools, the citizens provide fungible resources that can be deployed to attack particular performance problems. Indeed, these same taxes can help lessen the personnel constraints, for although the school system may have to follow the state's rules whenever it hires a teacher, the extra funds can help it to hire the teachers with the skills it really needs.[44]

Have the town's citizens complained about this extra flexibility? Not at all. Mostly they complain when their "charter agency" fails to produce its promised results—when the school superintendent fails to convert their extra taxes into improved educational performance.

If you want to become a charter agency—if you want to offer increased accountability for performance in exchange for fewer rules and constraints for finances and fairness—you had better make good on the deal. You had better produce the promised improvement in performance.

11

360-Degree Accountability for Performance

W hat do we mean by accountability? Whatever we mean today by the concept and process of accountability, it is—in practice—very linear, hierarchical, and unidirectional. The simple phrase we use—"hold people accountable"—dramatizes the character of the relationship. One person is holding another person accountable. There is an accountability holder and an accountability holdee—an accountability punisher and an accountability punishee. It is a superior-subordinate relationship. The superior holds the subordinate accountable. The superior punishes the subordinate. The subordinate has no rights or leverage. The subordinate can only cringe in fear.

What is accountability? Is it answerability—the public official's duty to explain and justify actions? Is it rules—a mechanism for preventing public officials from violating the public interest? Is it punishment—our collective need to penalize violations of the rules? Is it saluting—the faithful implementation of orders from hierarchical superiors? Or might it be responsibility—the moral obligation to work collectively with public employees, collaborators from nonprofit and for-profit organizations, and citizens in pursuit of the public interest?

What might accountability be? Is the accountability that we Americans have created through historical evolution right for today?[1] Is the accountability that we created for limited government—with limited aspirations, limited powers, and limited reach—applicable to contemporary government for which citizens have developed hefty expectations? Is the account-ability that we created for finances and fairness appropriate for perform-ance? Is the accountability that we created for hierarchical, governmental bureaucracies suitable for collaborative arrangements among public and private organizations? Is the accountability we created for a world in which administration merely but scientifically implemented policies relevant for an era in which we seek to improve performance through empowerment and flexibility in combination with entrepreneurship and innovation?

Or do we need to rethink our theory of democratic accountability and redesign how this accountability might work? As Edward Weber of Washington State University asks, "What does an effective system of ac-countability look like in a world of decentralized governance, shared power, collaborative decision processes, results-oriented management, and broad civic participation?"[2]

360-Degree Evaluation

In most large organizations, superiors regularly evaluate their subordinates. This annual ritual of performance appraisal is feared by the subordinates and dreaded by the superiors. It often isn't very pleasant and doesn't neces-sarily produce the desired results.[3] Such an "evaluation of performance, merit rating, or annual review," wrote W. Edwards Deming, "nourishes short-term performance, annihilates long-term planning, builds fear, demolishes teamwork, nourishes rivalry and politics." Just in case you thought he was equivocating on the effects of performance appraisals, Deming continues: "It leaves people bitter, crushed, bruised, battered, des-olate, despondent, dejected, feeling inferior, some even depressed, unfit for work for weeks after receipt of rating, unable to comprehend why they are inferior." Moreover, continues Deming, "It is unfair, as it ascribes to the peo-ple in a group differences that may be caused totally by the system that they work in."[4]

Behind performance appraisal lies a theory of human motivation and meritocratic rewards that is widely accepted (if only implicitly). Too often, however, the process fails to produce the desired results. Indeed, it often produces mostly undesirable results. "Not only is the conventional per-formance review failing to make a positive contribution, but in many executives' opinions it can do irreparable harm," writes Rensis Likert, long of the University of Michigan. "The fundamental flaw in current review procedures is that they compel the superior to behave in a threatening, rejecting, and ego-deflating manner with a sizable proportion of his staff."[5] All too often, linear, hierarchical, unidirectional performance appraisal just doesn't work.

From this dissatisfaction evolved the concept of 360-degree feedback. People are not merely evaluated by their hierarchical superior. They are also evaluated by their subordinates, their peers, and the people with whom they have worked on teams. They are evaluated by their internal and external customers as well as by their internal and external suppliers.[6]

The arguments for broadening the number and kind of people who provide evaluative feedback are many and obvious. First, although the boss may have a unique perspective on an individual's performance—particularly on how the individual's responsibilities fit within the organization's overall objectives—peers and subordinates know much more about the details of daily implementation. Multiple perspectives provide a richer understanding of how an individual is performing and of how he or she can improve. Moreover, when people get the same feedback from multiple sources, they are less able to dismiss it as the outgrowth of some minor misunderstanding or personal vendetta. Thus, 360-degree feedback has a greater chance of helping people to gain some self-awareness of their own behavior and to change it.[7] Moreover, 360-degree feedback can help the organization to make better choices about individual training and personnel development, as well as to improve organizational strategy and change organizational culture.[8]

This feedback is not just about evaluation. Primarily, 360-degree feedback is about performance—about improving performance. It is designed to help individuals improve their performance—to give them a clear picture of what they need to do to improve their personal performance. Moreover, 360-degree feedback is designed to help organizations improve performance—to give the organization's leaders a clear picture of what they need to do to improve organizational performance.

Employing 360-degree feedback doesn't automatically turn people and organizations around. It has its pitfalls and problems.[9] Nevertheless, 360-degree feedback is used extensively by Fortune 500 companies and even in the public sector.[10]

360-Degree Accountability

If organizations—even nominally hierarchical organizations—are employing 360-degree feedback to hold people accountable to a variety of stakeholders in the organization and to help individuals improve their performance (and thus to improve the performance of their organization), might not society employ some kind of 360-degree feedback to accomplish similar purposes? After all, within an organization, 360-degree feedback creates 360-degree accountability. Now people are not just accountable to their boss. They are accountable to their subordinates, peers, team members, customers and suppliers. They are accountable to everyone in their own, personal "accountability environment." Why can't we use a similar kind of 360-degree feedback to ensure that public managers and public agencies—and everyone else engaged in the public's business—are accountable to every other individual in their accountability environment?

In part, of course, we already do. That is how Kevin Kearns developed his concept of the "accountability environment."[11] Public managers and public agencies are accountable not just to their official superior in the governmental hierarchy. In America's pluralistic government, all sorts of people and organizations can legitimately claim to have the right to hold a public manager or public agency accountable.[12]

It is, however, always a superior-subordinate relationship. Only now the subordinate has multiple superiors. Still, this accountability relationship goes only one way: The accountability holders give feedback to their accountability holdee. For *some* public officials, we already have 360-degree accountability. But only for *some*. Others who are engaged in the public's business have zero-degree accountability.

Behind the concept of 360-degree feedback lies the recognition that *everyone* has some useful feedback to give to *everyone else* with whom he or she works. Every individual has the responsibility to accept and act on the feedback he or she receives. Every individual has the responsibility to provide honest and helpful feedback to all of those with whom he or she works.

In the public sector, we have not really created 360-degree accountability. It is more like 360-degree harassment. All of the clients, peers, partners, collaborators, customers, and suppliers get to provide a public agency with feedback. (So do all of the "designated accountability holders." People with this privileged status—call them the DAHs[13]—are assigned the wonderful task of holding other people accountable. But who holds these auditors, inspectors general, and special prosecutors accountable?) These accountability holders do not, however, expect to receive any feedback in return. Indeed, if they received any, they would be shocked and offended, and perhaps retaliate.

If we had true 360-degree accountability, each individual who is part of a public agency's accountability environment would be accountable to all the others. Each individual would have an opportunity to provide accountability feedback to every other person in the accountability environment. Each individual would be answerable to every other individual, Each individual could call another individual to account. Each individual could ask another to explain his or her behavior.

Think of the possibilities: Public managers providing accountability feedback to legislators for assigning vague and contradictory missions to their agencies.[14] Parents explaining to teachers why they neglected to read to their child even once in the last month.[15] Career civil servants providing accountability feedback to their political superiors for failing to provide the support or resources necessary to do their jobs. The regulators in overhead agencies answering to frontline supervisors for creating so many mind-numbing rules. Newspaper editors justifying to legislators why they ran that exposé without checking all of the facts or thinking through all of the ramifications. Political appointees asking legislators to account for their failure to provide the resources necessary to implement a new legislative mandate.

Why should anyone be unaccountable? James March of Stanford University and Johan Olsen of the University of Oslo set forth "the principle that power necessitates accountability." Yet they note that their principle "has not been implemented consistently" for individuals and organizations who function outside of formal government.[16] Nor, I might add, for many inside government too.

Today, if a traditional accountability holdee attempted to provide any such 360-degree feedback, the traditional accountability holders would label such behavior as outrageous, perhaps unethical, maybe even immoral: What makes legislators think that journalists should be accountable to them? What makes public managers think that inspectors general should be accountable to them? What makes teachers think that parents should be accountable to them? What makes public servants think that citizens should be accountable to them?

If we are to rethink democratic accountability, however, we need to do so from ground zero. We need to reconsider our unidirectional concept of accountability. If we are to revise our working doctrine of accountability as punishment, we need to reconsider our attachment to a hierarchical notion of accountability.[17] If we are to eliminate (or at least mitigate) the harm that the current accountability mechanisms for finances and fairness impose on performance, we need to reconsider our implicit division of the population of the accountability environment into two distinct species: the accountability holders and the accountability holdees. If we are to create accountability for performance, we need to accept the principle that everyone in a public agency's accountability environment has some responsibility for helping to improve that performance.[18]

Is it possible to think differently about what we mean by accountability— about what we mean by holding people accountable? Is it possible to think differently about who can hold whom accountable? Is it possible to think less about unidirectional executive-to-legislative accountability; less about unidirectional career-manager-to-political-appointee accountability; less about unidirectional politician-to-journalist accountability? Is it possible to think more about the mutual responsibility of everyone in the entire accountability environment to everyone else? Is it possible to think less about unidirectional, superior-subordinate accountability and more about webs of mutual responsibility? Is it possible to redefine accountability in a way that not only suppresses mistakes and punishes failure but also promotes performance? Is it possible to base accountability less on legally imposed strictures and more on mutually negotiated compacts? Is it possible to create accountability based less on competition and more on cooperation? Is it possible to renegotiate a new definition of shared accountability that binds people together in a web of mutual obligations for achieving accountability for finance, fairness, and performance? Is it possible to create a web of mutual responsibility that maintains our high standards for probity in finances and fairness for people and *also* enhances performance? Is it possible to create 360-degree accountability, including 360-degree accountability for performance?

The Bane of Performance Auditing

If we want to create 360-degree accountability for performance, who has to do what? If 360-degree accountability for performance is such a good idea, how might we foster some of it? Who needs to do what?

In particular, who should do what to compensate for the accountability bias: the inherent proclivity of accountability holders to focus on finances and fairness (and to ignore performance). Because the accountability bias exists—because it is hard-wired into our political behavior—we need to overcompensate for it. If we are unable to bring performance to the forefront of our political concerns, we will never create 360-degree accountability for performance.

An obvious solution is to create institutions with the specific responsibility of establishing accountability for performance. Why not simply create institutions that will ignore (or at least downplay) accountability for finances and fairness and, instead, emphasize accountability for performance? We have a lot of institutions, both within and outside of government that concentrate on finances and fairness. If we could somehow neutralize this explicit institutional bias, perhaps we could overcome our implicit cognitive bias.

More than thirty years ago, management mandarin Peter Drucker argued for such an institution—something that might be called a "performance auditor." "We need something much more urgently" than the auditing of every government agency for abuse of finances, wrote Drucker; we need "the clear definition of the results a policy is expected to produce, and the ruthless examination of results against these expectations." Thus Drucker advocated "an independent agency that compares the results of policies against expectations and that, independent of pressures from the executive as well as from the legislature, reports to the public any program that does not deliver."[19]

In the United States, the nation's chief auditor, the General Accounting Office, has indeed attempted to complement its traditional financial auditing by also examining organizational performance.[20] Moreover, Michael Barzelay of the London School of Economics and Political Science reports that "performance auditing" has become "a widespread phenomenon," though there do exist "important variations among countries" as to exactly what this means.[21]

What is "performance auditing"? Is it auditing the performance data reported by a public agency?[22] Is it auditing the procedures, processes, practices, and behavior of an agency to see whether it did what it promised to do? Is it auditing the procedures, processes, practices, and behavior of an agency to see whether it is following best practice? Or is performance auditing really a performance evaluation that seeks to link causes (an agency's actions) to effects (the societal outcomes that we seek)? Different institutions use the phrase "performance auditing" in quite different ways.[23]

The problem with performance *auditing* is that auditors believe that theirs is the only profession that is capable, authorized, or entitled to do it. And if the auditors manage to convert their version of "performance auditing" into the primary vehicle for creating accountability for performance, performance accountability will become compliance accountability. If this happens, accountability will come to mean nothing more than whether the agency—the performance auditee—has complied with the performance auditor's definition of performance. And for the performance auditor to do its audit, it will have to establish some rules, regulations, standards, or other criteria so that it can audit the agency's records and behavior to determine whether it has indeed complied with the performance criteria.[24]

The problem is that auditors audit. They have been trained to audit. They know how to audit. That is why some auditors could expand their institutional domain from accountability for finances to accountability for fairness. Both involve auditing. Both involve compliance. Both involve checking to see whether the accountability holdees followed the rules.[25]

Similarly, auditors may see an opportunity to expand their institutional domain into accountability for performance. But they will still audit. The only difference will be that, now, they will do performance audits. They will follow the standard operating procedures of the auditing profession, modifying them only as much as is necessary to adapt them to performance. They will still seek to determine whether the auditee has conformed to their performance standards. In the process, they will distort performance accountability, converting it into performance compliance. Consequently, we ought not to even use the phrase "performance audit,"[26] lest we give the auditors the excuse to assert a unique, professional claim to the task of creating performance accountability.

Achieving 360-Degree Accountability for Performance

Performance is qualitatively different from finances and fairness. It is not about compliance. It is not about rules. It is not about compliance with expectations that are defined by well-established rules. Thus we ought to think about creating accountability for performance in a way that is qualitatively different from the method we have employed to create accountability for finances or fairness. We ought not to create institutions with the singular task of being the accountability holders for performance. Nor should we assign this task to an existing institution. We should certainly not let one institution become the official accountability holder for performance. Given the many different perspectives on what good performance means, we ought to create 360-degree accountability by permitting a variety of individuals and institutions to contribute their feedback.

Fortunately, many institutions are already motivated to do this. Some even possess the analytical and political capacity. Universities and think tanks frequently evaluate government programs, policies, and agencies (and they tend to focus on performance rather than finances and fairness). Many stakeholder organizations have the capacity to examine government performance.[27]

Some, however, may need some help with the data. How can we shift our attention from finances and fairness to performance if there are so many more data on finances and fairness? Consequently, we might want to create an institution—an Office of Performance Data?—to collect and publish performance information for different agencies and programs. Such an institution would not be in the business of evaluating the meaning of the data, but it could verify (or report whether it could verify) the data it published.[28] Indeed, various components of the federal government (the Bureau of Justice Statistics, the National Center for Education Statistics, the Bureau of Labor Statistics) do publish data, some of which could be used for performance accountability. Usually, however, such data are social statistics, information that would not be particularly helpful for creating 360-degree accountability for a specific agency's performance.

Our ability to create 360-degree accountability will not, however, depend upon some clever institutional fix. Instead, it requires a mental reorientation. It requires us to get beyond the seductive (but fallacious) distinction between administration and policy—to reject the notion that administration is merely the scientific implementation of a policy by a hierarchical bureaucracy. It requires us to move beyond a fixation with simple accountability for finances and fairness to a more sophisticated conception of accountability for finances, fairness, *and* performance. And it requires us to escape from our simple dichotomous world occupied by accountability holders and accountability holdees. It requires us to immigrate to a more complex universe where every individual and every organization accepts that it ought to be accountable. This would not be some kind of brave new world where a few, select accountability holders rule, but a place where everyone is an accountability holdee (although with some complementary rights and obligations to be an accountability holder). It would be a world in which each individual would have responsibilities to everyone else in his or her personal accountability environment.

The big challenge to creating "360-degree accountability for performance" concerns both the *performance* and the *360-degree* aspects of the concept. The real challenge is not to create institutions with the capability to focus on performance. Instead, the challenge is really two challenges, both of which are more mental than institutional. The first is to recognize that we cannot simply adjust our conceptions about accountability for finances and fairness to create accountability for performance. When thinking about accountability for performance, we have to go back to basics. The second challenge is to recognize that true accountability for performance requires

360-degree accountability. Everyone must be accountable to everyone else. Otherwise, accountability for performance will deteriorate into a finger-pointing blame game.

Compact or Cabal?

One possible way to create 360-degree accountability is with a compact of mutual, collective responsibility. Within such a responsibility compact every member would, indeed, be accountable to everyone else.

But what about to outsiders? Will the members of such a responsibility compact also conclude that they should be accountable to those who have not signed on to the agreement? Will those in the compact accept that they should be accountable to citizens? Or will they possess a sense of personal accountability to their fellow members only? What will prevent such a compact from deteriorating into a cabal?

After all, one purpose of the compact is to deflect the public discussion about government from a narrow focus on small errors. The benign rationale for doing this is that such small errors consume much time, energy and resources, are insignificant compared to the necessity of improving performance, and discourage the experimentation that can produce innovations. But a less benign consequence of deflecting discussion from small errors could be that people become adept at hiding these errors and then graduate from hiding small ones to suppressing public awareness of significant deficiencies and large failures.

Can a compact of mutual, collective responsibility become nothing more than a cabal of narrow, selfish corruption? The advocates of the new public management argue that decentralized flexibility will improve performance. But it can also abet corruption. Lydia Segal of the John Jay College of Criminal Justice warns that "unless the new public management addresses the potential for corruption, it may unleash scandals that will generate pressure for top-down controls."[29]

Three decades ago, New York City decentralized its highly bureaucratic school system, in part to give it the flexibility and responsiveness to improve performance.[30] "The hope was that government would be forced to be accountable," observes Segal. "Local boards were to hold educators accountable by controlling district jobs, budgets, programs, and policies." Yet, she continues, "an important, unintended consequence of political decentralization was corruption." Specifically, Segal reports, "a majority of the city's 32 school boards carved their districts into fiefdoms where jobs were doled out to loyal campaign workers, lovers, and family or sold for cash." Another consequence was poor performance.[31]

How did this happen? Segal's basic answer is quite simple: "It is easier to engage in corruption when no one is watching," she explains. "The more discretion a system accords its officials without providing concomitant oversight or accountability, the farther it will move from facilitating corruption to inviting or even necessitating it." The New York City school system was divided not into charter schools but into what might be called charter districts. Yet Segal concludes that this "experience with school decentralization suggests that increasing discretion while decreasing oversight will only give employees additional opportunities for abuse with lower risks of detection."[32]

A cabal is—by definition—a secret cabal. Secrecy is what permits a cabal to form. Secrecy is what permits a cabal to function. A cabal needs secrecy. It needs to keep its deliberations and workings secret. And thus a cabal is—by definition—not accountable.

"Secrecy has been the great enemy of accountability," writes Garry Wills of Northwestern University. Indeed, he argues, secrecy gives us "the worst of both worlds—no accountability *and* no efficiency"—that is, no accountability for finances and fairness *and* no accountability for performance. Accountability is designed to "reassure the public that its interests are being properly served." Yet, Wills continues, secrecy does precisely the opposite: "Withholding information creates a general air of suspicion that has corroded public trust in government."[33] When does a compact of responsibility become a cabal of corruption? Answer: When it can operate in secret.

The history of American government is replete with cabals. Indeed, one of the basic objectives of traditional public administration was to create a cadre of civil servants whose professional ethics would ensure that they could not be seduced into joining such a cabal. In addition, the multiple rules for finances, personnel, procurement, and service delivery were designed to thwart any cabal. So were the requirements for public disclosure. Traditional public administration obligates public agencies to report on their adherence to the rules for finances, personnel, procurement, and service delivery. Such reporting—combined with the auditing done by accountability holders—inhibits secrecy and thus suppresses the temptation to form a cabal.

Moreover, recent additions to the accountability arsenal have created extra insurance. Sunshine laws and freedom-of-information acts are designed to ensure that government does not act in secret. And technology—from the photocopy machine to the Internet—helps spread what might once have remained secret. Today, unlike a century ago, public officials have a difficult time keeping their activities secret. Even national security secrets are reported on the front page.

Still, secrecy happens. Thus cabals happen. How can they be prevented? From her analysis of corruption in the New York City schools, Lydia Segal offers a number of suggestions. Some emphasize traditional accountability-holding mechanisms: "set up a central system for monitoring and investigation to deter wrongdoing"; "launch investigations"; "strengthen law enforcement." But her first suggestion is to "block corruption incentives by holding executives accountable for results." Why? Because, she found, nothing happened to the members of the district school boards when their schools failed to educate; indeed, the political system insulated the board members from any consequences for poor performance. Writes Segal: "If executives faced real consequences for doing poorly, including dismissal, and were rewarded for doing well, they would have incentives to hire the best people and make sure resources were not illegally siphoned off."[34]

Rethinking Accountability for Finances and Fairness

One critique of our accountability mechanisms for finances and fairness is that they inhibit performance. A more devastating critique is that these mechanisms don't work. They do not create accountability for finances or for fairness. After all, American government is full of people who abuse their power when dealing with citizens or handling their money:[35]

— In the U.S. Bureau of Land Management, employees profited from their agency's program for adopting wild horses and burros, paying reduced prices for the animals and then selling them for slaughter.[36]

— In the Indiana Family and Social Services Administration, an accountant was accused of embezzling $680,000—of using his computer access and skills to create fictitious child support cases, to send money to his various lovers, and then to delete the evidence.[37]

— In Massachusetts, the deputy treasurer, two other state employees, and four citizens were indicted for stealing $9.5 million from the state's Unpaid Check Fund.[38]

— In Durham, North Carolina, two police officers were accused of stealing $2,200 from two men in a traffic stop that the police department admitted should not have happened.[39]

From memory, each of us can produce a long list of public officials who violated both the explicit rules and the implicit norms for using the public's
money and for dealing with citizens.[40]

For traditional accountability holders, this is good news: Our existing
systems of accountability uncover numerous public officials who have violated some rule for finances or fairness. These offenders both create immediate work and justify continued employment. Unfortunately, our accountability systems fail to deter many violators and thus fail to eliminate the
problem. Indeed, the never-ending list of accountability violators suggests
that for real deterrence we need some new accountability concepts.

Yet how have we responded to each new scandal? Whenever we uncover
a failure in finances or fairness, we consistently choose to add more accountability rules and more accountability holders rather than to rethink
our concept of accountability. Creating new accountability holders is relatively cheap; it merely requires us to hire another, visible accountability
holder and staff a relatively small office.[41] And creating new rules is even
cheaper. As Frank Anechiarico and James Jacobs observe:

> Fiscal crisis and competition for scarce resources impose limits on the
> creation and maintenance of anticorruption mechanisms. However,
> scarce resources do not limit the proliferation of new laws and rules.
> It is always possible, and even advantageous, for politicians to throw
> law at a problem. By doing so, they can make a symbolic statement
> without expending significant resources.[42]

Yet such symbols do little to improve the probity of public officials.

Why do we assume that promulgating a new accountability rule or creating a new accountability holder to enforce an existing accountability rule
is the best way to enhance accountability for finances or for fairness? This
approach has clearly proven inadequate.[43]

Why do we assume that people will respect each individual rule when
everyone recognizes that the collectivity of rules is both internally contradictory and operationally absurd? Why would creating more rules—or
more aggressively enforcing the existing rules—encourage public officials to
take seriously their obligations to treat citizens fairly and handle their
money carefully? Why would creating more rules encourage more respect
for the rules when everyone working within the system recognizes that the
only way to survive, let alone accomplish anything, is to selectively ignore

the more absurd ones? In reality, the proliferation of rules fosters disrespect for all of the rules.[44]

Rethinking democratic accountability means rethinking our accountability mechanisms for deterring and preventing—not just for catching and punishing—those with the power or opportunity to violate our expectations for finances and fairness. In attempting to create an accountability system that promotes performance, we should not discard or emaciate our systems for creating accountability for finances or fairness. Instead, we need to rethink how we might actually ensure that public officials are duly diligent about finances, fairness, and performance.

The Conical Pendulum of Accountability

Any political system oscillates. Thus a traditional political metaphor is the pendulum. The accountability pendulum, some might argue, has swung too far in one direction. It has emphasized finances and fairness over performance. It has emphasized process over results. Consequently, we need to nudge it back toward the middle: We ought to accept a little less accountability for finances and fairness so that we can get a lot more accountability for performance.

This traditional metaphor is, however, too simplistic. The concept of an accountability pendulum suggests that any improvement in accountability for performance will automatically come at the expense of reduced accountability for finances and fairness. This accountability pendulum, to continue using this metaphor, is what in physics is labeled a "simple pendulum." It swings in a single plane (say, from east to west and back to east). At the eastern apogee on this pendulum's arc lies the maximum accountability for finances and fairness (and the minimum accountability for performance); at the other, western end of the arc lies maximum accountability for performance (and the minimum for finances and fairness).

A simple pendulum swings exclusively in a single plane. A conical pendulum, however, can swing east and west and, simultaneously, north and south. It can swing to the northeast, or to the northwest, or to the southeast. It can trace out complex patterns. And if you choose as your metaphor the conical pendulum, you can think about it swinging in a direction (say, to the northeast) that provides more accountability for performance *and* more accountability for finances and fairness.

Our approach to accountability for finances and fairness is a complex accumulation of rules, a collection of people to catch those who violate these rules, and a mélange of legal and extralegal methods for punishing the violators. This is hardly a "system." It is just a hodge-podge assembled over many years with each new component piled on top of its predecessors.[45]

If we really want to improve accountability for finances, we ought to obliterate the current system and start over. We ought to attempt to define what we expect of public officials in the handling of our money. We ought to examine the circumstances under which they abide by the spirit (not just the letter) of these expectations. Then we ought to develop basic values, generic strategies, and particular mechanisms that can foster such behavior.[46]

At the same time, we ought to take a serious look at the ways public officials have abused these expectations. We ought to analyze the circumstances under which individuals have violated not only specific rules for handling finances but also the universal principles behind these rules. Then we ought to devise the values, strategies, and mechanisms that can inhibit such impropriety.

We ought to do the same for fairness—although our expectations for what we mean by fairness are much more diverse than our expectations for finances.

The challenge will be to create a real accountability system—a coherent system, an effective system—not just to add to the existing jumble of accountability laws and accountability holders. For if we continue with our traditional approach, every contributor to the discussion can quickly think of another way that someone can somehow violate our expectations. Thus every individual can make a forceful argument for including another little, yet obviously "essential" rule to deter and catch such potential, if rare, behavior. But why should we think that an accountability system is simply a collection of rules? Why should we think that an accountability system is rules combined with punishment for violations? Why should we make this our implicit yet operating definition of accountability?

How can we create 360-degree accountability for performance? The answer is not to assign specific individuals to perform specific tasks. Instead, we need to change significantly our individual and collective thinking. We need to accept that accountability is not just about finances and fairness, but about finances, fairness, *and* performance. Traditional hierarchical accountability might make sense for finances and fairness. It might even make some sense when results are something that one person or one unit produces. It does not make sense, however, in a nonhierarchical world of collaboratives. Thus we need a new mental model of accountability; we need to shift from the implicit conception of linear, hierarchical, uni-directional, holder-holdee accountability to an explicit recognition that we need mutual and collective accountability. And we need to do both of these things simultaneously—to shift our accountability emphasis from finances and fairness to finances, fairness, and performance while rethinking what accountability (for all three) might mean.

Balancing Punishments with Rewards

In a book devoted to examining which public officials should be punished for what offenses, Dennis Thompson notes:

> In their efforts to hold officials accountable, citizens should care as much about honoring faithful officials as condemning felonious ones. . . . [T]he sanction of reward offers several benefits that punishment does not. . . . A system of reward could also help check the dangers of overdeterrence by counterbalancing the excessive caution that officials are said to show when working under the threat of the criminal sanction.[47]

Linguistically, the phrase "sanction of reward" is a contradiction, an oxymoron. Look up the word *sanction* in the dictionary. Mine offers several definitions, including:

— "the detriment, loss of reward, or coercive intervention annexed to a violation of a law as a means of enforcing the law."
— "a mechanism of social control for enforcing a society's standards."
—"an economic or military coercive measure adopted by several nations in concert for enforcing a society's standards."[48]

"A mechanism of social control" *could* be a reward as well as a punishment; but nothing in the other definitions of *sanction* suggests that it might be. Moreover, colloquially, the word *sanction* hardly conjures up the concept of a reward. When people talk about sanctioning a welfare recipient or a nation, they are talking about punishing the person or nation for violating some established rule or norm. If we want to create a concept of accountability that includes both punishments *and* rewards, we need to avoid using the word *sanction* to encompass all of the possible consequences.

Lydia Segal emphasizes not just punishments for doing poorly but also rewards for doing well. For if we continue to employ punishments for failure as the only accountability consequence, we will continue to explicitly encourage public officials to devote their full attention and resources to avoiding any failure to follow the rules for finances and fairness. We will do little to encourage them to worry about improving performance. Sanctions—that is, punishment—can only serve to reinforce the accountability bias.

Experimentation, Experience, and Evolution

By empowering civil servants to be responsive to citizens, by giving civil servants the authority to make innovative decisions, the advocates of a new public management seek to produce better results. But what about accountability? What might accountability for results look like? How might it work? The advocates of the new public management need not only to demonstrate that their strategy for organizing the apparatus of government is more effective or efficient. They also need to explain how it is accountable. They have to answer the accountability question for performance:

Q Is it possible to permit empowered, responsive civil servants to make decisions and be innovative and still have democratic accountability?

They have yet to do so.

The traditional systems of accountability were designed to establish and enhance the public's trust in government's probity. Now we need a new system of accountability to establish and enhance the public's trust in government's performance. The advocates of the new public management paradigm have a responsibility to help evolve a new paradigm of democratic accountability.

This is not a trivial task. After all, creating democratic accountability for process has not been easy. We Americans have been working at this for more than two centuries and still have not produced a completely satisfactory answer. The mechanisms that we have established to ensure accountability for process do not always work. Moreover, they have multiple, unintended consequences.

Our current mechanisms for establishing accountability are the product of years of experimentation and evolution.[49] Similarly, our future system of accountability will evolve only through experimentation.[50] We will not resolve the accountability dilemma through theoretical thinking. We will not answer the question about accountability for performance by debating, legislating, and codifying formal systems of accountability. Instead, we will have to experiment.

We will not learn much from cowards who are intimidated by multiple constraints or from outlaws who defy all of the rules. Instead, we will learn the most from a series of ad hoc experiments conducted by public managers and civic leaders who strive to accomplish public purposes that citizens value and who recognize their responsibility to explain what they are doing and what they have accomplished. The new kinds of accountability relationships will emerge from the efforts of those who take the lead in creating responsibility compacts and charter agencies such as those for special education in Madison, Wisconsin,[51] for health and social services in Oregon,[52] and for ecosystem management in rural communities throughout the American West.[53] These are the researchers who will answer the accountability questions. Indeed, the answer to the accountability questions can only emerge from practice—evolving from a variety of efforts by those new public managers who do not obscure their obligations but define and clarify them, from experimentation within collaboratives, and from efforts by others in the accountability environment to help create webs of mutual responsibilities.

Some of these experiments will be failures. (And, if there are too many failures, the entire effort will be abandoned.) Some, however, may be modest, qualified successes. And upon these small but real successes, public managers, legislators, stakeholders, and citizens will design other experiments and produce new successes. The task of answering the accountability questions falls not to the theoreticians of the new public management, but to its practitioners.[54]

The late Donald Campbell urged us to think of government reforms as experiments.[55] Yet we rarely follow his advice. To gain approval from all those who can veto any "reform," we must describe it as more than an "experiment." To gain authorization, we must call it a "solution." Graham Allison of Harvard University labels this "The 51-49 Principle." The nature of policy politics pressures people "to come down on one side of a 51-49 issue." This is Allison's "law of the game—he who hesitates loses his chance to play at that point and he who is uncertain about his recommendation is overpowered by others who are sure." Thus even "the reasonable player is forced to argue much more confidently than he would if he were a detached judge."[56]

The difference between an experiment and a solution is not just rhetorical. It is also operational. For if we have identified a "solution," then our operational task is to implement this solution as accurately and faithfully as possible. In contrast, if we consciously enter into an experiment, we must be willing to try several variations, collect data, look for successes while accepting that there will be failures, and then attempt to identify specific causal links between the specific features of various experiments and the indicators of success. Unfortunately, the political dynamics of policy debates favor those who confidently propose persuasive solutions and discriminates against those who can offer nothing more than an opportunity to experiment with some potential but untested improvements.

Not that we don't experiment with various public policies and management strategies. We certainly do. But we carefully avoid labeling any reform as a mere experiment. And thus we lose the opportunity to explore more possibilities—let alone to rethink basic premises.

Not that our policies don't evolve. They certainly do. But we are so obliviously captive to historical precedent, to well-defined if simplistic paradigms, and to our own overconfident rhetoric that we find it difficult to acknowledge any such evolution. We fail to accept that we are actually learning and, thus, improving. And thus we fail to recognize that we would learn and improve more if we would experiment consciously and more often.

It's one thing for tacit policy experiments to create the learning necessary to compel some incremental evolution in our political thinking, public policies, and managerial strategies. It's another to create conscious experiments that will challenge our existing paradigms—to accept from the outset that we may need to employ an entirely different mental framework.

Is it possible to create the experiments that are an essential feature of any new responsibility compact?[57] Or is our implicit working definition of accountability so fixed that we cannot even conceive of any different ways of making accountability work, let alone experimenting with some? To experiment, we must accept that our current systems, procedures, behaviors, rules, and expectations about accountability could be improved. To experiment with accountability, we must be willing to search for better ways of making the process work. To really experiment with accountability, we must accept that there exists more than one model of accountability—and that other, fundamentally different concepts of accountability might have some significant advantages that outweigh their disadvantages. Indeed, what makes us think that there exists one single model of accountability that will be best for all circumstances?[58]

The flexibility-performance tradeoff need not be a tradeoff between accountability for finances and fairness and accountability for performance.

It appears to be this only because we think of accountability for finances and fairness purely in terms of rules and punishments. But if we are willing to rethink accountability for finances and fairness, perhaps we will discover concepts and mechanisms for enhancing accountability for finances, fairness, *and* performance.

Accountability and Citizens

By definition, these experiments in accountability must, somehow, involve citizens. After all, the rationale for the new public management is that citizens need better performance. But what kind of performance? Citizens have a stake both in the choice of goals and in the achievement of these goals. Thus any accountability mechanism ought to permit citizens to participate in the debate over the choice of goals, and in the monitoring and evaluation of their achievement.

But how? Will the existing political system of periodic elections be adequate? Or will extra-electoral mechanisms be needed? If so, will they, too, be dominated by organized stakeholders? Or will they be irrelevant, with journalists, auditors, inspectors general, and prosecutors continuing to focus on process—particularly on minor errors in following the rules for finances and fairness? Or is it somehow possible to engage the citizenry's interest in the goals that its municipality sets for its school system, the goals that its state sets for its family support agencies, and the goals that the federal government sets for the nation's network of environmental organizations?

If so, when do citizens become involved in choosing goals and in monitoring and evaluating their achievement? In what kind of results and performance are citizens most interested? How do they like to engage in the responsibility to choose, monitor, and evaluate? How do they prefer to be presented with choices, with data? How can they be engaged but not too engaged?[59] These are the kinds of operational questions that the experiments with new accountability mechanisms will ask. The answers will only emerge as the experiments evolve.

In discussing the problem of "dirty hands"—when public "officials do wrong in order to do right"—Dennis Thompson emphasizes the importance of citizens and of their consent in such acts by public officials:

Democratic officials are supposed to act with the consent of citizens. . . . If they gain that consent, they are not uniquely guilty in the way that the [dirty-hands] problem in its traditional form presumes. If they act without that consent, they not only commit a further wrong (a violation of the democratic process), but they also cast doubt on the justifiability of the decision itself.[60]

"The idea of accountability," write James March and Johan Olsen, "becomes especially germane through the democratic emphasis on informed consent as the basis of governmental authority."[61]

But how does a public official know when he or she has gained that consent? How does a collaborative of public, nonprofit, and for-profit agencies know when it has gained that consent? Again, the answer will only emerge as the experiments evolve.

From Adversarial Accountability to Cooperative Responsibility

We have created an accountability system that focuses on finances and fairness. These are important values. Without frequent assurances that government agencies are handling their finances with complete probity, and without regular assurances that these agencies are treating citizens with absolute fairness, Americans will quickly lose faith in their government. But citizens also care about their public agencies' performance. For without repetitive assurances that these agencies are functioning both effectively and efficiently, Americans will also lose faith in their government. And rightly so.

We have, however, created an accountability system that depends upon the self-interested, competitive behavior of legions of accountability holders. But it isn't really a "system" of accountability—more like an anarchy of aggressively competitive accountability. In some ways, such self-interested behavior serves our accountability needs. It catches lots of violations in our standards for finances and fairness. Indeed, it catches too many "violations" that ought not to be labeled as such, while missing other more important failures. Exhibit A: the savings-and-loan scandal (which apparently was too complicated for any of the accountability holders).[62]

Adversarial accountability for finances and fairness works too well. By "too well," I mean that our existing institutions of accountability not only overemphasize accountability for finances and fairness. They also undercut performance. Indeed, they undercut the capacity of government's productive units from achieving the results they were created to pursue.

Our system of democratic accountability places too much emphasis on finances and fairness and not enough on performance—too much on rules and not enough on results. It also places too much emphasis on competition and not enough on cooperation. But to place more emphasis on accountability for performance, we need more cooperation. And to evolve such cooperation, we need to create mechanisms for evolving trust.

The first challenge, then, is not to scrap but to rethink the adversarial institutions that create accountability for finances and fairness. The second challenge is to create some new cooperative institutions that can promote accountability for performance. In the process, we might temper the zeal with which the accountability holders for finances and fairness attack the smallest failure to comply with our formal rules. As we create new concepts of accountability for performance, we might also redefine how we think about accountability for finances and fairness.

We need not worry that we will abolish accountability for finances or fairness. The institutions with this job are too well established to disappear, and the self-interest of those who lead and staff them will motivate continued vigilance. Americans will always be blessed with a herd of self-righteous accountability holders ready to pounce at the slightest hint of blood.

Instead, we need to worry that the aggressive, adversarial strategy pursued by these institutions of accountability is destroying the legitimacy and capabilities of many public agencies—and of government in general. We ought to let go of our fixation with finances and fairness. We ought not to let these legitimate concerns blind us to the need to enhance performance. Consequently, we need to invest some resources and time in experimenting with some alternative concepts and institutions—concepts that will not just enforce accountability but will also foster responsibility; institutions motivated less by personal, self-interest than by our mutual, collective public interest. We need to experiment with concepts and institutions that will not just hold public agencies and public officials accountable for improving performance. We need also to seek concepts and institutions that actively promote government's performance.

We need to rethink what we mean by democratic accountability.

Notes

Chapter One

1. General Accounting Office, *Federal Agencies Should Use Good Measures of Performance to Hold Managers Accountable*, GAO/FPCD-78-26 (November 22, 1978).

2. Bernard Rosen, *Holding Government Bureaucracies Accountable*, 2d ed. (Praeger 1989); and Helen F. Ladd, ed., *Holding Schools Accountable: Performance-Based Reform in Education* (Brookings, 1996).

3. For example, "the restraint of police brutality and other abuses of civil rights," argues Kathleen M. Sullivan, is "now more in the hands of enterprising litigators than elected representatives." "Put Politics Back Where It Belongs," *Washington Post*, January 3, 1998.

Note: when a lawyer no longer wants to be an accountability holder, he or she can switch sides and make a living defending accountability holdees. Lawyers get to work on both sides of the accountability-holding business.

4. "Livingston: 'To My Colleagues, . . . I Have Hurt You All Deeply,'" *Washington Post*, December 20, 1998, p. A29.

5. Bob Dole, "A Tough but Responsible Solution," *New York Times*, December 15, 1998, p. A27.

6. "Reno Taking Heat over Chinese Spying Probe," [Raleigh, N.C.] *News & Observer*, May 24, 1999, p. 6A.

7. Paul Light quotes one inspector general in President Carter's administration as saying: "Everyone wants a strong IG operation until it starts investigating them. The administration may start out thinking they want junkyard dogs, and what they

may end up with is French poodles." *Monitoring Government: Inspectors General and the Search for Accountability* (Brookings, 1993), p. 102.

8. Mark H. Moore and Margaret Jane Gates, *Inspectors-General: Junkyard Dogs or Man's Best Friend?* (Russell Sage Foundation, 1986), pp. 2, 1.

9. "Players Evaluate Umpires," [Raleigh, N.C.] *News & Observer,* April 1, 1999.

10. Peter Gammons, "Memories of a Starry Night Won't Dim," *Boston Globe,* July 18, 1999, p. D8.

11. No, you will not find the word "holdee" in your dictionary. But if someone is holding someone else accountable, that first person must be an accountability "holder"; and if there is an accountability holder, there must be an accountability "holdee."

Whom do auditors audit? Usually, auditors refer to the people or organizations that they audit as their "clients." After all, these are the people who hire them. And auditors want to be hired again. Nevertheless, at least one publication of the American Accounting Association refers to those being audited as the "auditee." Russell M. Barefield, *The Impact of Audit Frequency on the Quality of Internal Control,* Studies in Accounting Research 11 (Sarasota, Fla.: American Accounting Association, 1975).

12. For a number of different definitions of accountability, see Kevin P. Kearns, *Managing for Accountability* (Jossey-Bass, 1996), pp. 35–36. None, however, really provides much useful guidance.

Barbara S. Romzek and Melvin J. Dubnick write that "scholars and practitioners freely use the term [accountability] to refer to answerability for one's actions or behavior." "Accountability in the Public Sector: Lessons from the Challenger Tragedy," *Public Administration Review,* vol. 47, no. 3 (1987), p. 228. "Traditionally," write O. P. Dwivedi and Joseph G. Jabbra, accountability "has meant answerability for one's actions or behavior." "Public Service Responsibility and Accountability," in O. P. Dwivedi and Joseph G. Jabbra, eds., *Public Service Accountability: A Comparative Perspective* (Kumarian Press, 1988), p. 5. But converting accountability into answerability doesn't really help much either.

What does it mean to be answerable? In his analysis of the evolution of the concept of accountability, Gerald E. Caiden observes that it came to mean that the actions of public officials "had to be justified, their reasons explained and their deeds and misdeeds accounted before the court of public opinion." Does to be answerable mean that the public official must give a public account of his or her actions? Is that all? If the official explains what he or she did and why, is that sufficient? Caiden distinguishes three different concepts—responsibility, accountability, and liability—even though he accepts that "in normal use they are used interchangeably":

> To be responsible is to have the authority to act, power to control, freedom to decide, the ability to distinguish (as between right and wrong) and to behave

rationally and reliably and with consistency and trustworthiness in exercising internal judgment.

To be accountable is to answer for one's responsibilities, to report, to explain, to give reasons, to respond, to assume obligations, to render a reckoning and to submit to an outside or external judgment.

To be liable is to assume the duty of making good, to restore, to compensate, to recompense for wrongdoing or poor judgment.

"Public officials," writes Caiden, "should take responsibility for all that is done in the name of the public, should also be accountable to external bodies for what they have done or failed to do while in public office and should be liable, legally and morally, for correcting or compensating for their wrongdoing as judged internally or externally." Thus, to Caiden, accountability is answerability, while liability contains the potential for punishment or, at least, a reimbursement for past costs. "The Problem of Ensuring the Public Accountability of Public Officials," in Dwivedi and Jabbra, *Public Service Accountability,* pp. 20, 25.

In making the case for "deliberative democracy," Amy Gutmann and Dennis Thompson establish "the principles of reciprocity, publicity, and accountability." But what exactly do they mean by their "deliberative principle of accountability"? They never offer a specific definition, but the reader can easily infer that their "deliberative accountability" requires public officials to account for their decisions, to provide reasons, "to justify their actions in moral terms." (By public officials they appear to mean mostly elected representatives, but in addition to "prominent elected officials," they also include "far less conspicuous officials, professionals, corporate executives, union leaders, employers and employees, and ordinary citizens when they act in a public capacity.") Gutmann and Thompson write that "deliberative accountability requires representatives to give reasons to citizens and to respond to the reasons citizens give" and stress "the reason-giving demands of deliberative democracy." Yet they also lapse into conventional language of holding people accountable. They write about "voters" who can "hold officials accountable at the next election," though they clearly find this inadequate given "the arbitrary moments of accountability that elections offer." Indeed, they seem to suggest that there exists a difference between "deliberative accountability" and "electoral accountability." Occasionally Gutmann and Thompson seem to mix the two, writing about how "reiterated deliberation . . . enables citizens to hold their representatives accountable for making better decisions in the future." *Democracy and Disagreement* (Harvard University Press, 1996), pp. 8, 132, 128–29, 15, 138, 164, 142, 146, 144.

Accountability remains an elusive concept.

13. General Accounting Office, *Block Grants: Issues in Designing Accountability Provisions,* GAO/AIMD-95-226 (September 1995), p. 4.

14. This asymmetrical response to success and failure is a general human trait. For example, Andrew Beyer reports how "horseplayers" respond to the success and

failure of jockeys: "When a rider commits an error, we observe it and curse him; when he does something well, we take it for granted and pay little attention." "Looking for a Long-Shot Jockey? There Is A Good Reason to Take Pity," *Washington Post*, February 26, 2000, p. D3.

15. Theoretical writings on accountability usually report that it can be supported by reward as well as punishment. For example, John P. Burke examines "how officials can be held to account—blamed and praised, punished and rewarded—for what they do or fail to do." *Bureaucratic Responsibility* (Johns Hopkins University Press, 1986), p. 224. Similarly, Ronald J. Oakerson writes: "Accountability can bring either blame and censure or recognition for a job well done." "Governance Structures for Enhancing Accountability and Responsiveness" in James L. Perry, ed., *Handbook of Public Administration* (Jossey-Bass, 1989), p. 114. I suspect, however, that few public officials can recall when they were "held to account" by being "praised" or "rewarded," or when "accountability" brought them "recognition for a job well done."

16. Suzanne Garment, *Scandal: The Culture of Mistrust in American Politics* (Times Books, 1999), p. 9.

17. Frank Anechiarico and James B. Jacobs, *The Pursuit of Absolute Integrity: How Corruption Control Makes Government Ineffective* (University of Chicago Press, 1996), pp. 6, 102.

18. *Webster's Third New International Dictionary of the English Language*, Unabridged (Merriam-Webster, 1986), p. 13.

19. Jay M. Shafritz, *The Dorsey Dictionary of American Government and Politics* (Dorsey Press, 1988), p. 4. Shafritz also offers a definition of "administrative accountability": "That aspect of administrative responsibility by which officials are held answerable for general notions of democracy and morality as well as for specific legal mandates" (p. 8).

20. Barbara S. Romzek and Melvin J. Dubnick, "Accountability," in Jay M. Shafritz, ed., *International Encyclopedia of Public Policy and Administration* (Westview Press, 1998), p. 6.

21. Most dictionary definitions are only a paragraph or two long. In contrast, the "accountability" entry by Romzek and Dubnick in the *International Encyclopedia of Public Policy and Administration* runs six pages, with a page-and-a-half devoted to the "Problem of Blame Assessment" (pp. 7–8). They never use the word "punishment," though they do write about "reprimand" and "major sanctions (e.g., resignation)" (p. 8).

22. "The simple view of accountability" is, to Melvin Dubnick, "the *condition of being able to render a counting of something to someone.*" Dubnick, however, offers a more sophisticated view of accountability "as a genus encompassing a variety of [eight] species": liability, answerability, responsibility, responsiveness, obligation, obedience, fidelity, and amenability. "Clarifying Accountability: An Ethical Theory Framework," in Charles Sampford and Noel Preston, with C-A Bois, eds., *Public*

Sector Ethics: Finding and Implementing Values (Leichhardt, New South Wales: Federation Press, and New York: Routledge, 1998), pp. 76–79.

23. Romzek and Dubnick, "Accountability in the Public Sector," p. 228. William T. Gormley Jr., "Accountability Battles in State Administration," in Carl Van Horn, ed., *The State of the States*, 3d ed. (CQ Press, 1996), p. 175. Moore and Gates, *Inspectors-General*, p. 105. Kevin P. Kearns, "The Strategic Management of Accountability in Nonprofit Organizations: An Analytical Framework," *Public Administration Review*, vol. 54, no. 2 (1994), p. 187. Kevin P. Kearns, "Institutional Accountability in Higher Education: A Strategic Approach," *Public Productivity & Management Review*, vol. 22, no. 2 (1998), p. 141. Kearns, *Managing for Accountability*, p. 11.

Oakerson offers another explanation: "To be accountable means to have to answer for one's actions or inaction, and depending on the answer to be exposed to potential sanctions, both positive and negative." "Governance Structures for Enhancing Accountability and Responsiveness," p. 114. But this fails to specify what actions or inaction might be cause for sanctions.

24. Frederick C. Mosher, "The Changing Responsibilities and Tactics of the Federal Government," *Public Administration Review*, vol. 40, no. 6 (1980), p. 546.

25. Zechariah Chafee Jr., "The Press under Pressure," *Nieman Reports*, vol. 2, no. 2 (1948), p. 19.

26. Light, *Monitoring Government*, p. 173.

27. Caiden observes that when humans replaced the absolute monarch with "the rule of representative assemblies," they sought "to ensure that these new rulers would not place themselves above other persons." Thus, these new rulers "were to be subjected to the same laws as everybody else." "The Problem of Ensuring the Public Accountability of Public Officials," pp. 19–20.

28. This is, of course, an exaggeration. For example, a few federal inspectors general have been criticized for not being quick or determined enough at tracking down fraud, waste, or abuse. See Light, *Monitoring Government*, pp. 118–19, 144. Indeed, Light asks "whether the IG can be held accountable for the failure to catch and highlight problems earlier" (p. 75). Clearly, the most obvious political incentives under which these accountability holders operate encourage them to be aggressive instead of cautious in the pursuit of any errors committed by accountability holdees.

29. Garment, *Scandal*, p. 95. Anechiarico and Jacobs report a more bizarre story about a New York City executive, "K. P.," who was accused of establishing a policy of "forced abortion" for new recruits. (If they became pregnant, several female trainees alleged they had been told, they would have to either get an abortion or resign.) K. P. was given three options: "(1) termination; (2) resignation; or (3) demotion and a $10,000 fine, to be collected by withholding his next two paychecks." K. P. took the third option although he was advised to resign. Then K. P. hired an attorney, appealed his discipline, lost, filed a civil lawsuit, was then "cleared" by the city's corporation counsel and reimbursed the $10,000—but not reinstated to his previous

rank or reimbursed for his legal expenses. *The Pursuit of Absolute Integrity,* pp. 90–91.

30. Kearns distinguishes between the public trust and the public interest:

> In one sense, accountability involves preserving the public trust—being able to account for the organization's implied promises to its constituencies by pursuing its stated mission in good faith and with defensible management and governance practices. The public interest, on the other hand, is not so easily defined; it involves diverse perceptions and values regarding public needs and priorities. . . .
>
> While public trust and public interest are separate theoretical concepts, they generally become indistinguishable in any practical discussion of accountability. Again, the general public does not make clear distinctions between public trust and public interest when assessing the performance of government and nonprofit organizations. People want to know not only that we are doing what we promised to do or what we are legally obligated to do, but what they expect us to do, what they want us to do, what they think we should do.

Managing for Accountability, p. 40.

31. Ibid., p. 29.

32. Why is public sector accountability so complex? Principal-agent theory offers one explanation: Any government agency is an "agent" for many different "principals"—all of those people in the accountability environment who want the agent to pursue their disparate purposes.

33. Kearns also distinguishes three types of accountability—for resources, for outcomes, and for processes. These correspond rather closely to my three categories—for finances (resources), for performance (outcomes), and for fairness (processes). I, however, emphasize that the "processes" are designed to accomplish a fundamental democratic purpose: to ensure the equitable treatment of citizens. *Managing for Accountability,* p. 30.

Similarly, James W. Fesler and Donald F. Kettl define three types of accountability: "fiscal accountability"; "process accountability," which emphasizes not only "procedural fairness" but also "economy" and "efficiency"; and "program accountability," which "focuses on results." *The Politics of the Administrative Process* (Chatham House, 1991), p. 327.

Caiden writes about "traditional or compliance accountability and process accountability," which corresponds to my accountability for finances and fairness. He distinguishes these from "program accountability (which is concerned with the outcomes or results of government operations), and social accountability (which attempts to determine the societal impacts of government programs)"; these correspond to my accountability for performance. "The Problem of Ensuring the Public Accountability of Public Officials," p. 24.

Light also defines "three contemporary strategies of accountability—rule-based compliance, performance incentives, and improvements in basic governmental capacity." "Compliance accountability" employs "negative sanctions" to ensure that people follow the rules and regulations; "performance accountability" uses "positive sanctions" to create "incentives and rewards for desired outcomes"; and "capacity-based accountability . . . focuses on building organizations that are staffed, trained, structured, and equipped to be effective." Thus, Light's "compliance accountability" corresponds to my accountability for finances and fairness, while his "performance accountability" is obviously my accountability for performance (though I don't assume that it is based only on "positive" sanctions). Light's capacity-based account-ability is also a component of my accountability for performance; I think the task of creating organizational capacity is a basic step in producing the outcomes required by accountability for performance. *Monitoring Government,* pp. 11, 3–4.

In contrast, Moore and Gates use the word *accountability* primarily to mean accountability for finances, which they contrast with the "broader responsibility for promoting efficiency (in the sense that, over time, the quantity and quality of government production per unit of cost continues to increase)." In some circumstances, they write, "accountability differs from performance," and that "some tension exists between the ideas of improved accountability and improved performance." *Inspectors-General,* pp. 5, 75.

34. Robert K. Barnhart, ed., *The Barnhart Dictionary of Etymology* (H. H. Wilson, 1988), pp. 7, 200.

35. For a more detailed history of accountability, see Dubnick, "Clarifying Accountability," pp. 69–72. Dubnick calls accountability "an anglican concept" and emphasizes that many languages, such as Portuguese, have no word for accounta-bility and others, such as Japanese and Hebrew, only recently added the word by adopting it directly from English.

36. Eugene Bardach and Cara Lesser, "Accountability in Human Services Col-laboratives—For What? and To Whom?" *Journal of Public Administration Research and Theory,* vol. 6, no. 2 (1996), p. 197.

37. Joel G. Siegel and Jae K. Shim, *Dictionary of Accounting Terms,* 2d ed. (Bar-rons, 1995).

38. In the private sector, the definition of the wise stewardship of resources is more complex. Thus financial accountability in the private sector is different from financial accountability in the public sector. In business, the accountability holders want to know not only if you spent your money on what you were supposed to spend it on; they also want to know if you earned an acceptable return on this investment. In fact, in business, the accountability holders care less about how you spent your money (assuming that you didn't use it to bribe people or burn down your competitor's warehouse) than about how much of a return you earned. In the private sector, accountability for performance is a major part of accountability for finances.

In the public sector, however, the emphasis is not on what you earned. Public agencies get their funds from an appropriation rather than a market. Thus performance is not measured financially nor does increased performance automatically generate increased funding. In the public sector, accountability for finances and accountability for performance are not directly connected.

39. In 1921 Congress created the General Accounting Office to do precisely this. See Frederick C. Mosher, *The GAO: The Quest for Accountability in American Government* (Westview, 1979).

40. Robert B. Reich emphasizes that "public servants are accountable not only to the majority of voters" but also to the minority and to "those who do not vote," including "children, the retarded, [and] generations yet unborn." This "special kind of accountability" concerns "their basic rights as members (or future members) of society." *Public Management in a Democratic Society* (Prentice Hall, 1990), p. 76. I include this in my category of accountability for fairness.

41. This requires lots of forms. It also requires a lot of "accountants"—though real accountants want to deal only with money. So we give these accountability holders another name; we call them "bureaucrats." Still, we try to make accountability for fairness look very much like real, financial accounting.

42. Writing about police agencies, however, Mark H. Moore emphasizes that all of the rules and procedures (even if followed) do not necessarily guarantee that government treats citizens fairly: "It is no longer clear that police organizations can be free of error, corruption, and brutality by applying tighter rules, closer supervision, and stricter penalties for misconduct. Indeed, this bureaucratic apparatus increasingly looks like an expensive way to produce the form but not the substance of a disciplined, effective force." "Policing: Deregulating or Redefining Accountability?" in John J. DiIulio Jr., ed., *Deregulating the Public Service: Can Government Be Improved?* (Brookings, 1994), p. 201.

43. Okay, it's not completely straightforward. We don't all agree on even the abstract principles of fairness. Thus, we certainly don't all agree about the operational rules for guaranteeing fairness. One obvious example is the debate over affirmative action. Thus, while some official accountability holders examine whether the accountability holdees have abided by the formal rules, other, unofficial accountability holders can focus on whether the accountability holdees have abided by an informal perception about what is fair (or reasonable). And, of course, abiding by the formal rules may create other inequities. In fact, abiding by the formal rules can create conspicuously absurd inequities. When this happens, the accountability holdee—the individual or organization—that gets punished is often not the individual or organization that promulgated the rule but the individual or organization that obediently followed it. The formal rule looks reasonable enough in the abstract but becomes patently silly when implemented in some specific circumstances. So we blame the people who applied the rule for not think-

ing when, for years, we have been telling them that, when applying rules, they are not supposed to think.

For an example of a set of reasonable-sounding rules that proved absurd in practice, see Eric Black, "Why Regulators Need a Don't-Do-It-If-It's-Stupid Clause," *Washington Monthly,* January 1985, pp. 23–26.

44. Steven Kelman, *Procurement and Public Management: The Fear of Discretion and the Quality of Government Performance* (AEI Press, 1990), p. 3.

45. B. Guy Peters and Donald J. Savoie, "Managing Incoherence: The Coordination and Empowerment Conundrum," *Public Administration Review,* vol. 56, no. 3 (1996), p. 285.

46. Light, *Monitoring Government,* p. 12. As the discussion of the moving target of accountability suggests, however, what has really remained constant for years is not so much the *definition* of accountability as the *process* of holding people accountable for failing to follow the latest rules.

47. Sometimes a government agency is supposed to ensure that non-governmental organizations treat citizens fairly (for example, that the hiring practices of business are fair). In this case, the agency's performance depends upon how good a job it does ensuring private sector fairness.

48. Some aspects of performance may concern process more than real performance: Was the public service provided promptly? Was the service provided courteously? These could be issues of fairness: Did some people get services that were more prompt or more courteous than others? Or did *anyone* get services that could be reasonably described as prompt or courteous?

49. The book edited by Ladd, *Holding Schools Accountable: Performance-Based Reform in Education,* is not about holding schools accountable for finances or fairness; as the subtitle implies, it is about holding schools accountable for performance.

50. For example, the GAO prepares reports for Congress with titles such as *Park Service: Managing for Results Could Strengthen Accountability,* RCED-97-125 (April 1997).

51. Bardach and Lesser take a different view: "we like to think of *accountability for results* as a shorthand way of saying *accountability for a better quality of effort directed toward the results being measured.*" That is, to Bardach and Lesser, the expectations for performance accountability concern effort rather than results. "Accountability in Human Service Collaboratives," p. 201.

52. Mosher writes: "A major requirement of representative government is that the officials who decide and act for the citizenry be held accountable for their actions. This was a fairly simple concept—though never very easy to ensure—when one was concerned simply with legality, honesty, and correctness of actions by persons under direct electoral or hierarchical control. It has become far more difficult as the concept has extended to the efficiency and effectiveness of performance in terms of governmental purposes by organizations and persons outside

of the government." "The Changing Responsibilities and Tactics of the Federal Government," p. 546.

53. Many do view accountability for performance to be primarily accountability to customers (or clients) with market competition driving the government agency—or, more likely, its contractor from the nonprofit or for-profit sector—to improve performance (that is, to improve quantity and quality and to decrease costs). Thus the market becomes the mechanism for accountability.

This is certainly a key theme of "reinventing government": David Osborne and Ted Gaebler advocate "putting customers in the driver's seat" because "customer-driven systems force service providers to be accountable to their customers." Although Osborne and Gaebler also write of "political accountability" to executive-branch superiors and the legislature, and note that "voters demand some accountability," they emphasize accountability not to elected officials, voters, or the citizenry but "accountability to customers." *Reinventing Government* (Addison-Wesley, 1992), pp. 180, 181, 212, 254, and 169.

In *Banishing Bureaucracy,* Osborne and Peter Plastrik also emphasize "accountability to the customer," but their discussion of accountability is more subtle. They talk about "shifting some of the accountability to the customer," and of "dual accountability" to both customers and "to elected officials and the courts," who, they write, are analogous to the owners of a business. And, as in a business, they continue, "when there is a conflict, accountability to owners trumps accountability to customers." *Banishing Bureaucracy* (Addison-Wesley, 1997), pp. 184, 41, and 178.

54. Not only can accountability for finances and fairness conflict with accountability for performance, but accountability itself can conflict with other important political and social values. Mosher writes: "The values associated with public accountability have long been competitors of other values in our society, such as: the sovereignty of foreign nations; states' rights; local autonomy and self-government; the free-market economy; private initiative and experimentation; freedom of inquiry and academic freedom; avoidance of conflicts of interest; national security; and others." "The Changing Responsibilities and Tactics of the Federal Government," p. 547.

Elsewhere Mosher emphasizes "that accountability is not an absolute, that there are other values with which it must compete and to which it must accommodate." Here, Mosher adds other values including: "freedom of thought and expression," "personal privacy," "equity," "state sovereignty and rights[,] and of local self-determination," "the maintenance of a free, competitive market economy," "academic freedom and freedom of inquiry." "Comment," in Bruce L. R. Smith, *Improving the Accountability and Performance of Government* (Brookings, 1982), pp. 74, 72, 73, 74.

55. The Volcker Commission was formally titled the National Commission on the Public Service. The Winter Commission was formally titled the National Commission on the State and Local Public Service.

56. Paul A. Volcker and William F. Winter, "Introduction: Democracy and Public Service," in DiIulio, *Deregulating the Public Service*, pp. xv–xvi.

57. Some people think of this as a trade-off between accountability and efficiency—where this accountability implicitly means accountability for finances and fairness and efficiency measures performance by dividing the costs of outputs (or outcomes) by inputs.

For example, in his "history of American distrust of government," Garry Wills analyzes "our fear of government" and "the power of anti-government values." Wills also takes note of the accountability dilemma, which he defines as the "conflicting demands" and the "warring" between accountability and efficiency: "We want our government to be efficient yet we want it to be accountable. The one, if it does not preclude the other, continually impedes it." Accountability's reporting requirements can, alone, hinder efficiency, he writes; if a public official "has to keep explaining what he is doing while he is doing it," such frequent clarification (or justification) "slows anyone down."

Still, to Wills, accountability is necessary. After all, he writes, "there is ample reason to fear and distrust government, to probe it, to make it come clean, to demand access." Yet Wills is also struck by "one of the more astounding assumptions of our political life, the belief that government should be inefficient." Arguing that "government is a necessary good, not a necessary evil," Wills seeks a balance between accountability and efficiency. While he worries that our distrust of government creates inefficiency, he also notes that "we can stand some inefficiency when it is the necessary concomitant of accountability." *A Necessary Evil: A History of American Distrust of Government* (Simon & Schuster, 1999), pp. 17, 20, 309, 311, 309, 316, 318, 297, 316.

The trade-off between accountability (for finances and fairness) and efficiency does not, however, hold in all circumstances. For example, in their study of the offices of inspectors general (OIG), Moore and Gates write that "it sometimes may be possible to reduce fraud, waste, and abuse as well as reduce administrative costs by simplifying eligibility standards rather than complicating them." But they also observe that "it is possible to reduce fraud, waste, and abuse and at the same time *reduce* efficiency!" Moreover they note that through governmental procedures "financial integrity might be enhanced, but only at the expense of reduced performance in some attributes of the service and perhaps a reduced capacity to innovate in the future." Indeed, they "found some clear instances in which OIG interventions had important negative consequences for some performance attributes of programs." *Inspectors-General*, pp. 25, 27, 57, 80.

58. Peter Self, *Administrative Theories and Politics* (Allen & Unwin, 1972) pp. 277–78.

59. James G. March and Johan P. Olsen suggest a similar (but not quite identical) accountability dilemma: "The fundamental accountability dilemma is found in the way efforts to achieve accountability seem inexorably to reduce the capabilities of the political systems to maintain a long-run perspective." Noting "the trade-offs

between short-run accountability and long-run accountability," they observe that "contemporary democracies seem . . . to be more prone to risk the losses due to inadequate attention to the long run than the losses due to inadequate short-run accountability." *Democratic Governance* (Free Press, 1995), pp. 151, 152. If short-run accountability focuses primarily on finances and fairness and long-run accountability concerns mostly performance, my "accountability dilemma" is the same as March and Olsen's.

Romzek and Dubnick define a different accountability dilemma: "The essence of this dilemma is the inability of 'accountable' entities to resolve the problem of many masters and manage the government's business under conditions of multiple accountability relationships and systems." "Accountability," p. 10.

60. Anechiarico and Jacobs, *The Pursuit of Absolute Integrity,* p. 12.

61. Mosher, "Comment," p. 72.

62. Elmer B. Staats, "Governmental Performance in Perspective: Achievements and Challenges," in Smith, *Improving the Accountability and Performance of Government,* p. 25.

63. Organisation for Economic Co-operation and Development, Public Management Service, *Managing Government Ethics,* PUMA Policy Brief 1 (Washington, February 1997) (www.oecd.org//puma/ethics/symposium/polbrief.pdf [October 2000]).

64. Phillip J. Cooper, "Accountability and Administrative Reform: Toward Convergence and Beyond," in B. Guy Peters and Donald J. Savoie, eds., *Governance in a Changing Environment* (McGill-Queen's University Press, 1995), p. 174.

65. For a discussion of the importance of objective rules in accountability for finances, see Moore and Gates, *Inspectors-General,* pp. 19–22.

66. Light, *Monitoring Government,* pp. 7, 200.

67. Moore and Gates, *Inspectors-General,* pp. 21, 27.

68. Derek Bok, "On Our Best Behavior?" *New York Times Book Review,* October 19, 1997.

69. Mosher, "Comment," p. 72.

70. Volcker and Winter, "Introduction: Democracy and Public Service," p. xvi.

71. Kelman, *Procurement and Public Management,* pp. 24, 25. The General Accounting Office also discovered that several federal agencies "learned that the burdens and constraints that confronted their managers often were imposed by the agency itself or its parent department and were not the result of requirements imposed by central management agencies." General Accounting Office, *GPRA: Managerial Accountability and Flexibility Pilot Did Not Work as Intended,* GAO/GGD-97-36 (April 1997), p. 4.

72. Light, *Monitoring Government,* p. 166.

73. Of course, there is a third possibility: cheat. Produce the required numbers by the required date, but do so in a way that fails to achieve the agency's real purpose. See Robert D. Behn, "Cheating—Honest & Dishonest," *New Public Innovator,* no. 92 (1998), pp. 18–19.

74. Dennis F. Thompson, *Political Ethics and Public Office* (Harvard University Press, 1987), p. 16.

75. Quoted by Fesler and Kettl, *The Politics of the Administrative Process,* p. 329.

76. Quoted in Garment, *Scandal,* p. 1.

77. Thompson, *Political Ethics and Public Office,* p. 43.

78. Albert O. Hirschman, *Exit, Voice, and Loyalty: Responses to Decline in Firms, Organizations, and States* (Harvard University Press, 1970).

79. For an example of a federal executive who exercised both exit and voice, see H. George Frederickson, "Exit and Voice: When Enough Is Enough," *PA* [Public Administration] *Times,* December 1999, p. 8.

80. General Accounting Office, *Senior Executive Service: Reasons Why Career Members Left in Fiscal Year 1985,* GAO/GGD-87-106FS (1988). For other analyses of why government executives exit, see Barbara S. Romzek, "The Effects of Public Service Recognition, Job Security and Staff Reductions on Organizational Involvement," *Public Administration Review,* vol. 45, no. 2 (1985), pp. 282–91; Patricia A. Wilson, "Power, Politics, and Other Reasons Why Senior Executives Leave the Federal Government," *Public Administration Review,* vol. 54, no. 1 (1994), pp. 12–19.

81. David Pines, "Why Science Can't Be Done in Isolation," *Newsweek,* September 27, 1999, p. 11.

82. Alasdair Roberts, "Performance-Based Organizations: Assessing the Gore Plan," *Public Administration Review,* vol. 57, no. 6 (1997), p. 469.

83. James Q. Wilson, *Bureaucracy: What Government Agencies Do and Why They Do It* (Basic Books, 1989), p. 369.

84. Robert J. Samuelson, "Why I Am Not a Manager," *Newsweek,* March 22, 1999, p. 47.

85. Anechiarico and Jacobs, *The Pursuit of Absolute Integrity,* pp. 59, 61.

86. Garment, *Scandal,* pp. 291, 292, 301.

87. Jonathan Rauch, "Infinite Jeopardy," *National Journal,* March 14, 1998, p. 565.

88. Anechiarico and Jacobs, *The Pursuit of Absolute Integrity,* pp. 12, xvii, xi, 18, 62.

89. Frank Anechiarico, "Corruption Control *Means* Bureaucratic Pathology," *Public Integrity,* vol. 1, no. 1 (1999), p. 91.

90. Rauch, "Infinite Jeopardy," p. 570.

91. Quoted in Matthew Brelis, "Unfaithful Servants, Unfaithful Selves," *Boston Globe,* December 27, 1998, p. E3.

Chapter Two

1. The world is divided into two camps: people who use the word *paradigm* daily, and those who detest it. To those in the second camp, I apologize for employing this, now overused, word. It does, however, have a distinguished heritage, going back to the late Latin *paradigma* from the Greek *paradeiknynai.* Yet, the word *paradigm* did

not enter the popular lexicon until the publication of Thomas Kuhn's *The Structure of Scientific Revolutions* (University of Chicago Press, 1962). Then it quickly became a cliché. Still, the word does appear to be appropriate to this context under the third definition from *Merriam Webster's Collegiate Dictionary* (tenth edition): "a philosophical and theoretical framework of a scientific school or discipline within which theories, laws, and generalizations and the experiments performed in support of them are formulated." Certainly, those who support traditional public administration would argue that they have a "discipline," complete with "theories, laws, and generalizations" that focus their research.

2. B. Guy Peters, *The Future of Governing: Four Emerging Models* (University Press of Kansas, 1996), pp. 3–12.

3. Woodrow Wilson, "The Study of Administration," *Political Science Quarterly*, vol. 2, no. 2 (1887), pp. 206, 201.

4. Gerald E. Caiden reports that "in states where public administration is technically proficient, there have been relatively few instances of public scandal involving professional career public servants as opposed to elected political officials." "The Problem of Ensuring the Public Accountability of Public Officials," in O. P. Dwivedi and Joseph G. Jabbra, eds., *Public Service Accountability: A Comparative Perspective* (Kumarian Press, 1988), p. 22.

5. Derek Bok, "Measuring the Performance of Government," in Joseph S. Nye Jr., Philip D. Zelikow, and David C. King, eds., *Why People Don't Trust Government* (Harvard University Press, 1997), p. 55.

6. Larry Polivka and B. Jack Osterhold, "The Governor as Manager: Agency Autonomy and Accountability," *Public Budgeting & Finance*, vol. 5, no. 4 (1985), p. 97.

7. Quoted in Doreen Iudica Vigue, "Education Reform Funds May Be Cut: Disenchantment with Schools Taking Hold, State Leaders Say," *Boston Globe*, October 18, 1999, p. A1.

8. Zell Miller, "State of the State Address," January 10, 1996, photocopy.

9. "Williams: 'Our Citizens Deserve the Best City in America,'" *Washington Post*, January 3, 1999, p. A10.

10. John J. DiIulio Jr., ed., *Deregulating the Public Service: Can Government Be Improved?* (Brookings, 1996).

11. David Osborne and Ted Gaebler, *Reinventing Government: How the Entrepreneurial Spirit Is Transforming the Public Sector* (Addison-Wesley, 1992).

12. Christopher Pollitt, *Managerialism and the Public Services: The Anglo-American Experience* (Basil Blackwell, 1990).

13. Christopher Hood, "A Public Management for All Seasons?" *Public Administration*, vol. 69 (1991), pp. 3–19. Christopher Hood, "Economic Rationalism in Public Management: From Progressive Public Administration to New Public Management?" chap. 7 in *Explaining Economic Policy Reversals* (Open University Press, 1994), pp. 125–41.

14. Osborne and Gaebler, *Reinventing Government,* p. 328. Naturally, not everyone thinks this is a global revolution. See, for example, Christopher Hood, "Beyond 'Progressivism': A New 'Global Paradigm' in Public Management," *International Journal of Public Administration,* vol. 19, no. 2 (1996), pp. 151–77.

15. Donald F. Kettl, "The Global Revolution in Public Management: Driving Themes, Missing Links," *Journal of Policy Analysis and Management,* vol. 16, no. 3 (1997), p. 446.

16. Fred Thompson, untitled book review essay in *Journal of Policy Analysis and Management,* vol. 16, no. 1 (1997), p. 165.

17. Peters, *The Future of Governing,* p. 19. What is the difference between Peters's Model 3 of flexible government and Model 4 of deregulated government? After all, to get flexible government, we have to deregulate it; and if we deregulate government, it will have the opportunity to be more flexible. In describing each model's "conception of the public interest," Peters suggests that flexible government emphasizes "low cost; coordination," while deregulated government focuses on "creativity; activism." So perhaps flexible government (which is "experimental" in policymaking) focuses on better ways to achieve an established purpose through established means, while deregulated government (which is "entrepreneurial" in policymaking) seeks new purposes or employs new means (p. 19).

18. What went wrong with traditional public administration? Peters says "there is no single answer but a confluence of events" including less economic growth and more economic uncertainty; demographic changes, particularly the shift to older (and more expensive) populations; populist attacks on taxes from the political right and on bureaucracies from the political left; a "decline in government's capacity to regulate society" because of the diversity of its populations; the disagreements over moral absolutes; and a "decline of stable organizations" throughout society. Peters, *The Future of Governing,* pp. 13–16. Not all of these problems affect government performance; nevertheless, the strategies that I collect into the "new public management paradigm" are designed to improve the performance of public agencies and their partners.

Reschenthaler and Thompson offer (at least for Peters's Model 1) a different explanation: technology—specifically, information technology. Because cheaper, faster computers have lowered the costs of information, they argue, market solutions are preferable to hierarchical solutions: private organizations can perform better than public ones. G. B. Reschenthaler and Fred Thompson, "Public Management and the Learning Organization," *International Public Management Journal,* vol. 1, no. 1 (1998), pp. 59–106.

19. Improving the performance of the public sector might mean improving the performance of a specific public agency, or enhancing the performance of government in general, or upgrading the public services provided by government in cooperation with its nonprofit and for-profit collaborators.

20. Sandford Borins, "The New Public Management Is Here to Stay," *Canadian Public Administration*, vol. 38, no. 1 (1995), p. 122.

21. Sandford Borins, *Innovating with Integrity: How Local Heroes Are Transforming American Government* (Georgetown University Press, 1998), p. 9. Borins developed his definition of the new public management paradigm from evidence presented at a 1994 conference sponsored by the Commonwealth Association for Public Administration and Management. "Lessons from the New Public Management in Commonwealth Nations," *International Public Management Journal*, vol. 1, no. 1 (1998), p. 38.

22. For other conceptions of the new public management paradigm, see Peter Aucoin, *The New Public Management: Canada in Comparative Perspective* (Montreal: Institute for Research on Public Policy, 1995); Michael Barzelay with the collaboration of Babak J. Armajani, *Breaking Through Bureaucracy: A New Vision for Managing in Government* (University of California Press, 1992); Sandford Borins, "A Last Word," *Canadian Public Administration*, vol. 38, no. 1 (1995), pp. 137–38; Albert Gore, *From Red Tape to Results: Creating a Government that Works Better and Costs Less* (Report of the National Performance Review) (U.S. Government Printing Office, 1993); Public Management Service, *Governance in Transition: Public Management Reforms in OECD Countries* (Washington: Organisation for Economic Co-operation and Development, 1995); Public Management Service, *Responsive Government: Service Quality Initiatives* (Washington: Organisation for Economic Co-operation and Development, 1996).

23. This is the answer given by Laurence E. Lynn Jr.: "the variation in the models of reform being tried around the world strongly suggest that *there is no new paradigm*, if by paradigm we use Thomas Kuhn's original definition: achievements that for a time provide model problems and solutions to a community of practitioners." Lynn argues that there is no "community," no "accepted theoretical canon," and no "accepted methods of application." He concludes that "one cannot find evidence to support a claim of widespread transformation, much less a claim that a new paradigm has emerged." "A Critical Analysis of the New Public Management," *International Public Management Journal*, vol. 1, no. 1 (1998), pp. 115–16, 119.

24. David G. Mathiasen suggests that one way "to understand the new public management" is as "several fairly robust and widely used conceptual approaches to public and private sector management." And Mathiasen does believe that this is a paradigm shift; citing Kuhn ("each group uses its own paradigm to argue in that paradigm's defense"), he notes that this is precisely what is happening now in the debate over the new public management: "since each group uses its own paradigm to support its case, the arguments are essentially circular." "The New Public Management and Its Critics," in Lawrence R. Jones, Kuno Schedler, and Stephen W. Wade, eds., *International Perspectives on the New Public Management: Advances in International Comparative Management*, Supplement 3 (JAI Press, 1997), pp. 274–75, 279, 285.

25. OECD, Public Management Service, *Governance in Transition,* pp. 7, 8. Note that the OECD's mechanism for improving performance—a less centralized public sector" (p. 7)—reflects three of Peters's four models (market government, participative government, and flexible government), as well as two of Borin's four means (autonomy and competition).

26. Mathiasen reports that, when the OECD ministers responsible for public management in their nations got together in 1996, they "were surprised at the degree to which they shared this experience" of experimenting with the new public management. "The New Public Management and Its Critics," pp. 274–75, 291.

27. Kettl, "The Global Revolution in Public Management."

28. For a detailed description of the changes made in New Zealand, see Jonathan Boston, John Martin, June Pallot, and Pat Walsh, eds., *Reshaping the State: New Zealand's Bureaucratic Revolution* (Oxford University Press, 1991), as well as the symposium on "The New Public Management in New Zealand and Beyond" in *Journal of Policy Analysis and Management,* edited by Jack Nagel, vol. 16, no. 3 (1997), pp. 349–462.

29. Hood, "A Public Management for All Seasons?"

30. Improving performance is not the only challenge facing contemporary government. None of the strategies of the new public management will help resolve society's fundamental value conflicts over issues such as abortion or affirmative action.

31. For such a catalog of "the approaches other governments took in implementing management reforms that federal agencies may wish to consider," see L. Nye Stevens, *Managing for Results: Experiences Abroad Suggest Insights for Federal Management Reforms,* GAO/GGD-95-120 (General Accounting Office, May 1995), p. 1.

32. Stephanie Ebbert, "City Agency Is Accused of Bias by Employees," *Boston Globe,* August 16, 1999, pp. B1, B6.

33. Not everyone agrees. As Herbert Kaufman notes in his classic study of red tape: "Many people want more constraints, not fewer." *Red Tape: Its Origins, Uses and Abuses* (Brookings, 1977), p. 69.

34. The other actions that the NGA suggests help achieve a results-based government are "[to] articulate clear policy goals and measure progress toward achieving those goals; inform the public and mobilize communities to achieve desired goals; direct resources to achieve policy goals," and "manage for continuous improvement in service quality and effectiveness." *State Strategies for the New Economy* (Washington: National Governors' Association, 2000), p. 28.

35. David Osborne, "Bureaucracy Unbound," *Washington Post Magazine,* October 13, 1996, p. 8.

36. Paul C. Light, *Monitoring Government: Inspectors General and the Search for Accountability* (Brookings, 1993), pp. 177, 185, 182–83. Light notes that, "by breaking free of the burdens that most managers faced," inspectors general "lost some

measure of sympathy for those they oversaw because they became less sensitive to the colossal problems of managing in a tightly regulated environment and less understanding of the shortcuts some managers had to take to get their jobs done" (p. 185).

37. Only in 1995, by enacting the Congressional Accountability Act, did the U.S. Congress apply some of these rules to its own practices. See Public Law 104-1, 109 Stat. 3 (January 23, 1995).

38. Available from What on Earth, 2451 Enterprise East Parkway, Twinsburg, Ohio 44087. Give one to your favorite accountability holder. Or you might think it more appropriate to give him or her the t-shirt that declares "Power Corrupts. But absolute power is kinda neat." It is available from Wireless, Minnesota Public Radio, P.O. Box 64422, St. Paul, Minn. 55164-0422.

39. For example, see Constance Horner, "Beyond Mr. Gradgrind: The Case for Deregulating the Public Sector," *Policy Review*, no. 44 (1988), pp. 34–38; DiIulio, *Deregulating the Public Service;* James Q. Wilson, *Bureaucracy: What Government Agencies Do and Why They Do It* (Basic Books, 1989), p. 369.

40. Paul A. Volcker and William F. Winter, "Introduction: Democracy and Public Service," in DiIulio, *Deregulating the Public Service,* p. xvi.

41. Barbara S. Romzek and Melvin J. Dubnick suggest, however, that if American citizens are required to make a trade-off between accountability for finances, fairness, and performance, they will choose finances and fairness over performance: "the American system has consistently come down on the side of accountability [for finances and fairness], accepting the administrative inefficiencies as a necessary price to be paid." "Issues of Accountability in Flexible Personnel Systems," in Patricia W. Ingraham, Barbara S. Romzek and Associates, eds., *New Paradigms for Government* (Jossey-Bass, 1994), pp. 263–64.

42. The typical accountability system, which seeks to hold public managers accountable for both process and performance, reminds me of W. Edwards Deming's "stupid experiment" with the red and white beads. Public managers are supposed to "make" white beads from a box containing 800 red and 3,200 white beads. Unfortunately, the political authorities (that is, Deming) have failed to provide their public managers (volunteers from Deming's audience) with any mechanism for separating the red beads from the white ones, yet the political system (Deming again) berates its public managers for their "failure." Deming, *Out of the Crisis* (Center for Advanced Engineering Study, Massachusetts Institute of Technology, 1982), pp. 346–54; Mary Walton, *The Deming Management Method* (Perigee, 1986), pp. 40–51.

43. Frank Anechiarico, "Corruption Control *Means* Bureaucratic Pathology," *Public Integrity,* vol. 1, no. 1 (1999), p. 89.

44. Lisbeth B. Schorr, *Within Our Reach: Breaking the Cycle of Disadvantage* (Anchor Press/Doubleday 1988), p. 258. Schorr observes that "this suggests a fundamental contradiction between the needs of vulnerable children and families and the traditional requirements of professionalism and bureaucracy" (p. 259).

45. Martin A. Levin and Mary Bryna Sanger, *Making Government Work: How Entrepreneurial Executives Turn Bright Ideas into Real Results* (Jossey-Bass, 1994), pp. 216–17.

46. Marc D. Zegans, "The Dilemma of the Modern Public Manager: Satisfying the Virtues of Scientific and Innovative Management," in Alan A. Altshuler and Robert D. Behn, eds., *Innovation in American Government: Challenges, Opportunities, and Dilemmas* (Brookings, 1997), p. 115.

Steven Kelman has a different take on the impact of "rule-bound" organizations: "If an organization's tasks are standard and its environment slow to change, this [rules that deprive public managers of discretion] won't create any particular problems, since creativity or innovativeness are unnecessary. When that's not the case, rule-bound organizations are accidents waiting to happen." Kelman, *Procurement and Public Management: The Fear of Discretion and the Quality of Government Performance* (AEI Press, 1990), p. 28.

47. Kettl, "The Global Revolution in Public Management," pp. 447, 448.

48. Arguing that "it is far from clear [that] the reform measures adopted by different countries amount to a clear 'new paradigm,'" Hood derides "empowerment" as a "modish but conveniently vague idea." Hood, "Beyond 'Progressivism,'" pp. 164, 161.

49. To the frontline worker, how much difference does it make whether the agency head has been empowered or contracted? Maybe not much. In both situations, the agency head seeks to produce results as measured by improvements in some performance indicators (though for the contractor these indicators may be specified in the contract). In both situations, the agency head can experiment with different service-delivery mechanisms (though the empowered agency head may have more latitude to define the service to be delivered and to also experiment with performance indicators that reflect that particular service).

50. Kettl, "The Global Revolution in Public Management," p. 448.

51. Nagel, Editor's Introduction, *Journal of Policy Analysis and Management*, vol. 16, no. 3 (1997), p. 355.

52. Frank J. Thompson, and Norma M. Riccucci, "Reinventing Government," *Annual Review of Political Science*, vol. 1 (1998), pp. 235–37.

53. For an examination of the "pitfalls" of such performance contracts, see Robert D. Behn and Peter A. Kant, "Strategies for Avoiding the Pitfalls of Performance Contracting," *Public Productivity and Management Review*, vol. 22, no. 4 (1999), pp. 470–89.

54. Note that in Europe and elsewhere, privatization often means selling off public utilities that in the United States were never owned by a government.

55. For an analysis of such PBOs, see Alasdair Roberts, "Performance-Based Organizations: Assessing the Gore Plan," *Public Administration Review*, vol. 57, no. 6 (1997), pp. 465–78.

56. Peters, *The Future of Governing*, p. 19.

57. Ironically, the advocates of the new public management do not completely reject scientific management; instead of searching for the "one best way," however, they look for today's "best practice." They prefer "best practices" to the "one best way" because they accept that "best" is relative (not absolute): Tomorrow's best practice may be better than today's.

58. Peters concludes that the advocates of his "flexible government" model have "no clear recommendation" about accountability. *The Future of Governing,* p. 112.

59. The General Accounting Office notes that "Congress today faces the difficult question: Can grant programs be designed to promote flexibility at the state or local level as in traditional block grants, yet still provide the information needed to ensure accountability and support federal policy decisions?" Susan S. Westin, *Grant Programs: Design Features Shape Flexibility, Accountability, and Performance Information,* GAO/GGD-98-137 (General Accounting Office, June 1998), p. 1.

60. The challenge of creating public accountability for public work performed under contract by private organizations was not created by the new public management. It already existed. For a variety of analyses of this challenge, see the essays in Bruce L. R. Smith and D. C. Hague, eds., *The Dilemma of Accountability in Modern Government* (St. Martin's Press, 1971). For additional examinations of the accountability challenge for contracting out, see Lisa A. Dicke and J. Steven Ott, "Public Agency Accountability in Human Services Contracting," *Public Productivity and Management Review,* vol. 22, no. 4 (1999), pp. 502–16; John D. Donahue, "The Architecture of Accountability," chap. 2 of *The Privatization Decision: Public Ends, Private Means* (Basic Books, 1989), pp. 3–13; Robert S. Gilmour and Laura S. Jensen, "Reinventing Government Accountability: Public Functions, Privatization, and the Meaning of State Action," *Public Administration Review,* vol. 58, no. 3 (1998), pp. 247–58; Elke Loeffler, *Managing Accountability in Intergovernmental Partnerships* (Washington: Organisation for Economic Co-operation and Development, 1999); H. Brinton Milward, "Implications of Contracting Out: New Roles for the Hollow State," in Ingrahm, Romzek and Associates, *New Paradigms for Government,* pp. 41–62; H. Brinton Milward, "Symposium on the Hollow State: Capacity, Control, and Performance in Interorganizational Settings," *Journal of Public Administration Research and Theory,* vol. 6, no. 2 (1996), pp. 193–95 (as well as the other articles in this symposium).

61. Elsewhere I have argued that the study of public management should concentrate on "the big questions." See Robert D. Behn, "The Big Questions of Public Management," *Public Administration Review,* vol. 55, no. 4 (1995), pp. 313–24.

Basil Walker, the chief executive of New Zealand's Foundation of Research, Science, and Technology, reports that his nation's shift from traditional public administration to the new public management has not, however, created these problems. "The liberation of managers from central input controls," writes Walker, "has not lead [sic] to reckless behaviour as predicted by some. Instead, it has almost universally lead [sic] to responsible, innovative management and a focus on the real issues facing departments." "The New Zealand Experience, Reforming the Public Sector for Leaner Government and Improved Performance," a paper prepared for the Biennial Conference of the Commonwealth Association for Public Administration and Management, Malta, April 21–24, 1996, p. 11.

62. B. Guy Peters and Donald J. Savoie raise a different question: How can you have empowerment, contracting, and flexibility and also have policy coordination? Entrepreneurship and empowerment can "promote" what they call "policy incoherence." Thus they ask: "How will one be able to ensure a cross-cutting look at policy issues in a decentralized, empowered machinery of government?" "Managing Incoherence: The Coordination and Empowerment Conundrum," *Public Administration Review*, vol. 56, no. 3 (1996), pp. 282, 283, 288.

Donald F. Kettl makes a similar point: "Problems that, in particular, require horizontal coordination are difficult to attack within a system based on vertical control, from performance goals set by top officials to output measures gauging the behavior of bottom-level managers. More problems involve shared responsibility for results, which conflicts with the instinct toward ever-greater specification of every manager's responsibilities." "The Global Revolution in Public Management," p. 452.

Eugene Bardach implicitly responds that such horizontal coordination can take place at the service-delivery level through interagency collaboratives. *Getting Agencies to Work Together: The Practice and Theory of Managerial Craftsmanship* (Brookings, 1998).

For a discussion of the coordination challenge in New Zealand's version of the new public management, see Jonathan Boston: "The Problems of Policy Coordination: The New Zealand Experience," *Governance*, vol. 5, no. 1 (1992), pp. 88–103.

63. This critique, continues Borins, includes potential conflicts between entrepreneurship and the "equitable treatment of all citizens." *Innovating with Integrity*, p. 8.

64. Frederick C. Mosher, "The Changing Responsibilities and Tactics of the Federal Government," *Public Administration Review*, vol. 40, no. 6 (1980), p. 544.

65. Kenneth P. Ruscio, "Trust in the Administrative State," *Public Administration Review*, vol. 57, no. 5 (1997), p. 457.

66. Lynn, "A Critical Analysis of the New Public Management," pp. 120–21.

67. Kaufman, *Red Tape*, p. 4. Others offer similar contrasts in perspectives. B. Guy Peters observes that "one person's creativity might be another's malfeasance." Peters, *The Future of Governing*, p. 106. And Mark H. Moore and Margaret Jane Gates note that "One person's 'waste' is another person's 'quality service.'" *Inspectors-General: Junkyard Dogs or Man's Best Friend?* (Russell Sage Foundation, 1986), p. 20.

68. Larry D. Terry, "Why We Should Abandon the Misconceived Quest to Reconcile Public Entrepreneurship with Democracy," *Public Administration Review*, vol. 53, no. 4 (1993), pp. 393, 394; Larry D. Terry, "Administrative Leadership, Neo-Managerialism, and the Public Management Movement," *Public Administration Review*, vol. 58, no. 3 (1998), p. 198.

69. For various defenses of traditional public administration (and critiques of the new public management) see: H. George Frederickson, "Painting Bull's Eyes around Bullet Holes," *Governing,* December 1992, p. 61; H. George Frederickson, *The Spirit of Public Administration* (Jossey-Bass, 1997); Robert S. Gilmour and Laura S. Jensen, "Reinventing Government Accountability: Public Functions, Privatization, and the Meaning of 'State Action,'" *Public Administration Review,* vol. 58, no. 3 (1998), pp. 247–58; Ronald C. Moe, "Let's Rediscover Government, Not Reinvent It," *Government Executive,* June 1993, pp. 46–48, 60; Ronald C. Moe, "The 'Reinventing Government' Exercise: Misinterpreting the Problem, Misjudging the Consequences," *Public Administration Review,* vol. 54, no. 2 (1994), pp. 111–22; Ronald C. Moe and Robert S. Gilmour, "Rediscovering Principles of Public Administration: The Neglected Foundation of Public Law," *Public Administration Review,* vol. 55, no. 2 (1995), pp. 135–46; Donald J. Savoie, "What Is Wrong with the New Public Management?" *Canadian Public Administration,* vol. 38, no. 1 (1995), 112–21; and Donald J. Savoie, "Just Another Voice from the Pulpit," *Canadian Public Administration,* vol. 38, no. 1 (1995), 133–36. For a reflective analysis of such critiques, see Mathiasen, "The New Public Management and Its Critics."

70. Peters, *The Future of Governing,* p. 12.

71. In analyzing personnel systems, Romzek and Dubnick distinguish between those that are accountable and those that are flexible. "Issues of Accountability in Flexible Personnel Systems."

Certainly we need government's personnel systems to be accountable for fairness. But why do we need them to be flexible? Because (presumably) if line managers have more flexibility, they will be able to employ and deploy people in a way that improves performance. Flexibility itself is not an important political or even managerial value; flexibility is important only to the extent that it helps produce better results. Indeed, if we want to hold public managers accountable for performance, we have to give them some flexibility.

72. Peters, *The Future of Governing,* p. 8.

73. Moe and Gilmour, "Rediscovering the Principles of Public Administration," pp. 142, 135.

74. Ibid., pp. 138, 139, 140, 139. Moe and Gilmour construct accountability in a way that automatically precludes any nonhierarchical relationship from producing the "democratic accountability" that they desire. As Edward P. Weber observes of Moe's thinking about the new public management, he "has subjected the new arrangements to a scathing critique using a conceptualization of accountability that, by definition, finds them unaccountable." "The Question of Accountability in Historical Perspective: From Jackson to Contemporary Grassroots Ecosystem Management," *Administration & Society,* vol. 31, no. 4 (1999), p. 452.

75. Moe and Gilmour, "Rediscovering the Principles of Public Administration," pp. 135, 139, 141.

76. Ibid., pp. 135, 137, 138, 136, 138.

77. Ibid., pp. 142, 137, 140, 143, 141.

78. Ibid., p. 138.

79. At the beginning of World War II, Carl Joachim Friedrich and Herman Finer engaged in a similar debate, with Friedrich arguing that "administrative responsibility can no longer be looked upon as merely a responsibility for executing policies already formulated," and Finer responding that one kind of administrative "abuse of power" is "*over*feasance, where a duty is undertaken beyond what law and custom oblige or empower." Friedrich, "Public Policy and the Nature of Administrative Responsibility," in C. J. Friedrich and Edward S. Mason, *Public Policy: A Yearbook of the Graduate School of Public Administration, Harvard University* (Harvard University Press, 1940), p. 5; Herman Finer, "Administrative Responsibility in Democratic Government," *Public Administration Review,* vol. 1, no. 4 (1941), pp. 337–38.

Friedrich called the politics-administration dichotomy "a misleading distinction," asserted that it was based on "the metaphysical, if not abstruse, idea of a will of the state," and argued that "the idea that this state has a will immediately entangles one in all of the difficulties of assuming a group personality or something akin to it." Moreover, he emphasized the importance of improving government performance:

> Too often it is taken for granted that as long as we can keep the government from doing wrong we have made it responsible. What is more important is to insure effective action of any sort. To stimulate initiative, even at the risk of mistakes, must nowadays never be lost sight of as a task in making government's services responsible. An official should be as responsible for inaction as for wrong action.

To Friedrich, "responsible conduct of administrative functions is not so much enforced as it is elicited." Moreover, he concluded that the mechanisms "by which a measure of genuine responsibility can be secured under modern conditions appear to be manifold, and they must all be utilized for achieving the best effect." "Public Policy and the Nature of Administrative Responsibility," pp. 5, 6, 4, 10, 19, 24.

Finer disagreed: "Administrative responsibility is not less important to democratic government than administrative efficiency." Accepting the basics of the politics-administration dichotomy, Finer argued that civil servants "are not to decide their own course; they are to be responsible to the elected representatives of the public, and these are to determine the course of action of public servants to the most minute degree that is technically feasible." These public servants were to be subjected to external control, through the courts, through the "disciplinary controls within the hierarchy of the administrative departments," and through "sanctions exercised by the representative assembly." "Administrative Responsibility in Democratic Government," pp. 335, 336.

Finer observed that "we in public administration must beware of the too good man as well as the too bad." And thus he was wary of administrative discretion: "A system which gives the 'good' man freedom of action in the expectation of benefiting from all the 'good' he has in him, must sooner or later (since no man is without faults) cause his faults to be loaded on to the public." Indeed, Finer argued that "Professor Friedrich finds himself compelled to adopt quite an undemocratic view of government, and to throw scorn upon the popular will." "Administrative Responsibility in Democratic Government," pp. 338, 346.

80. Mathiasen, "The New Public Management and Its Critics," pp. 288, 290, 292.

81. Hugh Heclo, "OMB and the Presidency—The Problem of 'Neutral Competence,'" *The Public Interest*, no. 38 (1975), p. 81.

82. Article II, Section 3.

83. Woodrow Wilson, "The Study of Administration," *Political Science Quarterly*, vol. 2, no. 2 (1887), p. 212.

84. Ronald C. Moe, "'Law' Versus 'Performance' as Objective Standard," *Public Administration Review*, vol. 48, no. 2 (1988), p. 675. The other publications in this debate are Barry Bozeman, *All Organizations Are Public: Bridging Public and Private Organizational Theories* (Jossey-Bass, 1987); Ronald C. Moe, "Exploring the Limits of Privatization," *Public Administration Review*, vol. 47, no. 6 (1987), pp. 453–60; Barry Bozeman, "Exploring the Limits of Public and Private Sectors: Sector Boundaries as Maginot Line," *Public Administration Review*, vol. 48, no. 2 (1988), pp. 672–74.

85. B. Guy Peters and John Pierre suggest that it has been. They write that the advocates of the new public management have shown "little concern about these issues [of accountability], since accountability is seen as one of the strongest points of the model." "Governance without Government? Rethinking Public Administration," *Journal of Public Administration Research and Theory*, vol. 8, no. 2 (1998), p. 228.

86. Colin S. Diver, "Engineers and Entrepreneurs: The Dilemma of Public Management," *Journal of Policy Analysis and Management*, vol. 1, no. 3 (1982), pp. 402–06. The typical assignment given to a public manager, writes Diver, "is like asking an engineer to design some vaguely defined portion of a bridge to be built at an uncertain location over a river of constantly changing width, using materials whose characteristics are incompletely understood. Would it be any surprise if our engineer designed a ferry and called it a bridge? And then resigned a year later to become a government relations consultant to the ferry company?" (p. 405).

87. Alan A. Altshuler, "Bureaucratic Innovation, Democratic Accountability, and Political Incentives," in Altshuler and Behn, *Innovation in American Government*, p. 44.

Chapter Three

1. Woodrow Wilson, "The Study of Administration," *Political Science Quarterly*, vol. 2, no. 2 (1887), pp. 197–222.

2. Frederick Winslow Taylor, *The Principles of Scientific Management* (Harper & Brothers, 1911), reprinted in Frederick Winslow Taylor, *Scientific Management*

Comprising Shop Management, The Principles of Scientific Management, and Testimony before the Special House Committee (Harper & Brothers, 1947), p. 25 (of *The Principles of Scientific Management*).

3. Although they never worked together, Wilson, Taylor, and Weber were of the same generation. Wilson and Taylor were born in 1856; Weber in 1864. Thus, not surprisingly, their beliefs and proposals were quite compatible. After all, they were not merely shaping opinions; they were also reporting them and reflecting the culture and needs of their times. As Brian Fry observes of Taylor's scientific management, it "was clearly a movement right for its time." *Mastering Public Administration: From Max Weber to Dwight Waldo* (Chatham House, 1989), p. 68. Yet, of the three, only Taylor aggressively sought to convince the American public of the value of his ideas, and only Taylor had immediate influence.

Weber's thinking was not easily available in the United States until after World War II, when Hans H. Gerth and C. Wright Mills translated and published a collection of Weber's writings (*From Max Weber: Essays in Sociology* [Oxford University Press, 1946]), and A. M. Henderson and Talcott Parsons did the same (Max Weber, *The Theory of Social and Economic Organization* [Free Press, 1947]). Still, American businesses and governments created large bureaucracies very similar to those that Weber advocated.

Although Wilson became actively engaged in American politics, his essay "The Study of Administration" (1887) was not well known until decades after its publication. Much more influential in establishing the politics-administration dichotomy was Frank Goodnow's book, *Politics and Administration: A Study in Government* (Russell & Russell, 1900), published thirteen years later, though the 1941 republication of Wilson's article in *Political Science Quarterly* (vol. 56, December, pp. 481–506) did have an impact. For a discussion of the historical significance of Wilson's article, see Paul P. Van Riper, "The American Administrative State: Wilson and the Founders—An Unorthodox View," *Public Administration Review,* vol. 43, no. 6 (1983), pp. 477–90; Daniel W. Martin, "The Fading Legacy of Woodrow Wilson," *Public Administration Review,* vol. 48, no. 3 (1988), pp. 631–36; Jack Rabin and James S. Bowman, eds., *Politics and Administration: Woodrow Wilson and American Public Administration* (Dekker, 1984).

4. When government deliberately creates a policy that is designed to treat people differently—for example, affirmative action—it is difficult to evaluate the fairness of the implementation. Thus both the policy and implementation will be accused of being unfair.

5. B. Guy Peters and Donald J. Savoie, "Managing Incoherence: The Coordination and Empowerment Conundrum," *Public Administration Review,* vol. 56, no. 3 (1996), p. 285.

6. Richard D. White Jr. offers a history of the rise and fall of efficiency as an important value in American public administration, suggesting that it peaked in 1937 and then "falls quickly from intellectual grace." "More Than an Analytical Tool:

Examining the Ideological Role of Efficiency," *Public Productivity and Management Review*, vol. 23, no. 1 (1999), p. 8.

The theorists of public administration may no longer regard efficiency as highly as their predecessors did; still, it remains a resonant value in American politics. It is not, however, a neutral value. See Henry Mintzberg, "A Note on That Dirty Word 'Efficiency,'" in *Mintzberg on Management: Inside Our Strange World of Organizations* (Free Press, 1989), pp. 330–34.

7. John Urh, "Institutions of Integrity: Balancing Values and Verification in Democratic Governance," *Public Integrity*, vol. 1, no. 1 (1999), p. 102.

8. Hierarchical accountability also meshes with concepts of principal-agent theory. William R. Keech writes: "In democratic governments, public policy is made by elected officials who are accountable to the electorate, or by unelected officials who are accountable to elected officials and to the public. Implicitly, the issue of accountability involves delegation of decision-making authority from a principal to an agent." "Rules, Discretion, and Accountability in Macroeconomic Policymaking," *Governance*, vol. 5, no. 3 (1992), pp. 259–278.

9. Alexander Hamilton, James Madison, and John Jay, *The Federalist Papers* (Bantam Books, 1982), no. 51, p. 262.

10. Ibid., pp. 261, 263–64.

11. Ibid., no. 49, p. 257.

12. Ibid., no. 48, pp. 254, 250.

13. Ibid., no. 51, p. 262.

14. Ibid., pp. 262, 263.

15. Garry Wills, introduction to Hamilton, Madison, and Jay, *The Federalist Papers*, p. xv. Of the three authors, only Hamilton uses the words *checks* and *balances* together. In Federalist 9, he discusses several innovations in "the science of politics" including "the introduction of legislative ballances and checks." Hamilton, Madison, and Jay, *The Federalist Papers*, no. 9, p. 38.

Commenting on the "modern cult of checks as the primary virtue of the Constitution," Garry Wills notes that, in *The Federalist Papers*, Madison uses the word *check* nine times. *A Necessary Evil: A History of American Distrust of Government* (Simon & Schuster, 1999), p. 75.

16. Madison had faith in democracy—"the people are the only legitimate fountain of power"—but not too much faith: "The *passions* therefore not *the reasons*, of the public, would sit in judgment. But it is the reason of the public alone that ought to controul and regulate the government. The passions [of the public] ought to be controuled and regulated by the government." Hamilton, Madison, and Jay, *The Federalist Papers*, no. 49, pp. 255, 258.

17. In his review of our constitutional history and "constitution myths," Wills argues that these accountability mechanisms did not exist; in the Constitution, "there were no real checks, no balances, no separation of powers, no equality of

branches, no protection of rights (whether those of the states of those of individuals)." *A Necessary Evil,* p. 58.

18. Wilson, "The Study of Administration," pp. 209, 210.

19. Ibid., pp. 212, 211. Nonetheless, Wilson concedes that it is not obvious exactly where the line runs between politics and administration until one looks at the particulars of an issue (p. 211). Thus, writes Niels Aage Thorsen, "Wilson explicitly regarded the separation of administration from politics as a practical matter to be settled when concrete issues arose in the course of changing governmental functions and techniques." *The Political Thought of Woodrow Wilson: 1875–1910* (Princeton University Press, 1988), p. 119.

20. Wilson, "The Study of Administration," pp. 216–17, 210.

21. Ibid., p. 210.

22. Louis D. Brandeis, *Scientific Management and Railroads, Being Part of a Brief Submitted to the Interstate Commerce Commission* (New York: The Engineering Magazine, 1912).

23. Wilson, "The Study of Administration," pp. 210, 201. Indeed, one of "the most prominent features of Wilson's political scholarship," writes Thorsen, was "a maturing conviction that scientific knowledge of economic, political, and administrative practices could be introduced into the conduct of government." *The Political Thought of Woodrow Wilson,* pp. x–xi.

24. Wilson, "The Study of Administration," pp. 218, 220, 202.

25. Taylor, *Testimony before the Special House Committee,* p. 27.

26. Taylor, *The Principles of Scientific Management,* p. 7.

27. Taylor, *Testimony before the Special House Committee,* pp. 75, 61, 60.

28. Taylor, *The Principles of Scientific Management,* pp. 16, 32, 25.

29. Ibid., pp. 36–38.

30. Ibid., p. 39.

31. Charles D. Wrege and Ronald G. Greenwood, *Frederick W. Taylor, The Father of Scientific Management* (Business One Irwin, 1991), p. 194.

32. Taylor, *The Principles of Scientific Management,* p. 37.

33. Ibid., pp. 40, 142.

34. Taylor's concept of the manager as someone who was "responsible for the 'thinking' aspects of organizational activity," Roberts emphasizes, "was a novelty at the time":

> Even in the public sector, the role of the "manager" in the contemporary sense had not yet emerged. If you look at the classification plan for the U.S. federal civil service developed in 1920, you will see that most positions are for various kinds of clerks—right up to the top of the department, where you have head clerks and then assistant secretaries and so on. In Canada, you had the head clerk, deputy minister and minister. Below, you had principal clerks,

assistant clerks, etc. (The top civil servant in Canada is still called Clerk of the Privy Council.) No one had yet developed a view of activity within bureaucracies that was not premised on the notion that the work was essentially clerical.

Alasdair Roberts, personal communication, February 15, 2000.

35. Taylor, *The Principles of Scientific Management,* pp. 40, 142, 8. In his appearance before Congress on January 25, 1912, Taylor testified that baseball "represents one of the best illustrations of the application of the principles of scientific management," that on a baseball team, "you will find almost all of the elements of scientific management":

> Every single element of the game of baseball has been the subject of the most intimate, the closest study of many men, and, finally, the best way of doing each act that takes place on the baseball field has been fairly well agreed upon and established as a standard throughout the country. The players have not only been told the best way of making each important motion or play, but they have been taught, coached, and trained to it through months of drilling. And I think that every man who has watched first-class play, or who knows anything of the management of the modern baseball team, realizes fully the utter impossibility of winning with the best team of individual players that was ever gotten together unless every man on the team obeys the signals or order of the coach and obeys them at once when the coach gives those orders; that is, without the intimate cooperation between all members of the team and the management, which is characteristic of scientific management.

Testimony before the Special House Committee, p. 46. For a dissenting view of the existence of a "best way of doing each act on the baseball field" (as well as in public management), see Robert D. Behn, "The Futile Search for the One Best Way," *Governing,* July 1996, p. 82.

36. Gerth and Mills, *From Max Weber,* p. 197.

37. Ibid., pp. 198,199.

38. Herbert Kaufman, "Emerging Conflicts in the Doctrines of Public Administration," *The American Political Science Review,* vol. 50, no. 4 (1956), pp. 1057–73. Hugh Heclo offers a detailed definition of "neutral competence": "giving one's cooperation and best independent judgment of the issues to partisan bosses—and of being sufficiently uncommitted to be able to do so for a succession of partisan leaders. . . . Its motto is 'Speak out, shut up, carry up, carry out.'" "OMB and the Presidency—The Problem of 'Neutral Competence,'" *The Public Interest,* no. 38 (1975), pp. 81, 82. See also Francis E. Rourke, "Responsiveness and Neutral Competence in American Bureaucracy," *Public Administration Review,* vol. 52, no. 6 (1992), pp. 539–46.

39. Gerth and Mills, *From Max Weber,* p. 95. Weber would oppose the new public management with its politically entrepreneurial public managers exercising leadership. "To take a stand, to be passionate," he writes, "is the politician's element, and above all the element of the political leader." By contrast, even the "'political' administrator," he argues, "shall not do precisely what the politician, the leader as well as his following, must always and necessarily do, namely, *fight.*" (p. 95).

40. Quoted by Reinhard Bendix, *Max Weber: An Intellectual Portrait* (University of California Press, 1960), p. 421. Two centuries before Weber did so, Gottfried Leibniz, the co-inventor of calculus with Newton, suggested that computers would eventually make judicial decisions. Paul Strathern, *Turing and the Computer* (Anchor Books, 1997), p. 23.

41. Weber (trans. Henderson and Parsons), *The Theory of Social and Economic Organization,* p. 337.

42. Gerth and Mills, *From Max Weber,* p. 201.

43. Ibid., pp. 215, 216.

44. Why are Weber's bureaucratic rules more common in government than in business? Because, government needs to be fair to everyone and diligent in accounting for the taxpayer's money. "Government is properly conscious that it administers public funds and must account for every penny," writes Peter F. Drucker. We dare not even appear to accept the slightest misuse of the taxpayers' money. After all, Drucker continues, "a 'little dishonesty' in government is a corrosive disease. It rapidly spreads to infect the whole body politic." Thus, he concludes, "to fear corruption in government is not irrational." Government "is, of necessity, concerned with procedure"; it is "by definition, a 'government of paper forms.'" Indeed, "any government that is not a 'government of paper forms' degenerates rapidly into a mutual looting society." Unfortunately, catching every potential case of fraud, waste, or abuse is expensive; thus the need to catch and deter corruption, argues Drucker, inevitably means that "government is a poor manager." "The Sickness of Government," *The Public Interest,* no. 14 (1969), p. 15.

45. Gerth and Mills, *From Max Weber,* p. 214.

46. For a discussion of this problem, see Jeffrey Bradach, "The Challenge of Coordination," Harvard Business School Note 9-493-037 (June 9, 1993).

47. Robert D. Behn, "Public Management: Should It Strive to be Art, Science, or Engineering?" *Journal of Public Administration Research and Theory,* vol. 6, no. 1 (1996), pp. 100–02.

48. Behn, "The Futile Search for the One Best Way," p. 82.

49. Why did anyone ever believe that we could separate administration from politics? And why do people continue to believe it or, at least, behave as if they do? For a historical explanation, see Alasdair Roberts, "Demonstrating Neutrality: The Rockefeller Philanthropies and the Evolution of Public Administration, 1927–1936," *Public Administration Review,* vol. 54, no. 3 (1994), pp. 221–28.

50. Paul H. Appleby, *Policy and Administration* (University of Alabama Press, 1949), p. 43. Still, the politics-administration dichotomy is not dead. In most of the English-speaking world, it is very much alive. It is a cornerstone of New Zealand's reforms (which give politicians responsibility for outcomes and administrators responsibility for outputs) and of Britain's Next Steps agencies (with parliamentary ministers responsible for policy and the agency executives responsible for administration). For a defense of, as he calls it, the "policy-operations distinction," see Charles Polidano, "The Bureaucrat Who Fell under a Bus: Ministerial Responsibility, Executive Agencies, and the Derek Lewis Affair in Britain," *Governance,* vol. 12, no. 2 (1999), pp. 201–29.

51. Wilson, "The Study of Administration," p. 213.

52. Ronald C. Moe writes that, in the original report of the National Performance Review, "Congress is viewed largely as a nuisance that insists on micro-managing the beleaguered agency manager and should accept the lesser role in management implicit in the entrepreneurial management paradigm." "The 'Reinventing Government' Exercise: Misinterpreting the Problem, Misjudging the Consequences," *Public Administration Review,* vol. 54, no. 2 (1994), p. 117.

53. Edward P. Weber offers another historical interpretation with five different conceptions of accountability: Jacksonian, Progressives/New Deal, Public Interest Egalitarianism, Neoconservative Efficiency, and Grassroots Ecosystem Management (or GREM). My description of accountability (as drawn from the ideas of Wilson, Taylor, and Max Weber) is closest to his Progressives/New Deal model: "hierarchical control, trained meritocracy, written rules and procedures, specialization of tasks according to function, and clear lines of authority." "The Question of Accountability in Historical Perspective: From Jackson to Contemporary Grassroots Ecosystem Management," *Administration & Society,* vol. 31, no. 4 (1999), pp. 462–71, 472. Weber's "Grassroots Ecosystem Management" is a variant of the compact of mutual, collective accountability that I describe in chapter 7.

54. See Goodnow, *Politics and Administration;* Luther Gulick, "Notes on the Theory of Organization," in Luther Gulick and Lyndall Urwick, eds., *Papers on the Science of Administration* (New York: Institute of Public Administration, 1937), pp. 3–45; and Roberts, "Demonstrating Neutrality."

55. Gerald E. Caiden writes: "It took several centuries in the tortuous evolution of the modern nation state to develop a coherent, binding, respected ideology of public accountability." "The Problem of Ensuring the Public Accountability of Public Officials," in O. P. Dwivedi and Joseph G. Jabbra, eds., *Public Service Accountability: A Comparative Perspective* (Kumarian Press, 1988), p. 19.

56. Kaufman, "Emerging Conflicts in the Doctrines of Public Administration," p. 1057.

57. The initiative does not quite work in practice as it is supposed to in theory. In California, writes Peter Schrag, the initiative "had once been regarded as the people's weapon against the interests"—or what Charles Mahtesian calls "a populist

tool to wield against the business lobbies that possessed a stranglehold." No more. Now the special interests have learned to deploy their resources (money and people) to get on the ballot their bills that the legislature rejected. Mahtesian calls initiatives "doomsday weapons whose use by interest groups is controlled by a complex process of mutual deterrence." To Schrag, the initiative has become "a Rube Goldberg machine that has so divided and concealed responsibilities that it could do nothing but further alienate already cynical voters." Schrag, "California's Elected Anarchy: A Government Destroyed by Popular Referendum," *Harper's Magazine,* November 1994, pp. 54, 52; Mahtesian, "Grassroots Charade," *Governing,* November 1998, pp. 38, 40. For a detailed analysis of "the seductive simplicity of the up-or-down initiative vote," see David S. Broder, *Democracy Derailed: Initiative Campaigns and the Power of Money* (Harcourt, 2000), p. 243.

58. In the 1970s, by one estimate, the United States had approximately 7,000 public authorities. Annmarie H. Walsh, *The Public's Business* (MIT Press, 1978), p. 6.

59. For an analysis linking Wilson's politics-administration dichotomy and the theory of public authorities, see Jameson W. Doig, "'If I See a Murderous Fellow Sharpening a Knife Cleverly . . .': The Wilsonian Dichotomy and the Public Authority Tradition," *Public Administration Review,* vol. 43, no. 4 (1983), pp. 292–304.

60. Wilson, "The Study of Administration," p. 201.

61. When the desire to exploit technical expertise conflicted with hierarchical accountability, hierarchical accountability lost, and today's supporters of traditional public administration are not pleased: "The establishment of non-accountable, quasi-governmental bodies," writes Ronald C. Moe, "should cease, and entities now functioning largely at the margins of the state should be privatized or assigned regular agency status, where appropriate, and brought under democratic rules of accountability." "Let's Rediscover Government, Not Reinvent It," *Government Executive,* June 1993, p. 48.

62. For a discussion of professionalism and professional standards as a basis for accountability, see Carl Joachim Friedrich, "Public Policy and the Nature of Administrative Responsibility," in C. J. Friedrich and Edward S. Mason, *Public Policy: A Yearbook of the Graduate School of Public Administration* (Harvard University Press, 1940), pp. 3–24.

63. Gerth and Mills, *From Max Weber,* pp. 234, 232. Weber offers an interesting example: "All the scornful decrees of Frederick the Great concerning the 'abolition of serfdom' were derailed, as it were, in the course of their realization because the official mechanism simply ignored them as the occasional ideas of a dilettante" (p. 234).

64. Ibid., p. 233.

65. Marver H. Bernstein, *Regulating Business by Independent Commission* (Princeton University Press, 1955).

66. For example, see Dorothy Nelkin, *Jetport: The Boston Airport Controversy* (Transaction Books, 1974). (Full disclosure: I play a bit part in this "controversy.")

67. For a general critique of the accountability of independent government agencies, see Doig, "'If I See a Murderous Fellow Sharpening a Knife Cleverly . . .'"

68. Paul C. Light, *Monitoring Government: Inspectors General and the Search for Accountability* (Brookings, 1993), p. 39.

69. Mark H. Moore and Margaret Jane Gates, *Inspectors-General: Junkyard Dogs or Man's Best Friend?* (Russell Sage Foundation, 1986), pp. 12, 15. Congress, writes Light, liked the inspector-general concept for four reasons: it "would guarantee high rates of return—budgetary and political; create a new legislative arena in an era of fiscal restraint; provide protection, albeit minimal, against the growing lack of public confidence in government; and give Congress an opportunity to take a more aggressive role in federal management." *Monitoring Government*, p. 43.

70. Light comments on the irony that, at a time when the private sector was adopting the ideas of total quality management—in particular, the idea of building quality in at every stage rather than checking up for it at the end—the public sector was placing a greater emphasis on such post-hoc checking. Congress and the president, writes Light, put "their faith in compliance accountability" in part because it was a "less costly solution" than creating the organizational capacity necessary to produce quality up front. *Monitoring Government*, pp. 17, 57.

71. Light, *Monitoring Government*, pp. 160, 149, 156, 151, 102, 208, 211. Light argues that the Reagan administration sent its inspectors general a clear message: "The more statistical accomplishments produced in the war on waste—measured by dollars saved and cheaters caught—the more the IG office will grow and prosper" (pp. 103–04).

72. Moore and Gates, *Inspectors-General*, p. 5.

73. Light, *Monitoring Government*, pp. 194–97.

74. Ibid., p. 224. To reduce fraud, waste, and abuse, notes Light, Congress had options other than creating inspectors general to do compliance monitoring.

75. Moore and Gates, *Inspectors-General*, p. 74.

76. "No longer can it be said that nothing good came out of Whitewater, Monica and impeachment," wrote David S. Broder, when the Independent Counsel Act died. The concept "offends the constitutional principle of separation of powers and damages the political accountability that underlies our whole system of government. . . . The office of an independent counsel is, in effect, a fourth branch of government, accountable to no one." "Goodbye, Independent Counsel Law," *Washington Post*, June 27, 1999, p. B7.

Moreover, both Democrats and Republicans shared this concern about the independent counsel's lack of accountability: "There is no accountability," said Representative Bob Matsui (D-Calif.). Quoted by Michael Doyle, "Independent Counsels Endangered," [Raleigh, N.C.] *News & Observer*, February 13, 1999. "You can't have both [independence and accountability] at the same time," said Senator Fred Thompson (R-Tenn.). Quoted in "After Starr, Alternatives Considered," [Raleigh, N.C.] *News & Observer*, March 1, 1999.

77. John Delaware Lewis, *D. Iunni Iuvenalis Satirae with Literal English Prose Translation and Notes* (London: Rubner & Co: 1873), p. 71.

78. B. Guy Peters and John Pierre write: "Traditional models of public administration provide detailed rules concerning the deliberation process, partly because regulating the process is the Weberian method of output control; a legally correct deliberation process was believed to imply a correct outcome." "Governance without Government? Rethinking Public Administration," *Journal of Public Administration Research and Theory,* vol. 8, no. 2 (1998), p. 232.

79. Richard B. Stewart, "The Reformation of American Administrative Law," *Harvard Law Review,* vol. 88, no. 8 (1975), pp. 1670–71.

80. Charles Reich, "The New Property," *Yale Law Journal,* vol. 73, no. 5 (1964), pp. 733–87.

81. Stewart, "The Reformation of American Administrative Law," p. 1670; see also pp. 1681–82. In addition, Stewart argues, the standing in both administrative and judicial proceedings was broadened because administrative agencies tended to exercise their discretion in favor of narrow but organized interests rather than the general interest (pp. 1670, 1682–87).

82. Joseph L. Sax, *Defending the Environment: A Strategy for Citizen Action* (Alfred A. Knopf: 1971), p. 57.

83. Accountability by litigation, however, is no longer strictly an American phenomenon. David G. Mathiasen writes: "While the United States is well known as a litigious society, the trend toward more and more dispute resolution through administrative law tribunals or the courts is common to most OECD countries." "The New Public Management and Its Critics," in Lawrence R. Jones, Kuno Schedler, and Stephen W. Wade, eds., *International Perspectives on the New Public Management: Advances in International Comparative Management,* Supplement 3 (JAI Press, 1997), pp. 290–91.

84. Alexis de Tocqueville, *Democracy in America,* ed. Richard D. Heffner (New American Library, 1956), p. 126.

85. Phillip J. Cooper, "Accountability and Administrative Reform: Toward Convergence and Beyond," in B. Guy Peters and Donald J. Savoie, eds., *Governance in a Changing Environment* (McGill-Queen's University Press, 1995), pp. 181–82.

86. Gary E. Miller and Ira Iscoe, "A State Mental Health Commissioner and the Politics of Mental Illness," in Erwin C. Hargrove and John C. Glidewell, eds., *Impossible Jobs in Public Management* (University Press of Kansas, 1990), pp. 120, 122, 123, 122.

87. Mark H. Moore, "Realms of Obligation and Virtue," in Joel L. Fleishman, Lance Liebman, and Mark H. Moore, eds., *Public Duties: The Moral Obligations of Government Officials* (Harvard University Press, 1981), p. 30.

88. Cooper, "Accountability and Administrative Reform," p. 183.

89. Colin Campbell, "Public Service and Democratic Accountability," in Richard A. Chapman, ed., *Ethics in Public Service* (Ottawa: Carleton University Press, 1993), p. 111.

90. Barbara S. Romzek and Melvin J. Dubnick, "Accountability in the Public Sector: Lessons from the Challenger Tragedy," *Public Administration Review*, vol. 47, no. 3 (1987), pp. 227–38; Romzek and Dubnick, "Issues of Accountability in Flexible Personnel Systems," in Patricia W. Ingraham, Barbara S. Romzek and Associates, *New Paradigms for Government* (Jossey-Bass, 1994), pp. 263–94.

91. Kevin P. Kearns, *Managing for Accountability: Preserving the Public Trust in Public and Nonprofit Organizations* (Jossey-Bass, 1996), p. 27.

92. John W. Langford, "Responsibility in the Senior Public Service: Marching to Several Drummers," *Canadian Public Administration*, vol. 27, no. 4 (1984), pp. 520, 513, 515, 513.

93. Light, *Thickening Government: Federal Hierarchy and the Diffusion of Accountability* (Brookings, 1995), pp. 182, 140.

94. Joseph Nocera, "Who's Running This Country, Anyway? We, the Lawyers," *Fortune*, November 8, 1999, pp. 38–39.

95. John Maynard Keynes, *The General Theory of Employment, Interest, and Money* (Harcourt, Brace & Co., 1936), pp. 383–84.

Chapter Four

1. Others offer a different breakdown of the components of accountability:

Harvey C. Mansfield Sr. concludes there are four "main questions" of accountability: "for what, to whom, when, and by what means?" "Accountability and Congressional Oversight," in Bruce L. R. Smith and James D. Carroll, eds., *Improving the Accountability and Performance of Government* (Brookings, 1982), p. 61.

Kevin P. Kearns defines "three core elements that are at the heart of any accountability system: (a) a *higher authority* vested with the power of oversight, (b) an explicit *reporting mechanism* for conveying information to the higher authority, and (c) a *measure or criterion* used by the higher authority to assess compliance by subordinate institutions." "Institutional Accountability in Higher Education: A Strategic Approach," *Public Productivity and Management Review*, vol. 22, no. 2 (1998), p. 144.

The Alliance for Redesigning Government raises similar questions: "What does it mean for government to be responsible for results?" "What results?" "Who is to be held accountable for these results?" "What measures reliably indicate progress?" "What are the rewards for success and the consequences for failure?" *The Oregon Option: Early Lessons from a Performance Partnership on Building Results-Driven Accountability* (Washington: National Academy of Public Administration, 1996), p. 29.

2. Glen Hahn Cope, "Bureaucratic Reform and Issues of Political Responsiveness," *Journal of Public Administration Research and Theory*, vol. 7, no. 3 (1997), p. 466.

3. Marc D. Zegans, "The Dilemma of the Modern Public Manager: Satisfying the Virtues of Scientific and Innovative Management," in Alan A. Altshuler and Robert D. Behn, eds., *Innovation in American Government: Challenges, Opportunities, and Dilemmas* (Brookings, 1997), p. 109.

4. For example, from a study of the National Park Service, the General Accounting Office found:

> individual park managers have broad discretion in deciding how to spend park operating funds. . . . The most significant limitation associated with the Park Service's decentralized priority-setting and accountability systems is that they lack a focus on the results achieved with the funds spent. . . . No expectations have been established for the goals that are to be achieved in the parks, and there is no process for measuring progress towards these goals. As a result, the agency lacks a means to monitor progress towards achieving its goals and to hold park managers accountable for the results of park operations.

Victor S. Rezendes, *Park Service: Managing for Results Could Strengthen Accountability*, GAO/RCED-97-125 (General Accounting Office, April 1997), p. 2.

5. Cope ("Bureaucratic Reform and Issues of Political Responsiveness," p. 463) emphasizes that "responsiveness to customers is different from responsiveness to citizens." Michael A. Baer writes that we need "to distinguish between accountability and responsiveness." "Interest Groups and Accountability: An Incompatible Pair," in Scott Greer, Ronald D. Hedlund, and James L. Gibson, eds., *Accountability in Urban Society: Public Agencies under Fire, Urban Affairs Annual Review*, vol. 15 (Sage, 1978), p. 218. Indeed, it would seem that being responsive to some, individual citizens is, almost by definition, unfair to other, individual citizens.

6. To answer this Question of Entrepreneurship, Carl J. Bellone and George Frederick Goerl suggest that "if public entrepreneurs are to be held accountable, measures of accountability must shift from an input or process focus to one based on an outcome analysis." They recognize, however, that the challenge of reconciling "public-sector entrepreneurship" with "democratic values in government administration" requires more than traditional performance measurement. Thus, to resolve this fundamental conflict—"entrepreneurial autonomy versus democratic accountability"—they propose "a civic-regarding entrepreneurship." Public sector entrepreneurs, they argue, need "to facilitate increased citizen education and involvement." Thus Bellone and Goerl emphasize: "Only by testing entrepreneurial vision through a meaningful public participation process can public administrators and others ensure that public entrepreneurship is compatible with the values of democratic participation." "Reconciling Public Entrepreneurship and Democracy," *Public Administration Review*, vol. 52, no. 2 (1992), pp. 131–32. For a response to Bellone and Goerl, see Larry D. Terry, "Why We Should Abandon the Misconceived Quest to

Reconcile Public Entrepreneurship with Democracy," *Public Administration Review,* vol. 53, no. 4 (1993), pp. 393–95.

Eugene Lewis is also not very sanguine about the possibility for reconciling entrepreneurship and accountability. From his study of three public entrepreneurs (Hyman Rickover, J. Edgar Hoover, and Robert Moses), Lewis concludes that "freedom from accountability" is a "defining characteristic of the public entrepreneur." *Public Entrepreneurship: Toward a Theory of Bureaucratic Political Power* (Indiana University Press, 1980), p. 20.

7. B. Guy Peters, *The Future of Governing: Four Emerging Models* (University Press of Kansas, 1996), p. 6.

8. Under the new public management, New Zealand has attempted to do precisely this. See, for example, Donald F. Kettl, "The Global Revolution in Public Management: Driving Themes, Missing Links," *Journal of Policy Analysis and Management,* vol. 16, no. 3 (1997), pp. 450–52.

9. Dennis F. Thompson, *Political Ethics and Public Office* (Harvard University Press, 1987), p. 65. See also Dennis F. Thompson, "Moral Responsibility of Public Officials: The Problem of Many Hands," *American Political Science Review,* vol. 74, no. 4 (1980), p. 915.

10. O. P. Dwivedi and Joseph G. Jabbra, "Public Service Responsibility and Accountability," in Dwivedi and Jabbra, eds., *Public Service Accountability: A Comparative Perspective* (Kumarian Press, 1988), p. 2.

11. Certaintly Elliot Jaques believes that this is true in the private sector: "The hierarchical kind of organization we call bureaucracy did not emerge accidentally. It is the only form of organization that can enable a company to employ large numbers of people and yet preserve unambiguous accountability for the work they do." "In Praise of Hierarchy," *Harvard Business Review,* vol. 68, no. 1 (1990), p. 127.

12. Thompson, "Moral Responsibility of Public Officials," pp. 912, 914, 912, 915, 910, 913, 905, 907, 911, 912, 905.

13. Ibid., p. 908. Thompson, *Political Ethics and Public Office,* pp. 46–47.

14. Of course, it may be that the system permitted (or encouraged) these abuses. If so, someone should fix the system. But who should be accountable for fixing the system?

15. How should we set our expectations for performance? How high should we set a public agency's performance targets? We could demand that every public agency perform at its production-possibility frontier—if we could somehow determine this maximum level of effectiveness. But it would seem highly unrealistic to establish this as our expectation. After all, most businesses don't perform close to their production-possibility frontiers. So what should be our performance benchmark? Thompson proposes one possible baseline:

Even within the constraints of fixed routines, some officials perform worse than others; and these variations open some space for ascribing responsibility. A measure of actual variation—for example, an average performance—would not serve as a satisfactory base line from which to assess responsibility since all officials may be doing less well than they could, even given the constraints. We would need some criterion based on a hypothetical average performance—what the average official could reasonably be expected to do under the circumstances.

Thompson calls this the "'reasonable bureaucrat' test." "Moral Responsibility of Public Officials," p. 914.

Note that Thompson focuses on people who performs *worse* than others. This is because he seeks to identify public officials who have been negligent in fulfilling their moral responsibility—in this case, the moral responsibility to perform up to some satisfactory baseline. Why doesn't Thompson mention public officials who are performing better than others—better than his baseline? Is it because he is attempting to determine who should be punished?

16. Paul C. Light, *Thickening Government: Federal Hierarchy and the Diffusion of Accountability* (Brookings, 1995), pp. 64, 169.

17. Mary Walton, *Deming Management at Work* (G. P. Putnam's Sons, 1990), p. 20.

18. Rafael Aguayo, *Dr. Deming: The American Who Taught the Japanese about Quality* (Simon and Schuster, 1991), p. 59.

19. Michael Crowley, "Rage First in Line at Registry," *Boston Globe*, September 20, 1999, p. B8.

20. David Osborne and Ted Gaebler, *Reinventing Government* (Addison-Wesley, 1992), p. xviii.

21. The subordinate can, of course, offer a competing explanation: "I was just following orders. My boss made it extremely clear—though not in those precise words—what I was supposed to do. Given the way the system works, I had no choice." In fact, Mark Bovens offers ten "excuses that are commonly used by individual functionaries to clear themselves of the charge of individual accountability," *The Quest for Responsibility: Accountability and Citizenship in Complex Organizations* (Cambridge University Press, 1998), pp. 113–25.

22. On the Day of Atonement, the Lord commanded Moses to have his brother, Aaron, obtain "two goats for a sin offering;" one is to be sacrificed, while for the other, the Lord gave more detailed instructions: "Aaron shall lay both his hands upon the head of the live goat, and confess over him all the iniquities of the people of Israel, and all their transgressions, all their sins; and he shall put them upon the head of the goat, and send him away into the wilderness by the hand of a man who is in readiness. The goat shall bear all their iniquities upon him to a solitary land." Leviticus, 16:5, 21–22.

23. Sarah Lindenfeld, "Roof Collapses at Dorothea Dix," [Raleigh, N.C.] *News & Observer*, March 23, 1999, pp. 1B, 7B.

24. Steven Cohen and William Eimicke, "Is Public Entrepreneurship Ethical? A Second Look at Theory and Practice," *Public Integrity,* vol. 1, no. 1 (1999), p. 60.

25. Patrick B. Pexton, "Military Injustice," *Washington Post,* May 18, 1997.

26. For example, see Marin Landau, "Redundancy, Rationality, and the Problem of Duplication and Overlap," *Public Administration Review,* vol. 29, no. 4 (1969), pp. 346–58.

27. In the parliaments of the Westminster nations, ministerial accountability often requires the responsible minister to resign. But, Charles Polidano asks (primarily about the British government), when is "a failure of government . . . serious enough to justify the resignation of the responsible minister"? "Have the minister's personal actions (or inactions) contributed to the failure to such an extent that he or she can be held primarily to blame for it?" It is "very, very difficult to answer this question," writes Polidano, because (among other things) "government is complex. Complexity makes for convoluted reporting relationships and overlapping organizational jurisdictions." "The Bureaucrat Who Fell under a Bus: Ministerial Responsibility, Executive Agencies, and the Derek Lewis Affair in Britain," *Governance,* vol. 12, no. 2 (1999), p. 211. A similar answer (primarily in the Canadian context) comes from John W. Langford: "power is simply too widely diffused in most instances to hold specific individuals answerable or blameworthy in any meaningful sense." "Responsibility in the Senior Public Service, Marching to Several Drummers," *Canadian Public Administration,* vol. 27, no. 4 (1984), pp. 513–21.

28. I prefer Eugene Bardach's word *collaborative* to the traditional *network.* To me, the word *network* connotes a passive interconnection of people and organizations, whereas Bardach's collaborative suggests that its members are pursuing a specific, common purpose. Eugene Bardach, *Getting Agencies to Work Together: The Practice and Theory of Managerial Craftsmanship* (Brookings, 1998). Bardach and Cara Lesser define a collaborative as "two or more organizations that pool energies and perhaps funds (at least some of which are public) and seek thereby to overcome the fragmentation of services created by a host of current practices and institutional arrangements." "Accountability in Human Services Collaboratives—For What? and To Whom?" *Journal of Public Administration Research and Theory,* vol. 6, no. 2 (1996), p. 198.

Still, research on collaboration uses, almost exclusively, the word *network.* See, for example Ram Charan, "How Networks Reshape Organizations—For Results," *Harvard Business Review,* vol. 69, no. 5 (1991), pp. 104–15; Keith G. Provan and H. Brinton Milward, "A Preliminary Theory of Interorganizational Network Effectiveness: A Comparative Study of Four Community Mental Health Systems," *Administrative Science Quarterly,* vol. 40, no. 1 (1995), pp. 1–33; Laurence J. O'Toole Jr., "Treating Networks Seriously: Practical and Research-Based Agendas in Public Administration, *Public Administration Review,* vol. 57, no. 1 (1997), pp. 45–52; Laurence J. O'Toole Jr., "The Implications for Democracy in a Networked Bureaucratic World," *Journal of Public Administration Research and Theory*, vol. 7, no. 3 (1997), pp. 443–59; Robert Agranoff and Michael McGuire, "Multinetwork Management: Collaboration and the Hollow State in Local Economic Policy," *Journal of Public Administration Research and Theory*, vol. 8, no. 1 (1998), pp. 67–91; H. Brinton Milward and Keith G. Provan, "Principles for Controlling Agents: The Political Economy of Network Structure," *Journal of Public Administration Research and Theory*, vol. 8, no. 1 (1998), pp. 203–21; and B. Guy Peters and John Pierre, "Governance without Government? Rethinking Public Administration," *Journal of Public Administration Research and Theory*, vol. 8, no. 2, (1998), pp. 223–43.

29. Actually, collaboration is not a new idea; "most of the policies of a modern government," wrote Carl Joachim Friedrich more than half a century ago, "require collaboration rather than force for their accomplishment." "Public Policy and the Nature of Administrative Responsibility," in C. J. Friedrich and Edward S. Mason, eds., *Public Policy: A Yearbook of the Graduate School of Public Administration, Harvard University* (Harvard University Press, 1940), p. 17.

30. For example, DeWitt John and his colleagues define a "new governance" that "seeks to combine new and old ideas into a comprehensive approach, centered on collaboration, flexibility, results, and engaging citizens rather than announcing." DeWitt John, Donald F. Kettl, Barbara Dyer, and W. Robert Lovan, "What Will New Governance Mean for the Federal Government?" *Public Administration Review*, vol. 54, no. 2 (1994), p. 175.

31. "The predominance of intergovernmental processes raises important questions about accountability," wrote Catherine Lovell two decades ago. "The intergovernmental processes of today's administrative arena require us to develop new theories of accountability." "Where We Are in Intergovernmental Relations and Some of the Implications," *Southern Review of Public Administration*, vol. 3, no. 1 (1979), pp. 16, 17.

32. Sandford Borins, "The New Public Management Is Here to Stay," *Canadian Public Administration*, vol. 38, no. 1 (1995) p. 125.

33. Bardach, *Getting Agencies to Work Together*, p. 11.

34. For a discussion of accountability, governance, and the new public management in a world where collaboratives are important, see Peters and Pierre, "Governance without Government?"

35. Bardach writes that a collaborative "is not usually an entity that can be held accountable by an external constituency." *Getting Agencies to Work Together*, p. 197.

36. The General Accounting Office notes that federal financial support for state and local programs creates "puzzling performance accountability issues":

> While state or local program outcomes in total may be measurable, the component attributable to federal funding cannot be separated out. Thus, measuring performance at the level of the federal program may not be feasible. For accountability purposes, measuring overall performance of the state or local

program would not be appropriate, particularly when the federal grant contributes only a small fraction of the cost.

Susan S. Westin, *Balancing Flexibility and Accountability: Grant Program Design in Education and Other Areas,* GAO/T-GGD/HEHS-98-94 (General Accounting Office, February 11, 1998), p. 10.

37. Gerald E. Caiden, "The Problem of Ensuring the Public Accountability of Public Officials," in Dwivedi and Jabbra, *Public Service Accountability,* pp. 28, 31, 32, 31.

38. In a discussion of accountability for the block grants that the federal government makes to the states, the General Accounting Office notes that "assessments of state progress will need to recognize that outcomes are often affected by factors beyond state administrators' control." Paul L. Posner, *Block Grants: Issues in Designing Accountability Provisions,* GAO/AIMD-95-226 (General Accounting Office, September 1995), p. 3.

39. Bardach, *Getting Agencies to Work Together,* p. 144.

40. For a discussion of accountability within collaboratives, see Bardach and Lesser, "Accountability in Human Services Collaboratives."

41. Morris S. Ogul, *Congress Oversees the Bureaucracy: Studies in Legislative Supervision* (University of Pittsburgh Press, 1976), p. 182.

42. Harvey C. Mansfield Sr., "Accountability and Congressional Oversight" (p. 68), and Bruce L. R. Smith, "Major Trends in American Public Administration, 1940–1980" (p. 8). Both in Bruce L. R. Smith, ed., *Improving the Accountability and Performance of Government* (Brookings, 1982).

43. David Baumann, "Government on Autopilot," *National Journal,* March 13, 1999, pp. 689, 691.

44. Joel D. Aberbach, *Keeping a Watchful Eye: The Politics of Congressional Oversight* (Brookings, 1990), pp. 193, 202, 212.

45. Mathew D. McCubbins and Thomas Schwartz, "Congressional Oversight Overlooked: Police Patrols versus Fire Alarms," *American Journal of Political Science,* vol. 28, no. 1 (1984), pp. 166, 168.

46. Hugh Heclo, "Issue Networks and the Executive Establishment," in Anthony King, ed., *The New American Political System* (Washington: AEI Press, 1978), pp. 87–124.

47. John W. Gardner, "Comment," in Smith, *Improving the Accountability and Performance of Government,* p. 69.

48. Michelle Singletary, "Judge Rebukes Agency Regulating Credit Unions," *Washington Post,* December 5, 1996, pp. D1, D3.

49. Steve Cocheo, "Court Deals NCUA Another Blow, with Rigor," *ABA Banking Journal,* January 1997, p. 7.

50. In 1998, when the Supreme Court upheld Judge Jackson's ruling, Congress overwhelmingly modified the credit union statute to broaden significantly its "com-

mon bond" restriction on credit union membership. *National Credit Union Administration* v. *First National Bank & Trust Co.* 118 S. Ct. 927 (1998); Credit Union Membership Access Act, P. L. 105-219, 112 Stat. 913 (August 7, 1998).

51. For a discussion of who participates in administrative rulemaking, see Marrissa Martino Golden, "Interest Groups in the Rule-Making Process: Who Participates? Whose Voices Get Heard?" in H. George Frederickson and Jocelyn M. Johnston, eds., *Public Management Reform and Innovation* (University of Alabama Press, 1999), pp. 285–311.

52. Robert B. Reich, *Public Management in a Democratic Society* (Prentice Hall, 1990), p. 76.

53. Theodore J. Lowi calls this the "public philosophy" of "interest-group liberalism." For his critique, see his *The End of Liberalism: Ideology, Policy, and the Crisis of Public Authority* (W. W. Norton, 1969).

54. Indeed, Michael Baer argues that "the concept of an interest group holding the government accountable is antithetical to that of elected representative government." "Interest Groups and Accountability," pp. 217, 218.

55. Gerald E. Caiden cites "special interest government," which is "handicapped by interest group veto," as one of the "intractable problems of ensuring public accountability." "The Problem of Ensuring the Public Accountability of Public Officials," pp. 29, 30, 28.

56. Organized advocates will prefer policies that concentrate benefits on them and that, to avoid mobilizing opposition, either hide or diffuse the costs. If the advocates of a new public management paradigm want to focus the attention of government on results, they will need to define who exactly will be responsible for implementing an accountability process that focuses attention not only on the achievement of those results but also on both their direct and indirect costs.

57. Mark H. Moore and Margaret Jane Gates emphasize that accountability holders will use traditional oversight and accountability mechanisms to attack the administration of a program or policy with which they fundamentally disagree: "It is the widespread legitimacy of the values of 'tight' administration that makes the *administrative* weaknesses of both defense and welfare programs the focus of attacks even from those whose primary objection to these programs is substantive rather than procedural." For example, inspectors general may "disagree with the policy-makers about the value of a governmental enterprise but find it convenient to attack a program on its failure to comply with rules rather than on substantive grounds." When the inspector general for the Farmer's Home Administration critiqued the agency's loans for gasohol projects, "at least part of the motivation," report Moore and Gates, "was not the officials' failure to follow procedures, but a view among the auditors that the 'gasohol' enterprise was a foolish waste of government resources." *Inspectors-General: Junkyard Dogs or Man's Best Friend?* (Russell Sage Foundation, 1986), pp. 4, 21–22.

58. Political organizations that care deeply about a single public policy have learned to use the traditional accountability process of elections. Ignoring the

overall collection of policies, they have instead compared the candidates' positions on their own single important issue and then set out to elect those with whom they agree and to defeat those with whom they differ. Yet such single-issue organizations are denounced as a perversion of the democratic process.

59. In an analysis of international trends in accountability, Phillip J. Cooper distinguishes between the historical emphasis in the United States on "legal accountability" through the courts from the "political accountability" through "ministerial responsibility" employed by Canada and other parliamentary systems. Now, however, Cooper finds a "convergence," with the United States moving toward political accountability and parliamentary systems adopting legal accountability. "Accountability and Administrative Reform: Toward Convergence and Beyond," in B. Guy Peters and Donald J. Savoie, eds., *Governance in a Changing Environment* (McGill-Queen's University Press, 1995), pp. 173–99.

60. Joel Aberbach, however, points out that, although a parliamentary system may enhance accountability to the electorate, it also decreases the oversight that the legislative branch conducts of the executive. *Keeping a Watchful Eye,* p. 211.

61. Cooper also notes that "it is not all that clear precisely what accountability will look like in the new world of public service toward which we are moving or how it will operate." "Accountability and Administrative Reform," p. 174.

Chapter Five

1. This may be a little unfair to Weber, who argued that authority takes three forms: traditional, charismatic, and bureaucratic. Clearly traditional authority was based on trust. But modern, bureaucratic authority—with its rules and hierarchy— is necessary because of distrust. For an analysis of the thinking of Weber and Taylor about trust, see Francis Fukuyama, *Trust: The Social Virtues and the Creation of Prosperity* (Free Press, 1991), chap. 19 (pp. 221–30).

2. Woodrow Wilson, "The Study of Administration," *Political Science Quarterly,* vol. 2, no. 2 (1887), p. 197.

3. Ibid., p. 212.

4. Ibid., p. 213.

5. Ibid., p. 210.

6. Ibid., p. 214.

7. Some cooks are quite happy to be left no discretion as to the management of the fires and the ovens. Without discretion, they have no responsibility. This is why many cooks—that is, middle managers and frontline workers—do not want to be empowered, for to empower people is to give them responsibility. The fear of empowerment is the fear of responsibility. As the *Wall Street Journal* headlined a front-page article: "Not All Workers Find Idea of Empowerment as Neat as It Sounds." Timothy Aeppel, September 8, 1997, p. A1.

8. Harvey C. Mansfield Sr., "Accountability and Congressional Oversight," in Bruce L. R. Smith and James D. Carroll, eds., *Improving the Accountability and Performance of Government* (Brookings, 1982), pp. 61–62.

9. Wilson, "The Study of Administration," p. 213.

10. Ibid.

11. Kenneth P. Ruscio writes that I have it "only half right." To support this view, Ruscio notes that Madison wrote about both "distrust" and "confidence":

As there is a degree of depravity in mankind which requires a certain degree of circumspection and distrust: So there are other qualities in human nature, which justify a certain portion of esteem and confidence. Republican government presupposes the existence of these qualities in a higher degree than any other form.

Madison's government may have presupposed more "confidence" and less "distrust" than others. But this is only a relative statement; when actually designing a constitution, Madison worried more about the "degree of depravity" than the "other," more noble "qualities in human nature." "Trust, Democracy, and Public Management: A Theoretical Argument," *Journal of Public Administration Research and Theory,* vol. 6, no. 3 (1996), p. 470 (quoting Alexander Hamilton, James Madison, and John Jay, *The Federalist Papers* [Bantam Books, 1982], no. 55, p. 284).

12. Hamilton, Madison, and Jay, *The Federalist Papers,* no. 47, p. 244.

13. Distrust is not strictly an American phenomenon. "Accountability has been a 'buzzword' in both Japan's public and private sectors," writes Shun'Ichi Furukawa of the University of Tsukuba: "The emergence of the concept reflects distrust in authority." "Accountability Issues of Administrative Reform," a paper presented at "Accountability and Efficiency: Formal Controls and Performance Management," a conference sponsored by the International Institute of Administrative Sciences and the Civil Service College, at Sunningdale, United Kingdom, July 12–15, 1999, p. 1.

14. Kenneth P. Ruscio, "Trust in the Administrative State," *Public Administration Review,* vol. 57, no. 5 (1997), p. 457.

15. David Dery, "'Papereality' and Learning in Bureaucratic Organizations," *Administration & Society,* vol. 29, no. 6 (1998), p. 683.

16. Suzanne Garment, *Scandal: The Culture of Mistrust in American Politics* (Times Books, 1991), pp. 288, 2.

17. Garment, *Scandal,* pp. 99, 81–82, 10, 9.

18. Ed Regis, "Speed," *New York Times Book Review,* July 20, 1997.

19. Steven Kelman, "The Grace Commission: How Much Waste in Government?" *The Public Interest,* no. 78 (1985), pp. 62–82; and Steven Kelman, "A Reply," *The Public Interest,* no. 79 (1985), pp. 122–33.

20. Sydney J. Freedberg Jr., "The Myth of the $600 Hammer," *National Journal* (December 5, 1998), p. 2860.

21. Donald J. Savoie, "What Is Wrong with the New Public Management?" *Canadian Public Administration*, vol. 38, no. 1 (1995), pp. 114–15.

22. Robert D. Behn, "Innovation and Public Values: Mistakes, Flexibility, Purpose, Equity, Cost Control, and Trust," a paper presented at "The Fundamental Questions of Innovation," a conference held at Duke University, May 4, 1991, p. 1.

23. "Grace Panel Blames Congress for Wasted Federal Spending," *Congressional Quarterly,* January 14, 1984, p. 47.

24. Paul C. Light, *Monitoring Government: Inspectors General and the Search for Accountability* (Brookings, 1993), p. 19.

25. Garment, *Scandal,* p. 2.

26. Ibid., pp. 2, 291–96, 292, 288, 289.

27. For a more detailed discussion, see Joseph S. Nye Jr., Philip D. Zelikov, and David C. King, eds., *Why People Don't Trust Government* (Harvard University Press, 1997).

28. Hart-Teeter, "America Unplugged: Citizens and Their Government" July 12, 1999 (www.excelgov.org/publication/excel/usunplugged.htm [October 2000]). For an analysis of polling data on Americans' trust in their government see: Gary Orren, "Fall from Grace: The Public's Loss of Faith in Government," and Robert J. Blendon, and others, "Changing Attitudes in America," both in Nye, Zelikow, and King, *Why People Don't Trust Government,* pp. 77–107 and 205–16.

29. Paul Slovic, "Perceived Risk, Trust, and Democracy, *Risk Analysis,* vol. 13, no. 6 (1993), p. 677. Louis Barnes disagrees: "Trust may be easier both to create and to destroy, under some conditions, than we have assumed (it depends on how norms of reciprocity develop and take hold)." "Managing the Paradox of Organizational Trust." *Harvard Business Review,* vol. 59, no. 2 (1981), p. 112. But these norms of reciprocity are easier to develop *within* a single business organization than among those jostling for advantage in a very political environment.

30. Vice President Al Gore, *From Red Tape to Results: Creating a Government That Works Better and Costs Less* (U.S. Government Printing Office, 1993), p. i.

31. Alasdair Roberts, "The Paradox of Public Sector Reform: Works Better, Trusted Less?" October 25, 1998, photocopy, pp. 17, 1, 2. In Canada, Roberts argues, there exists a "control lobby" that seeks not more flexibility but to maintain "adequate controls over potentially errant bureaucrats." "Worry about Misconduct: The Control Lobby and the PS 2000 Reforms," *Canadian Public Administration,* vol. 39, no. 4 (1997), p. 491.

32. Executive branch agencies have "two basic kinds of discretionary authority," writes Gary Bryner: "(1) authority to make legislative-like policy decisions, and (2) authority to decide how general policies apply to specific cases." *Bureaucratic Discretion: Law and Policy in Federal Regulatory Agencies* (Pergamon Press, 1987),

p. 6. Bryner's concern for "the problem of bureaucratic discretion" focuses on the first group; in contrast, I concentrate on the second.

Olivia Golden makes a different distinction about the types of discretion: (1) "choices made by appointed public administrators that are not authorized by political overseers," and (2) "choices made by line workers in public bureaucracies that are not directly authorized by either their appointed managers or elected overseers." When the public administrators in Golden's first category exercise discretion, they could be making either Bryner's "legislative-like policy decisions" or simply applying general policies. In contrast, line workers would, presumably, be only applying general policies to specific cases. Olivia Golden, "Balancing Entrepreneurship, Line Worker Discretion, and Political Accountability: The Delicate Task of Innovators in Human Services," a paper presented at the Annual Meeting of the Association for Public Policy Analysis and Management, Seattle, October 27–29, 1988.

33. Steven Kelman, *Procurement and Public Management: The Fear of Discretion and the Quality of Government Performance* (AEI Press, 1990), pp. 10, 9, 10, 14. Three years after this book was published, Kelman went to work as the chief procurement guru in the U.S. Office of Management and Budget and increased significantly the discretion of federal procurement officials.

34. Ibid., p. 14.

35. Herbert Kaufman, *Red Tape: Its Origins, Uses, and Abuses* (Brookings, 1977), pp. 58–59.

36. Administrative Procedure Act, Section 10(e) (codified as amended at 5 U.S.C. § 706).

37. Citing the New Deal as an example, James Q. Wilson notes that, "on occasion, Americans have temporarily abandoned their fear of discretion and their insistence on rules." *Bureaucracy: What Government Agencies Do and Why They Do It* (Basic Books, 1989), p. 335.

38. Light, *Monitoring Government,* pp. 13, 12.

39. Ronald J. Oakerson, "Governance Structures for Enhancing Accountability and Responsiveness," in James L. Perry, ed., *Handbook of Public Administration* (Jossey-Bass, 1989), pp. 120–21.

40. The General Accounting Office examined 125 different regulatory concerns raised by 15 businesses. These covered "the perceived high cost of compliance [with federal regulations]; excessive paperwork; unreasonable, unclear, and inflexible requirements; and severe penalties for noncompliance." For "about one quarter" of these complaints (27), the responsible federal agency argued that the companies were really complaining about the "statutory requirements underlying their regulations." GAO checked these 27 cases and discovered that in 13 Congress "gave the rulemaking agencies no discretion in establishing the regulatory requirements at issue." L. Nye Stevens, *Regulatory Burden: Some Agencies' Claims Regarding Lack of Rulemaking Discretion Have Merit,* GAO/GGD-99-20 (General Accounting Office, January 1999), p. 1.

41. "Saccharin Ban Delay," *Congressional Quarterly Almanac*, 95th Congress, 1st sess. (Congressional Quarterly, 1997), pp. 495–99. Mary Link, "Proposed Saccharin Ban Causes Controversy," *Congressional Quarterly*, March 26, 1977, pp. 539–41. The ban was renewed in 1980, 1981, 1983, 1985, and 1987.

42. Oakerson, "Governance Structures for Enhancing Accountability and Responsiveness," p. 122.

43. David W. Walker, "Government Management: Addressing High Risks and Improving Performance and Accountability," testimony before the Committee on Government Reform, House of Representatives, GAO/T-OCG-99-23 (General Accounting Office, February 10, 1999), pp. 1–2.

44. Walker, "Government Management," pp. 3, 15.

45. This may be a little unfair to Walker. After all, he works for the Congress. Most people don't chew out their bosses—particularly on the record and in public. Still, it isn't obvious whether Walker's testimony is part of the solution or part of the problem—whether he moved congressional thinking or merely reinforced the members' preconceptions of agency incompetence.

It is not, however, unfair to Congress—or, at least, not to some members of Congress. Towards the end of Walker's testimony, Representative Dan Burton, chairman of the House Committee on Government Reform, told Walker: "I would like to figure out some way to give monetary rewards for people in government to come up with ways to streamline and create economies." Then, to illustrate his point about the need for rewards, Burton reported that, when he was a state senator, he overheard an agency head say: "We have only got what, 2 months left in the fiscal year. And if we don't spend the money we have got, we are not going to be able to ask for an increase in the next appropriation." This annoyed Burton: "That is the mind-set for people in all levels of government. They want to spend that money so they can get more in the next biennium or the next fiscal year." And, he continued, "the only way to turn that around is to really have financial incentives for people to cut wasteful spending." Apparently, it never occurred to Burton that one of the best "incentives" for saving money that a legislature can give any executive branch agency is to permit it to carry over a portion of its savings from one fiscal year to the next—or that the most common disincentive for saving money that a legislature imposes is not permitting an agency to keep any of its savings beyond the end of a fiscal year. *Fraud and Waste in Federal Government Programs*, Hearing before the Committee on Government Reform, House of Representatives, 106th Congress, 1st sess., February 10, 1999, Serial 106-3 (U.S. Government Printing Office, 1999), p. 241.

46. Elmer B. Staats, "Governmental Performance in Perspective: Achievements and Challenges," in Smith and Carroll, eds., *Improving the Accountability and Performance of Government*, pp. 26–27.

47. Richard P. Nathan, *The Administrative Presidency* (John Wiley & Sons, 1983), p. 30.

48. Golden, "Balancing Entrepreneurship, Line Worker Discretion, and Political Accountability," pp. 10, 12–13.

49. David G. Mathiasen, "The New Public Management and Its Critics," in Lawrence R. Jones, Kuno Schedler, and Stephen W. Wade, eds., *International Perspectives on the New Public Management: Advances in International Comparative Management,* Supplement 3 (JAI Press, 1997), pp. 292, 289. See, for example, Garry E. Miller and Ira Iscoe, "A State Mental Health Commissioner and the Politics of Mental Health," in Erwin C. Hargrove and John C. Glidewell, eds., *Impossible Jobs in Public Management* (University Press of Kansas, 1990), pp. 103–32.

50. I have used interchangeably "distrust" (the word employed by Light) and "mistrust" (the word used by Garment), for both mean "a lack of trust or confidence." But there is a slight distinction: Distrust "implies far more certitude that something is wrong than mistrust." Distrust "suggests conviction of another's guilt, treachery, or weakness"; mistrust "suggests domination by suspicion and, usually, fear." *Webster's New Dictionary of Synonyms* (G. & C. Merriam Co., 1968), p. 263.

51. Kelman, *Procurement and Public Management,* p. 188.

52. James P. Womack, Daniel T. Jones, and Daniel Roos, *The Machine That Changed the World: The Story of Lean Production* (New York: Rawson Associates, 1990), chap. 6, pp. 138–68.

53. Mathiasen, "The New Public Management and Its Critics," p. 287.

54. For an appraisal of PBOs, see Alasdair Roberts, "Performance-Based Organizations: Assessing the Gore Plan," *Public Administration Review,* vol. 57, no. 6 (1997), pp. 465–78.

55. L. Nye Stevens, *Performance-Based Organizations: Issues for the Saint Lawrence Seaway Development Corporation Proposal,* GAO/GGD-97-74 (General Accounting Office, May 1997), p. 19.

GAO discovered a similar phenomenon in the National Performance Review's effort to create "'reinvention labs,' which are designed to test ways that agencies could improve their performance and customer service by reengineering work processes and eliminating unnecessary regulations." "Over half," or 52 percent, of these "unnecessary regulations" were not imposed from the outside but created internally. L. Nye Stevens, *Management Reform: Status of Agency Reinvention Lab Efforts,* GAO/GDD-96-69 (General Accounting Office, March 1996), pp. 2, 39.

56. Sylvie Trosa, *Next Steps: Moving On* (London: Cabinet Office, 1994), p. 32.

57. Mathiasen, "The New Public Management and Its Critics," p. 292

58. For a collection of analyses of various types of discretion, see Douglas H. Shumavon and H. Kenneth Hibbeln, eds., *Administrative Discretion and Public Policy Implementation* (Praeger, 1986).

59. Some believe that executive branch discretion is not only inevitable but also good. Concentrating on executive branch discretion in policymaking, Jerry L. Mashaw writes: "Broad delegations recognize that tight accountability linkages at one point in the governmental system may reduce the responsiveness of the system

as a whole." "Prodelegation: Why Administrators Should Make Political Decisions," *Journal of Law, Economics, and Organization,* vol. 1, no. 1 (1985), p. 98.

Focusing on the second kind of discretion (applying general policies to specific cases), Joel F. Handler reaches the same conclusion: "Discretion is seen not only as inevitable but as necessary and desirable." *The Conditions of Discretion: Autonomy, Community, Bureaucracy* (Russell Sage Foundation, 1986), p. 11.

Olivia Golden (using her own distinction between executive and line-worker discretion) argues that "both kinds of discretion together may be valuable or even essential to innovative and successful human services programs, especially for hard-to-serve groups." "Balancing Entrepreneurship, Line Worker Discretion, and Political Accountability," p. 2.

60. Allan W. Lerner and John Wanat characterize such "vague marching orders" as "fuzzy charges." "Fuzziness and Bureaucracy," *Public Administration Review,* vol. 43, no. 6 (1983), p. 500.

61. Quoted by John M. Vandlik, "Voting for Smokey Bear: Political Accountability and the New Chief of the Forest Service," *Public Administration Review,* vol. 55, no. 3 (1995), p. 285. Vandlik further describes the act:

> It also directs the Secretary of Agriculture "to develop and administer the renewable surface resources of the national forests for multiple use and sustained yield of the several products and services obtained therefrom. In the administration of the national forest due consideration shall be given to the relative values of the various resources in particular areas."
>
> The statute defines "multiple use" and "sustained yield" in value-laden terms, prescribing a system of natural resources management that "will best meet the needs of the American people," makes "the most judicious use of the land," "conform[s] to changing needs and conditions," is "harmonious and coordinated," is conducted "without impairment of productivity," and is implemented "with consideration being given to the relative values of the various uses." (p. 285)

And you thought public managers did not have to make policy trade-offs and political choices?

Executive branch officials can, nevertheless, hide behind the politics-administration dichotomy, claiming that they are merely implementing the law. Indeed, argues Vandlik, "some Forest Service decision makers view the public involvement process as being counter to the exercise of their professional judgment" (p. 286). The politics-administration dichotomy, he continues, "provides cover for public administrators to engage in political issues without being held politically accountable for the outcome" (p. 288).

Moreover, Vandlik fears what happens when public managers exercise their inherent discretion without political guidance. First he notes what happens when political leaders buy into the politics-administration dichotomy: "To the extent the theory is accepted by the politicians themselves, it also protects public administrators from political forces that would otherwise attempt to influence the policies created by the administrator." Then he notes what happens when the administrators are, in fact, permitted to make decisions without any policy guidance: "When bureaucrats seek the public interest without political direction, they will never determine that the public interest is a position contrary to the view of the most active or cooperative interest group that participated in the decision making process. Interests of the broader society are ignored" (p. 288).

In a less emphatic discussion of the Forest Service's dilemma, GAO reports: "The National Forest Management Act and other multiple-use laws guiding the management of the national forests provide little direction for the Forest Service in resolving conflicts among competing multiple uses on its lands." Barry T. Hill, *Forest Service Priorities: Evolving Mission Favors Resource Protection Over Production*, GAO/RCED-99-166 (General Accounting Office, June 1999), p. 2.

62. The National Park Service doesn't have it much better. Its authorizing legislation directs it "to conserve the scenery and the natural and historic objects and the wild life therein and to provide for the enjoyment of the same in such manner and by such means as will leave them unimpaired for the enjoyment of future generations." The Park Service should let people enjoy the parks but make sure that they don't damage anything. Again, both vague and contradictory. Tom Kenworthy, "When Science Takes a Back Seat to Scenery," *Washington Post*, August 26, 1999, p. A23.

63. Angus A. MacIntyre argues that legislation that provides for such administrative discretion is not only "unavoidable," but also "prudent" and "desirable." "The Multiple Sources of Statutory Ambiguity: Tracing the Legislative Origins to Administrative Discretion," in Shumavon and Hibbeln, *Administrative Discretion and Public Policy Implementation*, p. 77.

64. Pamela Varley, "Ellen Schall and the Department of Juvenile Justice," C16-87-793.0 (Kennedy School of Government, Harvard University, 1987), p. 4.

65. Michael Lipsky, *Street-Level Bureaucracy: Dilemmas of the Individual in Public Services* (Russell Sage Foundation, 1980), pp. xi, 13, 161.

66. Ibid., pp. 14, 16. For a detailed analysis of why street-level bureaucrats necessarily possess such discretion, pp. 13–16.

67. Mark H. Moore, "Police Accountability and the 'Dirty Deal,'" *Governing*, August 1991, p. 9.

68. Fred Barbash and Al Kamen, "Blackmun Says 'Weary' Court Is Shifting Right," *Washington Post*, September 20, 1984, p. A42.

69. Gerald E. Caiden, "The Problem of Ensuring the Public Accountability of Public Officials," in O. P. Dwivedi and Joseph G. Jabbra, eds., *Public Service Accountability: A Comparative Perspective* (Kumarian Press, 1988), p. 17.

70. Garment, *Scandal*, pp. 96–97.

71. Kate Stith and José A. Cabrances, *Fear of Judging: Sentencing Guidelines in the Federal Courts* (University of Chicago Press, 1998).

72. Barnes, "Managing the Paradox of Organizational Trust."

73. Dale E. Zand, "Trust and Managerial Problem Solving," *Administrative Science Quarterly*, vol. 17, no. 2 (1972), pp. 229–39.

74. Nirmalya Kumar, "The Power of Trust in Manufacturer-Retailer Relationships," *Harvard Business Review*, vol. 74, no. 6 (November–December 1996), pp. 92–106.

75. Stewart Macaulay, "Non-Contractual Relations in Business: A Preliminary Study," *American Sociological Review*, vol. 28, no. 1 (1963), pp. 62, 64.

76. Carolyn Shaw Bell, "In Others We Must Trust," *Boston Globe*, September 23, 1997, p. C4.

77. Womack, Jones, and Roos, *The Machine That Changed the World*, p. 150.

78. Jon R. Katzenbach and Douglas K. Smith, *The Wisdom of Teams: Creating the High-Performance Organization* (Harvard Business School Press, 1993), p. 60.

79. David G. Carnevale, *Trustworthy Government: Leadership and Management Strategies for Building Trust and High Performance* (Jossey-Bass, 1995), p. 6.

80. Dennis M. Daley and Michael L. Vasu, "Fostering Organizational Trust in North Carolina: The Pivotal Role of Administrators and Political Leaders," *Administration & Society*, vol. 30, no. 1 (1998), p. 62. Trust doesn't cause increased productivity, but "the expression of trust in an organization's supervisory and managerial leadership is associated with job performance" (p. 62).

81. Fukuyama, *Trust*, p. 26. Fukuyama elaborates: "A high-trust society can organize its workplace on a more flexible and group-oriented basis, with more responsibility delegated to lower levels of the organization. Low-trust societies, by contrast, must fence in and isolate their workers with a series of bureaucratic rules" (p. 31).

82. Jane E. Fountain, "Trust as a Basis for Interorganizational Forms," a paper prepared for "Network Analysis and Innovations in Public Programs," a conference sponsored by the University of Wisconsin at Madison, September 30–October 1, 1994.

83. Eugene Bardach, *Getting Agencies to Work Together: The Practice and Theory of Managerial Craftsmanship* (Brookings, 1998), pp. 252–54, 274, 277, 252.

84. Such trust is one of the key ingredients of what people have labeled "social capital": the ability of people—in society, organizations, or teams—to work together to achieve common purposes and mutual gain. See Jane Jacobs, *The Death and Life of Great American Cities* (Random House, 1961), p. 138; James S. Coleman, "Social Capital in the Creation of Human Capital," *American Journal of Sociology*, vol. 94 supplement (1988), pp. S95–S120; Robert D. Putnam, "Bowling Alone," *Journal of Democracy*, vol. 6, no. 1 (1995), pp. 65–78.

85. Bell, "In Others We Must Trust."

86. Fukuyama, *Trust*, pp. 7, 9, 27–28.

87. Sissela Bok, *Lying* (Vintage, 1989), pp. 26–27.

88. Craig W. Thomas asks, "How can we create, maintain, or restore public trust in government agencies and their employees?" and suggests seven ways that agency managers do so:

(1) Select people to represent the agency whose "personal and professional characteristics" match those of the targeted outside groups and appoint outsiders to sit on advisory boards.

(2) "Encourage subordinates and peers to participate actively in professional communities as a means for signaling the agency's willingness to conform to institutional norms."

(3) "Cooperate with government regulators, perhaps even publicly requesting increased oversight of agency operations to increase fiduciary redundancy."

(4) When trust is weak, use "detailed contracts" to "align expectations."

(5) "Ceremonial attendance at various social functions . . . is a productive means for building trust with specific groups in the agency's environment."

(6) "Tenure longevity for street-level bureaucrats and midlevel managers is particularly important for building process-based trust."

(7) "Generate process-based trust by participating in consensus-building groups composed of multiple interests."

"Maintaining and Restoring Public Trust in Government Agencies and Their Employees," *Administration & Society,* vol. 30, no. 2 (1998), pp. 166, 187–88.

89. Ruscio, "Trust, Democracy, and Public Management," p. 462. Ruscio, "Trust in the Administrative State," pp. 454–55.

90. Carnevale, *Trustworthy Government,* pp. 23, 31.

91. Fukuyama, *Trust,* pp. 227, 263.

92. Oakerson, "Governance Structures for Enhancing Accountability and Responsiveness," p. 122.

93. Savoie, "What Is Wrong with the New Public Management?" p. 113.

94. Mark H. Moore, *Accounting for Change: Reconciling the Demands for Accountability and Innovation in the Public Sector* (Washington: Council for Excellence in Government, 1993), pp. 133–34. This tension—between the aggressiveness required to be effective as a public official and our collective fear of officials who are too aggressive—is a theme of Moore's research. Elsewhere, he observes that Americans do not want public officials to be too entrepreneurial: "The last thing we want is an official who takes liberties with (or even operates aggressively within) the mesh of process obligations to pursue an independent view of what the public interest requires." Mark H. Moore, "Realms of Obligation and Virtue," in Joel L. Fleishman, Lance Liebman, and Mark H. Moore, eds., *Public Duties: The Moral Obligations of Government Officials* (Harvard University Press, 1981), p. 3.

95. James A. Stever, *The End of Public Administration: Problems of the Profession in the Post-Progressive Era* (Transnational Publishers, 1988), p. 99.

96. Eugene Lewis, *Public Entrepreneurship: Toward a Theory of Bureaucratic Political Power* (Indiana University Press, 1980), pp. 9, 10, 17, 18.

97. In his public administration textbook, Gerald Garvey devotes an entire chapter to "Democratic Accountability versus Administrative Discretion," though the chapter focuses mostly on Bryner's "legislative-like decisions" rather than the application of general policies to specific situations. *Public Administration: The Professions and the Practice* (St. Martin's Press, 1997), pp. 127–66.

98. Ruscio, "Trust, Democracy, and Public Management," p. 474.

99. Lipsky takes the opposite view: "bureaucratic accountability is virtually impossible to achieve among lower-level workers who exercise high degrees of discretion, at least where qualitative aspects of the work are involved." *Street-Level Bureaucracy,* p. 159.

100. Wilson, *Bureaucracy,* p. 149.

101. Robert D. Behn, "The Big Questions of Public Management," *Public Administration Review,* vol. 55, no. 4 (1995), pp. 313–24.

102. Oakerson, "Governance Structures for Enhancing Accountability and Responsiveness," p. 120.

Chapter Six

1. Such a performance goal would necessarily be an output: a specific measurable result that a public agency could *produce* in a year. The real policy objective, however, is an "outcome," which is not something that an agency can directly *produce;* often, an outcome will not exhibit an improvement for several years. The management task is to produce specific annual outputs while continuously checking to see whether this short-term output performance is creating any long-term outcome improvements. See Robert D. Behn, "Broken Windows and Production Targets," *Governing,* March 1997, p. 68.

2. Andreea M. Serban and Joseph C. Burke report that numerous states are using performance funding "to achieve two major goals: increased accountability and improved institutional performance." "Meeting the Performance Funding Challenge: A Nine-State Comparative Analysis," *Public Productivity & Management Review,* vol. 22, no. 2 (1998), p. 157.

3. This may require more back-and-forth negotiation than might happen between an executive agency and the legislature, though it is clearly a private negotiation.

4. John W. Gardner, "Comment," in Bruce L. R. Smith and James D. Carroll, eds., *Improving the Accountability and Performance of Government* (Brookings, 1982), p. 70.

5. B. Guy Peters and John Pierre make a similar (but not identical) distinction between governance and the new public management (NPM): "Governance is about process, NPM is primarily about outcomes," they write. "Governance is essentially a political theory," they continue, "whereas NPM is an organizational theory."

"Governance without Government? Rethinking Public Administration," *Journal of Public Administration Research and Theory,* vol. 8, no. 2, (1998), p. 232.

6. *State Strategies for the New Economy* (Washington: National Governors' Association, 2000), p. 28

7. Donald J. Savoie, "Just Another Voice from the Pulpit," *Canadian Public Administration,* vol. 38, no. 1 (1995), p. 135.

8. Morris P. Fiorina, *Congress: Keystone of the Washington Establishment* (Yale University Press, 1977), pp. 48, 71.

9. David Schoenbrod, *Power without Responsibility: How Congress Abuses the People through Delegation* (Yale University Press, 1993), p. 92.

10. "Delegation of Legislative Power," *IPA Report,* Fall 1995, pp. 3, 4. "Legislators are more likely to delegate if doing so would shift blame away from them significantly or would fail to shift away much credit," writes Schoenbrod. Conversely, they are "more likely to avoid delegation if doing so significantly would shift credit away from them or would fail to shift away much blame." Schoenbrod, *Power without Responsibility,* pp. 92, 90.

11. United States Senate, Committee on Governmental Affairs, *Government Performance and Results Act,* Report 103-58 (U.S. Government Printing Office, June 16, 1993), pp. 57, 59.

12. "Executive Report: Ford Endorses 172 Goals of 'Management by Objective' Plan," *National Journal,* October 26, 1974, p. 1601.

13. Commodity Futures Trading Commission, "Vision and Strategies for the Future: Facing the Challenges of 1997 through 2002," Strategic Plan, September 1997 (www.cftc.gov/strplan97/home.html [October 2000]).

14. Commodity Futures Trading Commission, "Quarterly Performance Review," Fourth Quarter, FY 1999 (www.cftc.gov/ofm/qpr1fy2000/QPRMasterDocument.htm [October 2000]).

15. In its customarily temperate style, the General Accounting Office reported that "most of CFTC's performance goals and measures focus on program outputs—such as the number of meetings attended and number of research projects or reports completed." But GAO also chided the commission in unusually direct language: "A key shortcoming of CFTC's performance plan is that it relies on output measures that describe completed activities, not program results. Also, these measures are weighted toward measuring the quantity of completed activities, rather than the quality, cost, or timeliness of performance outcomes." Richard J. Hillman, "Results Act: Observations on CFTC's Annual Performance Plan," GAO/T-GGD-99-10 (General Accounting Office, October 8, 1998), p. 5.

Further, from a survey of the performance plans prepared by twenty-four federal agencies for fiscal 2000, GAO reported blandly that although these plans showed "moderate improvements," they also exhibited "an important weakness": an "inattention to ensuring that performance data will be sufficiently timely, complete, accurate, useful and consistent." Nancy Kingsbury, *Managing for Results: Opportunities for Continued Improvements in Agencies' Performance Plans,* GAO/GGD/AIMD-99-215 (General Accounting Office, July 1999), pp. 3, 7.

16. Robert D. Behn, "Performance Measures in State Administrative Agencies: Bureaucratic Hoop Jumping or Management Tool?" remarks prepared for the Annual Conference of the National Association of State Chief Administrators, Salt Lake City, August 23, 1999.

17. Gardner, "Comment," p. 70.

18. During the New Deal, writes Richard B. Stewart, one justification for administrative discretion was that federal agencies were charged with achieving very specific (economic) goals, and thus what was really delegated to the agencies was not so much administrative discretion but the scientific task of determining the best way to achieve those goals. Thus, writes Stewart: "Two basic types of directives may be distinguished: rules and goals." And, if the agency is given a goal to pursue (instead of rules to follow), "the discretion that the administrator enjoys is more apparent than real." A skilled administrator may employ a trial and error process in finding the best means of achieving the posited goal," continues Stewart, "but persons subject to the administrator's control are no more liable to his arbitrary will than are patients remitted to the care of a skilled doctor." Stewart calls this "the 'expertise' model of the New Deal period." "The Reformation of American Administrative Law," *Harvard Law Review,* vol. 88, no. 8 (1975), pp. 1678, 1684. (Today, we have no more respect for scientifically skilled doctors than we do for scientifically skilled administrators. In all of the professions, the "expertise model" has taken a big hit.)

19. The "outputs" are what government directly produces; the "outcomes" are what government actually wants to accomplish. Unfortunately, it is much harder to determine whether we have achieved our desired outcome than whether we have produced our targeted output. Even if we produce our targeted output, that is no guarantee that we will realize our desired outcome.

For a school system, the desired outcome is graduates who mature into productive employees and responsible citizens. Unfortunately, it is difficult to determine how much the school system is contributing to this outcome. It will be years before the necessary data will be available; it will be difficult to collect these data; and, even if we get the data, they will be difficult to interpret. If a school system's students do grow up to be productive employees and responsible citizens, how would we determine how much the school system contributed to this outcome? Given these problems in evaluating how well a school system is doing (or has done) to achieve our desired outcome, we rely on its outputs, that is, today's students' test scores. Robert D. Behn, "Linking Measurement and Motivation: A Challenge for Education," in Paul W. Thurston and James G. Ward, eds., *Advances in Educational Administration: Improving Educational Performance: Local and Systemic Reforms,* vol. 5 (JAI Press, 1997), pp. 15–58.

20. To some elected officials, the inputs are the outputs. To them, the inputs (rather than the outputs) provide the measure of the benefits. The benefits to whom? The benefits to their constituents—to the members of their district who get the jobs, or the contract, or the special program. To a member of Congress, for example, the benefits of military programs are the inputs—the dollars and jobs—rather than their contribution to the nation's defense. They may feel compelled to argue publicly for their favorite weapon systems in terms of national defense (output). When they privately evaluate the program, however, they will use the local inputs as the measure of benefit. This simplifies the evaluation task. It is much easier to define, measure, and predict the inputs than the outputs. When evaluating a weapons system, it is much easier to determine the profits and jobs that it will produce than its marginal contribution to national security. Robert D. Behn, "Policy Analysis and Policy Politics," *Policy Analysis*, vol. 7, no. 2 (1981), pp. 206–07.

21. Gerald E.Caiden, "The Problem of Ensuring the Public Accountability of Public Officials," in O. P. Dwivedi and Joseph G. Jabbra, eds., *Public Service Accountability: A Comparative Perspective* (Kumarian Press, 1988), p. 27.

22. Woodrow Wilson, "The Study of Administration," *Political Science Quarterly*, vol. 2, no. 2 (1887), pp. 213–14.

23. Hugh Heclo, "OMB and the Presidency—The Problem of 'Neutral Competence,'" *The Public Interest,* no. 38 (1975), pp. 80–98; Herbert Kaufman, "Emerging Conflicts in the Doctrines of Public Administration, *American Political Science Review,* vol. 50, no. 4 (1956), particularly pp. 1059–62.

24. For the Canadian parliamentary system, Phillip J. Cooper wonders "whether ministers can be held responsible at all for events in their departments about which they were not aware"? For, he continues, "as organizations and their functions are becoming more complex, the range of activity of which ministers may be unaware is substantial." "Accountability and Administrative Reform: Toward Convergence and Beyond," in B. Guy Peters and Donald J. Savoie, eds., *Governance in a Changing Environment* (McGill-Queen's University Press, 1995), p. 179.

25. Peters and Pierre, "Governance without Government?" p. 228.

26. Sandford Borins, "The New Public Management Is Here to Stay," *Canadian Public Administration,* vol. 38, no. 1 (1995), pp. 125–26.

27. For a general discussion of how specific goals can help public managers, see Robert D. Behn, *Leadership Counts: Lessons for Public Managers* (Harvard University Press, 1991), chap. 4; Robert D. Behn, "Bottom-Line Government" (The Governors Center at Duke University, 1994); Behn, "Linking Measurement and Motivation."

The business management literature contains numerous analyses of the value of goals in improving organizational performance. See, for example, the following articles from the *Harvard Business Review:* Jim Collins, "Turning Goals into Results: The Power of Catalytic Mechanisms," vol. 77, no. 4 (1999), pp. 71–82; Christopher Meyer, "How the Right Measures Help Teams Excel," vol. 72, no. 3 (1994), pp. 95–103; Robert Schaffer and Harvey A. Thomson, "Successful Change Programs Begin with Results," vol. 70, no. 1 (1992), pp. 80–89.

28. Again, can an agency head be accountable for the implementation of the plan by individuals with civil-service protection who work several layers down in the agency's bureaucracy? Can an individual legislator be accountable for the performance of a policy he or she helped enact when it will be implemented by people who have been carefully insulated from political control?

29. This was the case in the Massachusetts Department of Public Welfare in the mid-1980s. The department had ten goals, and each division and each unit within each division also had its own goals. Behn, *Leadership Counts,* chap. 4.

30. Ibid.

31. This suggestion could also eliminate the anonymity of the various members of the collaborative. If a collaborative accepted responsibility for a given program or policy, it would be asked to create a specific goal that it would achieve by the end of the fiscal year. In turn, the collaborative could ask each member to create its own specific goal for the fiscal year. Then, if the collaborative failed to achieve its fiscal year goal, these component goals would highlight responsibility—either that of the individual members who failed to achieve their own goals, or that of the leadership of the collaborative that failed to create a collection of member goals whose achievement would automatically realize its overall goal. But before we try using subordinate goals to highlight responsibility and enhance accountability within collaboratives, we ought to do it in more traditional, hierarchical organizations. For a discussion of accountability in collaboratives, see Eugene Bardach and Cara Lesser, "Accountability in Human Services Collaboratives—For What? and To Whom?" *Journal of Public Administration Research and Theory*, vol. 6, no. 2 (1996), pp. 197–224.

32. Wilson, "The Study of Administration," p. 216.

33. Finley Peter Dunne, *Mr. Dooley's Opinions* (R. H. Russell, 1901), p. 26.

34. Wilson, "The Study of Administration," pp. 214, 215, 217, 222.

35. Derek Bok, "Measuring the Performance of Government," in Joseph S. Nye Jr., Philip D. Zelikow, and David C. King, eds., *Why People Don't Trust Government* (Harvard University Press, 1997), p. 62.

36. Alasdair Roberts, "Worrying about Misconduct: The Control Lobby and the PS 2000 Reforms," *Canadian Public Administration,* vol. 39, no. 4 (1997), p. 518.

37. "Deconstructing Distrust: How Americans View Government," The Pew Research Center for the People and the Press, March 10, 1998 (www.people-press.org/trustrpt.htm [October 2000]).

38. Behn, *Leadership Counts,* p. 88.

39. Panel on Civic Trust and Citizen Responsibility, *A Government to Trust and Respect: Rebuilding Citizen-Government Relations for the 21st Century* (Washington: National Academy of Public Administration, 1999), p. 19.

40. Behn, "Linking Measurement and Motivation," p. 20.

41. David G. Carnevale, *Trustworthy Government: Leadership and Management Strategies for Building Trust and High Performance* (Jossey-Bass, 1995), p. 12.

Chapter Seven

1. In their "deliberative democracy," Amy Gutmann and Dennis Thompson argue, "each is accountable to all." Yet they recognize that this "universal accountability is obviously difficult to realize in practice." *Democracy and Disagreement* (Harvard University Press, 1996), p. 128.

2. Over time, the accountability environment of business has become more complex as well. Managers in the private sector are now accountable for their environmental performance as well as their financial performance. And they are accountable for fairness in their hiring practices and even in their service-delivery practices. Business is becoming more like government in terms of the number and diversity of the stakeholders to whom it is accountable. Nevertheless, public managers remain accountable to many more stakeholders. As James Q. Wilson writes, "Government bureaucracies must satisfy principles of accountability that are fundamentally different from those in industry." "Can the Bureaucracy Be Deregulated? Lessons from Government Agencies," in John J. DiIulio Jr., ed., *Deregulating the Public Service: Can Government Be Improved?* (Brookings, 1994), p. 37.

3. Elsewhere I have argued that public managers not only have a right but an obligation to exercise such leadership. "What Right Do Public Managers Have to Lead?" *Public Administration Review,* vol. 58, no. 3 (1998), pp. 209–24.

4. Unfortunately, new mistakes and new scandals are constantly creating pressure for new regulations. Every time someone makes a new mistake, the obvious response is to create another rule that, its advocates assure us, will prevent this mistake from ever happening again. Thus any effort to focus the accountability rules for finances and fairness on the most frequent, most egregious errors can be thwarted by the constant pressure to add new rules to prevent the recurrence of minor, one-time, but nevertheless troubling, mistakes.

5. The United States is currently engaged in a major debate about the theoretical meaning of fairness: What does it mean to treat people with different, discernible characteristics equitably? To treat men and women equitably? To treat people with different ethnic heritages equitably? To treat people from different economic backgrounds equitably? To treat people with different abilities or disabilities equitably? Because this debate is very political and divisive, public managers have avoided the conflict. They have avoided the discussion of theoretical issues or the shaping of operational practicalities. They could become involved, but they have decided that the costs of appearing to choose sides and of offending key stakeholders are not worth the benefits—particularly in a debate in which they perceive they have little influence.

6. Theologians lined up on both sides of President Clinton's 1999 trial in the United States Senate. Yonat Shimron, "Theologians Divvy Up the Moral High Ground," [Raleigh, N.C.] *News & Observer* January 16, 1999, pp. 1A, 14A.

7. In embracing accountability, Mark H. Moore wants public managers to be strategic; they ought not to expose their "organization haphazardly to political overseers." Instead, he wants public managers to "seek out those overseers who are likely to demand" what the managers "think is most valuable to deliver." Rather than get locked in to "political coalitions supporting the old strategies of their organizations," Moore recommends that they "forge new political coalitions that demand from them an organization whose substantive purposes are more to their [the public managers'] liking." *Creating Public Value: Strategic Management in Government* (Harvard University Press, 1995), pp. 274, 275, 274.

8. Public managers need not, however, reveal these insights. They need not reveal how society (or government) could improve the managers' accountability for finances, for fairness, or for performance. In fact, if they believe that any new accountability arrangement has mostly the potential to punish them even more, they will offer nothing meaningful—though, if required to suggest something, they will figure out how to jump through this hoop too. To convince public managers to help us rethink managerial accountability, we first need to convince them that any new accountability will not automatically increase their chances of being punished.

9. These managers are not completely wasting their knowledge. They are not, however, using it to improve accountability. Rather, they are using their insider knowledge to escape from the sillier and more onerous forms of accountability. But should only the inventors of the loopholes be able to take advantage of them? Shouldn't all agencies be able to benefit? Shouldn't the public managers who best understand the perverse incentives and wasted resources that result from various accountability mechanisms be accountable for helping to fix them?

As the system is constructed now, the managers have no incentive to reveal their secrets. If they do, the result may not be the elimination of the dysfunctional form of accountability. Instead, someone might simply close the loophole. For the strategic manager, this is the worst of both worlds. The perversity is not fixed; and the loophole no longer exists. Public managers will not reveal their knowledge of the errors in the system without some guarantee that the problem—not the loophole—will be fixed.

10. Alasdair Roberts, "Performance-Based Organizations: Assessing the Gore Plan," *Public Administration Review,* vol. 57, no. 6 (1997), pp. 465–77.

11. A PBO requires an agreement about some very specific performance targets that the agency should achieve. Moreover, these performance targets have to be widely accepted by the accountability environment. It is not easy to create a PBO for agencies whose performance is difficult to measure or whose missions are controversial.

12. For a critique of performance under PBOs, see Roberts, "Performance-Based Organizations."

13. David Osborne and Ted Gaebler, *Reinventing Government: How the Entrepreneurial Spirit Is Transforming the Public Sector* (Addison-Wesley, 1992).

14. Larry Polivka and B. Jack Osterhold, "The Governor as Manager: Agency Autonomy and Accountability," *Public Budgeting & Finance*, vol. 5, no. 4 (1985), pp. 91, 92, 94, 100, 95.

15. Ibid., pp. 102, 101, 98, 101.

16. When Derek Lewis was dismissed as chief executive of Britain's Prison Service, he sued. He had, he claimed, meet fifteen of the sixteen performance targets in his contract. His administration had cut the number of prison escapes significantly, but a few politically embarrassing escapes precipitated his dismissal. So Lewis sued—and won £280,000. Charles Polidano, "The Bureaucrat Who Fell under a Bus: Ministerial Responsibility, Executive Agencies, and the Derek Lewis Affair in Britain," *Governance*, vol. 12, no. 2 (1999), pp. 201–09.

17. Francis Fukuyama, *Trust: The Social Virtues and the Creation of Prosperity* (Free Press, 1991), pp. 226, 223.

18. "Responsibility is something more than accountability," writes Philip Selznick. "To be accountable is to be subject to judgment or, as we sometimes say, to be *held* responsible. The focus is on conformity to an external standard." In contrast, "a responsible enterprise, like a responsible person, must have an inner commitment to moral restraint and aspiration." *The Moral Commonwealth: Social Theory and the Promise of Community* (University of California Press, 1992), p. 345.

19. Jane J. Mansbridge distinguishes between "adversary democracy" and "unitary democracy." Adversary democracy (as practiced in the United States and other modern democracies) assumes conflicting interests, emphasizes the equal protection of interests, and makes decisions by majority rule using a secret ballot. In contrast, unitary democracy (as practiced in town meetings and participatory workplaces) assumes common interests, emphasizes equal respect for each individual, and makes decisions by consensus through face-to-face contact. *Beyond Adversary Democracy* (Basic Books, 1980). In this sense, my compact of mutual, collective responsibility is an effort to move from adversary democracy towards unitary democracy.

20. Within such a compact, each individual would both compete and cooperate. Each individual would cooperate with other individuals to quickly uncover and fix small errors in process, to obtain the flexibility and resources necessary to fulfill their common purpose, to experiment with alternative strategies, to improve performance, to make a positive impression, and thus to demonstrate that the compact deserves to survive and prosper. Simultaneously, each individual would compete with other individuals, to obtain the resources necessary to fulfill his or her responsibility to the compact, to perform well, to make a positive impression, and thus to survive and prosper.

This is similar to the concept in evolutionary biology of competition within groups and competition between groups. For competition within a group, cooperation (or altruism) puts the individual at a disadvantage; for competition between groups, however, such cooperation puts the group (but not the individual) at an advantage. See Elliott Sober and David Sloan Wilson, *Do Unto Others: The Evolution and Psychology of Unselfish Behavior* (Harvard University Press, 1998). The cooperative behavior that I am advocating (relinquishing the personal advantage of being an accountability holder and accepting the less immediately rewarding task of creating some kind of mutual and collective responsibility) will not, however, be transmitted through genes but through communication. One group can simply observe another group's success and copy it; they don't have to interbreed.

21. A compact of mutual, collective responsibility might be government wide—covering, for example, an entire town, city, county, or even state. It will be much easier, however, to create a more narrow compact that focuses on a particular policy area. A city or a state could have one compact for housing, another for education or health.

22. Kevin P. Kearns argues that "the mission is one of an organization's primary accountability contracts with the public. It is the document in which we say to the public, 'Here is what we promise to do for you. You may hold us accountable for this.'" *Managing for Accountability* (Jossey-Bass, 1996), p. 52.

23. The compact actually *helps* the public manager accomplish performance targets. By making these targets very explicit and very public, the manager creates the leverage necessary to win resources from outside and production from inside. "By committing their organizations to quite specific objectives, and anchoring those objectives in specific agreements with powerful overseers," writes Moore, public managers can "increase their ability to challenge their organizations." Moreover, "their embrace of accountability attracts confidence from overseers. That confidence, in turn releases money and authority for operations." *Creating Public Value*, pp. 274, 282.

24. Moore argues that to make the "deregulation" of government work—to eliminate many of the rules and procedures designed to ensure accountability for equity—public employees must accept personal, professional responsibility for achieving the fundamental, underlying purposes that these narrow rules were designed to produce. Specifically, he applies this idea to policing: "police officers must become true professionals and be controlled through the methods that are used to control professionals. It is not enough to deregulate the bureaucratic structures of traditional policing; the norms and values of public accountability that motivate deregulation must be internalized by the officers themselves." "Policing: Deregulating or Redefining Accountability?" in DiIulio, *Deregulating the Public Service*, p. 226.

25. My concept of a compact of mutual, collective accountability is similar to what Edward P. Weber calls "Grassroots Ecosystem Management" (or GREM) found in rural communities with a natural-resources economy and a desire to maintain

the quality of their environment. Weber describes them as "collaborative partnerships among diverse government, civic, and business actors at the state and local levels" who are "committed to direct citizen participation in governance arrangements; collaborative, consensus-based decision processes; and a holistic policy mission that seeks to meld ecology with economics and the needs of the community." Moreover, he writes, "GREM accepts that a key part of the accountability equation centers on government performance—the ability of government to actually deliver on its promises." GREM places an "emphasis on direct (political) accountability flowing from bottom-up self-governance" and uses "nonhierarchical networks." But "the real key," he continues, "is the reconnection of citizens to governance arrangements." "The Question of Accountability in Historical Perspective: From Jackson to Contemporary Grassroots Ecosystem Management," *Administration & Society*, vol. 31, no. 4 (1999), pp. 452, 459, 471.

26. Eugene Bardach and Cara Lesser "conjecture that professional norms, interpersonal loyalties, and a shared desire to work together in the future do more to promote peer accountability among partners than do more formal agreements." Indeed, they write, "informal and norm-based means of projecting accountability are the most significant methods available to collaborative partners." For example, line staff told them "that the quality of individual performance—not only their own, they thought, but that of their peers—improved when individuals knew they would have an audience for their performance, an audience that could be appreciative but that could also be critical." They "heard the same from middle managers," and from upper management the story was "essentially the same." "Accountability in Human Services Collaboratives—For What? and To Whom?" *Journal of Public Administration Research and Theory*, vol. 6, no. 2 (1996), p. 205. What audience will most appreciate any individual's performance? Besides that individual's mother, the most supportive audience will be the most knowledgeable one—an audience of the individual's peers.

27. As head of the Tactical Air Command (TAC) in the late 1970s, General William Creech established performance targets with his wing commanders. But a wing's targets were contingent on it receiving from TAC the resources (including planes, fuel, and mechanics) necessary to achieve its targets. Robert D. Behn, "Homestead Air Force Base" (The Governors Center at Duke University, 1998).

It would seem that executive branch superiors would cause agency heads much less trouble than would legislators, or journalists, or stakeholders, or overhead regulators. Nevertheless, "parent departments are also reluctant to give flexibilities" to their agencies, observes Roberts. Moreover, the heads of these agencies have little leverage when their superiors renege on the contract. Roberts notes "the inability of chief operating officers to compel cabinet secretaries to live by the terms of annual performance agreements." "Performance-Based Organizations," pp. 470, 474.

28. B. Guy Peters and Donald Savoie suggest that the new public management is not having much of an impact on the traditional, controlling behavior of central (or

overhead) agencies. In a government that has decentralized decisions, empowered frontline workers, and converted managers into entrepreneurs, "central agencies appear to be anachronisms," they write, and thus obvious targets for reform, Yet, they observe, "the fundamental nature of central agencies has not been transformed." "Managing Incoherence: The Coordination and Empowerment Conundrum," *Public Administration Review,* vol. 56, no. 3 (1996), pp. 283, 281.

29. One of the "fourteen points" established by W. Edwards Deming was "Eliminate slogans, exhortations, and targets for the workforce." Why did Deming dislike goals? Because, he wrote, "the bulk of the causes of low quality and low productivity belong to the system and thus lie beyond the power of the work force." Indeed, argued Deming, "I have yet to see a quota that includes any trace of a system by which to help anyone to do a better job." *Out of the Crisis* (Center for Advanced Engineering Study, Massachusetts Institute of Technology, 1982), pp. 24, 71. Clearly, this applies to the kind of targets, goals, or quotas set by a legislature; they create the goal, but they fail to provide a system to help anyone to do a better job. Indeed, the legislature often creates a system that causes low quality and low productivity. By establishing goals without fixing the underlying system, legislatures are setting executive branch agencies up to fail.

In business, Jean-François Manzoni and Jean-Louis Barsoux argue, a boss sets subordinates up to fail by placing them in an "out-group" whose members "are regarded more as hired hands and are managed in a more formal, less personal way with more emphasis on rules, policies, and formal authority" than for those in the in-group. Manzoni and Barsoux list several aspects of this boss's behavior towards those in the out-group: "Pays close attention to unfavorable variances, mistakes, or incorrect judgments." "Usually imposes own view in disagreements." "Emphasizes what the subordinate is doing poorly." "The Set-Up-to-Fail Syndrome," *Harvard Business Review,* vol. 76, no. 1 (1998), pp. 103, 109. This is how some legislators treat those in their governmental out-group—that is, the executive branch.

30. If "citizens have greater opportunities to participate in the design and delivery of their public goods and services," write Carl J. Bellone and George Frederick Goerl, they "can be held accountable, in part, for current deficiencies in public services and financial resources." "Reconciling Public Entrepreneurship and Democracy," *Public Administration Review,* vol. 52, no. 2 (1992), p. 132.

31. Kearns, *Managing for Accountability,* pp. xix, 197, 192.

32. Ibid., pp. 80, 81.

33. James Q. Wilson, "Can the Bureaucracy Be Deregulated?" p. 45.

34. Moore, "Policing: Deregulating or Redefining Accountability?" p. 214.

35. Ibid.

36. Morton H. Halperin offers an explanation for this unwillingness of public agencies to exploit unique and significant organizational capabilities to obtain authorization to pursue new purposes—and thus to broaden its mission and consequently its base of support. This is his concept of "organizational essence": "the view

held by the dominant group in the organization of what the mission and capabilities should be." For example, "Naval officers agree on the general proposition that the essence of the Navy is to maintain combat ships whose primary mission must be to control the seas against potential enemies." (This organizational essence does not include getting relief supplies quickly to developing countries.) And, Halperin argues, "an organization is often indifferent to functions not seen as part of its essence or necessary to protect its essence." Indeed, "sometimes an organization attempts to push a growing function out of its domain entirely. It begrudges expenditures on anything but its chosen activity." *Bureaucratic Politics and Foreign Policy* (Brookings, 1974) pp. 28, 32, 39, 40. Even when the purpose behind the various organizational essences of the U.S. military services—defeating the Soviet Union—has largely disappeared, the services are so locked into their original essence that they find it difficult to think about using their existing capabilities for new purposes.

37. John E. Chubb and Terry M. Moe, *Politics, Markets, and America's Schools* (Brookings, 1990) pp. 26, 187, 226, 186. Chubb and Moe think that bureaucracy and politics share the blame for the failure of American schools: "The bureaucracy problem is the more immediate explanation for the schools' poor academic performance. The politics problem is the more fundamental: it explains the bureaucracy problem" (pp. 26–27). Because of this "politics problem," Chubb and Moe would permit government to establish a school's accountability for finances and fairness— but not for performance: "The state will hold the schools accountable for meeting procedural requirements," they write, but it "will not, on the other hand, hold the schools accountable for student achievement or other dimensions that call for assessments of the quality of school performance." Instead, schools would be held accountable for performance by parents, students, and the market (pp. 224–225).

38. During the mid-1990s, as Congress was debating welfare reform, the nation's governors argued that they could accomplish more with the same federal dollars, provided that they had fewer constraints. "We are asking you to give us flexibility to design our own programs and the guaranteed funding we need," Governor Tommy Thompson of Wisconsin told Congress, "and we will transform the welfare system into a program of transitional assistance that will enable recipients to become productive, working members of our society." Quoted in Frank A. Aukofer, "Partisanship Hinders Governors' Welfare Reform: Thompson Takes Direct Hits in Hearing on Plan," *Milwaukee Journal Sentinel,* February 21, 1996, p. 1.

39. Although the leaders of a charter agency could negotiate for some waivers and flexibility, they could not escape accountability for either finances or fairness. They would still be subject to bureaucratic accountability to their hierarchical superiors, political accountability to the legislature, and legal accountability to the courts; these traditional accountability mechanisms would always exist as both a constraint and a vulnerability. Dissatisfied individuals could always seek to establish accountability by taking their case to political executives, to the courts, to the legislature, or to journalists and other watchdogs. For example, Weber observes that his

grassroots ecosystem management is always subject to these forms of accountability: "Decisions must necessarily accord with the well-established superstructure of
national law[,] and clearance is required from hierarchical superiors." "The
Question of Accountability in Historical Perspective," p. 457.

40. A "charter agency" is obviously similar to Britain's Next Steps executive agencies and the performance-based organizations proposed by Vice President Gore's
National Partnership for Reinventing Government. These two organizational
designs, however, include the opportunity for the agency head to earn a performance bonus if the agency achieves its annual performance goals. For three reasons,
my charter agency would have no provision for an annual performance bonus.

First, such bonuses are extremely controversial. Legislators are reluctant to enact
them and quickly attack the awarding of any specific bonus that they deem unfair
or unwarranted. See Roberts, "Performance-Based Organizations," pp. 473.

Second, initial enthusiasm quickly wanes; legislators may fund the bonus in the
first year but appropriate less in subsequent years. Richard A. King and Judith K.
Mathers studied four of the earliest educational-accountability systems (in South
Carolina, Texas, Indiana, and Kentucky) and found that three of these states even-
tually reduced their funding for financial incentives significantly. "Improving
Schools through Performance-Based Accountability and Financial Rewards,"
Journal of Education Finance, vol. 23 (1997), pp. 147–76.

Third, I do not think that such a bonus will do much to motivate improved
agency performance; after all, the only person who can earn the bonus is the agency
head (plus, perhaps, a few top lieutenants). How motivating is this for the other
people within the organization?

41. DiIulio, *Deregulating the Public Service;* Osborne and Gaebler, *Reinventing
Government;* David Osborne and Peter Plastrik, *Banishing Bureaucracy* (Addison-
Wesley, 1997).

42. Mark Friedman, "Trading Outcome Accountability for Fund Flexibility"
(Baltimore: Fiscal Policy Studies Institute, December 1995). Lisbeth B. Schorr, "The
Case for Shifting to Results-Based Accountability" (Washington: Center for the
Study of Social Policy, Fall 1994).

43. The basic reports of the two commissions are: National Commission on the
Public Service, *Rebuilding the Public Service* (Washington: National Commission on
the Public Service, 1989); National Commission on the State and Local Public
Service, *Hard Truths/Tough Choices: An Agenda for State and Local Reform* (Albany:
Rockefeller Institute of Government, State University of New York, 1993).

44. Charles T. Clotfelter, and Helen F. Ladd, "Recognizing and Rewarding Success
in Public Schools," in Helen F. Ladd, ed., *Holding Schools Accountable: Performance-
Based Reform in Education* (Brookings, 1996), p. 36.

45. Richard F. Elmore, Charles H. Abelmann, and Susan H. Fuhrman, "The New
Accountability in State Education Reform: From Process to Performance," in Ladd,
Holding Schools Accountable, p. 70.

46. If we did this, argues David Osborne, "accountability would increase, rather than be lost." Osborne, "Make 'Em All Charter Schools," *Washington Post,* November 14, 1999, p. B3.

47. Roberts, "Performance-Based Organizations," p. 468.

48. General Accounting Office, *GPRA: Managerial Accountability and Flexibility Pilot Did Not Work As Intended,* GAO/GGD-97-36 (April 1997), pp. 1, 3.

49. Ibid., pp. 12, 14, 12. For another example of how public agencies, when given the opportunity to request waivers from regulations that they believe to be too restrictive, can focus on minor annoyances, see Susan Rosegrant, "The Coast Guard's Model Unit Program: Testing the Waters of Change," (A), (B), and (C), C16-93-1194.0, C16-93-1195.0, and C16-93-1196.0 (Kennedy School of Government, Harvard University, 1993).

50. General Accounting Office, *GPRA,* pp. 3, 29, 30, 32, 28.

51. Ibid., pp. 31, 32, 33. GAO talked with another fifteen agencies that had planned to seek such a waiver but were discouraged by OMB (pp. 10–11).

52. Ibid., p. 11.

53. Unfortunately, the objective rules also create the accountability bias that diverts the attention of the accountability holders—and of the holdees—from performance to finances and fairness.

54. The uncertainties of grassroots ecosystem management, combined with a focus on performance, "leads GREM proponents toward an adaptive management style," writes Edward Weber. "Instead of locking-in the best solution, or automatically employing the same administrative structure for every program," GREM emphasizes "learning through experimentation." "The Question of Accountability in Historical Perspective," p. 461.

55. Lawyers, legalisms, and formal contracts undermine long-term working relationships, reports Stewart Macaulay in a frequently cited article, and thus businesses resort to contracts infrequently. Macaulay illustrates this nonlegalistic thinking with two quotations from business executives:

> If something comes up, you get the other man on the telephone and deal with the problem. You don't read legalistic contract clauses at each other if you ever want to do business again. One doesn't run to lawyers if he wants to stay in business.

> You can settle any dispute if you keep the lawyers and accountants out of it. They just do not understand the give-and-take needed in business.

"Non-Contractual Relations in Business: A Preliminary Study," *American Sociological Review,* vol. 28, no. 1 (1963), p. 61.

56. David S. Broder, "Fine-Tuned Lawyering," *Washington Post,* December 1, 1998, p. A25.

57. Quoted by Gutmann and Thompson, *Democracy and Disagreement,* p. 114.

58. Kenneth P. Ruscio writes: "high levels of trust are associated with thick, well-established social networks in which citizens recognize their interdependence and the norms they have in common." In a small group, individuals have more of an opportunity to create such a social network, understand their interdependence, and discover their common norms. "Trust, Democracy, and Public Management: A Theoretical Argument," *Journal of Public Administration Research and Theory,* vol. 6, no. 3 (1996), p. 475.

59. Jon R. Katzenbach and Douglas K. Smith, *The Wisdom of Teams: Creating the High-Performance Organization* (Harvard Business School Press, 1993), p. 60.

60. Ibid.

61. Ibid.

62. For one example of how this can happen, see Eugene Bardach, *Getting Agencies to Work Together: The Practice and Theory of Managerial Craftsmanship* (Brookings, 1998), particularly chap. 8, pp. 269–305.

63. Thus the responsibility compact is a *contingent* compact; individual contributions are always contingent upon conditions and upon the contributions of others. They resemble contingent contracts (rather than iron-clad ones); see Max H. Bazerman and James J. Gillespie, "Betting on the Future: The Virtues of Contingent Contracts," *Harvard Business Review,* vol. 77, no. 6 (1999), pp. 155–60.

64. Katzenbach and Smith express their "six basic elements of teams" in questions, the first of which is "Are you small enough in number?" *The Wisdom of Teams,* p. 62.

65. Such cooperation would require the nominal accountability holders—those whose constitutional or organizational position puts them higher in the formal, governmental hierarchy—to refrain from attempting to change the terms of the accountability relationships too frequently, too fast, or too much. Multiple accountability holders, note Mark Moore and Margaret Janes Gates, may differ about "the very terms of accountability" and "often change their minds" so that "the terms of accountability are always changing." Moreover, such "conflict and frequent changes in the terms of accountability threaten the commitment of the executives to their overseers, for it seems that there is nothing they can do to satisfy them." *Inspectors-General: Junkyard Dogs or Man's Best Friend?* (Russell Sage Foundation, 1986), p. 105.

66. It is now Part B of the Individuals with Disabilities Education Act (IDEA) (codified as amended at 20 U.S.C. §§ 1411–19).

67. Joel F. Handler, *The Conditions of Discretion: Autonomy, Community, Bureaucracy* (Russell Sage Foundation, 1986), p. 3.

68. For a description of Madison's approach to special education, see ibid., particularly pp. 83–117.

69. Ibid., particularly pp. 93, 94, 95, 99.

70. When capable, the student is also a member of the team. Ibid., p. 88.

71. The atomic element temporarily named *Ununbium* appears in the periodic table of the elements not because it exists in nature but because (like other elements with atomic numbers 93 and higher) it has been created by scientists. On February 9, 1996, German scientists at Gesellschaft für Schwerionenforschung in Germany created Ununbium by bombarding a lead target with zinc atoms ($^{208}Pb + {}^{70}Zn \rightarrow {}^{277}Uub + {}^{1}n$). Unfortunately, Ununbium has a half-life of only 240 microseconds and only a few atoms have ever been made (www.webelements.com/webelements/elements/text/key/Uub.html [October 2000]). The special-education responsibility compact in Madison has existed for substantially longer.

72. John P. Burke, *Bureaucratic Responsibility* (Johns Hopkins University Press, 1986), pp. 216, 39, 216, 217.

73. Burke (*Bureaucratic Responsibility,* p. ix) cites the "ethics of responsibility" that Max Weber proposed for political leaders. Specifically, Weber argued that "the politician" should have "three pre-eminent qualities": "passion [for a cause], a feeling of responsibility, and a sense of proportion." *From Max Weber: Essays in Sociology* ed. H. H. Gerth and C. Wright Mills (Oxford University Press, 1946), p. 115. Although most politicians can mobilize their own passion, they often lack Weber's "sense of proportion," let alone his "feeling of responsibility."

Chapter Eight

1. Cooperation that must emerge or evolve without any government or other formal institution to impose it is frequently called cooperation under anarchy: Kenneth A. Oye, ed., *Cooperation under Anarchy* (Princeton University Press, 1986); Michael Taylor, *Community, Anarchy and Liberty* (Cambridge University Press, 1982).

2. Alasdair Roberts, "Performance-Based Organizations: Assessing the Gore Plan," *Public Administration Review,* vol. 57, no. 6 (1997), pp. 465–77.

3. Robert Axelrod calls this "the problem of cooperation." *The Evolution of Cooperation* (Basic Books, 1984), pp. 3–24.

4. If we choose to deregulate government and give public managers greater freedom, writes B. Guy Peters, "a certain amount of error will have to be accepted." *The Future of Governing: Four Emerging Models* (University Press of Kansas, 1996), p. 96.

5. John Mayne, "Accountability for Program Performance," in John Mayne and Eduardo Zapico-Goñi, eds., *Monitoring Performance in the Public Sector* (Transaction Publishers, 1997), p. 171. Mark Bovens and Paul 't Hart, however, make an implicit distinction between assigning accountability and assigning blame; they write of the "political processes of allocating blame and accountability" and of the "pivotal role of accountability and blame." *Understanding Policy Fiascoes* (Transaction Publishers 1996), pp. 135, 139.

6. John J. DiIulio Jr., Gerald Garvey, and Donald F. Kettl, *Improving Government Performance: An Owner's Manual* (Brookings, 1993), p. 76.

7. In his analysis of collaboratives, Eugene Bardach defines trust as "confidence that the trustworthiness of another party is adequate to justify remaining in a condition of vulnerability." "The situation in which trust operates," writes Bardach, is "a situation of vulnerability, uncertainty, personal risk, and the power of others over oneself." *Getting Agencies to Work Together: The Practice and Theory of Managerial Craftsmanship* (Brookings, 1998), p. 252.

8. This is not necessarily true. For example, the compact could consist of everyone in the accountability environment except journalists, who could continue to write nasty stories about agency incompetence and about the cabal that is protecting it. Still, if every member of the compact concluded that the benefits he or she was gaining from cooperation more than compensated for the costs of the journalists' additional attacks on the cabal, they would continue to work together.

Philip Pettit distinguishes between two types of multi-person prisoner's dilemmas. In one case, a "foul dealer" defects and imposes on at least one other party costs that are large enough to make this party worse off than if everyone defected; thus to reduce its own costs, the abused party will also defect. In the other case, a "free rider" defects and imposes costs on some of the other parties, but no one is worse off than he or she would be if everyone defected. Thus the compact's members ignore the defector, continue to cooperate, and still reap some benefits from their cooperation. "Free Riding and Foul Dealing," *Journal of Philosophy,* vol. 83, no. 7 (1986), pp. 361–79.

9. Even inspectors general (IGs), those prototypical accountability holders, need cooperation. If their accountability holdees ignore their brilliant ideas, IGs will accomplish nothing. Moreover, they cannot create practical recommendations without the operational knowledge possessed by line managers. These facts, write Mark H. Moore and Margaret Jane Gates, "impel IGs toward managers and encourage them to want to join the 'management team.'" As Paul C. Light observes, most inspectors general "have no authority to compel their bosses to respond"; they have "but one power; the power to persuade." Thus some IGs build alliances; in the 1980s, Light reports, the federal Office of Management and Budget (OMB) formed such alliances with various IGs: The IGs provided OMB with information; OMB protected the IGs' operational freedom. Moore and Gates, *Inspectors-General: Junkyard Dogs or Man's Best Friend?* (Russell Sage Foundation, 1986), p. 70. Light, *Monitoring Government: Inspectors General and the Search for Accountability* (Brookings 1992), pp. 75, 115 (also, 106–20, 225).

Of course, IGs can always threaten to run to Congress. But if they actually do so, they may destroy a working relationship with line managers or the possibility of creating one. Thus, conclude Moore and Gates, threatening to defect works but actually defecting doesn't: "The effectiveness of IGs is greatest when they can operate with the implicit threat of publicity and congressional attention rather than its reality." Indeed, they continue, "the impact of the IGs may be greatest when they allow management to assume much of the initiative for solving their agencies' problems and much of the credit for doing so." Conversely, Moore and Gates write, "program managers must develop a 'tolerance' for the traditional OIG functions of investigation and audit," and recognize their IG's "desire to contribute to the prevention of fraud and abuse and to the promotion of efficiency." Thus they recommend that, if political executives, legislators, inspectors general are to work together to improve "the efficiency of public sector programs," they will need to "reach more or less durable agreements about the terms in which a given program's performance will be measured." *Inspectors-General,* pp. 72–73, 83–84. Sounds like a responsibility compact.

10. Bruce L. R. Smith, "Major Trends in American Public Administration, 1940–1980," in Bruce L. R. Smith and James D. Carroll, eds., *Improving the Accountability and Performance of Government* (Brookings, 1982), p. 8.

11. Union presidents make their living by protecting their existing employees. Obtaining their commitment to a responsibility compact may, however, be relatively easy: Simply promise that all existing employees will be grandfathered into their current positions and salaries and that many of them will have an opportunity for advancement or, at least, for more interesting jobs. A union president has no direct stake in the wages denied potential future employees who may never be hired and, thus, who will never know that they might have been employed if the responsibility compact had not been created. Francis Fukuyama argues that "the implicit bargain that underlies the successful implementation of lean production, in both Japan and the United States, is a trade-off of relaxed work rules for long-term job security." *Trust: The Social Virtues and the Creation of Prosperity* (Free Press, 1997), p. 263. When automobile firms attempt to introduce lean production, report James Womack and his colleagues, "workers respond only when there exists some sense of reciprocal obligation." James P. Womack, Daniel T. Jones, and Daniel Roos, *The Machine That Changed the World: The Story of Lean Production* (New York: Rawson Associates, 1990), p. 99.

12. Smith, "Major Trends in American Public Administration," p. 7.

13. Anatol Rapoport and Albert M. Chammah, *Prisoner's Dilemma: A Study in Conflict and Cooperation* (University of Michigan Press, 1965); William Poundstone, *Prisoner's Dilemma* (Doubleday, 1992).

14. Thomas C. Schelling, *Micromotives and Macrobehavior* (Norton, 1978), pp. 217–37.

15. Garrett Hardin, "The Tragedy of the Commons," *Science,* vol. 162, no. 3859 (1968), pp. 1243–48.

16. For a discussion of self-enforcing agreements, see L. G. Telser, "A Theory of Self-Enforcing Agreements," *Journal of Business,* vol. 53, no. 1 (1980), pp. 27–44.

17. Mancur Olson: *The Logic of Collective Action: Public Goods and the Theory of Groups* (Harvard University Press, 1965), p. 2.

18. For an analysis of collective action in small groups, see ibid., pp. 22–36.

19. This policing arrangement solves two problems that Kenneth A. Oye identifies as inhibiting a strategy of reciprocity: It clearly identifies who is cooperating and

who is defecting, and it clearly punishes defectors (without punishing cooperators). "Explaining Cooperation under Anarchy: Hypotheses and Strategies," in Oye, *Cooperation under Anarchy*, pp. 15–16.

20. Hardin advocates "mutual coercion mutually agreed upon." He believes that responsibility won't work; indeed, Hardin thinks that any effort to exploit another's sense of responsibility is itself irresponsible: "When we use the word responsibility in the absence of substantial sanctions are we not trying to browbeat a free man in a commons into acting against his own interest? Responsibility is a verbal counterfeit for a substantial *quid pro quo*. It is an attempt to get something for nothing." Hardin prefers explicit coercion to the coercion implicit in appeals to responsibility: "The social arrangements that produce responsibility are arrangements that create coercion." "The Tragedy of the Commons," p. 1247.

21. Olson, *The Logic of Collective Action*, p. 2.

22. For a discussion of how the assumption that humans are motivated almost exclusively by self-interest has come to dominate much of academic research (and popular thinking) about political behavior, see Jane J. Mansbridge, "The Rise and Fall of Self-Interest in the Explanation of Political Life," in Jane J. Mansbridge, ed., *Beyond Self-Interest* (University of Chicago Press, 1990), pp. 3–22.

23. For example, Joel D. Aberbach analyzes the difficulties that the president and the Congress have in cooperating and concludes that "sharing [power] isn't easy." "Sharing Isn't Easy: When Separate Institutions Clash," *Governance*, vol. 11, no. 2 (1998), pp. 137–52.

Chapter Nine

1. See Kenneth A. Oye, ed., *Cooperation under Anarchy* (Princeton University Press, 1986). Given that cooperation among nations is difficult, Robert Jervis observes, "the central question is not, 'Why do wars occur?' but 'Why do wars not occur more often?'" "From Balance to Concert: A Study of International Security Cooperation," in Oye, *Cooperation under Anarchy*, p. 58.

2. Elinor Ostrom, *Governing the Commons: The Evolution of Institutions for Collective Action* (Cambridge University Press, 1990). Elinor Ostrom, "A Behavioral Approach to the Rational Choice Theory of Collective Action," *American Political Science Review*, vol. 92, no. 1 (1998), pp. 1–22.

3. David W. Brown, *When Strangers Cooperate: Using Social Conventions to Govern Ourselves* (Free Press, 1995), p. 16.

4. Mary Douglas, *How Institutions Think* (Syracuse University Press, 1986), p. 25.

5. Robert Axelrod, *The Evolution of Cooperation* (Basic Books, 1984), pp. 2, 6. See also Robert Axelrod and Douglas Dion, "The Further Evolution of Cooperation," *Science*, December 9, 1998, pp. 1385–90.

6. Axelrod, *The Evolution of Cooperation,* pp. 54, 20, 22. See also Axelrod and Dion, "The Further Evolution of Cooperation," p. 1385.

7. Axelrod, *The Evolution of Cooperation,* p. 5. For a discussion, see Alvin W. Gouldner, "The Norm of Reciprocity: A Preliminary Statement," *American Sociological Review,* vol. 25, no. 2 (1960), pp. 161–78.

8. Axelrod, *The Evolution of Cooperation,* pp. 22–23, and chapter 6, pp. 109–23.

9. Ibid., pp. 24, 124, 20. Axelrod also recommends (pp. 133–34) attempting to change the payoffs, by, for example, lowering the benefits and raising the costs of defection.

10. In fact, explains Axelrod, "TIT FOR TAT never once scored better in a game with the other player." Yet, over the long run, it proved to be extremely effective. Moreover, Axelrod describes how a small cluster of tit-for-tat cooperators can invade a group of "meanies" who always defect, and take over a population so that all of the meanies are gone and only tit-for-tat cooperators remain. Axelrod, *The Evolution of Cooperation,* pp. 134, 136, 112, 137, 112, chapter 3 (pp. 55–69).

11. What is fair? Journalists and public officials have different definitions. A public official may believe that what is said in a social setting outside of government is not reportable. In contrast, a journalist may make no such distinction between the personal and the professional. The journalist is always on duty, prepared to report anything that is said by anyone at anytime unless it is preceded by a complete and explicit statement that the following is off the record. To public officials, this may seem extremely unfair. To journalists, however, it conforms with their professional ethics.

Of course, public officials can establish some different rules by becoming friends with journalists—not social friends (though that might work quite well) but professional friends. Professional friends craft their own set of cooperative and mutually supportive rules: You feature me favorably in your coverage; I'll make sure that you get useful information before others. But like any treaty between two nations, such an agreement lasts only as long as it benefits both parties. As soon as a journalist perceives a gain to be made by voiding the unwritten agreement and attacking the public official, he or she will do so. As soon as the public official perceives a gain to be made by withholding information (or giving it to another, more useful journalist), he or she will do so.

The late George Frazier, a curmudgeonly columnist for the *Boston Herald* and the *Boston Globe,* never wanted to meet the people about whom he wrote. Why? Because it might turn out that he would like them. And, if he liked an individual, Frazier knew, he would have a much more difficult time wielding his poison pen. Frazier practiced witty, sarcastic journalism, and he well knew that it would be more difficult to assail someone who had become a friend. Charles Fountain, *Another Man's Poison: The Life and Writing of Columnist George Frazier* (Globe Pequot Press, 1984), p. 254.

It is easier to compete with strangers than with friends. Conversely, it is easier to cooperate with friends than with strangers.

12. If someone else is watching, and if we know that we will have to deal with this person in the future, we will want to convince this individual that we are nice, retaliatory, forgiving, and clear.

13. If the rulers of a nation that is about to lose a war assume that they will be executed after their defeat, they will see no value in abiding by the international rules of warfare. Thus they have an incentive to fight brutally to the end (even if their soldiers don't and won't). Consequently, the winning nation may decide that it will not execute the rulers of the losing nation (though it may have a difficult time convincing these rulers that they will abide by this commitment).

14. Dashiell Hammett, *The Maltese Falcon* (Vintage Books, 1929, 1989), pp. 213–14.

15. Axelrod, *The Evolution of Cooperation*, p. 115.

16. Both you and the dealer recognize that, unless you research the performance characteristics and dealer's price for each automobile model, the dealer will have a lot more information about what is a fair deal. Thus how fair the deal actually is depends upon how fairly the dealer treats you.

17. The dealer's strategy of creating reciprocal relationships with its car-buying customers includes its service department. If these customers also bring their cars back for service, and if the service department also treats them fairly, these customers are even more apt to evolve a reciprocal relationship with the dealer—perhaps even a professional friendship with someone in service.

18. Even an owner who plans to sell the business soon wants to treat you fairly. For the franchise's value includes its goodwill, which depends, in part, on its reputation for treating customers fairly.

19. Brown, *When Strangers Cooperate*, p. 98.

20. Both Axelrod and Gouldner use the phrase *tit for tat* to describe reciprocity for both cooperation and defection. Axelrod, *The Evolution of Cooperation*, p. 20; Gouldner, "The Norm of Reciprocity," p. 172.

21. In rock climbing and other professional relationships, you need to trust not only your partner's willingness to reciprocate your cooperative behavior; you also need to trust your partner's competence. You need to trust your partner's ability to reciprocate cooperatively with skill and judgment. To trust people to do something, you have to believe not only that they *will try* to do it; you also have to believe that they *will be able* to do it.

22. Axelrod, *The Evolution of Cooperation*, pp. 187, 20, 182.

23. What do we mean by *trust*? Is trust our unquestioning faith in the personal behavior of another individual? Or is trust merely our confidence in our ability to predict another individual's behavior? Usually we think about placing our "trust" in the altruistic behavior of a friend or relative: I cooperate with these people because I trust them to take my interests into account when they do something that affects me. Yet we

can also "trust" in the not-necessarily-altruistic behavior of an institution with which we have no experience or an individual whom we have never met strictly because we have the knowledge necessary to predict that behavior with some confidence: I cooperate with people I do not know personally because I have somehow concluded that they have the incentives or reputation for behaving in a way that I can predict. In both cases, the trust reflects a belief that someone will behave very predictably.

Axelrod argues that we can predict that another individual will engage in reciprocal behavior *if* we know that this individual knows that he or she will have to deal with us frequently in the future: To establish from zero a cooperative relationship with an unknown individual, I want to ensure that this relationship will last for a long time—creating the opportunity for the two of us to play tit for tat and to commit and signal that we each will, indeed, continue to play tit for tat.

24. Axelrod includes the second condition only because he believes that it will produce the first. This, however, is not guaranteed. Even people who accept that they will have to work a lot with each other in the future still have to evolve a mutual recognition of the value of reciprocity. And they might never get there. Consequently, for a professional friendship to exist (in my definition), the individuals must not only expect that they are in a durable relationship; they must also already have evolved the norm of reciprocity that ensures that they will not defect in their next interaction.

25. If a small group of tit-for-tat cooperators can invade a group of "meanies" (see note 10), why can't the cooperators in a responsibility compact invade the non-cooperators and drive them out? Because the tit-for-tat cooperators in a responsibility compact may not possess any *tits* with which to retaliate for the *tats*; the cooperators have no way to punish the defectors. The members of the compact simply have no sanctions that they can impose on a defecting auditor, or a defecting inspector general, or a defecting journalist, or a defecting candidate.

26. For a discussion of why this is so, see Kenneth A. Oye, "Explaining Cooperation under Anarchy: Hypotheses and Strategies," in Oye, *Cooperation under Anarchy*, pp. 18–20. The essays in Oye's volume were designed to employ a common framework to analyze international cooperation in both military-security and political-economic relationships. Yet this framework also helps to analyze the relationships among those in a public agency's accountability environment.

27. Axelrod, *The Evolution of Cooperation*, p. 60.

28. Ibid., p. 41.

29. Brown, *When Strangers Cooperate*, pp. 12–16.

30. Oye, "Explaining Cooperation under Anarchy," p. 15.

31. Oye writes: "In two-person games, Tit-for-Tat works well because the costs of defection are focused on only one other party. If defection imposes costs on all parties in an N-Person game, however, the power of strategies of reciprocity is undermined." Oye, "Explaining Cooperation under Anarchy: Hypotheses and Strategies," p. 20.

32. Robert Axelrod, *The Complexity of Cooperation: Agent-Based Models of Competition and Collaboration* (Princeton University Press, 1997), p. 41.

33. For a discussion of the ease of creating group identity and its value in inducing cooperation, see Robyn M. Dawes, Alphons J. C. van de Kragt, and John M. Orbell, "Cooperation for the Benefit of Us—Not Me, or My Conscience," in Jane J. Mansbridge, ed., *Beyond Self-Interest* (University of Chicago Press, 1990), pp. 97–110.

34. Mancur Olson: *The Logic of Collective Action: Public Goods and the Theory of Groups* (Harvard University Press, 1965), p. 2.

35. Organizations, write Peter B. Clark and James Q. Wilson, can employ three kinds of incentives; one is quite concrete, while the other two are strictly intangible: (1) "Material incentives" are the traditional, "tangible rewards." (2) "Solidary incentives" come from "the act of associating" and include "such rewards as socializing, congeniality, the sense of group membership and identification, the status resulting from membership, fun and conviviality, the maintenance of social distinctions, and so on." (3) "Purposive incentives" come "from the stated ends of the association rather than from the simple act of association." "Incentive Systems: A Theory of Organizations," *Administrative Science Quarterly*, vol. 6, no. 2 (1961), pp. 134–35. To create a responsibility compact, it would help to employ both solidary and purposive incentives.

36. Dennis Chong, *Collective Action and the Civil Rights Movement* (University of Chicago Press, 1991), p. 232.

37. Alasdair Roberts, "Performance-Based Organizations: Assessing the Gore Plan," *Public Administration Review*, vol. 57, no. 6 (1997), pp. 469–70. Roberts notes that support agencies with a monopoly on the services they provide to line agencies fear that flexibility will cut into their revenue (p. 471).

38. Richard F. Fenno Jr. writes that all members of Congress have a "disposition to run and hide when a defense of Congress might be called for. Members of Congress run *for* Congress by running *against* Congress. The strategy is ubiquitous, addictive, cost-free, and foolproof. . . . In the short run, everybody plays and nearly everybody wins. Yet the institution bleeds from 435 separate cuts." *Home Style: House Members in Their Districts* (Little Brown, 1978), p. 168.

39. Frank Anechiarico and James B. Jacobs, *The Pursuit of Absolute Integrity: How Corruption Control Makes Government Ineffective* (University of Chicago Press, 1996), pp. 25, 23.

40. A group may sanction only a few of its defectors, yet still establish a reputation for playing tit for tat aggressively.

41. The political and intellectual competition among legislators, candidates, and journalists not only holds people accountable; it also generates policy innovation. See Nelson W. Polsby, *Political Innovation in America: The Politics of Policy Initiation* (Yale University Press, 1984).

42. Brown, *When Strangers Cooperate.*

43. Axelrod, *The Complexity of Cooperation*, p. 7.

44. For a discussion of how norms emerge, see Robert Axelrod, "Laws of Life: How Standards of Behavior Evolve," *The Sciences,* vol. 27, no. 2 (1987), pp. 44–51.

45. Karl-Dieter Opp writes that norms can be established in three ways: Institutions can prescribe norms; people may create norms with a voluntary social contract; or the norms "may gradually emerge without either bargaining or the involvement of a norm-making institution." But how can norms "emerge" in large groups? Opp suggests that recurrent behavior can lead to the formation of a norm, that direct rewards and imitation are two mechanisms that foster recurrent behavior, and that "social structures" (such as communication systems and group cohesion) can help or hinder the spread of any behavior. He also argues that the recurrent behavior shapes preferences. Then people who have adopted these new preferences speak out in favor of the behavior, and, from such public support, the behavior becomes accepted as a norm. "The Evolutionary Emergence of Norms," *British Journal of Social Psychology,* vol. 21 (1982), pp. 139–49.

46. Axelrod lists eight "mechanisms" that "can serve to support a norm:" (1) "metanorms," or norms that require the punishment of people who defect from a norm and of people who fail to punish such defectors, (2) "dominance" of one group over another, (3) "internalization" of a norm, (4) "deterrence" by someone who pays the immediate cost of punishing a defection to ensure wide acceptance of the norm in the future, (5) "social proof," in similar behavior by others, (6) voluntary "membership" in a group, (7) a "law" that mandates the norm, or (8) the "reputation" that an individual establishes by abiding by the norm. These mechanisms would not, however, be very effective in encouraging the acceptance of a responsibility compact's norm of reciprocity by those journalists, candidates, auditors, and prosecutors who (1) are not particularly interested in improving performance and (2) have already accepted a different (and conflicting) set of professional norms. "An Evolutionary Approach to Norms," *American Political Science Review,* vol. 80, no. 4 (1986), pp. 1095–1111 (reprinted in Axelrod, *The Complexity of Cooperation,* pp. 44–68).

47. In a discussion of cooperation among nations, Axelrod and Robert O. Keohane observe that international "regimes"—which consist of principles, norms, rules, and decision-making procedures—can foster cooperation. Indeed, "international regimes may also help to develop new norms." "Achieving Cooperation under Anarchy: Strategies and Institutions," in Oye, *Cooperation under Anarchy,* pp. 249–51.

48. Any simple benefit-cost analysis would certainly reveal that the costs of your time exceed the benefits that you, personally, receive from a very slightly cleaner environment.

49. Even if your community had mandatory recycling, you would have several simple and obvious ways to cheat, some of which would cost you less than abiding by the recycling rules.

50. Or because we do not want to incur the wrath of our neighborhood's environmental enforcer?

51. For a discussion of the line, see Brown, *When Strangers Cooperate,* particularly pp. 23–28.

52. Ibid., pp. 18, 23.

53. David K. Lewis, *Convention: A Philosophical Study* (Harvard University Press, 1969), p. 208. For Lewis's formal definition of a convention, see pp. 78–79.

54. Brown distinguishes between a "convention" and a "norm": "A norm is a model of correct behavior and, more than likely, an end in itself. Something is simply done or not done for its own sake or to avoid disapproval." In contrast, he writes, "with a convention, we are usually focused on the satisfactory outcome that our cooperation can produce, not the behavior itself." Still, Brown continues, "as a convention becomes established, however, a norm will in all likelihood emerge to support that particular regularity of behavior"; indeed, "fragile conventions stand a better chance when there are norms that support them." *When Strangers Cooperate,* pp. 50, 51. (Lewis calls conventions "a species of norms." *Convention,* p. 98.)

The convention is our mutual agreement to form an orderly line rather than fight. The norm that supports this convention is the first-come, first-served principle.

55. Someone with a little authority can provide a rationale that permits someone to cut in, despite it being a clear violation of the first-come, first-served norm that supports the line: It is 9:30 at the airline ticket counter, and an airline official walks down the long line asking: "Is anyone here on the 10:00 plane?" Anyone on this plane is immediately escorted to the front of the line. Yet no one complains. Why? Because a different, widely accepted, and simple norm now dominates: People ought to be given a chance to make their plane. Even if they were late to the airport, they should be given this chance. We accept this norm because even the most prompt of us may be late some day. Thus we are pleased that the airline has provided for this contingency.

56. Donna Harrison, personal communication, January 1, 2000.

57. Why ignore the violators? Because enforcing a convention imposes costs on both the violators and the enforcers.

58. A responsibility compact cannot be based on formal rules. Any such rules for performance accountability would require another set of accountability holders, exacerbating the current excesses of accountability for process. Silly. Instead, a responsibility compact has to convince enough people that improving performance is sufficiently important that they will voluntarily accept the compact's conventions and behave in a manner consistent with its underlying norms.

59. Brown, *When Strangers Cooperate,* p. 45.

60. For the latest tenting rules, see www.duke.edu/dsg/kville/tenting/policy.html (October 2000).

61. Brown, *When Strangers Cooperate,* p. 53.

62. We Americans are constantly trying to outlaw reciprocity in politics. We pass laws to ensure that no campaign contribution, plane ride, or meal is reciprocated with a favor. Yet it is very hard to outlaw such a well-established and widely accepted norm as reciprocity.

63. Donald R. Matthews, *U. S. Senators and Their World* (University of North Carolina Press, 1960), pp. 100, 253, 101, 116, 92, 102–03, 101.

64. Legislators, however, can speak in code. In 1945 Senator Alben William Barkley (D-Ky.) offered some "Advice to Newly Elected Senators": "If you think one of your colleagues is stupid in debate, which you will think if you are here long, refer to him as 'the able, learned and distinguished senator.' If you *know* he is stupid, which you probably will, refer to him as 'the *very* able, learned and distinguished senator.' " Alben W. Barkley, *That Reminds Me* (Doubleday & Co., 1954), pp. 253, 255.

65. Matthews, *U.S. Senators and Their World,* p. 99.

66. Matthews predicted that trends in American politics would "encourage departure from the norms of Senate behavior," and, as a result, "nonconformity to the folkways will increase in the future." Ibid., p. 117.

67. Ibid., p. 92.

68. Other "new rules of engagement" include "Define your opponent to the voters before he or she can define him-/herself or you." "If attacked, hit back even harder." "It's easier to give voters a negative impression of your opponent than it is to improve their image of you, especially if you are already viewed negatively. The best way to win is by bringing the other guy down, not by bringing yourself up." Victor Kamber, *Poison Politics: Are Negative Campaigns Destroying Democracy?* (Insight Books, 1997), p. 46.

69. As Axelrod and Keohane argue about cooperation and noncooperation in Europe in 1914 (and in international affairs in general): "Beliefs, not realities, governed conduct." "Achieving Cooperation under Anarchy," p. 231.

Chapter Ten

1. Okay. Not every state's charter school legislation establishes how they will be evaluated. North Carolina's law simply says that a school's charter may be revoked for (among other things) its "failure to meet the requirements for student performance contained in the charter." "Charter Schools Act of 1996," House Bill 955, section 2, General Assembly of North Carolina, 1995 Session (ratified June 21, 1996) (codified at North Carolina General Statutes, § 115C-238.29A).

This ambiguity about expectations for performance appears to be common. "Unclear laws and lax implementation in many states cloud charter schools' relationships with government and threaten to replace performance with compliance as the basis of charter school accountability," report Paul T. Hill, Lawrence C. Pierce, and Robin Lake. From their study of charter school accountability in six states, they found that "few school districts have created the capability of judging individual schools on the basis of performance, and few want to." "How Are Public Charter Schools Held Accountable," University of Washington (December 1998), photocopy, pp. 3, 11.

2. As Kenneth A. Oye observes, one way improve the prospects for cooperation in a multi-person game is to simply reduce the number of players. He also notes, however, that "reductions in the number of actors can usually only be purchased at the expense of the magnitude of gains from cooperation." "Explaining Cooperation under Anarchy: Hypotheses and Strategies," in Oye, *Cooperation under Anarchy* (Princeton University Press, 1986), p. 21. That is, the potential gains from a charter agency will be less than from a complete compact of mutual, collective responsibility; it will, however, be easier to create a charter agency.

In international affairs, write Robert Axelrod and Robert O. Keohane, institutions "may enable N-person games to be broken down into games with smaller numbers of actors." In accountability relationships, this may also be an important role for the institution of a charter agency. Moreover, in fostering cooperation, the institution of a charter agency will necessarily have to cope with the four problems, defined by Axelrod and Keohane, that make cooperation difficult:

1. how to provide incentives for cooperation so that cooperation would be rewarded over the long run, and defection punished;
2. how to monitor behavior so that cooperators and defectors could be identified;
3. how to focus rewards on cooperators and retaliation on defectors;
4. how to link issues with one another in productive rather than self-defeating ways and, more generally, how to play multilevel games without tripping over their own strategies.

"Achieving Cooperation under Anarchy," in Oye, *Cooperation under Anarchy,* pp. 238–39, 249.

3. David W. Brown, *When Strangers Cooperate: Using Social Conventions to Govern Ourselves* (Free Press, 1995), p. 45.

4. Ibid., p. 59.

5. Ibid., pp. 59, 54.

6. In the lexicon of "complex adaptive systems," a compact of mutual, collective responsibility is not an "emergent" phenomenon. After all, if it was truly emergent, it would not only have emerged already; it would also have reproduced and propagated. I think, however, it can be evolved (if you can think of "to evolve" as a transitive verb with someone or some group actively doing the evolving). Like Axlerod's tit-for-tat strategy, however, a responsibility compact will not necessarily evolve spontaneously from random mutations in some political or organizational DNA. Instead, someone must exercise conscious and intelligent leadership to create it,

grow it, and to sustain it—that is, to evolve it. For a discussion of the application of complex adaptive systems to public management, see Robert D. Behn, "Can Public Managers Usefully Exploit the Principles of Complex Adaptive Systems? No; Yes; Maybe; But Is It Worth It?" a paper presented at the Twenty-First Annual Research Conference of the Association for Public Policy Analysis and Management, Washington, D.C., November 5, 1999, and at the Fifth National Public Management Conference, College Station, Texas, December 3, 1999.

7. If a responsibility compact does become a "law" (imposed by some central authority), it ought to be a "common law"—one that has evolved over time, through use and reinforcement, from a custom into a law. In the process, it would also evolve a widely appreciated value and publicly accepted legitimacy that a legislatively imposed law often lacks. Thus the responsibility compact would be in the Anglo-American "common-law tradition," which, writes Philip Selznick, reflects "a preference for law that is more emergent than imposed." *The Moral Commonwealth: Social Theory and the Promise of Community* (University of California Press, 1992), p. 463.

8. Brown, *When Strangers Cooperate*, p. 65.

9. Brown observes how "successful coordination solutions" provide "prominent analogies" that can be adapted to solve other coordination problems. Ibid., p. 139. Nevertheless, it may not be at all obvious what key elements are common to most charter agencies and what singular, specific components are idiosyncratic to a particular charter agency (reflecting the particulars of its political context or social history). Thus scholars and practitioners will need to distinguish between the necessary, helpful, and purely particular features of charter agencies.

10. This charter team is like one of Francis Fukuyama's "moral communities": "Their shared languages of good and evil give their members a common moral life," and "create a degree of trust among its members." Indeed, Fukuyama argues, such "communities depend on mutual trust and will not arise spontaneously without it." *Trust: The Social Virtues and the Creation of Prosperity* (Free Press, 1995), pp. 36, 25.

11. It is a prisoner's dilemma only if for each player mutual cooperation is not as good as defecting while the others cooperate. If mutual cooperation produces the best outcome for everyone, the game becomes Rousseau's "stag hunt." See Kenneth N. Waltz, *Man, the State and War: A Theoretical Analysis* (Columbia University Press, 1959), pp. 167, 183, 192; Brown, *When Strangers Cooperate*, p. 15; Oye, "Explaining Cooperation under Anarchy," pp. 8, 12, 14–15; Axelrod and Keohane, "Achieving Cooperation under Anarchy," pp. 229, 244.

12. Brown, *When Strangers Cooperate*, p. 106.

13. Ibid., p. 20.

14. The Alliance for Redesigning Government, *The Oregon Option: Early Lessons from a Performance Partnership on Building Results-Driven Accountability* (Washington: National Academy of Public Administration, July 1996), pp. 2, 22, 21. "The Memorandum of Understanding is useful symbolically, but it has no inherent

muscle," notes the Academy's report; it "does not hold anyone accountable for the success of the Oregon Option" (p. 23).

The report argues that three important conditions made it feasible for the two governments to create this partnership: (1) "A credible statewide system was in place"; (2) Oregon possessed "catalytic state and local leadership dedicated to results"; and (3) "The political and policy environment in Washington was right" (pp. 8–9). The report also lists a set of "state/local readiness factors" plus some "federal readiness factors" that can be organized under three general preconditions for creating this kind of partnership, collaborative, responsibility compact, or charter agency: (1) general political acceptability, (2) leadership, and (3) resources, particularly infrastructure and staff (p. 11).

15. Robert D. Behn, "Partnerships Require Trust," *New Public Innovator,* no. 94 (Winter 1999), p. 16.

16. You might call this "engineered emergence," or "negotiated emergence," or "facilitated emergence," or "assisted emergence." A mini responsibility compact is not emergent unless someone or some group engineers, negotiates, facilitates, or otherwise assists its emergence.

17. Robert H. Schaffer, *The Breakthrough Strategy: Using Short-Term Success to Build the High Performance Organization* (Ballinger Publishing Co., 1988), pp. 5, 63.

18. Can this work in Washington, D.C.? I don't know. I have seen it work in state and municipal governments. Public managers who do a few mediocre things well can significantly improve performance and quickly establish their reputation for managerial competence. But Washington is different—as many a business executive has learned.

At the beginning of President Jimmy Carter's administration, Michael Blumenthal left Bendix, where he was the chief executive officer, to become secretary of the Treasury. "One very important thing you have to learn in Washington is the difference between appearance and reality," reports Blumenthal; moreover, "appearance is as important as reality." In Washington, he observes, "since your power is based on what people think you have in the way of influence, the appearance [of influence] is very important." Indeed, he continues, "when it comes to having and exercising influence, appearance matters a great deal." Consequently, people work hard to create appearances. W. Michael Blumenthal, "Candid Reflections of a Businessman in Washington," *Fortune,* January 29, 1979, pp. 36, 37, 38.

19. Each such charter agency will, of course, be competing with every other one for resources. Every public agency is always attempting to convince society at large that its policy area both needs and warrants more resources and flexibility. And although there is no limit on the total amount of flexibility to be allotted to agencies, there is a clear budgetary limit on the resources to be distributed. How does society judge the comparative worth of these policy areas? The relative distribution of resources will be influenced by the usual political factors: contributions, connec-

tions, reputations, and luck. Competence could also be an important (though rarely decisive) factor: Which charter agencies are doing a better job holding their members to high ethical standards? Which have avoided messy scandals and petty disputes? Which have improved performance? Which have improved performance significantly? Which have produced results that society values? Such agencies will gain society's respect and thus be in a better position to compete politically for resources and flexibility.

Will society really value ethics, competence, performance, and results? Will the citizenry really allocate more resources and flexibility to a public agency that has established a mini responsibility compact and demonstrated its collective accountability to the electorate? Will the citizenry really deliver on such rewards? More important, can the citizenry convince public agencies and public officials that it will reward in significant ways agencies that produce results? After all, if a charter agency is an intangible concept, the citizenry is even more ephemeral.

But maybe we need not evoke the concept of a conscious, thinking, acting, capital-C Citizenry to create productive competition between agencies for resources and flexibility. After all, the Citizenry doesn't have to sit down and send specific signals. All that has to happen is that the members of existing compacts (and the prospective members of potential compacts) receive these signals. If they simply believe that they will get more resources and flexibility if they are ethical and competent, that will be adequate. And who thinks that, given its track record, the U.S. Department of Housing and Urban Development warrants (or will get) more flexibility or resources? If we can manage to shift—if only at the margin—resources from incompetent to competent agencies, from corrupt to ethical agencies, that may be a sufficient signal to encourage useful competition.

20. Tracy Kidder, *The Soul of a New Machine* (Atlantic Monthly Press, 1981), pp. 63, 160, 120.

21. John P. Kotter reports that business managers "seldom give orders." *The General Managers* (Free Press, 1982), p. 133.

22. Brown, *When Strangers Cooperate*, p. 123.

23. Ibid., pp. 120–21.

24. Dennis Chong, *Collective Action and the Civil Rights Movement* (University of Chicago Press, 1991), pp. 131, 231, 235. Chong also notes that initiating collective action requires people who are not "too easily frustrated by their lack of success" (p. 235).

25. In another context, Thomas C. Schelling notes that people can take clues for solving a coordination problem from "focal points" with "some kind of prominence or conspicuousness," but the nature of this prominence "depends on time and place and who the people are" and "some kind of uniqueness." *The Strategy of Conflict* (Harvard University Press, 1960), pp. 57–58.

26. Albert O. Hirschman, *Exit, Voice, and Loyalty: Response to Decline in Firms, Organizations, and States* (Harvard University Press, 1970), pp. 99, 100, 98, 99.

27. Karl E. Weick, "Small Wins: Redefining the Scale of Social Problems," *American Psychologist,* vol. 39, no. 1 (1984), pp. 48, 40, 41, 40, 43.

28. Ibid., pp. 46, 44, 46.

29. Ibid., pp. 43, 47, 43.

30. The Alliance for Redesigning Government, *The Oregon Option,* p. 16. They also identified three targets to be realized in four to six years and three more to be accomplished in eight years.

31. Weick, "Small Wins," p. 47. Schaffer, *The Breakthrough Strategy,* pp. 73, 135, 101.

32. Frances S. Berry, Richard Chackerian, and Barton Wechsler suggest that one of the "lessons" from the reinventing government efforts in Florida is "When reforms accomplish less than was promised, they are perceived as failures and tend to lose support." "Reinventing Government: Lessons from a State Capitol," in H. George Frederickson and Jocelyn M. Johnston, eds., *Public Management Reform and Innovation: Research, Theory, and Application* (University of Alabama Press, 1999), p. 347.

33. In retrospect, all of this will appear logical, organized, and well planned. Indeed, Weick suggests that a series of small wins can be "gathered into a retrospective summary that imputes a consistent line of development." The reality, however, will have been quite different, argues Weick; the "careful plotting of a series of wins to achieve a major change is impossible because conditions do not remain constant." Thus, he emphasizes, any "post hoc construction should not be mistaken for orderly implementation." Weick, "Small Wins," p. 43. Indeed, it will be much more like "management by groping along." Robert D. Behn, "Management by Groping Along," *Journal of Policy Analysis and Management,* vol. 7, no. 4 (1988), pp. 643–63.

34. Some might argue: (1) the leaders of these charter agencies have an obligation to help improve the performance of all of the state's agencies; (2) they have an obligation to help all of the agencies in state government learn how to become a charter agency; and (3) they have an obligation to help the legislature create a formal process for creating more charter agencies. But arguments (1) and (2) are different from (3). Charter agency leaders could well have an obligation to help other public agencies (1) improve performance and (2) learn how to evolve into a charter agency. But that does not mean that they have an obligation to help (3) the legislature create a formal process for creating more charter agencies. Indeed, in doing (3) they might undermine both (1) and (2).

35. Alasdair Roberts, "Performance-Based Organizations: Assessing the Gore Plan," *Public Administration Review,* vol. 57, no. 6 (1997), p. 471.

36. In Britain's parliamentary system, notes Roberts, the legislature is relatively weak, and thus the negotiation that produces the performance goals for each Next Steps executive agency is primarily between the minister who heads the department and the agency executive. In the United States, however, the legislative branch—be

it the Congress or a board of aldermen—is much more powerful. Thus, when it comes to creating an American-style performance-based organization, the legislature (or, at least, some legislators) will have to be at the bargaining table. For if the legislature isn't at the table, it has many tools with which to undermine or destroy the agreement over the targets. Indeed, even an individual legislator possesses a variety of powers (both formal and informal) to undermine the agreement. For example, the legislature can add (through the authorization or appropriations process) additional restrictions or cut the budget of any agency that it believes is behaving inappropriately. Roberts, "Performance-Based Organizations," p. 472.

But for a "charter agency," which accumulates flexibility through a strategy of small wins, neither its performance goals nor its flexibility may ever make it on to the legislative agenda. The legislature enacts a bill establishing a PBO, but it never formally "creates" a charter agency. Instead, it would implicitly ratify various incremental increases in performance targets and their accompanying incremental relaxations in constraints by never overriding or even discussing them.

37. Moreover, with increased success, a charter agency may be unable to focus on its own self-defined performance targets. Legislators or stakeholders may try to add specific goals to the agency's list of performance targets. After all, if it is such an effective agency, it ought to do even more. (In several states, the revenue agency established a reputation for effectiveness in collecting taxes, so the legislature gave it the task of collecting child support payments. Congratulations!)

Further, even if the legislature establishes a few specific performance targets, a charter agency will face additional pressures to pursue even more. "Senior executives in a congressional system of government are compelled to serve many masters," observes Roberts in an analysis of PBOs. "This basic constitutional problem is unlikely to be resolved by legislatively-mandated performance agreements." Thus, he concludes, cabinet "secretaries will continue to worry about many aspects of organizational performance [not just those specified in a formal, PBO performance agreement], and chief operating officers will diffuse their efforts in order to accommodate this fact." Similarly, political executives will pressure their senior-level career managers to broaden their efforts beyond the narrowly focused small-win targets. "Performance-Based Organizations," p. 474.

38. For a discussion of how to ensure that such reports have the desired impact, see Robert D. Behn, "Making Measures Media Friendly," *New Public Innovator,* Fall 1998, pp. 10–11.

39. For an example of how one agency did this kind of repetitive marketing, see Robert D. Behn, *Leadership Counts: Lessons for Public Managers* (Harvard University Press, 1991), pp. 83–88.

40. Linda T. Kohn, Janet M. Corrigan, and Molla S. Donaldson, eds. (Institute of Medicine, Committee on Quality of Health Care in America), *To Err Is Human: Building a Safer Health System* (National Academy Press, 1999), p. 1.

41. B. Guy Peters and Donald J. Savoie, "Managing Incoherence: The Coordination and Empowerment Conundrum," *Public Administration Review,* vol. 56, no. 3 (1996), p. 287.

42. If there are fewer rules, Peters and Savoie also note, "there will be less consistency in how errors are dealt with. We are likely to be left with a situation where the punishment will be designed on an ad hoc basis to fit the crime." Ibid., pp. 287, 288.

43. One such charter agency is The Door, a nonprofit, social service agency that offers a variety of education, employment, and drug treatment services to youth in New York City. See Eugene Bardach and Cara Lesser, "Accountability in Human Services Collaboratives—For What? and To Whom?" *Journal of Public Administration Research and Theory,* vol. 6, no. 2 (April 1996), p. 216; Eugene Bardach, *Getting Agencies to Work Together: The Practice and Theory of Managerial Craftsmanship* (Brookings, 1998), pp. 94–96, 147.

44. The need to ensure fairness in financing education undercuts these charter (school system) agencies. In recent years, many state courts have invalidated the method that their states use to finance elementary and secondary education—forcing wealthier communities to share their resources with other school districts and thus reducing their ability to buy the flexibility a charter agency requires.

Chapter Eleven

1. Gerald E. Caiden observes that "the public accountability of public officials does seem inadequate in contemporary society." Why? He cites several reasons, one of which is offered by V. Subramaniam: "the concept of public accountability and public responsibility [was] developed in Britain in a very narrow context of limited governmental expenditure, limited governmental activity, limited liberal democracy, and a limited administrative structure." "The Problem of Ensuring the Public Accountability of Public Officials," in O. P. Dwivedi and Joseph G. Jabbra, eds., *Public Service Accountability: A Comparative Perspective* (Kumarian Press, 1988), p. 23.

2. Edward P. Weber thinks that Americans may "be on the verge of redefining the constituent elements of a broadly acceptable system of democratic accountability." "The Question of Accountability in Historical Perspective: From Jackson to Contemporary Grassroots Ecosystem Management," *Administration & Society,* vol. 31, no. 4 (1999), pp. 486, 454.

Other scholars have observed that the changes in how we perform public functions will require us to rethink accountability and our mechanisms for obtaining it. Phillip J. Cooper writes: "It is not all that clear precisely what accountability will look like in the new world of public service towards which we are moving or how it will operate." "Accountability and Administrative Reform: Toward Convergence and Beyond," in B. Guy Peters and Donald J. Savoie, eds., *Governance in a Changing Environment* (McGill-Queen's University Press, 1995), p. 174.

3. Douglas McGreagor, "An Uneasy Look at Performance Appraisal," *Harvard Business Review,* vol. 50, no. 5 (1972), pp. 133–38.

4. W. Edwards Deming, *Out of the Crisis* (Center for Advanced Engineering Study, Massachusetts Institute of Technology, 1982), pp. 101–02.

5. Rensis Likert, "Motivational Approach to Management Development," *Harvard Business Review,* vol. 37, no. 4 (1959), p. 75.

6. For descriptions of 360-degree feedback, see Richard Lepsinger and Anntoinette D. Lucia, *The Art and Science of 360° Feedback* (San Francisco: Pfeiffer, 1997); David A. Waldman and Leanne E. Atwater, *The Power of 360° Feedback: How to Leverage Performance Evaluations for Top Productivity* (Houston: Gulf Publishing, 1998); Mark R. Edwards and Ann J. Ewen, *360° Feedback: The Powerful New Model of Employee Assessment and Performance Improvement* (New York: AMACOM, 1996).

7. Allan H. Church and Janine Waclawski, "Making Multirater Feedback Systems Work," *Quality Progress,* vol. 31, no. 4 (1998), pp. 81–87. Brian O'Reilly, "360 Feedback Can Change Your Life, *Fortune,* October 17, 1994, pp. 93–94, 96, 100.

8. Lepsinger and Lucia, *The Art and Science of 360° Feedback,* chap. 9, pp. 197–222; Waldman and Atwater, *The Power of 360° Feedback,* chaps. 6 and 7, pp. 98–127.

9. Scott Wimer and Kenneth M. Nowack, "Thirteen Common Mistakes Using 360-Degree Feedback," *Training & Development,* vol. 52, no. 5 (1998), pp. 69–80.

10. Waldman and Atwater, *The Power of 360° Feedback,* pp. 2–4. For example, in 1994 the Florida Department of Revenue began using 360-degree feedback for all employees in its senior management service and its select exempt service.

11. Kevin Kearns, *Managing for Accountability: Preserving the Public Trust in Public and Nonprofit Organizations* (Jossey-Bass, 1996), p. 29.

12. Although the linear, unidirectional, hierarchical model dominates our thinking about accountability, the United States employs a variety of accountability mechanisms. I am not advocating that we rely upon one method of accountability. Instead, following Landau's "theory of redundancy," I think we need multiple means for establishing accountability. That is what 360-degree accountability could create. Martin Landau, "Redundancy, Rationality, and the Problem of Duplication and Overlap," *Public Administration Review,* vol. 29, no. 4 (1969), p. 350.

Will responsibility compacts and charter agencies displace traditional accountability mechanisms? I don't think this is a big problem. The danger is not that the existing forms of accountability will wither—or that the parties to any responsibility compact will drive them out. This strikes me as unlikely—indeed, impossible. Instead, I worry that the existing forms of compliance accountability will continue to dominate—and will quickly tear apart the trust fostered by any fledgling effort to create a compact of collective and mutual responsibility.

13. A DAH is like the DH, the designated hitter in baseball. Every day you get to hit. But you never have to worry about the ball dribbling through your legs for a run-scoring double.

14. "Because legislators ought to be accountable for rationalizing the system of delivering publicly financed human services," write Eugene Bardach and Cara Lesser, "they should to some degree be accountable to the people who work the system and who know the most about it. It is not enough to say that legislators are accountable to the voters; for the delegate model of representation needs to be supplemented by a trusteeship model which, properly understood, implies a duty to consider advice from all sources that have a reasonable probability of making a helpful contribution to legislators' performance of the trusteeship function." "Accountability in Human Services Collaboratives—For What? and To Whom?" *Journal of Public Administration Research and Theory,* vol. 6, no. 2 (1996), p. 220.

15. Ed Doherty, president of the Boston Teachers Union, writes that "people who attempt to place all accountability for a child's education on teachers and schools do not understand the difference between education and 'schooling.'" Ed Doherty, "Sharing Responsibility for Teaching our Children," *Boston Globe,* September 18, 1999, p. A19. For a further discussion of parental responsibility for their children's education, see Robert D. Behn, "Standards, Assessments, and Accountability: *How Should Who* Hold *Whom* Accountable for *What?",* a paper presented at the Second Business and Education Symposium, Kennedy School of Government, Harvard University, Cambridge, Mass., April 14, 1999.

The idea that parents should be accountable for their children has expanded from education to criminality. "Parents should be accountable for their kids' actions," declared John P. Stone, the sheriff of Jefferson County in Colorado, after Eric Harris and Dylan Klebold shot up Columbine High School. Indeed, at least fifteen states have enacted laws designed to hold parents accountable for their children's criminal behavior. William Glaberson, "Parental Culpability Dubious," [Raleigh, N.C.] *News & Observer,* April 27, 1999, p. 4A. Jillian Lloyd, "Holding Parents Accountable for Children," *Christian Science Monitor,* April 29, 1999, p. 3.

16. James G. March and Johan P. Olsen, *Democratic Governance* (Free Press, 1995), p. 153.

17. Even though March and Olsen advocate "the principle that power necessitates accountability," their conception of accountability seems to be implicitly (but unambiguously) hierarchical and unidirectional: "This idea of accountability builds on more general ideas of social order, ideas about the links between agents and principals, professionals and clients, subordinates and superiors, individuals and their gods." Ibid., p. 150.

18. Not that 360-degree accountability will make everyone happy. By giving more people a say, a new accountability system will, inevitably, reduce the say of others. As Weber points out, "even if a new configuration of accountability does make government accountable to more people, at least some of the beneficiaries of past systems of accountability may suffer total or relative declines in the accountability of government to their self-proclaimed interests." "The Question of Accountability in Historical Perspective," p. 486.

19. Peter F. Drucker, "The Sickness of Government," *The Public Interest,* no. 14 (1969), p. 16. Note that Drucker's independent agency can't compare "the results of policies against expectations" unless there is some mechanism for establishing these performance expectations.

20. For discussions of this effort by two GAO staffers, see Eleanor Chelimsky, "Comparing and Contrasting Auditing and Evaluation: Some Notes on Their Relationship," *Evaluation Review,* vol. 9, no. 4 (1985), pp. 483–503; and Ray C. Rist, "Management Accountability: The Signals Sent by Auditing and Evaluation," *Journal of Public Policy,* vol. 9, no. 3 (1989), pp. 355–69.

21. Michael Barzelay, "Performance Auditing and the New Public Management: Changing Roles and Strategies of Central Audit Institutions," in *Performance Auditing and Modernization of Government* (Washington: Organisation for Economic Co-operation and Development, 1996), p. 27.

22. Barzelay calls this a "performance information audit." Ibid., p. 25.

23. For analyses of what different central audit agencies in different countries mean by "performance audit," see Michael Barzelay, "Central Audit Institutions and Performance Auditing: A Comparative Analysis of Organizational Strategies in the OECD," *Governance,* vol. 10, no. 3 (1997), pp. 235–60, plus Barzelay, "Performance Auditing and the New Public Management," and the other chapters in *Performance Auditing and Modernization of Government* (Washington: Organization for Economic Cooperation and Development, 1996).

24. For a discussion of traditional auditor behavior (in contrast with evaluator behavior), see Chelimsky, "Comparing and Contrasting Auditing and Evaluation."

25. Auditing for fairness is very similar to auditing for finances. First, you establish very specific rules (the standards) for how the organization should handle money or people. Second, you determine how the organization has actually handled its money or its people. Third, you compare the actual behavior with the original rules. If the organization's behavior matches the rules, you do nothing. If, however, the organization failed to follow the rules, you punish it.

This approach will not work, however, for performance; how do you establish rules for performance? Indeed, the philosophy of the new public management— that performance is best achieved through flexibility and empowerment, not rules and regulations—conflicts with any effort to create performance standards that performance auditors can audit.

26. Barzelay argues that the phrase *performance audit* is "something of a misnomer" and "a misleading label." "Performance Auditing and the New Public Management," p. 19; "Central Audit Institutions and Performance Auditing," p. 242.

27. This is most true for large, national stakeholder organizations like the Sierra Club or the National Alliance of Business. But even small neighborhood organizations have this capacity to think in terms of performance. In 1988, when Mayor Kurt Schmoke of Baltimore attempted to close three fire stations, neighborhood groups challenged him not only politically but also analytically: What would closing these

fire stations do to the fire department's response time? Harvey Simon, "How to Bite the Bullet: Baltimore Mayor Kurt L. Schmoke and Fire Station Closings" (B), C16-92-1130.0 (Kennedy School of Government, Harvard University, 1992).

28. We should not pretend, however, that any Office of Performance Data would merely implement the scientifically correct or best way to collect and publish performance data. It would have to make choices about what data to publish and how. (What data are performance data?) It would publish only available data, though it could push for more data. (What kind of performance data should be collected?) Such an office would, necessarily, make a variety of political choices.

29. Lydia Segal, "The Pitfalls of Political Decentralization and Proposals for Reform: The Case of New York City Public Schools," *Public Administration Review,* vol. 57, no. 2 (1997), p. 147.

30. In New York City in the 1960s, decentralization of the school system was also a civil rights issue. Segal, "The Pitfalls of Political Decentralization and Proposals for Reform," pp. 141–42.

31. Ibid., pp. 141, 142, 141.

32. Ibid., pp. 144, 143, 147.

33. Garry Wills, *A Necessary Evil: A History of American Distrust of Government* (Simon & Schuster, 1999), pp. 310, 315.

34. Segal, "The Pitfalls of Political Decentralization and Proposals for Reform," pp. 148, 147, 144–47, 147.

35. Larry J. Sabato and Glenn R. Simpson, *Dirty Little Secrets: The Persistence of Corruption in American Politics* (Times Books, 1996).

36. Martha Mendoza, "Crackdown Aims to Limit Killings of Wild Horses," [Raleigh, N.C.] *News & Observer,* April 25, 1997.

37. "Ind. Accountant Accused of Using State Funds to Support His Lovers," *Washington Post,* January 31, 1999, p. A12.

38. Tina Cassidy, "Seven Charged with Theft of Millions at Treasury," *Boston Globe,* September 29, 1999, pp. A1, A12.

39. John Sullivan, "Officer Took Offer to Quit," [Raleigh, N.C.] *News & Observer,* February 19, 2000, pp. 1B, 5B.

40. If I have failed to cite an accountability breakdown in your state or municipality, don't feel too smug. That's only because I haven't been reading your local newspapers.

41. Paul C. Light, *Monitoring Government: Inspectors General and the Search for Accountability* (Brookings, 1993), p. 57.

42. Frank Anechiarico and James B. Jacobs, *The Pursuit of Absolute Integrity: How Corruption Control Makes Government Ineffective* (University of Chicago Press, 1996), p. 13.

43. Mark H. Moore has consistently emphasized that creating more rules will not create more accountability. See, for example, "Realms of Obligation and Virtue," in

Joel L. Fleishman, Lance Liebman, and Mark H. Moore, eds., *Public Duties: The Moral Obligations of Government Officials* (Harvard University Press, 1981), pp. 3–31.

44. Frank J. Thompson and Norma M. Riccucci note that "a high density of rules can undermine respect for the law. As anyone who has worked in rule-dense agencies knows, administrators find ways to dodge the rules." "Reinventing Government," *Annual Review of Political Science,* vol. 1 (1998), p. 246.

45. Our process for constructing accountability systems for finances and fairness is similar to our process for constructing our tax laws. To our basic tax code, we continually add special provisions—some law or regulation that compensates for particular problems brought to our attention by the individuals or organizations most directly affected. Thus, the tax code becomes so complicated that no normal human can figure it out. Eventually, in response to this overwhelming complexity, we drastically simplify the tax code (as the U.S. government did in the Tax Reform Act of 1986). Immediately, however, new special provisions are proposed to compensate for new special problems. Thus, over time, the tax laws become more complicated, until we again decide to simplify them.

The challenge of simplifying the tax laws is always intimidating. And although some people are always calling for simplification, many others (particularly those who benefit from the existing provisions) are quite happy with the current code. This is why we undertake to simplify our tax code so infrequently.

A similar dynamic affects our behavior toward our accountability systems. Obviously, they are complicated, and simplifying them is at least as complicated. But there is one important difference: With the tax system, there are pressures for simplification. The benefits of any individual tax provision are concentrated and the costs diffuse. As the number of special provisions increases, however, the accumulated costs become greater; eventually, these costs become so large that organizations (and individuals) begin agitating for change. Moreover, accountants and lawyers who, through their work, uncover the inconsistencies and complications in the tax laws and regulations, often publicize these problems.

Who, however, will discover and publicize the inconsistencies and incongruities of the accountability laws and regulations? The accountability holders? Not necessarily. For to catch accountability holdees, they need not even be aware of the entire range of accountability rules and regulations; to catch any individual accountability holdee, they need only employ the few accountability rules that they enforce. The accountability holdees? By the time people have been caught by some weird feature of the accountability rules and become accountability holdees, they will have lost all credibility. Outside observers? The calls for major modifications in the accountability mechanisms have created little momentum for change. The institutional and human dynamics appear to move the conical accountability pendulum into the quadrant that contains lots of micro-mechanisms for finances and fairness *and* undermines accountability for performance.

46. Moore suggests "that we will depend on the moral character of our officials much more in the future than we have in the past." "Realms of Obligation and Virtue," p. 4. If this is true, we might devote less of our personnel resources to writing job descriptions and testing whether individuals can perform the required tasks and more to selecting for character, and then training and reinforcing it.

47. Dennis F. Thompson, *Political Ethics and Public Office* (Harvard University Press, 1987) p. 93.

48. *Merriam-Webster's Collegiate Dictionary,* 10th ed. (Merriam-Webster, 1996), p. 1034.

49. As Weber observes, "The conceptualization of democratic accountability, rather than being a sacrosanct concept that all can agree on, varies dramatically over time." "The Question of Accountability in Historical Perspective," p. 453.

50. In Britain, Charles Polidano reports, the experiment with accountability under Next Steps "is evolving with experience," and "the doctrine of ministerial responsibility has evolved, and continues to evolve." Charles Polidano, "The Bureaucrat Who Fell under a Bus: Ministerial Responsibility, Executive Agencies, and the Derek Lewis Affair in Britain," *Governance,* vol. 12, no. 2 (1999), pp. 206, 223.

51. Joel F. Handler, *The Conditions of Discretion: Autonomy, Community, Bureaucracy* (Russell Sage Foundation, 1986).

52. The Alliance for Redesigning Government, *The Oregon Option: Early Lessons from a Performance Partnership on Building Results-Driven Accountability* (Washington: National Academy of Public Administration, 1996).

53. Weber, "The Question of Accountability in Historical Perspective."

54. During and after these experiments, however, scholars will help by codifying the failures, successes, and lessons, and by suggesting new directions for experimentation. Weber suggests that "we devote greater effort to studying the *is* of effective accountability as opposed to the *ought*." Indeed, he raises several questions that scholars could address:

— What does a framework for effective democratic accountability look like in a world of decentralized governance, shared power, and collaboration?
— Are there conditions under which accountability is more likely than others?
— What are the conditions under which collaborative, community-based decision-making arrangements are most likely to be democratically accountable?

"The Question of Accountability in Historical Perspective," pp. 454, 484.

55. Donald T. Campbell, "Reforms as Experiments," *American Psychologist,* vol. 24, no. 4 (1969), pp. 409–29. Donald T. Campbell, "The Experimenting Society," *Methodology and Epistemology for Social Science: Selected Papers* (University of Chicago Press, 1988), pp. 290–314.

56. Graham T. Allison, *The Essence of Decision: Explaining the Cuban Missile Crisis* (Little Brown, 1971), pp. 178, 172, 171, 178.

57. Mark H. Moore notes that, collectively, we are not enthusiastic about experimentation: "Society remains enormously ambivalent about the kind of leadership it wants from public executives. It may not tolerate gambling with public resources to find better ways to do a job." *Accounting for Change: Reconciling the Demands for Accountability and Innovation in the Public Sector* (Washington: Council for Excellence in Government, 1994) p. 231.

58. All concepts of accountability will have advantages and disadvantages. None will be perfect. Some will be more effective in some situations; others may work better under other conditions. "There is no perfect model of accountability," argues Weber; "an acceptable system of democratic accountability can take a variety of forms rather than adhering to some sacrosanct, overarching notion of accountability." "The Question of Accountability in Historical Perspective," pp. 480, 483.

59. Dennis Thompson notes that to make his concept of "personal responsibility" work "may require citizens to know more about what more officials do, and to make more nuanced judgments about what they do." *Political Ethics and Public Office*, p. 64.

60. Ibid., pp. 38, 11.

61. March and Olsen, *Democratic Governance*, p. 150.

62. Howard Kurtz, "Asleep at the Wheel," *Washington Post Magazine*, November 29, 1992, pp. 10–13, 24–31.

Index